Bloodless Atonement?

Princeton Theological Monograph Series
K. C. Hanson, Charles M. Collier, D. Christopher Spinks,
and Robin A. Parry, Series Editors

Recent volumes in the series:

Steven C. van den Heuvel
*Bonhoeffer's Christocentric Theology and Fundamental
Debates in Environmental Ethics*

Andrew R. Hay
God's Shining Forth: A Trinitarian Theology of Divine Light

Peter Schmiechen
*Gift and Promise:
An Evangelical Theology of the Lord's Supper*

Hank Voss
*The Priesthood of All Believers and the Missio Dei:
A Canonical, Catholic, and Contextual Perspective*

Alexandra S. Radcliff
*The Claim of Humanity in Christ: Salvation and
Sanctification in the Theology of T. F. and J. B. Torrance*

Yaroslav Viazovski
*Image and Hope:
John Calvin and Karl Barth on Body, Soul, and Life Everlasting*

Anna C. Miller
*Corinthian Democracy:
Democratic Discourse in 1 Corinthians*

Thomas Christian Currie
*The Only Sacrament Left to Us: The Threefold
Word of God in the Theology and Ecclesiology of Karl Barth*

Bloodless Atonement?
A Theological and Exegetical Study of the Last Supper Sayings

BENJAMIN J. BURKHOLDER

☙PICKWICK *Publications* · Eugene, Oregon

BLOODLESS ATONEMENT?
A Theological and Exegetical Study of the Last Supper Sayings

Princeton Theological Monograph Series 219

Copyright © 2017 Benjamin J. Burkholder. All rights reserved. Except for brief quotations in critical publications or reviews, no part of this book may be reproduced in any manner without prior written permission from the publisher. Write: Permissions, Wipf and Stock Publishers, 199 W. 8th Ave., Suite 3, Eugene, OR 97401.

Pickwick Publications
An Imprint of Wipf and Stock Publishers
199 W. 8th Ave., Suite 3
Eugene, OR 97401

www.wipfandstock.com

PAPERBACK ISBN: 978-1-5326-0571-0
HARDCOVER ISBN: 978-1-5326-0573-4
EBOOK ISBN: 978-1-5326-0572-7

Cataloguing-in-Publication data:

Names: Burkholder, Benjamin J.

Title: Bloodless atonement? : a theological and exegetical study of the last supper sayings / by Benjamin J. Burkholder.

Description: Eugene, OR : Pickwick Publications, 2017 | Series: Princeton Theological Monograph 219 | Includes bibliographical references and index(es).

Identifiers: ISBN 978-1-5326-0571-0 (paperback) | ISBN 978-1-5326-0573-4 (hardcover) | ISBN 978-1-5326-0572-7 (ebook)

Subjects: LCSH: Jesus Christ—Person and offices. | Lord's Supper—Biblical teaching. | Salvation.

Classification: BT420 .B87 2017 (print) | BT420 .B87 (ebook)

Manufactured in the U.S.A.   06/14/17

English Scripture quotations are from New Revised Standard Version Bible with OT Apocrypha, copyright © 1989 National Council of the Churches of Christ in the United States of America. Used by permission. All rights reserved worldwide.

Greek New Testament quotations are from *Novum Testamentum Graece*, 28th revised edition, Edited by Barbara Aland and others, © 2012 Deutsche Bibelgesellschaft, Stuttgart. Used by Permission.

Greek Old Testament quotations are from *Septuaginta*, edited by Alfred Rahlfs, © 1935 and 1979 Deutsche Bibelgesellschaft, Stuttgart. Used by permission.

Hebrew Old Testament quotations are from *Biblia Hebraica Stuttgartensia*, edited by Karl Elliger and Wilhelm Rudolph, Fifth Revised Edition, edited by Adrian Schenker, © 1977 and 1997 Deutsche Bibelgesellschaft, Stuttgart. Used by permission.

I dedicate this work to my wife, Jennifer, who has encouraged, supported, and sacrificed much. Together, we are "Living the Dream!"

Contents

List of Tables | viii

Acknowledgments | ix

Abbreviations | x

Introduction | xiii

1. Girard's Soteriology and Salvation History | 1
2. Reading the Bible with the Girardians | 27
3. Jesus as Savior in Which Story (Part 1)?—Israel's Hopes for Restoration | 51
4. Jesus as Savior in Which Story (Part 2)?—The Restoration of Israel as the Leitmotif in the Gospels | 91
5. The Cross of Christ in Mark | 134
6. Matthew and Jesus' Death for the Forgiveness of Sin | 158
7. The Cross, Covenant, and Forgiveness in Luke | 168
8. Assessing the Biblical and Theological Foundations of Girardian Soteriology | 193
9. Girard, Renewing the Covenant, and Ways Forward | 222

Bibliography | 235

Subject Index | 257

Ancient Document Index | 261

List of Tables

Comparison of the Words of Institution in Mark and Matthew | 160

Comparison of the Words of Institution in Mark and Luke | 170

Acknowledgments

THIS WORK COULD ONLY have reached its current form with the help of a number of individuals for whom I am eternally grateful. Larry Cain's generous gift in the summer of 2014 allowed me to "get my oars in the water." Temporarily relieving me of the onus of providing financially for my family, his generous gift permitted the full devotion of my energy to the chapters on the Gospels, which still remain the sections of this volume that give me the most satisfaction. William Wright IV also deserves special thanks. His perspicacious observations and gentle suggestions helped refine the work that now sits before you. Without his circumspect guidance, the work would have been far less polished. Elizabeth Vasko and Bodgan Bucur also provided informative feedback on earlier drafts that have helped to refine it. All the mistakes and overstatements, however, are fully mine. To the many unnamed individuals who have aided me in all of my academic endeavors and encouraged me in various ways, you too share in the completion of this volume. For all of your support and help, I am eternally thankful.

Abbreviations

Ant.	*Jewish Antiquities*
As. Mos.	*Assumption of Moses*
AThR	*Anglican Theological Review*
2 Bar	*2 Baruch*
BDAG	Bauer, W., Frederick W. Danker, W. F. Arndt, and F. W. Ginrich, eds. *A Greek-English Lexicon of the New Testament and Early Christian Literature*. 3d. ed. Chicago: University of Chicago Press, 2000.
Bib	*Biblica*
BBR	*Bulletin for Biblical Research*
CBQ	*Catholic Biblical Quarterly*
CTQ	*Concordia Theological Quarterly*
1 En.	*1 Enoch*
ExAud	*Ex Auditu*
ExpTim	*Expository Times*
Her.	*Quis rerum divinarum heres sit*
JBL	*Journal of Biblical Literature*
JETS	*Journal of the Evangelical Theological Society*
JTS	*Journal of Theological Studies*
J.W.	*Jewish War*
HTR	*Harvard Theological Review*
Int	*Interpretation*

MT	*Modern Theology*
NTS	*New Testament Studies*
Neot	*Neotestamentica*
NovT	*Novum Testamentum*
OTP	*The Old Testament Pseudepigrapha.* Edited by James H. Charlesworth. 2 vols. Garden City, NY: Doubleday, 1983–1985.
m. Pesaḥ	Mishnah tractate Pesaḥim
m. Zebaḥ	Mishnah tractate Zebaḥim
Pss. Sol.	Psalms of Solomon
Sib. Or.	Sibylline Oracles
SJT	*Scottish Journal of Theology*
SBLSP	Society of Biblical Literature Seminar Papers
SLJT	*St. Luke's Journal of Theology*
T. Dan.	Testament of Dan
T. Jud.	Testament of Judah
Tg. Isa.	Targum Isaiah
TS	*Theological Studies*
TD	*Theology Digest*
VT	*Vetus Testamentum*
ZAW	*Zeitschrift für die alttestamentliche Wissenschaft*
ZNW	*Zeitschrift für die Neutestamentliche Wissenschaft*

Introduction

Despite the shared affirmation among Christians that Jesus brings salvation to humanity, there has rarely been agreement on *how* he saves humankind. Some find it intuitive that Jesus dies on the cross in order to assume the punishment for sin. Others find such a notion morally reprehensible. Such disagreements have not been uncommon. Consider, for instance, how Anselm's *Cur Deus Homo?*—a text written around 1099 CE that argued only the God-man could make satisfaction to God the Father as recompense for human sin—was shortly met with Abelard's rejoinder that God did not need a payment to forgive sins.[1] In modern discourse, such disagreement has only escalated. If anything has changed, it is the growing assurance expressed by some writers that atonement theories sharing some relationship to Anselm stand in stark contradiction to Jesus himself. One can point here to Nelson-Pallmeyer who argues that all the violent God images in the Bible should be discarded, and this would include any form of violence, even the notion of God punishing wrongdoers. Regarding the violent images of God buttressing many models of the atonement, he contends that Christianity and the Bible severely misunderstand Jesus.[2] According to him, this cleansing of violent God images should include the celebration of the Eucharist as well since it suggests Jesus' death is necessary for atonement. Such thinking, he avers, comes from the early church and not from Jesus.[3] In a similar vein, Stephen Finlan, in *Options on Atonement in Christian Thought*, follows up an analysis of Paul's sacrificial metaphors of Christ's death with a section entitled "None of This Was in Jesus," in which he argues that Jesus never thought of his death in a sacrificial way.[4] Although Finlan does not

---

1. He attacks both Christus Victor and Anselm's satisfaction theory. See Abelard, *Epistle to the Romans*, 114–17.

2. He concludes, "it is doubtful that the atonement would make any sense to Jesus in light of his image or experience of God." Nelson-Pallmeyer, *Jesus Against Christianity*, 156.

3. Ibid., 341.

4. Finlan, *Options on Atonement*, 35–42. Other authors who share a similar interpretation of the Gospels include Weaver, *Nonviolent Atonement*; Baker, *Executing God*, esp. 78; Gorringe, *God's Just Vengeance*, 67; and Northey, "The Cross," 366.

ignore the presence of verses contrary to his view in the Gospels—like the ransom sayings or the Last Supper sayings—he doubts such passages stem from Jesus himself or, if they do, they were not intended in a sacrificial way.[5] Instead, Paul and the Gospel writers introduce the expiatory meaning in the cross where Jesus never had it.[6] This cursory glance at some contemporary authors reveals that, though almost a millennium has transpired since the squabble between Anselm and Abelard, the debate smolders on.

With the addition of new voices, the soteriological debates have increased in complexity as different groups have identified flaws with both Anselm and Abelard. In the past few decades, feminist theologians have criticized many traditional models of atonement. For several such authors, the traditional notions of atonement, including satisfaction (Anselm) and moral exemplar models (Abelard), have the negative potential of glorifying suffering and encouraging acquiescence in the face of abuse. As a result, some feminists have called for a reformulation of atonement theology altogether. Instead of depicting Christ's death as a glorious martyrdom, some contend the cross should be seen as an affront to evil in the world.[7] One provocative criticism from some feminist theologians has been that atonement models like Anselm's constitute a case of divine child abuse and need to be abandoned since they perpetuate a passive approach to abuse.[8] The fear is that if Jesus' death is portrayed as God's will from eternity past and is glorified as a good action, then women and children suffering from domestic abuse will consequently assume it is God's will for them to suffer as well.

Modern soteriological discourse has certainly become quite interesting to say the least. Nevertheless, among the various figures reshaping contemporary soteriology, few stand taller than René Girard. In fact, it is hard to over-exaggerate his influence on contemporary discussions of soteriology. Some theologians herald Girard's soteriology as an entirely new theory that deserves to be mentioned alongside other traditional approaches to the atonement like Christus Victor, satisfaction, or moral exemplar theories.[9] Others realize that Girard's influence has become so pervasive that their

---

5. The ransom sayings are those in which Jesus describes his death as a "ransom for many" (Matt 20:28; Mark 10:45). The Last Supper sayings are the institution of the Eucharist by Jesus in the Synoptic Gospels (Matt 26:26–29; Mark 14:22–25; and Luke 22:14–20).

6. Finlan, *Options on Atonement*, 39.

7. Williams, *Sisters in the Wilderness*, 161–67 and Ray, *Deceiving the Devil*, 58–70.

8. Brown and Parker, "For God so Loved," 9. See also Brown, "Divine Child Abuse?" 24–28 and Brock, "And a Little Child Will Lead Us," 42–61.

9. See Daniels, "Passing the Peace," 125–48; Park, *Triune Atonement*, 27–30; and Placher, "How Does Jesus Save?" 23–27.

summaries of soteriology must engage it to remain relevant in contemporary discourse.[10]

Like Nelson-Pallmeyer, Girard sees the sacrificial interpretation of Jesus' death as directly opposed to the Gospel message. Girard has written, "There is nothing in the Gospels to suggest that the death of Jesus is a sacrifice, whatever definition (expiation, substitution, etc.) we may give for that sacrifice."[11] In fact, he categorizes an interpretation of Christ's death like expiation or penal substitution "as a most enormous and paradoxical misunderstanding" of the Gospel.[12] Although Girard has become more amenable to associating Christ's death with the terminology of "sacrifice," he continues to note that in doing so he still sees Christ's death as discontinuous with the archaic rituals of sacrifice that had some kind of atoning function. For him, Christ's death is a "(self)-sacrifice" which is "against all blood sacrifices," and hence their undoing.[13] Despite adopting this qualified use of sacrificial language to interpret Christ's death, Girard still sees the Gospels as essentially non-sacrificial in that they deconstruct sacrificial theology instead of portraying Christ as the ultimate once-for-all-sacrifice for sin. Any view that assumes Christ's death is such a sacrifice, whether it is Anselm's satisfaction theory or the Reformer's penal substitution theory, is antithetical to the New Testament Gospels. As Girard's views have been disseminated to broader audiences, some have unequivocally endorsed Girard's view of the cross as essentially correct.[14]

For as influential and persuasive as Girard's view has proven for some, one can question whether Girard's interpretation of the Gospels accounts for all they have to say about the importance of Christ's death. Careful readers have noted that Girard does ignore certain passages, particularly

10. E.g., Eddy and Beilby, "The Atonement," 10; Long, *Sacrificial Theology of Atonement*, 62–64; and Scott, *What About the Cross?*, 127–29.

11. Girard, *Things Hidden*, 180. Later Girard makes a similar claim: "the sacrificial interpretation of the Passion and the Redemption cannot legitimately be extrapolated from the text of the New Testament . . . ." (ibid., 227; cf. 243). The only exception in the New Testament that he initially gave was the Epistle to the Hebrews (ibid., 224–25, 243).

12. Ibid., 180.

13. Vattimo and Girard, *Weakening Faith*, 93. On his acceptance of using the term "sacrifice" for Christ's death, see also Girard, "Mimetische Theorie und Theologie," 15–29 and Girard, *Evolution and Conversion*, 215. Regarding the mature position of Girard on sacrificial language, see Kirwan, "Saved from Salvation," 40–43.

14. See, for example, Girard, *Things Hidden*, 180. Some follow Girard here without reserve. E.g. Henriksen readily affirms that Girard is right in this assertion: "Girard claims that there is nothing in the Gospels to suggest that the death of Jesus is a sacrifice, whatever definition (expiation, substitution, etc.) we may give for that sacrifice. He is right in this, insofar as the Gospels are concerned." *Desire, Gift, and Recognition*, 260.

those that might jeopardize his interpretation of the cross.[15] Even those who regard his work favorably have called for a more sustained investigation of the biblical texts in relation to Girard's work. For example, Depoortere notes that "a verse-by-verse study of the New Testament in light of Girard's theses and a critical evaluation of them in light of the letter of the Biblical texts are necessary if we want to consolidate his view on the uniqueness of Christianity."[16] In light of this, we have good reason to investigate whether Girard can reasonably and justifiably claim that the Gospels do not depict Jesus' death as an expiation or satisfaction for sin.

The goal of this work is to contribute to a critical evaluation of Girard's soteriology by engaging some of the very passages in the Synoptic Gospels that are most difficult to assimilate into his theory. As we will see, some of the passages in the Gospels undermine rather than confirm Girard's soteriology. Of all the passages in the Gospels that seem to imply and infer an atoning element to Christ's death, the words of institution that Jesus utters at the Last Supper (Mark 14:22–24; Matt 26:26–29; Luke 22:15–20) provide the richest and densest articulation of the cross's significance. As a result, a significant portion of this study is devoted to understanding how these passages reveal the significance of the cross for the Gospel writers and why they should be central in an evaluation of Girard's soteriology. This study of the Gospels, however, will not be limited to the Last Supper sayings, but it will also engage other passages that reinforce and corroborate the theological implications found in the Last Supper sayings, which collectively challenge several of Girard's assertions. Admittedly, drawing so heavily on the Last Supper sayings could be faulted for being too narrowly centered on a limited set of passages. It must be noted at the outset that the point of this work is not to develop an all-encompassing account of the Gospels' soteriology but merely to evaluate critically the veracity of Girard's claims. Because Girard makes such a global claim that expiation and substitution are foreign to the New Testament Gospels, a full account of the Gospels' soteriology is unnecessary. As will be seen shortly, if Girard's claims are true, they must be true on all accounts, even with the passages that are potentially problematic.[17]

---

15. While some theologians have identified the Last Supper sayings as problematic for Girard's view, they have failed to extrapolate how they contravene his thesis. See Long, *Sacrificial Theology of Atonement*, 64 and Wink, *Engaging the Powers*, 153.

16. Depoortere, *Christ in Postmodern Philosophy*, 90; cf. 147.

17. One of Girard's interlocutors in *Things Hidden Since the Foundation of the World* observed something along these lines and noted that "it is crucial that the non-sacrificial reading should demonstrate a clear superiority to all the sacrificial readings that have been given so far." Girard, *Things Hidden*, 185. This interlocutor correctly realized that the viability of Girard's reading of the Gospels requires it to be better supported than other interpretations.

Though the crux of the matter lies in the exegesis and theological understanding of the Gospels, this study additionally presumes that any interpretation of the Gospels depends upon the larger theological narrative and intertextual relationships presumed by interpreters. As it will be demonstrated, Girard's interpretation of the Gospels is contingent upon the intertextuality that he presupposes as operative in the Gospels, namely, a polemical exchange between the Gospels and mythology. Part of the contention in this volume is that the Gospel writers are actually quite clear about the other written texts and the larger story that they presuppose for their narratives about Jesus. It will be argued that if we are going to read the Gospel writers on their terms, we should read them in light of the stories and texts the authors explicitly employ to illuminate the person and ministry of Jesus of Nazareth.

Like all inquiries, this work has its limitations. For one, the emphasis upon the Last Supper sayings limits the focus to the Synoptic Gospels. This is not to dismiss the Gospel of John as an important contributor to a Christian understanding of the cross. John surely has much to offer any understanding of the cross rooted in the Gospels, and it is my belief that John shares much of the Synoptics' theological understanding of the cross, though it will be clothed in its own unique Johannine garb. John was not included in this work simply because John's account of the Last Supper lacks the words of institution over the bread and wine and includes a substantial portion of unique material not shared with the Synoptics. As a result, the material that has been deemed central to the evaluative purpose did not demand the use of John in this instance.

Methodology

The interpretive methodology adopted here approaches the New Testament Gospels as narrative compositions, seeking to read individual passages in light of the whole. Though other texts and historical events will be utilized to situate the Synoptic Gospels within their historical contexts, this will be primarily a literary investigation rather than a historical one. As a result, defending the historicity or authenticity of any one saying, even that of the Last Supper sayings, is beyond the purview of this particular endeavor, though some comments are made from time to time in the footnotes for the interested reader. The reason for this lies with Girard himself. Girard, though not unaware of historical questions, approaches the Gospels as literary narratives not as a collection of sayings to be verified. Moreover, he never attempts to dismiss potentially problematic passages by labeling them as unhistorical, making engagement with questions of authenticity superfluous for an actual evaluation of Girard.

When it comes to the primary interlocutor, René Girard, he will be analyzed from a theological point of view by employing the tools of biblical and theological analysis. Some readers might question whether Girard fully fits within the rather rigid disciplines that comprise biblical studies and theology. Certainly, Girard would neither claim the mantle of a theologian proper nor that his work perfectly fits within its auspices. Rather, his work is a fascinating synthesis of various fields like literary theory, psychology, and anthropology, to name a few. As a result, his work is much broader than theology, and some might think it unfair to subject his work to such analyses. Nevertheless, Girard does make interpretive and exegetical claims about the biblical texts, the very texts which are foundational for Christian theology. Furthermore, based upon his exegetical observations, Girard makes theologically relevant assertions about the cross and how this event rescues humankind, constructing what many would identify as a soteriology. Although Girard might not be exclusively working in theology, his work is theologically relevant, which is demonstrated by the number of theologians who have adopted his framework as their own. Therefore, it seems entirely justified to analyze Girard where his work intersects the disciplines of biblical and systematic theology.

Outline of the Chapters

The inaugural chapter provides an overview of Girard's thought in two parts. In the first half, a basic overview of Girard's three major theses will be given, namely, mimetic desire, the scapegoat mechanism, and the revelation of the Gospels. The first half of this chapter is standard fare for books on Girard and could be skipped by readers familiar with Girard. However, the second half of the chapter provides an essential overview of Girard's "salvation history" in order to sketch Girard's broader reading of the Christian Bible. While this latter portion is rare among books on Girard, it will be essential for the argument developed in subsequent chapters to the effect that Girard's account of salvation history contains significant departures from the version of salvation history that seems operative in the biblical canon.

The second chapter recounts the ways in which Girard's work has been adopted and adapted by other theologians like Schwager, Alison, Heim, and Bartlett to name a few. Though notable differences are present among these thinkers, there is a detectable "family resemblance." This chapter also purposely introduces some of the interlocutors that will appear in the following chapters since the continuing conversation is not solely with Girard but also with those who have championed his thought.

The third chapter begins a hermeneutical critique of Girard, which extends into the following chapter, contending that the Gospels need to be read in light of Israel's story of exile and restoration rather than presuming a polemical relationship with mythology as the dominant hermeneutical key in the Gospels. To establish the point, the third chapter recounts the Old Testament's story of Israel, her punishment in the exile, and the promises of her restoration, which continue to reverberate throughout important intertestamental texts. The argument that was begun in the third chapter culminates in the fourth. With a close reading of the Gospels, I argue that the Gospel writers, through their use of Old Testament allusions and their citations of important prophetic texts, situate their narratives about Jesus—and thus his saving efficacy—in the larger story of Israel waiting for restoration. As a result, if we are to understand the importance of the cross, we must read the Passion narratives not within a narrative foreign to the Gospels—as Girard does by reading the Gospels over against mythical texts—but within the very story that the Gospel writers utilize.

After situating the Gospels within Israel's story of exile and restoration in the previous chapters, the fifth chapter focuses on the Markan Last Supper account, which depicts Jesus' death as a covenant sacrifice through allusions to Old Testament passages ("my blood of the covenant"), the most notable of which is Exodus 24:8 where Moses offers a sacrifice to inaugurate the covenant. Drawing upon Hebrews and relevant Jewish texts, I argue that covenant sacrifice was often assumed to possess atoning efficacy and should be interpreted in this way in Mark. Furthermore, the Last Supper in Mark should not be made to stand on its own, even though it certainly could. When we interpret the Last Supper sayings as infusing Christ's death with atoning value, this interpretation resonates with a number of other portions of the Gospel like the predictions sayings, the ransom saying, and Mark's framing of the Passion account. Thus, if Mark is to be read correctly, we must in fact see Jesus' death as an atonement for sin, opening up a more direct access to God.

Journeying in a chronological order, assuming Markan priority, the sixth chapter turns to the Gospel of Matthew. While Matthew contains a good many of the details found in Mark's account of the Last Supper, Matthew is much more explicit about connecting the crucifixion and death of Christ to the acquisition of forgiveness. Moreover, as will be demonstrated, Matthew's Last Supper account is not an isolated affirmation of atonement theology, but the culmination of a number of Matthean glosses and redactions that ultimately lead to the robust formulation one finds at the Last Supper account.

Chapter seven concludes the portion of this work devoted to biblical exegesis by analyzing Luke's Gospel. Though Luke also adopts several elements present in Mark, he is most noted for his supposed lack of atonement theology. This chapter is a sustained engagement with the prevailing views in biblical scholarship about Luke's supposed dearth of atonement theology. In contrast to the consensus view, I contend that Luke's pronounced theme of forgiveness is directly connected to the inauguration of the new covenant, which was announced at the Last Supper. Thus, if we are to understand Luke correctly, we cannot suppress atonement theology but rather understand how it unlocks the implicit connection between Luke's theme of forgiveness and Jesus' death on the cross as the beginning of the new covenant era, a point which finds its chief expression in the Last Supper account.

Drawing upon the biblical exegesis of chapters five through seven, the eighth chapter will identify how the data drawn from the exegesis of the Gospels challenges the assertions made by Girard and his followers. In addition, this chapter will also contain a theological analysis of Girardian soteriology, showing that it contains a problematic contradiction at the very center of the theory, which inherently weakens its viability.

Despite having some sharp criticisms of Girardian soteriology in the previous chapter, the ninth chapter will show how contemporary interpretations of the cross could assimilate prescient insights from Girardian thought without jeopardizing the soteriology of the Gospels. What is more, the biblical exegesis performed in the previous chapters also opens up the possibility of utilizing covenant renewal as a more encompassing approach to soteriology that is able to incorporate the essential elements noted throughout, even assimilating elements of Girard's soteriology.

Before we can get to such analysis and assimilation, though, we must first discuss Girard's theory and to that we now turn.

I

Girard's Soteriology and Salvation History

TRYING TO SUMMARIZE GIRARD's work is a daunting affair for it comprises a robust synthesis of various fields of study. In fact, his interdisciplinary approach has been so fascinating for countless thinkers because it weaves together literature, philosophy, ethnology, and biblical studies. Nevertheless, Girard's primary contributions can be distilled into three main theses that constitute his mimetic theory. The opening half of the chapter will summarize Girard's mimetic theory, which constitutes the essential core of Girard's thought and his soteriology. At the same time, these theses also inform how Girard reads the Christian Bible. The latter half of this chapter consequently sketches Girard's account of salvation history as contained within the Christian Bible, beginning with the Old Testament and culminating in the New Testament. As Christians before him, Girard affirms that a unique stage of salvation history is attained in Christ.

Introduction to Girard

Mimetic Desire

Girard's soteriological conclusions are built upon three integrated theses regarding the nature of humanity and the Bible's revelation of this truth. Since his soteriology comes in the final thesis, the first two are necessary precursors for understanding his soteriology. Girard articulated the first of these theses—that human desire is mimetic—in his first major work, *Deceit, Desire, and the Novel*. In this work, Girard observed that the great literary masters like Cervantes, Dostoevsky, Proust, Shakespeare, and Stendahl all articulate an understanding of human desire that departs from the common notion that humans autonomously choose their desires and that desires proceed directly from the desiring subject to a desired object. As Girard describes it, human desire is essentially "triangular"—hence, not a linear connection of subject to object—because an individual's desires are induced by the desires of another person, who functions as a model.[1] Because a valued or esteemed model desires a particular object, others come to desire the same object, not because it is inherently valuable, but because it possesses value in the eyes of others. One has to look no further than the advertising on television to see some truth in his proposal.[2] Every day glamorous and attractive people introduce us to products and services that we have survived without. However, seeing the products being valued and modeled by someone else with a higher social status often evokes desires for such objects within the viewers. In light of this discovery, which he finds present in the great novelists, Girard concludes that humans, most often unconsciously, pattern their desires after the objects—and these range from physical objects to the more intangible "objects" like beauty or wisdom— that others already desire or possess.[3] Thus, Girard's first thesis offers an innovative understanding of human desire.

Scapegoat Mechanism

While mimetic desire can occur apart from conflict, the fact that other people induce one's desires easily leads to conflict between the model and the follower when both individuals converge on the same object.[4] This leads to the second important thesis of Girard's anthropology, namely, that mimetic desire can and will eventually escalate into widespread social conflict to such a degree that resolution can only be found through what will be called throughout as the "scapegoat mechanism."

For Girard, the convergence of two individuals on the same object or status of being mutually reinforces the desire for a particular object.[5] The more the other desires the object of contention, the more it is deemed valuable, further augmenting one's own desire for the object. Such contests are unlikely to remain isolated between two individuals. They, in turn, serve as models for other people as well. The more people involved in the mimetic contagion, the more compelling and attractive it is to the others in the community.

---

1. Girard, *Deceit, Desire, and the Novel*, 2, 43, 61, 83, 183.

2. While Girard has persuaded me that *some* of our desires are mimetic, it is not apparent that *all* of our desires are therefore mimetic.

3. Girard does differentiate between biological needs and mimetic desire. See Fleming, *René Girard*, 11.

4. Girard, *Deceit, Desire, and the Novel*, 9, 26, 45.

5. Girard, *Violence and the Sacred*, 145–48; Girard, *Things Hidden*, 26; and Girard, *I See Satan*, 23.

As the rivalry increases, people are likely to lose sight of the objects they originally desired and become more focused on supplanting the other person in what Girard—at least in his earlier works—terms the switch from "acquisitive mimesis" to "conflictual mimesis."[6] As the social conflict spreads its tentacles ever wider, the entire community is threatened with absolute decimation in the "war of *all against all.*"[7] At the peak of a mimetic conflict, rivalries become much more volatile and the crowd can exchange its object of hate quite quickly. Near the zenith of the conflict, "the opposition of everyone against everyone else is replaced by the opposition of all against one."[8] Girard believes that: " . . . it is inevitable that at one moment the entire community will find itself unified against a single individual."[9] At this point, the wild pogrom suddenly morphs from a war of all against all to a "war of *all against one*" as it arbitrarily pins the guilt for the conflict on a single individual.[10] The community, unanimously united against a solitary victim, projects the guilt for the community's problems onto it, believing "in the unshakable conviction that it has found the one and only cause of its trouble."[11] With unassailable conviction, the community condemns the "guilty" one, the scapegoat. The execution—or sacrifice—of the presumed culprit does in fact pacify the community, at least temporarily. The presumed reason for their conflict disappears, and this only serves to substantiate that the victim was indeed the culprit. Hence, the scapegoat mechanism is born, and it functions as a means of purging conflict and violence from a community.

According to Girard, the scapegoat mechanism not only serves to expunge conflict and violence in a community, it also serves to generate cultural order.[12] Because the execution of the victim brings reconciliation to the community, the scapegoat mechanism becomes the generator of culture by creating corresponding prohibitions and rituals. Prohibitions arise because people will be forbidden "to repeat any action associated with the crisis, to abstain from all mimicry, from all contact with the former antagonists, from any acquisitive gesture toward objects that have stood as causes or pretexts for rivalry."[13] Thus, all of the precursors that led to the original

6. Girard, *Things Hidden*, 26–29. See also Girard, *Violence and the Sacred*, 169.
7. Girard, *I See Satan*, 24.
8. Girard, *Things Hidden*, 24; cf. 26.
9. Girard, *Things Hidden*, 26.
10. Girard, *I See Satan*, 24.
11. Girard, *Things Hidden*, 27.
12. Ibid., 32.
13. Ibid., 28.

scapegoat are banned in the community's effort to insulate itself against further violence. Consequently, this system of prohibitions and taboos erects a wall of cultural differentiation that separates safe insiders from outsiders who threaten communal order. Additionally, Girard believes that the scapegoat mechanism generates rituals. In order to preserve the fragile peace within the community, they will try to reproduce the effects of the victim's death by offering new victims that attempt to recreate the original setting as much as possible.[14] Religious rituals like sacrifices are therefore attempts to remember and recreate the peace ensuing the death of the victim. As a result, fear of future violent outbreaks and a desire to preserve the hard-won peace generates the prohibitions and rituals of human culture.

The scapegoat mechanism also generates another important dimension of human culture: religion. Girard suggests that once the victim's death brings unexpected peace to the community, they begin to credit the victim with numinous powers.[15] Only a god, after all, could bring such beneficence. Over time, the victims are deified as gods, and the entire cultural order of prohibition and ritual is buttressed by the threat of divine violence and future catastrophes. Such gods possess the bipolar ability to cause malevolence if angered and benevolence if appeased.[16] In light of this, Girard concludes that archaic religion is a profound misunderstanding of the nature and effects of mimetic violence, which simply deifies its victims, even though its desire to mitigate violence is not unwarranted.[17]

Against this backdrop of human culture and its origins in violence, Girard then explains how mythology substantiates the new cultural order. For Girard, myths, with their fantastic stories of divine-human encounters, are retellings of victims who have been apotheosized through the community's retelling of the story. A brief summary of Girard's analysis of *Oedipus Rex*, his myth of choice in many writings, will demonstrate his hermeneutical approach to myths. For Girard, Oedipus functions as the quintessential scapegoat in the myth for several reasons.[18] First, Oedipus is unequivocally deemed guilty because he has transgressed two hefty taboos by committing parricide against his father and incest with his mother. Second, as a result of these transgressions, Oedipus becomes culpable for the plague decimating

---

14. Ibid., 28. See also pages 48–83 for a fuller articulation and explanation of the various kinds of cultural order.

15. Girard, *Violence and the Sacred*, 94–95, 307.

16. Girard, *Things Hidden*, 46, 107, 116.

17. Hence, Girard's main thesis in *Violence and the Sacred* is: "Violence is at the heart and secret soul of the sacred." Girard, *Violence and the Sacred*, 31.

18. René Girard, "What is a Myth?" 287–88. This essay was originally published in his work, Girard, *The Scapegoat*, 24–44.

Thebes. In order for the plague to cease, the guilty party, Oedipus, must pay. Third, Oedipus is described as someone marginalized within the community: he is a foreigner, he possesses a physical deformation, and he is the king. For Girard, all of these indictments and descriptions of Oedipus correlate precisely with scapegoat victims that are always deemed guilty for the community's problems. While many people treat myths as erroneous fictions, Girard avers that a myth is "the transfigured account of a real violence."[19] In other words, myths have taken a real event, a scapegoat lynching, and obfuscated the reality of what happened in order to justify the community's actions. To put it bluntly, myths are outright conspiracies. The only accurate truth found in them is the community's agreement that the victim bears culpability for the community's strife.[20] Ultimately, myths eliminate the victim's voice when the perspective of the persecutors extinguishes the cry of the victim once and for all.

Revelation of the Gospels

Girard arrived at the final thesis of his work when he placed his anthropological findings of mimetic desire and the scapegoat mechanism alongside the Christian Scriptures, which he did not do until he published *Things Hidden Since the Foundation of the World*.[21] While Girard observes that there is much in the biblical texts that corresponds to mythology and the accounts of collective murders, he asserts that only in comparing mythology and the biblical texts can one discover the true uniqueness and message of the Bible.[22] The startling difference he discovers is that the biblical texts vindicate the victim, whereas the myths inculpate the victim. One can point to various biblical texts that prove his point. For example, in Genesis 4 where Cain murders his brother Abel, the Bible clearly depicts Abel as the recipient of unjustified violence.[23] Likewise, the narrative cycle devoted to Joseph un-

---

19. Girard, *Things Hidden*, 109; cf. 119. To substantiate this reading of myths as real persecutions, Girard turns to stories where modern critics will acknowledge the presence of a victim: Middle Age narratives of persecution that include anti-Semitic texts, witch trials, and records of the Inquisition. Herein, Girard identifies a "half-way" step between the persecution that has been completely effaced in mythology and the persecution that is partially camouflaged in the texts from the Middle Ages that cast inordinate guilt on certain individuals. While these medieval accounts include the exaggerated and pernicious qualities of the condemned, they lack the deification and "sacralization" of myths. See Girard, *Scapegoat*, 1–23 and Girard, *Things Hidden*, 127–30.

20. Ibid., 113–17.

21. Girard, *Violence and the Sacred*, 66, 309.

22. Girard, *Things Hidden*, 141–44.

23. Girard, *Things Hidden*, 146–47. For instance, the narrative of Cain and Abel

equivocally shows Joseph undeserving of a host of injustices done to him.[24] From this consistent biblical tendency, he concludes that the biblical texts are fundamentally opposed to ancient mythology. Instead of justifying the persecutors like the myths do, the biblical texts vindicate the victim and condemn the crowds.

Moreover, Girard observes that the biblical texts persistently repel the mythical desire to divinize the victims.[25] Whereas ancient cultures divinized their victims, a process that is obliquely visible in mythology, the Christian Bible refuses to divinize such victims. Individuals like Abel and Joseph are shown to be human victims, but never gods. In light of the refusal to divinize the victims and the continual defense of the victims, Girard concludes that the biblical texts possess an anti-mythological thrust because they seek to undermine the scapegoat mechanism that has surreptitiously governed human culture from its inception.

This is not to say that the entirety of the Christian Bible speaks with the same degree of insight into the scapegoat mechanism. As will be shown in more detail shortly, according to Girard, although the Old Testament progressively unveils key anthropological insights about human nature's tendency to justify its violence, it never fully arrives at a complete, pristine revelation of the scapegoat mechanism.[26] Moreover, it continues to perpetuate a view of God wherein he is willing to utilize violence in retribution and punishment, even at the points where the Old Testament seems closest to revealing the scapegoat mechanism.[27] For Girard, associating threats of punishment with the divine constitutes evidence of mythical thought. Thus, by itself, Girard finds the Old Testament ambiguous. Only with Christ, as the hermeneutical key, is one able to look in retrospect at what God was revealing through the Old Testament.[28] The Old Testament thus heralds and prefigures the revelation that is to come in Jesus and the Gospels, though it never arrives at this destination itself.[29]

---

shares many similarities with the founding murders of other societies like Rome where Romulus slays his brother Remus, but Girard observes a significant difference: the slaying of the brother is condemned in the biblical account.

24. Ibid., 149–53.
25. Girard, *I See Satan*, 119.
26. Girard, *Things Hidden*, 200.
27. Ibid., 154–58.
28. Girard, *Evolution and Conversion*, 256. Here he writes, "God provided the text, but also the hermeneutical key with which to read it: the Cross. The two cannot be separated." See also Girard, *Job*, 163.
29. Girard, *Things Hidden*, 205.

Jesus' crucifixion constitutes the quintessential example of the biblical defense of victims. Like other classic examples of the scapegoat mechanism, Jesus' crucifixion results from mimetic conflict, and the social forces—the Jewish leaders, the Romans, etc.—have once again found that the only way to make peace is at the expense of a victim.[30] Unlike the manifold perpetrators in the crucifixion, the Gospel writers see through the charges concocted to indict Jesus, for the Gospels unwaveringly attest to his innocence.[31] The Gospels do this in various ways, but perhaps the clearest expression of Jesus' innocence is his declaration in John 15:25 that "They hated me without a cause," which affirms the vacuous rationality behind the mob's lynching of Jesus.[32] At the cross, the scapegoat mechanism fixes its crosshairs on Jesus in the way it had so many times in the past, except something happens differently this time, which leads to its undoing.

In *I See Satan Fall Like Lightning*, Girard notes that the New Testament possesses a third point of correspondence with mythology that was missing in the Old Testament: the divinity of the victim. The Old Testament narratives of collective violence only include two of the three stages within myths: the initial mimetic crisis and collective violence. The final stage, however, the one in which "the resurrection ... reveals the divinity of the victim," is absent because the victims are never apotheosized in the Old Testament.[33] However, the Gospels brazenly introduce this final element, placing the Gospels in a direct correspondence to myths on all three accounts. For Girard, this correspondence does not jeopardize the veracity of the resurrection accounts but serves to bring the revelation to its climax.

For Girard, the resurrection is the moment at which the tide that has engulfed Jesus' followers in a sea of fear and preposterous charges, demanding his death, begins to ebb. The resurrection illumines the disciples who have been temporarily swept up in the opposition to Jesus.[34] Because of the resurrection, they become assured of Jesus' innocence because God has definitely intervened on behalf of the victim. As a result, the disciples break from their solidarity with the mob and become witnesses to the innocence of Jesus.[35] In the end, the death and resurrection of Jesus reveal the inanity of the human pattern of maintaining social order at the expense of innocent

30. Thus, Girard finds it significant that Pilate and Herod became friends over the execution of Jesus. See Girard, *I See Satan*, 132–33.

31. He cites John 15:25 here; see Girard, "Are the Gospels Mythical?" 30.

32. Girard, *I See Satan*, 127–28. Cf. Girard, *Evolution and Conversion*, 210 and Girard, *Scapegoat*, 102–4.

33. Girard, *I See Satan*, 106–7; cf. 121.

34. Ibid., 125; cf. 133–36, 189, 191 and Girard, *Evolution and Conversion*, 218.

35. Girard, "Are the Gospels Mythical?" 31.

victims. Jesus was a victim that was needlessly put to death, like so many victims before him.

Most importantly, in the cross and resurrection, the scapegoat mechanism which had remained buried in the subconscious of human culture "since the foundation of the world" becomes clearly manifest for those with the eyes to see. For Girard, these events reveal the truth about humans. Moreover, this revelation becomes the vehicle of salvation because it constitutes the fullest revelation of the violent nature of humanity and demonstrates that human culture has been founded and sustained by the murder of innocent victims.[36] In revealing this truth about human nature, humans are invited to relinquish their penchant for mimetic violence and follow Jesus' positive example of eschewing all violence. Thus, Jesus offers humanity a conversion away from the complicity in violence that has plagued humanity since its origins.

While the cross and resurrection reveal something profound about humans, they also reveal something about the nature of God. In the Christ event, humans are finally emancipated from "the illusion of a violent God."[37] Instead of being a God who would punish or threaten humans—which is equated with "violence" in Girardian thought—God is the God against such violence. To prove his character, "God himself accepts the role of the victim of the crowd so that he can save us all."[38] This is in direct contrast to the mythic gods that threaten to annihilate recalcitrant devotees or punish them with plagues. Instead of encouraging more victims, God in fact becomes a victim at the cross to reveal that he desires no more violence. God now offers human beings a better mimetic model, one free of violence and rivalry if they follow the model set forth in Jesus.[39] According to Girard, through being a victim that exposes humanity's violent nature and displays God's true nature, God rescues and saves human beings, and it is for this reason that one can rightly say that Girard offers a soteriological account of Jesus Christ.

Girard's Salvation History

For Girard, the saving revelation unleashed by the cross and resurrection comprises the conclusion to a long arduous process. The cross and resurrection were not surds tossed up on the shores of time, but events that finalized

---

36. Girard, "Are the Gospels Mythical?" 30.
37. Girard, *Evolution and Conversion*, 216.
38. Girard, *I See Satan*, 130.
39. Girard, *Battling to the End*, 80–82, 101, 106, 109.

God's attempts to reveal the truth throughout human history. With an explanation of the three theses informing Girard's soteriology in place, we can turn to how Girard understands this revelation being progressively conveyed over the course of the biblical canon. What follows traces Girard's salvation history through the various stages and genres of the Christian Bible.

Human Origins and the Fall

Though Girard adopts an evolutionary account for human origins, his account of human origins is closely wed to the Fall. For Girard, humans separate from their primal ancestors at the point when victimizing scapegoats begins.[40] In fact, he equates the mimetic behavior that culminates in the lynching of the innocent victim with original sin.[41] It is, therefore, not surprising that Girard's interpretation of Genesis 3 emphasizes the presence of mimetic desire and scapegoating. For him, when the serpent seduces Adam and Eve into eating the fruit, the text betrays the problem of the first humans, namely, that they allow a being other than God to mediate their desires. Eve allows the serpent to mediate her desires while Adam allows Eve to mediate his.[42] In addition, this narrative of the Garden reveals the scapegoating nature of human beings. When God confronts the errant humans, they try to affix blame on a culpable scapegoat. Adam blames Eve, and Eve blames the serpent.[43] Thus, in Genesis 3 Girard finds evidence that the biblical texts understand the nature of mimetic desire and its disastrous social consequences. Despite the corroboration Girard finds in this account, he still sees the account of Adam and Eve as "mythic" when it ends with God expelling sinful humankind from his presence.[44]

Fuller support for Girard's equation of mimetic theory with original sin is found in Genesis 4 with Cain's murder of Abel. Whatever was left unsaid in Genesis 3 about the primal murder, Girard finds on full display in the following chapter when Cain murders his innocent brother. Here Girard indicates one can see the lucid difference between the Bible and myth:

> The theme of the founding murder is not only mythical but also biblical. We find it in the book of Genesis, in Cain's murder of his brother, Abel. The account of this murder is not a founding myth; it is rather the biblical interpretation of all founding

---

40. Girard, *Things Hidden*, 95–96.
41. Girard, *Evolution and Conversion*, 198–99.
42. Girard, *A Theater of Envy*, 324.
43. Ibid., 324–25.
44. Girard, *Things Hidden*, 275.

myths. It recounts the bloody foundation of the beginnings of culture and the consequences of this foundation, which form the first mimetic cycle narrated in the Bible.[45]

For Girard, the story of Cain and Abel is not simply an account about two brothers but the story about human culture more generally: human culture derives from the murder of the innocent. Moreover, true to Girard's observation about the biblical texts, Abel is never seen as deserving his death, and Cain's action is condemned. Thus, according to Girard, the opening chapters of the Bible depict the biblical intelligence of the victim with great acuity, even if they resemble mythical texts in some respects.[46]

Patriarchal Narratives

In addition to grounding his mimetic theory in the opening chapters of Genesis, Girard also identifies a significant development during the later patriarchal narratives of Genesis. In particular, the account of Abraham's sacrifice of Isaac in Genesis 22 is significant. At the climax of the narrative, God forbids Abraham to sacrifice his son. In Isaac's place, they sacrifice a ram. For Girard, this episode is an important first step in the process of deconstructing the human penchant for human victims present in ancient cultures.[47] At this juncture, animal victims displace human victims in sacrificial practice. Though sacrifice itself maintains its existence, it no longer needs to be sustained by human victims. In fact, substituting animals for humans begins a process that will eventually lead to the dissolution of such practices altogether.

In the Joseph cycle of Genesis, Girard finds further support that the Bible defends victims over against the persecutors.[48] Joseph, who is hated by his own family, sold into slavery, charged with attempted rape, and incarcerated, is deemed to have suffered all of these afflictions unworthily, which exhibits the biblical truth of the victim's innocence.[49] Despite rising

---

45. Girard, *I See Satan*, 83; cf. Girard, *Things Hidden*, 144–49.

46. Noah's escape from the flood and Lot's rescue from Sodom and Gomorrah are other examples of the single victim escaping the threat of communal violence. Girard, *Things Hidden*, 143.

47. Girard, *Evolution and Conversion*, 203; cf. Girard, *I See Satan*, 119.

48. Girard, *I See Satan*, 106–20. Throughout, he compares the charges against Joseph and Oedipus showing that the charges never seem credible in the case of Joseph, but are assumed to be legitimate for Oedipus. Cf. Girard, *Evolution and Conversion*, 199–203.

49. See Girard, "The Bloody Skin of the Victim," 63. He writes, "If you have the Joseph story and the Gospels as point-counterpoint, you have the whole Bible, its whole truth, its whole beauty."

to power and providing salvation for his people and the Egyptians, Joseph is never divinized nor does he threaten retribution against the perpetrators. As a result, Joseph delivers an excellent example of the Bible's support of the victim against the accusations of the crowd. Thus, even in Genesis, Girard sees the beginnings of the Bible's deconstruction of sacrificial theology, even it is not completely dismantled at this point in salvation history.

Exodus and Conquest

Although Girard does not write much about the Exodus narratives, they seem to follow in the same mixed pattern of partially revealing the victimization of the Hebrews in Egypt while also participating in the mythic delight of seeing divine vengeance meted out upon Israel's enemies.[50] In addition, Moses seems to fit the characteristics of a "scapegoat-legislator" according to Girard.[51] His inability to speak well betrays the usual physical deformation of a scapegoat. Moreover, he is deemed guilty for slaying an Egyptian, not to mention the plagues on the Egyptians. Thus, the book of Exodus again gives a voice to the persecuted Israelites and Moses who were victimized in the narrative.

However, the biblical book of Exodus contains more than just the Israelites' escape from Egypt. It also contains the commandments and the laws that regulated ancient Israelite society. Based upon Girard's belief that prohibitions derive from the scapegoat mechanism, one might expect Girard to utter an entirely negative pronouncement regarding the Old Testament law codes. Nevertheless, Girard is able to maintain a cautiously positive evaluation of the Old Testament law for several reasons. First, although Girard concludes that certain laws seem archaic by today's standards, he notes that many laws were born out of the desire to suppress or even eliminate human violence.[52] Thus, the end that some laws sought to accomplish was honorable. Second, some of the laws demonstrate an awareness of mimetic desire. Girard cites the final command in the Decalogue as an example of this awareness: "You shall not covet your neighbor's house; you shall not covet your neighbor's wife, or male or female slave, or ox, or donkey, or anything that belongs to your neighbor" (Exod 20:17).[53] Girard privileges this commandment above the rest because it most directly strikes at the core of human violence and conflict since it reveals the way in which one's neigh-

---

50. Williams, Foreword in *I See Satan Fall Like Lightning*, xx.
51. Girard, *Scapegoat*, 178.
52. Girard, *Things Hidden*, 423. See also Girard, *I See Satan*, 12.
53. All biblical and apocryphal citations are from the NRSV.

bor inspires covetousness.[54] Furthermore, Girard argues that the previous four prohibitions—the ones outlawing murder, adultery, theft and bearing false witness—are subsumed under this final command.[55] As a result, the law codes significantly contribute to the biblical revelation of humanity's problem: mimetic desire crescendos in the victimization of the innocent person. Thus, at least some of the Old Testament laws are "necessary warnings against behavior that heightens violence by awakening jealous rivalries and vendettas."[56]

In spite of such affirmations about the Old Testament law codes, Girard maintains several criticisms of them. For one, Girard thinks their current formulation actually exacerbates mimetic desire rather than abates it. He writes, "Their primarily negative character ... inevitably provokes in us the mimetic urge to transgress them."[57] In other words, by prohibiting a particular action or object ("Thou shalt not ... "), they serve to elevate its desirability and the likelihood that others would crave it. Secondly, following the Apostle Paul's negative judgment of the law, he concludes that, after the fullness of the revelation available in Christ, the law can only function "as veils and obstacles that obstruct the fullness of revelation."[58] In their contexts, the Old Testament laws were meant to progress revelation to the next level. However, since we are reading them after the fullness of the revelation in Christ, we should not privilege them as being of equal fullness as that which is available in Christ. To accord them equal weight with the revelation of Christ is to regress to a stage previously surpassed. To summarize, Girard affirms that there is positive revelation present in Exodus and the law codes but also qualifies his positive statements in light of his understanding of revelation's progression in the biblical canon.

Girard seems to offer a similar assessment of Joshua and Judges, though they receive minimal treatment in his work. Based on his few brief statements, one could say that such books still possess a strong degree of the mythic tendency. For example, he makes the following comments about Judges: "In fact, in the Old Testament one still finds a good deal of violence: in Judges and other historical books, there is still a mythical valorization of

---

54. Girard, *I See Satan*, 11–13. This is adopted by Alison too. Alison, *Joy of Being Wrong*, 148.

55. Girard's elevation of the final commandment differs from the approach of others like Luther. Luther elevates the first command, arguing that living out faith in God will lead one to obey the remaining commandments. See Luther, *Works*, 31:353; 44:110–14.

56. Cowdell, *René Girard*, 89.

57. Girard, *I See Satan*, 14.

58. Girard, *Things Hidden*, 190–91.

the community against the scapegoat victim."[59] Thus, though Girard affirms that Exodus and conquest narratives proclaim the innocence of the victim, they have not pried themselves free from what he calls the "mythical" point of view.

Wisdom Literature

Like other Old Testament texts, Girard believes the wisdom literature possesses the same duality. While they do defend the victim against the crowds, they also promulgate a notion of God as angry and vengeful. In the book of Psalms, Girard finds the psalms of lament particularly striking and indicative of the biblical revelation in that they give a voice to the victims of ancient Israel. He writes, "As far as I know, these texts are the first in human history to allow those who would simply become silent victims in the world of myth to voice their complaint as hysterical crowds besiege them."[60] For example, the psalmist of Psalm 17 asks for God's protection against unjust violence:

> Guard me as the apple of the eye; hide me in the shadow of your wings, from the wicked who despoil me, my deadly enemies who surround me. They close their hearts to pity; with their mouths they speak arrogantly. They track me down; now they surround me; they set their eyes to cast me to the ground. They are like a lion eager to tear, like a young lion lurking in ambush (Ps 17:9b–12).

In Psalms like this, the cries of the innocent are preserved in spite of the mob's desire to extinguish it. What has been preserved is not the mythical condemnation of the victim, but his cry to YHWH. For this reason, Girard believes the Psalms make an important step forward in salvation history.

Still, the Psalms do not speak with all of one voice. While some side with the victim as noted above, others expect God to mete out judgment upon evildoers, which reifies a "mythical" perspective according to Girard.[61] In fact, because of this, Girard once reminded one of his interviewers that the Psalmist is "not a Christian yet."[62] Psalm 137 is a prime example in this regard when it relishes the thought of future conquerors smashing the infants of Babylon against the rocks as recompense for their decimation of the

---

59. Girard, *Evolution and Conversion*, 207.
60. Girard, *I See Satan*, 115–16; Girard, *Job*, 8; and Girard, "Bloody Skin," 62.
61. Girard particularly finds Psalm 73 an example of this tendency. See Girard, *Job*, 55–59, 122.
62. Girard, "Bloody Skin," 62.

Israelites (Ps 137:8–9). Due to Psalms like this, Girard still thinks the Psalms perpetuate a mythical point of view, despite the milestone that is attained. However, the mythical viewpoint seems to be gradually eroding because Girard concludes that "the cry for revenge is quite secondary" in the Psalms.[63] As a result, the biblical revelation has not simply gained a foothold but is beginning to overcome the opposite point of view in the texts of the Psalms.

Girard also devoted an entire book to analyzing Job and came to similar conclusions as he discovers in other portions of the Old Testament, namely, that the book of Job possesses both pieces that share the biblical support of the victim and passages that buttress the victimary tendencies of humans and their corresponding views of God. Girard's exegesis of Job emphasizes a strand of argumentation within the book that contains Job's revolt against the indictment being forced upon him by his visiting friends. Here he notes that in spite of the theology being brandished against him, namely, that God is punishing him for his wrongdoing, Job still manages to affirm that God will come to his defense (Job 16:19–21; 19:25–27). Admittedly, Job struggles to hold on to this insight in opposition to his friends' point of view since they are persuasively trying to elicit an admission of guilt from him (Job 30:9–15).[64] However, despite second guessing himself at points in the dialogues with his friends, Girard identifies Job's assertion of innocence as the true message of the exchanges between Job and his friends. Consequently, if one affirms alongside of Job that he is innocent regarding the calamities that have struck him, then the calamities plaguing Job have no divine origin, but are solely the creation of his fellow humans.[65] Hence, Girard concludes that Job is "the victim of his people," who, as a result of the mimetic crisis plaguing his community, finds himself being forced to become a scapegoat for his people.[66]

Despite a collection of verses that corroborate his understanding of biblical revelation, Girard does recognize that there is much in the book of Job that supports a view that God punishes the wicked and perhaps Job too. For instance, even the opening prologue (Job 1:1—2:10) seems to credit God with some degree of responsibility for Job's calamities since he allows Satan to plague Job. Furthermore, the ending monologue by God brings Job to silence, attenuating his protests of innocence (Job 38:1—42:6). These portions of Job stand in conflict with Girard's emphasis on God's defense of

---

63. Ibid., 63.

64. Girard, *Job*, 125–26; cf. Girard, *Evolution and Conversion*, 196–97 and Girard, *I See Satan*, 117. In the latter, he calls Job a "super-psalm."

65. Girard, *Job*, 3–4.

66. This is the subtitle of Girard's book on Job, *Job: The Victim of his People*.

Job's innocence. As a result, Girard asserts that the prologue and concluding speeches of God constitute the theology of the victimizers who are attempting to suppress the insights expressed by Job himself.[67] In the end, Girard concludes that the prologue and conclusion derive from a different author than the one who wrote the dialogues of Job. If Girard is right, the current form of Job is the record of a clash between the biblical revelation of the victim's innocence and the attempts of mythical theology to smother it.[68]

Prophetic Literature

For Girard, the zenith of Old Testament revelation is attained in the prophetic corpus, even if it still falls short of the revelation that will come in the Gospels.[69] In the prophets, one finds the starkest repudiation of all sacrifice, human and animal.[70] Girard writes, " . . . in the prophetic texts . . . animal sacrifices will not work any more . . . . In other words, the Bible provides not merely a replacement of the object to be sacrificed, but the end of the sacrificial order in its entirety . . . ."[71] The prophets, therefore, deconstruct the institution of sacrifice itself rather than simply trying to displace or suppress its harmful effects like earlier stages of salvation history. In addition, the prophets recalibrate Israel's maintenance of the law codes. Instead of allowing their adherence to degenerate into a rigid form of legalism, the prophets emphasize the law's ethical focus as its *"raison d'etre,* which is the maintenance of harmonious relationships within the community."[72] Thus, the prophets take the process of revelation to the next stage by revealing that God's primary intention was the creation of a social order void of victimization.

---

67. Girard, *Job*, 141–43. Brueggemann, in contrast, suggests that interpreters should let the tensions in the book stand and that we should treat the work holistically. See Brueggeman, *Theology of the Old Testament*, 489–91.

68. Girard's interpretation of Job, however, has not been compelling to everyone. E.g., Levine, "René Girard on Job," 125–33.

69. Kirwan demarcates the prophets as the second phase of scriptural interpretation of the scapegoat mechanism. The final stage comes with the Gospels. See Kirwan, *Philosophy and Theology*, 84. To my knowledge, Girard does not make this designation.

70. Girard, *Things Hidden*, 240. This view of the prophetic denouncement of sacrifice is debated, even by some who adopt pieces of Girard's thought. E.g. Daly, *Sacrifice Unveiled*, 33–34.

71. Girard, *Evolution and Conversion*, 203; cf. Girard, *I See Satan*, 119.

72. Girard, *Things Hidden*, 154. As Girard notes though, the prophets are simply carrying out the inherent implications found in the law itself rather than completely disparaging sacrifice (e.g. Lev 19:18).

For all the accolades that Girard confers on the prophetic texts, Girard still sees mythological accretions present. A closer look at his handling of the final Servant Song from Isaiah (Isaiah 52:13—53:12) demonstrates the problematic nature of the prophets that Girard identifies, though it occurs less frequently than it does in other portions of the Old Testament.[73] Girard equates the marring and deformation of YHWH's servant as a classic example of a mob lynching. Since the plight of the servant resembles the classic story of the innocent victim so well, Girard avers that ultimately God had nothing to do with the death: it was caused solely by humans.[74] However, the author of the text, at least in Girard's estimation, jeopardizes this reality by crediting God with the violence. Speaking of the servant, Isaiah 53:4 says, "Surely he has borne our infirmities and carried our diseases; yet we accounted him stricken, struck down by God, and afflicted." Thus, God is reintroduced as a cause of the violence when, according to Girard's theory, God would have nothing to do with such violence. As a result, Girard concludes, "This ambiguity in the role of Yahweh corresponds to the general conception of the deity in the Old Testament. In the prophetic books, this conception tends to be increasingly divested of the violence characteristic of primitive deities. . . . Yet all the same, in the Old Testament we never arrive at a conception of the deity that is entirely foreign to violence."[75] According to Girard, in Isaiah 53, the Old Testament comes closest to most fully revealing the scapegoat mechanism but falters at the finish line. As a result, another impartation of divine revelation will be required, namely, Jesus Christ, to make this point unequivocally.

The Gospels

The Old Testament, though progressively unveiling the anthropological insights about human nature, never fully arrives at a complete, pristine revelation of the scapegoat mechanism and the innocence of the victims.[76] It

---

73. Girard, *Things Hidden*, 200. In other places, he seems more positive about how Isaiah 53 correlates with his thesis. See Girard, *I See Satan*, 28–31.

74. Girard, *Things Hidden*, 157, 227.

75. Ibid., 157.

76. There is some tension here within Girard's thought. In a desire to affirm continuity with the Old Testament, there is a concerted effort to see the Gospels as fulfilling the Old Testament itself and thus of one piece. If one posits too strong of a rupture, one risks reinstituting a system of differentiation. However, Girard seems to jeopardize this at times when he describes the New Testament as constituting a "decisive break" from the Old Testament with its conclusive vitiation of sacrifice. See Girard, *Things Hidden*, 200.

remains ambiguous apart from the New Testament. Girard sees the Gospels, in particular the cross of Christ, as the hermeneutical key, which unlocks the intended revelation of the Old Testament.[77] He affirms that Jesus is "a clearer and more definite revelation" of sacrifice who thereby becomes the savior of "all human beings."[78] The Old Testament thus heralds and prefigures the revelation that only fully comes in Jesus and the Gospels.[79]

Jesus' Ministry

While the Old Testament never finishes the task of revealing the human penchant for scapegoats, Jesus' ministry takes the process begun in the Old Testament to its logical conclusion. Girard finds this present in the way that the Gospels apply Old Testament texts to Jesus. For instance, Second Isaiah has often been noted as containing important prophetic hopes for the restoration of Israel, which will be more fully discussed in subsequent chapters. The opening verses of Second Isaiah look forward to God's restoration of Israel: "A voice cries out: 'In the wilderness prepare the way of the LORD, make straight in the desert a highway for our God. Every valley shall be lifted up, and every mountain and hill be made low; the uneven ground shall become level, and the rough places a plain" (Isaiah 40:3–4). Although most commentators take these verses as a reference to Cyrus' edict that allowed the exiled Jews to return to their native soil, Girard departs from the academic guild at this point by using a figural interpretation. For him, the leveling of the terrain constitutes "the most tremendous *figura* of the sacrificial crisis, of the violent undifferentiation process."[80] In other words, it is an allusion to the scapegoat mechanism's erasure of difference in a community. When the Synoptic writers use this verse to introduce the ministry of Jesus in this way, they are indicating "that Jesus emerges at the cynosure of a crisis which calls for the designation of a new scapegoat, and this would be Jesus; this new scapegoating will be the occasion for God to reveal himself."[81] In this way, Girard situates Jesus and his ministry within the larger prophetic context, which is taken to be one anticipating another cataclysmic victimization.

In the Gospels, Jesus' main message proclaims the advent of the kingdom of God. For Girard, Jesus' announcement of the kingdom constitutes

77. Girard, *Evolution and Conversion*, 256. See also Girard, *Job*, 163.
78. Girard, *Evolution and Conversion*, 206.
79. Girard, *Things Hidden*, 205.
80. Girard, *Evolution and Conversion*, 209; cf. Girard, *I See Satan*, 29–31.
81. Girard, *Evolution and Conversion*, 210.

an invitation for the Jewish people to forsake the violence constitutive of culture and to embrace the peace offered in the kingdom of God.[82] According to Girard, the Kingdom brings an unmediated relationship with God. Instead of relating to God through means of sacrifices, the relationship is now based upon the "rules of the kingdom."[83] These new rules of the kingdom bring social reconciliation apart from violence: "The Kingdom of God means the complete and definitive elimination of every form of vengeance and every form of reprisal in relations between men."[84] In fact, it is fair to say the Kingdom ushers in the cessation of violence altogether.

As the various audiences refuse the offer of the Kingdom, Jesus responds with dire warnings—basically, the Apocalyptic sections of the Gospels—of how a failure to embrace the Kingdom will affect his listeners. For Girard, Jesus' Apocalyptic teachings are not resorting to threats of divine vengeance for refusing the Kingdom but demonstrating a rather prescient understanding of human evil: refusing to relinquish human violence will result in bringing destruction upon oneself.[85] In summary, violence delivers its own punishment. The Apocalypse is not a divine thunderbolt falling from heaven upon humans, but the inherent return of violence upon its perpetrator.[86] As a result, Jesus offers his contemporaries two alternatives: embrace the Kingdom of God without violence or the Apocalyptic return of violence will be the end result.

Not only does Jesus offer a kingdom of non-violence, but his teaching also exhibits an uncanny insight into the scapegoat mechanism. For example, in John 8:43–44, Jesus states that the devil was a liar and a murderer from the beginning, and Girard claims this as evidence corroborating his thesis that humanity originated in a founding murder.[87] According to Girard, designating Satan as a murderer from the beginning is a direct allusion to Cain's murder of Abel.[88] Such an allusion, according to Girard, acknowledges the foundation of human culture upon the murder of innocent victims, which is precisely what Cain does. Furthermore, the lie associated with the devil refers to the ultimate deception that surrounds the scapegoat mechanism and keeps humanity from acknowledging its reality. Additionally, Jesus'

---

82. Girard, *Things Hidden*, 201–3.
83. Ibid., 183.
84. Ibid., 197.
85. Ibid., 203.
86. Ibid., 260.
87. Girard, *Things Hidden*, 161 and Girard, *I See Satan*, 85–94.
88. Girard, "The Evangelical Subversion of Myth," 33. Here he makes the connection more explicit by pointing to a similar text from Matthew 23:35.

teaching contains several allusions to Satan as the adversary or opponent. In interpreting the passages about Satan, Girard demythologizes Satan in such a way as to equate him and his persona with the mimetic desire that results in communal conflict.[89] In fact, "Satan" for Girard denotes the entire mimetic process from the solicitation of initial desire to the hostile opposition generated between rivals and its consequent elimination of the victim.[90] In one particular discourse in the Gospels, Jesus rhetorically asks about the manner in which Satan casts out Satan (Mark 3:23).[91] In the conversation, Jesus verbalizes another insight into the mechanism by recognizing that Satan works by casting out Satan. According to Girard, when the social conflagration reaches the pinnacle moment at which it finds release, it does so at the expense of the victim. With each new victim a new form of social "order" is constructed. As such, the former evil is cast out but only by introducing a new form of victimary culture, hence establishing Satan once again.[92] Thus, Satan is willing to be cast out, but only when a new form of satanic culture has been generated.

Other additional passages in the Gospel are taken as supporting Girard's conclusions. For example, there are themes of unjustified violent lynching as seen in the parable of the wicked tenants and suggested in Jesus' quotation of Psalm 118:22: "The stone that the builders rejected has become the chief cornerstone."[93] Moreover, Girard finds further examples in the curses against the Pharisees that deride them for being "like whitewashed tombs, which on the outside look beautiful, but inside they are full of the bones of the dead and of all kinds of filth" (Matt 23:27). For Girard, the reference to tombs can be connected to funeral rites, which, in his view, ultimately derive from the scapegoat mechanism.[94] Thus, the allusion to tombs reminds Jesus' listeners that human culture is founded upon the graves of past innocent victims.

89. Girard, *I See Satan*, 32–46. See also Girard, *Scapegoat*, 165–83.

90. Girard, *I See Satan*, 43.

91. Girard's exegesis here is a bit troubling. Jesus embarks on this discourse not to talk about Satan per se, but to disprove the claims of his detractors, who are claiming that he is possessed by Beelzebul. He explains in another work that Jesus is here quoting the logic and beliefs of his interlocutors. See Girard, *Scapegoat*, 186.

92. Girard, *I See Satan*, 34–35.

93. Jesus cites Psalm 118 in Matt 21:42, Mark 12:10–11, and Luke 20:17. Girard, "The Evangelical Subversion of Myth," 37. I will point out that Girard fails to cite Psalm 118:23 ("This is the Lord's doing; it is marvelous in our eyes"), which suggests divine involvement in the rejection of the cornerstone. The passages in Matthew and Mark both include Psalm 118:23; it is only absent in Luke.

94. Girard, "The Evangelical Subversion of Myth," 39–41.

In *I See Satan Fall like Lightning*, Girard explicitly labels Jesus' warnings about coming scandals as warnings about scapegoat mechanisms (e.g. Matt 18:6–9).[95] For Girard, the warning against scandals refers most directly to:

> ... the behavior of mimetic rivals who, as they mutually prevent each other from appropriating the object they covet, reinforce more and more their double desire, their desire for both the other's object of the desire and for the desire of the other. Each consistently takes the opposite view of the other in order to escape their inexorable rivalry, but they always return to collide with the fascinating obstacle that each one has come to be for the other.[96]

In short, Jesus' warnings about scandals inform his audience about the nature of mimetic rivalry and its proliferation within a community.[97]

Finally, and most importantly, Girard sees Jesus continuing the prophetic rejection of sacrifice. Citing Matthew 9:13 where Jesus quotes from Hosea 6:6, saying, "Go and learn what this means, 'I desire mercy, not sacrifice,'" Girard sees Jesus corroborating the prophetic critique of sacrifice, which is not simply a critique of impure motives in the sacrificial act but the sacrificial enterprise itself.[98] In fact, when Girard ventures into a theological exploration of what it means for Jesus to be the incarnate Word of God, he equates the Word with the prophetic oracle: "I wish for mercy and not sacrifices."[99] Thus, the various emphases in Jesus' ministry—the kingdom of God, his awareness of the scapegoat mechanism along with its generation of human culture, and the rejection of sacrifice—all combine to provide Girard grounds for concluding that Jesus sought to reveal the mimetic nature of humanity in his ministry and to repudiate the ideology supporting sacrifice.

The Passion of Christ

Although Jesus operates with an intelligent awareness of the scapegoat mechanism, it is not until the death and resurrection of Christ that sacrifice itself is finally deconstructed. For Girard, the events precipitating the

---

95. Girard, *I See Satan*, 16–24; cf. Girard, *Scapegoat*, 162 and Girard, *Evolution and Conversion*, 223–24.

96. Girard, *I See Satan*, 16.

97. Even the disciples are not exempt. See Girard, *Scapegoat*, 158.

98. Girard, *Things Hidden*, 180.

99. Ibid., 210. Elsewhere he affirms that this is the incarnation of the nonviolence of the Father (ibid., 269).

crucifixion of Jesus correspond precisely to the snowballing of mimetic rivalry that has consumed a host of human victims throughout history. Girard finds confirmation of this correlation littered throughout the portrayal of the Passion. First, Jesus' persecutors articulate a rather explicit belief in the efficaciousness of the scapegoat mechanism. In the Gospel of John, the religious leaders conclude: " . . . it is better for you to have one man die for the people than to have the whole nation destroyed" (John 11:50). For Girard, this is further evidence that the sacrificial logic has been deeply ingrained in Jesus' antagonists who will eventually seal his fate on the cross.[100] Second, the entire social structure turns upon Jesus. Together, the religious and political leaders consent to his death, being pulled into the conflagration by the violence of the mob and their own desire to maintain power.[101] What is more, the disciples also seem to acquiesce in this moment. By failing to stand by him, they give "their explicit or implicit assent to his death . . . ."[102] Thus, Jesus dies abandoned by all, just like the solitary victim, which generated human culture. Third, Girard also identifies places in the Gospels where the community experiences the reconciliatory effects of aligning against a common foe. Here he points to Luke 23:12 where it says, "That same day Herod and Pilate became friends with each other; before this they had been enemies."[103] Thus, the common alliance against Jesus brings two political leaders together in friendship, just like the victims of the past. By combining these various elements together, Girard concludes that Jesus' crucifixion bears structural similarities typical of the scapegoat mechanism.

Although the events leading up to Jesus' death correspond precisely to the stages of the mimetic contagion, Girard observes that the Gospels continue the biblical defense of the victim by affirming Jesus' innocence. Girard's quintessential observation is that, despite the array of people aligned against Jesus, he is never presented as guilty or worthy of such opprobrium as myths would depict the victim of the crowd. He writes, "In fact the opposite is the case: the Passion is presented as a blatant piece of injustice. Far from taking the collective violence upon itself, the text places it squarely on those who are responsible."[104] The Gospels place responsibility on the perpetrators in various ways. The clearest expression of Jesus' innocence is Christ's declaration in John 15:25 that "They hated me without a cause,"

100. Girard, *Scapegoat*, 112-14.

101. Ibid., 105-6.

102. Girard, *Things Hidden*, 167. He corroborates the point in another work *The Scapegoat*: "The fact that even the disciples cannot resist the effect of the scapegoat reveals the power exerted by the persecutors' account over man" (105).

103. Girard, *I See Satan*, 132-33.

104. Girard, *Things Hidden*, 168.

which affirms the vacuous rationality behind the mob's lynching of Jesus.[105] Like other victims throughout human culture, the charges against Jesus were *ad hoc* constructions that had little purchase on reality. This is not to forget that the persecutors think they are doing justice. The main point, for Girard, is the contrast made by Jesus and the Gospel narrators to the effect that the persecutors' assiduous allegiance to their notions of "justice" is actually injustice at its worst. The Gospels also capture Jesus' innocence in other ways. For example, the Gospel of John refers to Jesus as the Lamb of God, which emphasizes "the innocence of this victim, the injustice of the condemnation, and the causelessness of the hatred of which it is the object."[106] Moreover, Jesus' constant comparison with the prophets—i.e. the scapegoats of the Old Testament—shows Jesus receives the same unjust persecution.[107] Therefore, although Jesus is portrayed as a victim of the mimetic contagion, the Gospel writers never capitulate to the pressure to believe Jesus deserved his fate.

The Resurrection of Christ

It would be a mistake to say that Jesus being the innocent victim on the cross is the only thing necessary to attain human salvation in Girard's soteriology, for the resurrection also plays an essential role. Girard notes that the Old Testament narratives of collective violence only include two of the three stages of mimetic theory: the initial mimetic crisis and collective violence. The final stage, however, the one in which "the resurrection . . . reveals the divinity of the victim" is absent because the victims are never apotheosized in the Old Testament.[108] However, the Gospels brazenly introduce this final element, placing the Gospels in a direct correspondence to myths in all three stages. For Girard, this correspondence does not jeopardize the veracity of the accounts but serves to bring the revelation to its culmination.

In fact, the resurrection is the moment at which the tide that has engulfed Jesus, demanding his death, begins to abate. The resurrection

---

105. Girard, *I See Satan*, 127–28. Cf. Girard, *Evolution and Conversion*, 210 and Girard, *Scapegoat*, 102–4.

106. Girard, *Scapegoat*, 117.

107. Ibid. Interestingly, here he takes the sign of Jonah as a reference, not to three days or to resurrection, but as a reference to Jonah's victimization by the sailors. Girard, also sees Jesus as mirroring Isaiah 53, which also describes the fate of a solitary victim, making Isaiah 53 a proto-evangelium in the Old Testament. See Girard, *The Girard Reader*, 274.

108. Girard, *I See Satan*, 106–7; cf. 121.

illumines the disciples who have been swept up in the pogrom against Jesus.[109] It is only after the resurrection that the disciples break from their solidarity with the mob and become witnesses to the innocence of Jesus. Moreover, the resurrection is not simply a revelation about Jesus' innocence, but it also constitutes the final revelation of humanity.[110] It is the resurrection, in conjunction with the collective victimization of Jesus that reveals what human culture has always sought to cover up, namely, the manner in which its own violence has generated deities. By revealing this fact more lucidly than any other event, the resurrection "opposes so decisively the power of the mythic cover-up that once we perceive this opposition, the thematic resemblances between myth and Gospel fade into insignificance by comparison."[111] Thus, it brings all the edifices that have supported humankind, including archaic religion and its derivatives, crumbling to the ground.

Due to his comparison with mythology, Girard must defend the veracity of the resurrection accounts from the charge of being another mythic story of a dying and rising god. Much of his defense lies in the uniqueness of Jesus' resurrection in contrast to myths. The chief difference lies in "the power of revelation" found in Jesus' death and resurrection by which he insinuates that it alone is capable of revealing the violent origins of human culture.[112] From the unparalleled "power of revelation" found in the Gospel accounts, Girard makes two conclusions. First, this revelation cannot derive from humans who have been mired in the lies and mythology of victims made sacred. It can only come from the divine realm. The fact that only God can exist above the mimetic fray serves to support the affirmation of Jesus' divinity.[113] Moreover, Jesus is declared divine before the collective victimization occurs and not as a result of it.[114] Second, because the Gospels never succumb to the invectives of Jesus' persecutors and assiduously hold to the truth of his innocence, one is warranted in assuming that their proclamation of the resurrection is true as well. Christ's resurrection is the resurrection of an innocent victim at the hands of God, not one that is mythically generated by human violence.[115] Moreover, the Gospels depart from the myths in the fact that the mob never proclaims Jesus as divine but only a small group

---

109. Girard, *I See Satan*, 125; cf. 133–36, 189, 191 and Girard, *Evolution and Conversion*, 218.

110. Girard, "Are the Gospels Mythical?" 31.

111. Girard, *I See Satan*, 135.

112. Ibid.

113. Girard, *Things Hidden*, 218–19; cf. Girard, *I See Satan*, 131.

114. Girard, *Battling to the End*, 104.

115. Girard, *I See Satan*, 135.

of disciples, a minority that has managed to break away from the mob.[116] Girard's chief defense of the resurrection again derives from the fact that, though the Gospels might mirror other examples of a dying and rising god, a closer comparison reveals many significant differences that support the veracity of the Gospel accounts.

For additional support of the resurrection, Girard notes that the Gospel writers openly mention a supposed resurrection that they believe to be false. He points to the fact that Matthew and Mark both contain Herod's comment betraying his personal belief that John the Baptist had been resurrected (Mark 6:16).[117] He argues that if the Gospel writers were conniving propagandists, they would have never allowed the threat of another person being resurrected to stand in contest with the resurrection of Christ.[118] The Gospel writers, however, were secure in their affirmation of the resurrection to the point that they were willing to let the true and the false resurrection stand side by side. Moreover, they allow themselves this luxury because the false resurrection, that of John the Baptist, once again reveals the usual way in which humans create deities: John the Baptist was murdered like a collective victim under Herod. It is little wonder that Herod feared him coming back from the dead as a malevolent deity.

Salvation

At this point, salvation history has arrived at an essential destination. The death and resurrection of Christ procure salvation for humankind by emancipating humans from the cultural edifices of the scapegoat mechanism. Once the scapegoat mechanism has been exposed, as it has been in the death and resurrection of Jesus, it loses its power to conceal and re-mythologize victims. Girard describes it in the following manner: "Once understood, the mechanisms can no longer operate; we believe less and less in the culpability of the victims they demand. Deprived of the food that sustains them, the institutions deprived from these mechanisms collapse one after the other about us."[119] As a result of the revelation found in the Gospels, human culture has now been liberated from its own self-inflicted imprisonment. It no longer needs to continue scapegoating innocent victims to procure its own survival.

---

116. Ibid., 123.
117. Girard, *Girard Reader*, 263.
118. Girard, *I See Satan*, 133–36.
119. Girard, *The Scapegoat*, 101.

Although the revelation is primarily about the nature of humanity, the Gospels do reveal something of God according to Girard. For one, it demonstrates to humans "that God himself accepts the role of the victim of the crowd so that he can save us all."[120] This is a direct contrast to the mythic gods that threaten to annihilate disobedient followers. Instead of encouraging more victims, God in fact becomes a victim. In light of this, the revelation of God in the person of Jesus Christ disabuses humankind, through his victimhood, "of the illusion of a violent God, which must be abolished in favour of Christ's knowledge of his Father."[121] God is thus a God of nonviolence.

Conclusion

For Girard, salvation history is the progressive revelation of the nature of mimetic desire and its corresponding demand for innocent victims to sustain human culture. The substitution of animal sacrifices for humans in the patriarchal narratives is an important step forward in this regard. The law codes also contribute to this process by suppressing mimetic desire and rivalry within the community. The Psalms come to the defense of the innocent victims and record their plaintive cries, even as they yearn for divine recompense against their enemies. With the prophets, there is a noticeable step forward as the institution of sacrifice is rejected entirely. However, the Old Testament contains an ambiguous view of God for Girard and thus it never arrives at the fullness of revelation. Only with the Gospels, which contain the death and resurrection of Jesus, where God becomes a victim of his people to emancipate them from the practice of scapegoating has the revelation arrived *in toto*.

Although Girard weaves a compelling narrative of salvation history and finds passages that suggest the biblical texts are aware of mimetic desire and the human tendency to scapegoat, Girard has avoided some of the texts in the Gospels that are problematic for his case, which will be analyzed in later chapters. While the Gospels can be said to be aware of humanity's tendency to scapegoat, it does not necessarily follow that the Gospels entirely undermine atonement theology as a result and future chapters will return to a closer evaluation of passages that jeopardize the account of salvation history offered by Girard. For the next chapter, however, our attention turns to scholars who have been significantly informed by Girard. Some of them

---

120. Girard, *I See Satan*, 130.
121. Girard, *Evolution and Conversion*, 216.

26   BLOODLESS ATONEMENT?

have been more attentive to problematic passages and offered varying responses to them. To these thinkers we now turn.

2

Reading the Bible With the Girardians

NOT SURPRISINGLY, RENÉ GIRARD's thought has received varied responses. Many have found Girard's work compelling and have taken up the basic elements of Girard's theories, adding particular nuances and developments to Girard's fundamental insights. Although some theologians and scholars have embraced Girardian soteriology wholly, others have offered cautious and sometimes strident critiques of his work. In light of this divergent reception, Girard remains a controversial figure, heralded by some and questioned by others. In what follows, I elucidate some of the ways in which Girard's soteriology and exegesis of the Gospels has been both adopted and employed by various authors, particularly noting interaction with the Last Supper sayings when such is present in the author's work since these passages will play a substantial role in my own evaluation of Girard's claims.

Since Girard's interdisciplinary approach spans several different disciplines, even within theological studies, this particular chapter has divided Girard's interlocutors into two categories. The first includes those who engage Girard's exegesis of the Gospels and the Bible, that is, those working primarily as biblical theologians. The second group focuses primarily on the theological implications of Girard's thought. While these authors are not devoid of biblical interpretation, their approach is more theological than exegetical in nature.

Biblical Interpretation and Girard

Raymund Schwager

Raymund Schwager was among the first to corroborate Girard's biblical anthropology and soteriology across a broader swath of biblical texts than what Girard himself used.[1] Written as an evaluation and development of

---

1. See North, "Violence and the Bible," 14.

Girard's *Violence and the Sacred*, Schwager's *Must There be Scapegoats?* still constitutes one of the most sweeping attempts at reading the Christian Bible from a Girardian perspective wherein the biblical God is completely disassociated with violence.[2] Schwager's analysis of the Old Testament reveals that, for the great majority of the time, much of the violence that is credited to God simply comprises humans perpetrating violence against one another when the fuller context is taken into account.[3] At the same time, Schwager does not deny the presence of some texts, ostensibly few in his analysis, that attribute violence directly to the hand of YHWH, which leads him to the conclusion that YHWH's relationship to violence is ambiguous in the Old Testament.[4] Appropriating a manner of Old Testament exegesis akin to the early church fathers, Schwager suggests that the true nature of the Old Testament can only be read in light of the New Testament, which posits Jesus as the center of God's saving action for humanity and the hermeneutical key for unlocking the biblical texts.

In his approach to interpreting the New Testament, Schwager uses a particular set of texts to guide his reading of the New Testament. Following Girard quite closely, he finds in the summary to the parable of the wicked tenants (Matt 21:33–44; Mark 12:1–11; Luke 20:9–18) the hermeneutical key to the New Testament: "The stone that the builders rejected has become the cornerstone" (Mark 12:10).[5] As he points out, this citation from Psalm 118:22 finds itself repeated across several sectors of the New Testament, ranging from the Gospels to Acts, 1 Peter, and some allusions in Paul.[6] The violent rejection of Jesus—rather than his substitutionary or expiatory death on behalf of others—comprises the key to understanding the cross, and Schwager avers that this theme is "a summation of the contents of the primitive Christian kerygma."[7] Christ, the rejected one, thus maps onto Girard's portrayal of Jesus as the innocent scapegoat who is rejected by the community. At this point, Schwager proceeds in reading New Testament

2. Schwager, *Must There be Scapegoats?*. The work was formerly published in German as Schwager, *Brauchen wir einen Sündenbock?*.

3. Schwager, *Scapegoats*, 55–70. These observations influence the direction in which he interprets the apocalyptic and judgment pronouncements by Jesus in his later work. See, for example, Schwager, *Jesus in the Drama of Salvation*, 159. This was originally published as *Jesus in Heilsdrama*.

4. Schwager, *Scapegoats*, 55–70, 135.

5. This intrabiblical quotation of Psalm 118:22 is placed in a similar location in Luke 20:17 and Matthew 21:42. Schwager makes use of this verse as a hermeneutical key in other works as well. See also Schwager, *Jesus in the Drama*, 140.

6. Matt 21:42; Mark 12:10–11; Luke 20:17; Acts 4:11; 1 Cor 3:11; Eph 2:20; and 1 Pet 2:7.

7. Schwager, *Scapegoats*, 145.

soteriology along Girardian lines: Jesus' innocence reveals the sinfulness of humanity and their pent up anger directed at God.[8]

While it is clear that Schwager's soteriology is rooted in the fertile soil of Girard's exegesis, Schwager does advance a soteriology more nuanced than what one finds in Girard. While Girard seems to avoid the biblical passages that describe Jesus' death as "necessary" (e.g. Luke 24:26), Schwager contends that the cross was necessary on two accounts. First, Schwager sees the incarnation as necessarily culminating in the cross. Unlike Girard, Schwager's notion of sin sees God, rather than the human other, as the ultimate rival. In fact, he sees this animosity toward God underlying all human scapegoating, which he believes is ultimately—though indirectly and unconsciously—targeted at God.[9] Thus, when Christ claims to be God, the suppressed human vitriol against the divine is unleashed upon him with fury. As a result, the cross was not the arbitrary selection of a victim, but the colluding hatred of humankind against the divine directed at the one who claimed to be God. Second, the cross was necessary in order to reveal the goodness of God. Situated in the larger context of Jesus' proclamation of the kingdom of God, which was met with firm denial by his contemporaries, the only way the light of the kingdom could cast out the darkness was to make the ultimate demonstration of love and forgiveness. For Schwager, human recalcitrance against Jesus' proclamation of the kingdom had become obstinate to the point that only the experience of forgiveness in response to the lynching of the Son could pierce the darkness.[10] The cross, therefore, manifests God's unceasing love, which does not return evil for evil, but instead responds with forgiveness and acceptance of sinners. In making the cross more about the revelation of God's goodness and forgiveness, Schwager differs from Girard. Whereas the emphasis in Girard's soteriology seems to fall upon revealing and emancipating humans from their sinful patterns, Schwager subordinates the exhibition of humanity's sin to the larger objective of seeing the Christ event as the revelation of God's forgiveness and goodness. As such, the cross is not simply the revelation and negation of human sin, but the revelation of God's positive and welcoming response to human depravity.

Schwager's exegesis of the Last Supper sayings is woven into the fabric of his broader soteriology. Although some scholars question whether the sayings derive from Jesus, Schwager affirms that they originate with Jesus

---

8. Ibid., 214.

9. Ibid., 190–200.

10. Schwager, "Christ's Death and the Prophetic Critique of Sacrifice," 120. See also Schwager, *Banished from Eden*, 60–63.

himself and that they do in fact offer readers an indication of how Jesus thought about his imminent death.[11] Upon this conclusion, he argues that these sayings must be interpreted in line with Jesus' kingdom proclamation, which never made forgiveness contingent upon the satisfaction of God's justice.[12] As a result, Schwager's understanding of the kingdom limits what kind of soteriological implications can be derived from the Last Supper sayings because they must corroborate his understanding of the kingdom.[13] For him, the Last Supper sayings are to be read as a prediction of how Jesus' death would be the way in which "the goodness of his Father can reach human hearts . . . ."[14] Because the Jewish people had rejected the kingdom up to that point, Jesus' death would penetrate such obstinacy with a nonviolent demonstration of God's love, which would overwhelm the hardened hearts opposing the kingdom.

Although Schwager has a lengthy treatment of the Last Supper sayings, the intertextual elements seem underdeveloped. He downplays the obvious connections with the sacrifice and covenant inauguration on Sinai that will be discussed later in order to affirm that the Last Supper sayings corroborate Girard's assertion that sacrificial theology is absent from the Gospels. While he suppresses the connection with Sinai, he does argue that there is a strong connection with Isaiah 53 that emerges in the Last Supper sayings, which seems to be more tenuous and is certainly not as overt as the connections with Sinai.[15] For him, the connection with Isaiah 53 revolves around the similar vicarious, nonviolent offerings that both Jesus and the servant make. Jesus willingly offers himself up for the purposes of demonstrating to all that God responds to human violence with love and forgiveness. What he does on the cross in turn defines the nature of the kingdom as one of forgiveness and nonviolence.

In Schwager's soteriology, the cross does not stand alone, but the resurrection provides further affirmation that God, even after the death of his

---

11. Schwager, *Jesus in the Drama*, 101–3, 150.

12. For him, it seems that one is forced into an either-or situation. One is forced to see Jesus' soteriology either solely as the coming kingdom or as an expiatory death. See Schwager, "Christ's Death," 111. One can rightly wonder if such an either-or scenario confronts biblical interpreters at this point.

13. In fact, Schwager notes that the manner in which someone interprets the Last Supper sayings depends upon his or her presupposition about God's relationship to justice. See Schwager, *Jesus in the Drama*, 101.

14. Ibid., 111.

15. On the debated impact that Isaiah 53 had on early Christian thought, see Bellinger and Farmer, eds., *Jesus and the Suffering Servant*.

own Son, offers a kingdom of pure forgiveness to all.[16] Basically, it is a tangible corroboration of the truth of Jesus' message, which once again shows humanity that God operates differently than they expect. When it comes to defending the veracity of the resurrection accounts, Schwager appeals to Girard himself, saying that the biblical accounts are more realistic than myths in that they follow the expulsion of the victim from the victim's point of view.[17] His response to the history of religions questions concerning the similarity of the Christian kerygma with other religions that proclaim the death and resurrection of a god is simply to say that no one has arrived at any solid solution regarding the origin of the accounts.

Although Schwager's work is monumental in its scope, one can still question his final conclusion about the biblical texts being non-sacrificial in character. His reading of the Old Testament is ultimately dependent upon his reading of the New Testament, which is further contingent upon the selection of texts he makes paradigmatic for the New Testament.[18] Thus, his choice of a hermeneutical lens—Jesus as the rejected cornerstone—for the New Testament has become the rudder that steers the ship of his reading of the biblical texts more broadly. While Schwager is able to demonstrate the existence of the rejected cornerstone motif across a wide swath of New Testament texts, his claim for this being *the* hermeneutical key is taken up with little defense other than its widespread presence. He is, at this point, open to the criticism that he has uncritically adopted Girard's hermeneutical approach. Certainly other portraits of Christ's death are just as widespread, and Jesus as inaugurating the new covenant seems just as, if not more, prevalent than the description of his death as the rejected cornerstone.[19] What is more, covenantal imagery pervades not simply the New Testament but the Old Testament as well and could serve as a more encompassing soteriological motif.[20]

Furthermore, Schwager's efforts at portraying God as offering pure forgiveness is undermined in his treatment of judgment. Schwager's theology of judgment, drawn from his observation that humans perpetrate much of the violence ascribed to God in the Bible, sees many of the warnings

---

16. Schwager, *Jesus in the Drama*, 135–36.

17. Ibid., 127–30.

18. One reviewer observed that Schwager's work has primarily sought to corroborate Girard's hermeneutics, rather than subject it to "possible falsification." See Galvin, "The Marvelous Exchange," 691.

19. See, for instance, Matt 26:28; Mark 14:24; Luke 22:20; 1 Cor 11:25; 2 Cor 3:6; Heb 7:22; 8:1–10:39; 12:24; and 13:20.

20. Shelton, "A Covenant Concept of Atonement," 91–108; Shelton, *Cross and Covenant*; and Blocher, "Old Covenant, New Covenant," 140–70.

about judgment as simply informing us about the natural consequences of evil. He affirms along Pauline-like lines, that sin and violence inherently revert back upon the perpetrator.[21] At first, such affirmations seem to remove God from being the direct cause of violence.[22] However, Schwager still constructs a notion of natural judgment that posits God as its source when this notion of "self judgment" is described as a result of what God "inscribed in nature."[23] By affirming that God constructed nature in such a way as to recompense sin with further evil and human violence, Schwager does not succeed in removing God from the causal chain of violence entirely, but simply introduces a string of intermediaries causes. Perhaps the introduction of other causal agents like humans and nature lessens the direct role God plays, making the judgment language of Scripture more palatable to some, but it does not remove God from the equation altogether.

Schwager also does not repudiate a notion of future punishment in Hell, making it a real possibility for those who consistently refuse God's overtures. People who reject the offer of the kingdom's forgiveness "condemn themselves to ultimate isolation and to hell."[24] Jesus, therefore, "had to speak of hell as the last imminent consequence of humans being closed up within themselves."[25] Though Schwager uses the language of self-condemnation, his resuscitation of eschatological punishment as "isolation" means that not all are welcomed into the eschaton. God's eschatological future will exclude some. Though this is in keeping with traditional Christianity, for many Girardians, the threat of eschatological punishment reifies the notion of a violent deity who threatens to punish and exclude unless certain conditions are met. Thus, although Schwager assiduously tries to free God from the violence attributed to him in Scripture, Schwager seems forced to credit God with certain aspects of violence displayed in judgment, which can be either the natural effects of sin or the eschatological effects of repudiating God altogether.

Finally, Schwager leaves one aspect of human salvation, the forgiveness of willful sin, unhelpfully ambiguous.[26] On the cross, Schwager sees Christ dying in solidarity with all victims: "Jesus on the cross identified himself as victim with all the others as victims."[27] On the one hand, Schwager sees all

21. Schwager, *Banished from Eden*, 61.
22. Schwager, *Scapegoats*, 66.
23. Ibid., 61.
24. Schwager, "Christ's Death," 113.
25. Schwager, *Banished from Eden*, 85
26. Marshall, "Review of *Jesus in the Drama of Salvation*," 592–93.
27. Schwager, "Christ's Death," 118.

humanity suffering as some kind of victim, and, as a result, Christ's cross is identified with their suffering *qua* victim. On the other hand, Schwager sees all humans as victimizers too.[28] The nebulous aspect of his soteriology is how humans, as the victimizers (which is equally true of all people according to some of his assertions), are excused from such sin.[29] He complicates the issue further by pitting God against any form of victimization in order to maintain that Jesus does not approve of his executioners' actions. He writes that Jesus "will have nothing to do with the evil-doers as evildoers . . . ."[30] If Jesus stands opposed to the aspects of humans that are complicit in evil, what redemption is there when humans act in the role of victimizer rather than the role of victim? Unfortunately, there is no clear answer to my knowledge in his work.

His explanation of Jesus' warnings of judgment also fails to identify what God does with willful victimizers. When it comes to Jesus' identification of the just and the unjust at the final judgment (Matt 25:31–46), Schwager furtively sidesteps the category of willful sin (i.e. victimization) altogether. When he identifies the two parties that Christ demarcates in the final judgment, "the just" are those who have "the justice of Christ . . . directly mirrored in their good works."[31] However, instead of calling the other party at the judgment the "unjust," he calls them "the rejected," and they are the ones who "are victims of sin."[32] By taking the two groups who are welcomed into Christ's eternal bliss as those who do the works of Christ and those who suffer the violence of others, Schwager misses a vital opportunity to explain how salvation is possible for violent perpetrators—which he avows is true of every human. While he seems to suggest at one point that Jesus might see evil tendencies as a result of being victimized by sin, this does not explain how intentional human violence is forgiven or redeemed.[33]

---

28. Schwager, *Jesus in the Drama*, 193.

29. His qualification, repeated in several different works, is that Jesus "*identifies* himself with his enemies insofar as they themselves are *victims* of evil . . . ." While he operates with the assumption that humans are a mixture of victim and victimizer, it is not clear what Jesus specifically does to redeem our victimizing tendencies. At most, he sees Jesus as interceding for those who are victimizers. Schwager, "Christ's Death," 121.

30. Ibid., 118; cf. 121.

31. Schwager, *Jesus in the Drama*, 196.

32. Ibid., 196. One can question Schwager's exegesis on this point. The parable in Matthew suggests the "rejected" are those handed over to eternal punishment, not the victims of other people's sins.

33. Ibid., 194. He writes, "The event of the cross shows that individual people are far more victims of evil than responsible agents, for even those who condemned, handed over, and crucified the Son of God did not know what they were doing . . . ." Even here, it seems he is talking about the degree of victimization, which still does not eliminate

If God truly does offer salvation for all humanity, then it needs to be clear how God deals with willful violence.

Nevertheless, Schwager has done much to disseminate Girard in academic theology. To this day, his work is still one of, if not, the most extensive efforts undertaken to compare Girard's theology with the biblical texts. His work was simply prodigious in size. While we will have cause for disagreement over the interpretation of the Last Supper accounts, he nevertheless has done much to advance Girard in theological discourse.

James Williams

While Schwager was among the first on the scene, he has not remained alone. Other scholars have also performed similar studies of the Bible, and James Williams has likewise conducted a more holistic reading of the Bible from a Girardian perspective. His work is distinguished by a number of significant features. For one, he ventures onto a wider scale analysis of sibling rivalry within the Old Testament, specifically within the book of Genesis, noting the many instances of mimetic rivalry between the various sets of brothers in the book. Important in this regard is his observation that, in Genesis, the older brothers are not simply supplanted but are often "redeemed or 'won back' for the larger story" as in the case of Esau and Joseph's older brothers.[34] In addition, an elucidating comparison between certain Old Testament accounts and later Hellenistic Egyptian retellings of the stories informs his reading of some Old Testament narratives.[35] Almost predictably, the later Hellenistic recounting of the Joseph narrative has been transformed into what a Girardian theory of culture and literature would expect, namely, the elimination of victimization in the story's retelling. According to the Hellenistic version of the Joseph narrative, the prior stability of Egypt was supposedly disrupted by a group of outcasts who, for the sake of communal welfare, had to be banished in order to regain peace and unity.[36] Again,

---

the fact that we as humans are perpetrators of violence as well as victims of it. The one place where he potentially sidesteps this problem is that Jesus, the judge over "the just" and "the rejected" sides with the rejected. But he then clarifies that the "rejected" are not the unjust perpetrators of violence but the "victims of sin" (ibid., 196). Cf. Schwager, "Christ's Death," 119.

34. Williams, *The Bible, Violence, and the Sacred*, 63.

35. The Hellenistic Egyptian authors he uses are Hecataeus, Manetho, Diodours, Pompeius Trogus, Lysimachus, Apion, and Chaeremon. His sources for these authors are: Josephus' *Against Apion* as well as other fragments collected in Sterm, *From Herodotus to Plutarch*. See Williams, *Bible, Violence, and the Sacred*, 89–91. Regarding his sources for this conclusion, see Ibid., 270n34.

36. Ibid., 59–60.

unlike the biblical account, Joseph's dream-interpreting abilities award him divine status, corroborating what Girardian theory would suspect from the normal progression of the scapegoating mechanism, which culminates in the divinization of the victim. This comparison between Genesis and later Hellenistic Egyptian accounts supports Girard's predictions, showing that scapegoats are often viewed as detrimental to normative society on the one hand and that the biblical texts have a unique perspective in championing the innocence of a non-divinized victim, in this case Joseph.

Along the same lines, Williams marshals a similar retelling of the Exodus accounts in the Hellenistic era that likewise casts the Hebrews as culprits, deserving of expulsion from Egypt. Even more intriguing are his observations that Freud's recounting of the Exodus functions in a similar manner, blotting out the victimization of the Jewish people in Egypt and deleting their Jewishness altogether.[37] In light of such later attempts to delete the victimization of persons like Joseph or people like the Jews, Williams indicates, even if he does not fully spell this out, that Girard's theory can be substantiated in the desire of later authors to legitimate the expulsion of the Hebrews and suppress their victimization through various literary emendations.

In another way his work is distinguishable from others, Williams' biblical exegesis takes up the theme of covenant more readily than other Girardian commentators. For him, the covenant with Israel functions as a communal center, wherein the commandments mitigate the potential for the community to disintegrate into mimetic rivalry.[38] Similar to Girard, the prohibitions and the punishments in the legal codes of the Old Testament are taken in stride as necessary for the gradual movement from a violent view of the sacred to nonviolence.[39] However, even the legal codes are critiqued and transcended as revelation progresses. Here, Williams turns to the prophetic literature as the saving grace of the Old Testament. According to him, the prophets became victims in order to protect other victims and therefore stymie violence.[40] For Williams, the eradication of violence is progressive in the Bible, just as it is in Girard, beginning with the substitutions developed in the sacrificial cult, which are later displaced altogether by the revelation of their inherent violence. As a result, Williams possesses a form of salvation history similar to Girard, wherein the saving knowledge and revelation are gradually disclosed over the course of God's history with

37. Ibid., 91–98.
38. Ibid., 105.
39. Ibid., 109.
40. Ibid., 147.

his people in a transition from outright mimetic crisis to its suppression under the covenantal law. Despite its advances, even covenant law must be further critiqued by the prophets and the Gospels to inaugurate the ultimate emancipation from violence.

When he comes to the Gospels, he distances himself from Girard—at least Girard's early statements about the Gospels—by saying that sacrificial language still appears in the course of the Gospels.[41] However, as his argument progresses, it becomes clear that the sacrificial language of passages like the ransom sayings are in some sense necessary evils in order to help people transition from a sacrificial view of the world to a non-sacrificial one.[42] One cannot transition from one view of the world to the next without using the structure and categories of the old world. His exegesis of the ransom sayings is compelling in some respects, for he observes that the ransom saying of Mark 10:45 occurs in response to a quarrel among the disciples who are vying for power and prestige among themselves. According to Williams, they have become ensnared in mimetic rivalry. He then shows that the model of Jesus offering a ransom is actually a model of good mimesis, which cuts against the grain of his disciples' narcissistic aspirations. The Son of Man offering his life as a ransom therefore provides a different model than the mimetic rivalry typical of human culture.

Nevertheless, Williams still wrestles with the reason why the offering of Christ's life is necessary as a ransom offering. Remaining true to Girard, he explains his thoughts on what Mark meant by depicting the death of Christ as ransom in the following manner:

> ... I think that Mark probably intends to say, in effect, "The human condition is such that only the price of the Son of Man's suffering and death will have the effect of loosening the bonds of the sacred social structure, enabling human beings to see what their predicament is and the kind of faith and action that will bring liberation."[43]

Thus, by using the sacrificial language of "ransom," the Gospel writers are diffusing the sacrificial theology implicit in the term. To corroborate his non-sacrificial reading of the ransom sayings, he turns to Luke, who, despite using Mark's Gospel as a source, does not employ the ransom sayings at all. Williams then concludes that Luke is correcting what was potentially misleading in Mark's utilization of sacrificial language.[44] In the end, Luke's

41. Ibid., 188.
42. Ibid., 223–24.
43. Ibid., 224.
44. Ibid., 202.

handling of the ransom saying governs the understanding of the similar saying in Mark and Matthew.

Williams likewise reads the Last Supper sayings in a non-sacrificial manner. As he notes, the usual sacrificial transaction, which goes from humans to God, has been inverted. In the Last Supper sayings, God is giving "himself as victim to the worshipers."[45] As a result, it presages the death of Christ where he will be handed over to the mimetic contagion of the crowds. Similar to his treatment of the ransom sayings, he notes that Luke has a different version of the Last Supper discourse which is less sacrificial in nature—the blood "poured out for many" is not present—and instead depicts the solidarity formed through participation in the Eucharist. Thus, the Last Supper discourse does not portray Jesus' death as a sacrifice in his understanding.[46]

In the final analysis, Williams' work offers some valuable corroboration with Girard's thesis by comparing later accounts of Joseph and the Exodus with the biblical narrative. In addition, Williams is at least willing to concede the presence of sacrificial language in select passages like the ransom saying and the Last Supper accounts. However, in doing so, he does raise the question of how the authors are using this language. In his view, sacrificial language is present as a means of accommodating a previous outlook that assumed God demanded sacrifice and atonement in order to undermine it. While we might have good reason to question the validity of this claim, it is important to note that the debate, at least according to Williams, is not simply over the presence of sacrificial language but about the end towards which the language aims.

Robert Hamerton-Kelly

Schwager and Williams have both evaluated Girard's reading across Old and New Testaments. Others have read more specific portions of the New Testament from a Girardian perspective. For instance, Robert Hamerton-Kelly, in *Sacred Violence*, reads the Pauline literature from a Girardian vantage point.[47] More pertinent to our concern is his reading of Mark from a Girardian perspective, published in *The Gospel and the Sacred*. In this work on Mark, he begins with what he sees as the central aspect of Jesus' ministry,

45. Ibid., 194.
46. Ibid., 202.
47. Hamerton-Kelly, *Sacred Violence*. See also his following articles: Hamerton-Kelly, "Paul's Hermeneutic of the Cross," 247–54; Hamerton-Kelly, "Allegory, Typology and Sacred Violence," 53–70; Hamerton-Kelly, "Sacred Violence and Sinful Desire," 35–54; and Hamerton-Kelly, "A Girardian Interpretation of Paul," 65–81.

the temple cleansing. He argues that Jesus' action in the temple constitutes the demystification of the temple, which sat at the sacred center of first-century Judaism. Jesus' expulsion of the money changers spelled the end of the sacrificial system, calling for its replacement by a different kind of order no longer centered on the violent sacred and its practices.[48] Not only is the sacrifice of animals in the temple cult problematic, all kinds of substitutional exchanges—even monetary substitutions—are equally problematic because they continue to repress the actual violence taking place in the temple cult.[49]

Hamerton-Kelly does engage biblical themes that will be discussed in future chapters. For instance, he is cognizant of Israel's restoration theology and the hope for a new exodus in his exegesis of Mark, which will be an essential component of the discussion in future chapters. There is a significant difference between Hamerton-Kelly's approach and the one I will take up later. Basically, in his view, Israel's hope for a new exodus anticipates the emancipation from "sacred violence" rather than a physical or spiritual restoration of Israel.[50] For him, the hope for a new exodus is freedom from sacrificial religion altogether, which was incomplete in the first exodus since the sacrificial rituals and the destruction of the Egyptians were an essential part of the first exodus. Though we will have reason to disagree with Hamerton-Kelly's understanding of Israel's hope for restoration, it is a helpful step forward to place Girard's interpretation of the Gospels in conversation with aspects of restoration theology.

Hamerton-Kelly does address the verses that appear to credit Jesus' death with atoning value. Not surprisingly, these are interpreted in light of Girard's mimetic theory. When it comes to the renowned ransom saying in Mark where Jesus says the Son of Man came "to give his life a ransom for many" (Mark 10:45), he explains the ransom not as a payment for sin but as Jesus going "into captivity to the [Generative Mimetic Scapegoat Mechanism] in order that we might be released from it."[51] In other words, Jesus gives himself to the process of mimetic scapegoating in order to save us. This, he notes, is still a substitutionary death since Jesus becomes the victim in place of others. However, in affirming the substitutionary nature of Christ's death, he does not relinquish the non-sacrificial reading by maintaining that the purpose was to reveal the pathology of scapegoating.

---

48. Hamerton-Kelly, *The Gospel and the Sacred*, 2; cf. Hamerton-Kelly, "Sacred Violence and the Messiah," 467–71.

49. Hamerton-Kelly, *Gospel and the Sacred*, 3.

50. Ibid., 68.

51. Ibid., 71.

When he comes to the Last Supper sayings, he sees the Last Supper as a corollary to the Temple cleansing and therefore as another inversion of sacrifice instead of a sacrifice in the atoning sense, despite the presence of sacrificial language.[52] Rather than humans bringing their offerings to God, he notes that Jesus describes God, in the person of Jesus, giving himself to human beings. In fact, according to Hamerton-Kelly, the Last Supper introduces a new form of substitution meant to displace the Temple cult, namely, the Eucharist. In his understanding, the upper room correlates with the Temple while the body and blood stand in the place of the sacrificial victim, making the Last Supper the replacement of sacrifice. Thus, even though the Last Supper might contain sacrificial language, it is interpreted as the subversion of it rather than its affirmation.

Even though Hamerton-Kelly has produced a thoroughgoing Girardian reading of Mark, it is not without its problems. He has, for instance, been liable to the charge of pressing the Gospel of Mark into a solitary mold where the divergent voices and counter evidence are silenced.[53] In fact, his reading of Mark seems to hinge upon an *a priori* commitment to Girard. Furthermore, his understanding of the Jewish hopes for restoration has been unnecessarily reduced to the scapegoat mechanism. The next several chapters will provide a more robust understanding of restoration theology and its influence upon the Gospel writers. Nevertheless, by reducing the soteriological problem informing restoration theology into freedom from scapegoating, Hamerton-Kelly has read the ransom saying and the Last Supper saying in this light. Unfortunately, this causes him to miss some of the soteriological implications present in the passages, including the covenantal language in the Last Supper, which would allow him to see that Jesus' death does not simply produce reconciliation among his followers but also between them and God.

Theological Reflection and Girard

In addition to the various biblical scholars that have taken up Girard's work, numerous theologians and philosophers have also adopted his approach in varying degrees.[54] Indeed, as Girard's work has been digested by ever widening circles, his influence can be detected in a number of contempo-

52. Ibid., 43–45; cf. Hamerton-Kelly, "Messiah," 484–85.

53. Finamore, *God, Order, and Chaos*, 125.

54. Some of the notable authors that we will not get to discuss are the following: Bailie, *Violence Unveiled*; McKenna, *Violence and Difference*; Fleming, *René Girard*; Golsan, *René Girard and Myth*; Kirwan, *Discovering Girard*; and Kirwan, *Girard and Theology*.

rary authors. For several authors, Girard's understanding of the scapegoat has become the foundation for their own personal theological reflections, which is seen in the following scholars.

James Alison

Of the various appropriators of Girard, few match the voluminous endeavor of James Alison who has taken up Girard's theory of atonement and placed it into a more explicitly Catholic approach.[55] Alison's work constitutes a rather significant step forward in many regards. First, Alison seems to blend the soteriological emphases in Schwager and Girard together to form a much more balanced soteriology. Alison manages to balance evenly Girard's dominant emphasis on the revelation of human sin and Schwager's primary emphasis on the revelation of the goodness of God by positing the Christ event as equally revealing both the depth of human sin *and* the goodness of God's grace in response to human sin.[56] As a result, he manages to harness the emphases of both authors in a balanced fashion.

Second, Alison has sought to make the resurrection more central to his soteriology and anthropology than other followers of Girard, which is an advance beyond Girard's own sporadic and often underdeveloped references to it. In fact, in the *Joy of Being Wrong*, Alison argues that Christianity's understanding of the human problem (i.e. original sin) needs to be constructed from the vantage point of the resurrection.[57] For him, a doctrine of original sin cannot be known antecedent to the Christ event, but is an *a posteriori* construction that can only be constructed after the resurrection. He writes, " . . . the doctrine of original sin is not prior to, but follows from and is utterly dependent on, Jesus' resurrection from the dead and thus cannot be understood at all except in the light of that event."[58] The resurrection of Jesus, which Alison affirms is literal and historical, reveals for the apostles the innocence of Christ thereby exposing the scapegoat mechanism that had led to his death.[59] Not only does the resurrection validate the innocence

---

55. Some of his works include: Alison, *Knowing Jesus*; Alison, *Raising Abel*; Alison, *Living in the End Times*; Alison, *Being Wrong*; and Alison, *Undergoing God*.

56. Alison, *Being Wrong*, 83.

57. For various reasons, I would question whether Alison's account of original sin is wholly an *a posteriori* construction. In my view, mimetic theory and the Christ event are mutually explicatory in his work, and he does not fully demonstrate how "original sin" can be extracted and deduced by the resurrection alone without some prior awareness of Girard's hypotheses. See also Kirwan, *Philosophy and Theology*, 60; cf. 68.

58. Alison, *Being Wrong*, 3; cf. Alison, *On Being Liked*, 24.

59. Alison, *Raising Abel*, 26–27 and Alison, *Knowing Jesus*, 11, 26.

of Christ, it also demonstrates that God responds to human violence with pardon, not revenge.[60] As God's final word in the Christ event, the resurrection illuminates two important theological ideas: humans are violent and God is wholly other, "entirely without violence."[61]

Third, like Schwager, Alison willingly takes up the Gospels' depiction of Jesus' death as necessary and outlines two distinct reasons for this necessity. First, the repeated fulfillment motif in Scripture, which he calls the "theological" dimension, shows that Jesus' death was anticipated as a part of God's redemption.[62] While this reason could potentially lead one to see Jesus' death as demanded by some divine choice, Alison argues that the theological reason is only present because of the second reason for this necessity, namely, that human depravity could not see its sordidness through any other means.[63] The only way for God to reveal the true gift of himself to the world is "taking the form of a man substituting himself for the sacrificial lamb proper to the social order based on murder."[64] According to Alison, the nature of human sin is the only factor that truly necessitates the death of Jesus.

Fourth, Alison goes much further than Girard in trying to construct an ecclesiology.[65] Following Girard, Alison endorses "the slow pruning of violence from God"[66] by portraying God as the one who is without violence because he does not enforce identity boundaries.[67] As a result, Alison sees

60. Alison, *Being Wrong*, 74, 98.
61. Ibid., 83.
62. Ibid., 171.
63. Ibid., 171–72.
64. Ibid., 174.
65. I have reservations regarding the viability of Alison's ecclesiology as he seeks to construct it over against exclusionary practices. In his other works, he still affirms God's eschatological judgement as being "very real and very terrible" (Alison, *Raising Abel*, 158). Eschatological judgement seems to imply that God possesses some kind of moral boundary, one that he actually enforces. Moreover, even though he seeks to construct a community without boundaries, Alison only succeeds in gerrymandering the boundaries for those who seem too self-righteous to love social outcasts become excluded. See Alison *Being Wrong*, 158. See also his criticisms of evangelical protestants and pietists in Alison, *Knowing Jesus*, 29, 102–6. One of the tensions that arises is that in appropriating Girard, Alison still wants to retain an ability to separate from other viewpoints that are inferior, but this can become problematic. As Sandor Goodhart has cautioned, one cannot use Girard's assertion of the victim's innocence in order to align oneself against the perpetrators. This simply perpetuates the scapegoat cycle. Rather, the innocence of the victim is to heighten one's own sense of culpability, not find a new target. See Goodhart, *The Prophetic Law*, xxvi–xxvii.
66. Alison, *Raising Abel*, 108.
67. Alison, *Being Wrong*, 83.

the Gospel as the toppling and subversion of human culture in order to erect "a new sacred order, the order which is built *without victims* . . . ."[68] Consequently, Alison concludes that such an order implies that there are no divisions between "insiders" and "outsiders."[69] If there is any division of judgment between insiders and outsiders, this division derives from the human choice to reject the offer to live from a different basis, namely, from the victim.[70] As a result, the victim becomes the foundation of a new kind of ecclesiology, one where the community exists to protect the excluded and outcast. All of these contributions to the discussion take Girard's theological implications to a deeper level of development.

When it comes to the Last Supper sayings in the Gospels, Alison's interpretation bears many similarities with other Girardian interpreters as well as introducing some of his own innovations. Alison strongly avers that Jesus' Last Supper was indeed a Passover celebration.[71] The connection with the Passover is important for Alison, because the Passover was a meal that connoted the exodus, which presumed two separate themes. First, the Passover represented God's call for Israel to be his covenant people. As God's covenant people, their society was to be distinguished from their neighbors because the widows and orphans would not be disenfranchised.[72] Second, the Passover signified Israel's expulsion by the Egyptians and hence reminded them of the way in which they had been victims at the hands of the Egyptians. God's covenant with the Jewish people set them apart as people who were protectors of the victims, all of which was bound up in the Passover festival.

By connecting the Last Supper with the Passover and its surrounding context of exodus and covenant, Alison sees Jesus assuming Israel's identity and mission in his final meal.[73] Furthermore, the manner in which Jesus alludes to his death against the backdrop of the exodus categorizes Jesus' death as another instance of expulsion and victimization.[74] Just as Israel was birthed through its expulsion, so Jesus, in his expulsion, would generate a new covenant community while simultaneously revealing the "victimary

---

68. Alison, *Raising Abel*, 107.

69. Ibid., 127. See also Alison, *On Being Liked*, 29. This is consistent with Girard's own formulations. See Girard, *Things Hidden*, 202.

70. Alison, *Being Wrong*, 124.

71. Alison, *Knowing Jesus*, 66.

72. Ibid., 65.

73. Alison, *Being Wrong*, 172.

74. Alison, *Knowing Jesus*, 66–68.

basis of all societies, including even, sadly, Jewish society."[75] In the confluence of impending death and the Last Supper, Jesus revealed that the community he was founding was one that worshipped God "*from* the victim, and not *over against*, or by exclusion of, the victim."[76] As such, the community founded by Christ was the logical fulfillment of God's covenant with Israel and was to provide humanity with a model for constructing social structures that no longer require exclusion and subjugation of others to survive. In fact, instead of producing victims, it now comes to their aid.

While much of Alison's interpretation of the Last Supper sayings focuses on the connection with the covenant and the exodus, he is aware of the sacrificial terminology present in them as well as possible allusions to Isaiah's Suffering Servant.[77] Instead of interpreting the Last Supper sayings as an indication that Jesus is bearing Israel's sin, he interprets them, like Hammerton-Kelly, as depicting the inversion of the sacrificial order. To substantiate this interpretation, Alison believes YHWH's covenant with Israel set Israel on a path away from the sacrificial order. Since Jesus is the culmination of the covenant and hastening its *telos*, then it only seems logical, in his view, to understand the sacrificial terminology present there as subversive of sacrificial theology. The irony present in Alison's interpretation is that he is aware that the covenant sacrifice on Sinai (Exodus 24:8) was interpreted as an expiation in the first century, something which will be developed in future chapters.[78] Unfortunately, Alison does not use his knowledge of these interpretive traditions to understand the cross but instead interprets it in precisely the opposite manner.

Despite Alison's impressive work, there are some areas that call for reservation. Although one can credit Alison with reading the biblical texts carefully, he often admits the presence of counter-evidence, which sometimes beg for a reconsideration of his conclusions. For example, he is very much aware that when the early Christians, informed by the Old Testament, sought to interpret the Christ event, they would have readily seen him as assuming the punishment for Israel's sin. In fact, he even goes so far as to concede that Jesus himself possessed this same "victimary self-understanding" that flowed from the Old Testament knowledge of God.[79] However, he qualifies this as a "provisional" understanding of God, one that

75. Alison, *Being Wrong*, 172.
76. Alison, *Knowing Jesus*, 72 (emphasis is his).
77. Alison, *Being Wrong*, 172.
78. Alison, *Knowing Jesus*, 68. Regarding the covenantal sacrifices on Sinai in Exodus 24, he writes: "This was not, in all probability, a sacrifice for the expiation of sins, when it was first performed, but by Jesus' time it was understood as such."
79. Alison, *Being Wrong*, 108.

must be transcended in order to see God as completely free from violence. Interestingly, this view of God was only possible after the resurrection, which means that Jesus' entire ministry might have been conducted with this understanding.[80] With these admissions in view, Alison's readers are justified in asking why, in light of the counter-evidence, one should follow Girard's interpretation of the cross as Alison does. Moreover, one can certainly ask whether his understanding of the covenant as solely in defense of the victim is comprehensive enough to govern his interpretation of the Last Supper discourse.[81]

At the same time, Alison is to be credited with recognizing the "victimary" language that is present in Jesus' discourse. Furthermore, he neither denies nor ignores the sacrificial terminology used at the Last Supper. The question that will confront us in future chapters is how one is to determine the purpose or telos of the Last Supper sayings. There is clearly a trajectory by followers of Girard to see the statements as subversive rather than affirming a theology of atonement. Thus, one of the governing issues concerns how one is to interpret the passages in question. It is for this reason that establishing the historical and theological context for the Last Supper sayings will be essential for any interpretation of these key passages.

S. Mark Heim

In addition to Alison's rather comprehensive work, S. Mark Heim's *Saved from Sacrifice*, delivers one of the most thorough and erudite adoptions of Girard's soteriology to date. In a very meticulous fashion, Heim works his way through the labyrinth of modern questions about the viability of Christ's cross as a saving event and shows how a Girardian perspective helps to answer these questions. In short, the work constructs a way to acknowledge, on the one hand, the saving efficacy of Jesus' violent crucifixion while rejecting the divine origin of this violence. Heim notes on numerous occasions that Girard's reading of the Gospels solves the paradoxical presentation of the crucifixion as a thing that benefits Jesus' followers all the while being something that should have never happened.[82]

The resurrection does play a prominent role in Heim's soteriology because the vindication of Jesus affirms the spurious nature of the charges

---

80. See ibid., 127–28.

81. While there is certainly emphasis that the covenant expected Israel to defend the victims, he errs by saying that the covenant demands "that slaves not be made" (ibid., 134). Slaves were indeed permitted by the covenantal stipulations (e.g., Exod 21).

82. Heim, *Saved from Sacrifice*, 108.

against him, declaring his innocence.[83] At the same time, the resurrection also makes the cross an effective exposition of human violence. The human impetus to suppress the cries of their innocent victims means that only an invincibly innocent victim could really challenge our adherence to the system. The resurrection therefore indubitably proves Jesus' innocence, shattering the illusions.[84] In addition, Heim makes the resurrection the causal event that effects our justification. While our sin implicates us in the lynching of Christ, the fact that he lives means that we cannot be held responsible for his death since the victim is no longer dead. The only way to avoid forgiveness is to refuse to admit one's guilt.[85]

Although the bulk of the work focuses on interpersonal relationships, Heim is able to appropriate Girard in a way that speaks to our reconciliation with the divine. However, he makes it clear that the reconciliation with the divine happens because humans are first rescued from their violent sacrificial tendencies, which puts us at odds with God.[86] Thus, our rescue from bondage is the condition upon which the relationship with the divine is restored. In fact, it reveals that God has chosen to accept humanity in spite of its moral failings. Likewise, Heim argues that Christ's death results in forgiveness for all sins in general, even though the primary sin forgiven at the cross is sacrificial violence. In order to affirm this, Heim labels all other forms of sin as "tributary to sacrifice in that they sow the conflicts that flower in social crisis and lead to redemptive violence."[87] Whether all sins do in fact have sacrifice as their intrinsic *telos* is something worth exploring further, but it at least begs an analysis of sin within the Christian tradition.

In his work, Heim does acknowledge the presence of atonement theology in the Gospels, but asserts that "it is Jesus' antagonists who view his death as a redemptive sacrifice, one life given for many."[88] Interestingly, he avoids the Last Supper sayings almost entirely, only briefly providing a single line gloss on the Last Supper sayings: "Jesus' 'new covenant' in his blood is an end to the justification for shedding blood."[89] The rationale for this interpretation, unfortunately, is never given. Further insight might be provided in his understanding of the Eucharist, which is supposed to func-

83. Ibid., 127.
84. Ibid., 197.
85. Ibid., 147.
86. Ibid., 320.
87. Ibid., 321–22.
88. Ibid., 125. For evidence, he points to John 11:45–53 and the reconciliation between Pilate and Herod.
89. Ibid., 231.

tion as a substitute for normal human sacrificial practices, which likewise reconcile the community together.[90] In other words, the Eucharist now delivers the same reconciliatory effects among the community without the lynching of a victim.

On the surface, Heim's treatise seems to answer all of the problems of those who have desired to distance themselves from the divine violence inherent in Christian soteriology. However, buried in a footnote, Heim alludes to the Achilles heel of Girardian soteriology: in order to be the scapegoat that exposes the irrationality of human violence, Jesus must choose to become "an accomplice of Satan in something that is unqualifiedly evil."[91] God, in order to attain human salvation, must join paths, even if for a moment, with the devil. For Heim, and Girard as well, this means that God must participate in the very system that he is trying to overturn.[92] What justifies God's participation in this regard is the future goal and result of this endeavor. If taken to heart, this admission by Heim means that Girard's theory does not emancipate God from being complicit in the violence at the cross but permits it as a means to a better end.

Heim's work is robust and intricately argued. At the same time, his thesis, or at least his hope, that Girardian soteriology can help theologians affirm the salvific nature of the cross in concert with Christian tradition while agreeing with critics of atonement that the violence of the cross should not be condoned, seems to run into a conflict when it acknowledges that God must dance with evil one fateful time in order to secure salvation for humanity. Furthermore, his lack of attention to the Last Supper sayings means that there are important passages that have not been incorporated into a fuller understanding of the cross.

Anthony Bartlett

Like Heim, Bartlett adopts Girardian thought in a circumspect manner. While some have criticized Girard for meshing science and biblical faith into a monstrous hybrid, Bartlett attempts to keep the discourse of scientific research and that of the biblical narrative distinct, preferring to employ the biblical narrative as the primary mode of entry into mimetic theory.[93] In

90. Ibid., 236.

91. Ibid., 153n12. Such an admission sounds reminiscent of Gregory of Nyssa's soteriology in which God employs deception in order to trick the devil. See Gregory of Nyssa, "The Great Catechism," 24.

92. The same critique is directed at Girard in Finlan, *Problems with Atonement*, 93; cf. Putt, "Violent Imitation or Compassionate Repetition?" 40–41.

93. Bartlett, *Cross Purposes*, 12, 165.

addition, although Girard focuses on the negative power of mimesis that is revealed by the Gospel, Bartlett successfully moves past Girard to a "redemptive anthropology" through Christ that not only reveals the human problem but also points the way beyond the problems Girard identifies.[94] Faulting Girard's soteriology for potentially being just "information," Bartlett seeks to channel mimetic anthropology into a direction where Christ's death opens up a path to mimetic transformation wherein humans are not just saved *from* something (so Girard) but in which humans are freed *for* something.[95] Instead of being simply the impartation of knowledge, for Bartlett, the cross is the moment when God enters the "abyss" of human experience. For him this experience of God entering the abyss has both existential and philosophical implications. On the existential side, it means God has infiltrated the violent context of humanity, experiencing its loneliness and isolation, which culminates in the cross. On the philosophical side, it means God manifested himself in a world where deconstruction has shorn the metaphysical grounding from beneath its feet.[96] The abyss is the world without philosophical foundations. In this abyss, the cross pours forth compassion in response to human violence and meaninglessness. This demonstration of compassion invites humans to mimetic transformation where they turn from the hostility of the world to an unselfish movement toward others.[97] Taking up Kierkegaardian repetition, he suggests that the cross is a moment of invitation to conversion, to be repeated throughout one's life where one desists from violence and exclusion.[98] As he explains, "It is a dream of the enemy as friend," which beckons one to enter a radically different reality.[99] This movement entails a loss of one's self, which is the essence of what happens at the cross. Interestingly, when it comes to the question of the necessity of the cross, Bartlett sides with Girard against Schwager and Alison. Bartlett argues against any kind of "necessity" compelling God's offer of himself in the cross, asserting that any kind of necessity erases com-

---

94. Ibid., 40.

95. Ibid., 13.

96. Ibid., 18–27. See also Eagle, "Anthony Bartlett's Concept of Abyssal Compassion," 66–81.

97. Bartlett, *Cross Purposes*, 39.

98. Ibid., 150. He does note that he is going a good deal beyond Kierkegaard at this point. In taking up the notion of repetition, though, he is avoiding a potential weakness in Girard where one might overlook the fact that imitating Christ requires "nonidentical repetition" in order to preserve the uniqueness of Christ and also avoid a new form of mimetic rivalry. See Fodor, "Christian Discipleship as Participative Imitation," 261–62.

99. Bartlett, *Cross Purposes*, 157.

passion altogether and the likelihood that such an action would result in human transformation via mimesis.[100] Thus, Christ's death offers the pattern that is to be made ever new in the lives of his followers.

The resurrection is an essential piece to his understanding of atonement as the offer of forgiveness and love in the human abyss. Unlike other resurrections, he notes that Christ's does not obfuscate the victimization, but rather affirms its reality and responds with forgiveness instead of violence.[101] In the end, it affirms that all violence is forgiven. In addition, he clarifies that the resurrection "is not a transcendent miracle vindicating Christ against his human history" but is instead an "affirmation of the anthropological revolution of the cross."[102] The resurrection does not necessarily add new revelation, but it affirms that God does not return violence for violence.

When Bartlett turns to the New Testament in the final portion of his book, he boldly states that, despite differing interpretations, any notion of an exchange at the cross is "highly prejudicial" and results from a culture that erroneously embraces the notion of sacred violence rather than deriving from the actual texts themselves.[103] When dealing with the possible sacrificial theology in the Gospels, he treats the Last Supper sayings and the ransom sayings together, and interprets the Last Supper sayings through the prism of the ransom sayings. To support this exegetical move, he points to Luke's Gospel, which does not use the word "ransom," but has a similar form of the saying *following* the Eucharist (Luke 22:24–27), a point to which we will return in a few chapters. In light of Luke's deletion of the ransom language, Bartlett concludes " . . . the Eucharistic institution is interpreted in terms of abyssal service rather than cultic sacrifice, and precisely over against an anthropology modeled in the image of kings, lords, great ones, and mimetic desire in relation to their power . . . ."[104] For the most part, it seems Luke's absence of the ransom language is taken as indicative of how the ransom sayings should be interpreted in Mark 10:45 and Matthew 20:28 as well, namely, as lacking any kind of cultic reference. For support, he draws on two Old Testament antecedents of ransom. The first is a connection between the notion of ransom and the money that is paid in exchange for damage of life or property in the Old Testament. This notion of exchange for life is augmented by the second, which is basically the Old Testament depiction of God as the kinsman redeemer who rescues his people. Pulling

100. Ibid., 24, 224, 251.
101. Ibid., 153–54.
102. Ibid., 154.
103. Ibid., 189.
104. Ibid., 212.

these Old Testament antecedents together to interpret the ransom offered by the Son of Man in Mark 10:45 and Matthew 20:20, Bartlett explains these sayings as "a statement of divine solidarity working a redemption from the consequences of human violence and death rather than of a divine anger from which God also strangely redeems."[105] Thus, Bartlett's understanding of the use of "ransom" in Mark and Matthew has everything to do with God redeeming humans from themselves and their patterns of violence rather than a sacrificial payment for human sin.

In the end, Bartlett's study takes Girardian soteriology to new specificity in its understanding of sanctification and fleshes out a fuller picture of imitating Christ. This alone constitutes a substantial contribution to Girardian scholarship. At the same time, Bartlett also makes the Last Supper sayings theologically subservient to Luke's choice to emend the ransom saying away from the connotation of "ransom" that is present in Mark and Matthew. In future chapters, we will have good reason to question whether this is a fair representation of Luke as well as Mark and Matthew. Nevertheless, Bartlett has delivered a provocative account and has provided an articulation of Girard that provides more guidance for how Girard's mimetic theory can inform Christian living.

Conclusion

Despite the many positive adoptions of Girard's work for biblical and theological reflection, there is room for a more focused conversation on Girard's soteriology vis-à-vis the Last Supper sayings. While Girard never engages these important passages, several of Girard's prominent followers have. However, even in their engagement with these key texts, several fail to acknowledge the fact that the Last Supper sayings directly allude to the sacrifice on Sinai ("blood of the covenant") in Matthew 26:28 and Mark 14:24.[106] This, as we will see, is not something minor but does impact how they are to be understood. Many of Girard's adopters also fail to engage the way in which the Synoptics' Last Supper sayings bring Israel's story of being in covenant with YHWH into the foreground and consider how this story would impact how we are to interpret these passages.[107] In fact, it seems to be a common strategy that emerges in both Williams and Bartlett to allow the Gospel of Luke, who has putatively less of an emphasis on atonement, to determine the meaning of Mark and Matthew. Such an exegetical decision

---

105. Ibid., 215.
106. E.g., Schwager, Williams, Heim, and Bartlett.
107. E.g., Schwager, Williams, Hamerton-Kelly, Heim, and Bartlett.

forces the Synoptics into a uniform mold in order to support a certain exegetical conclusion. In future chapters, each of the Synoptics will be dealt with on an individual basis in order to hear their unique voice. Moreover, I contend that only with Israel's story of being in a covenant relationship with YHWH in view and only by acknowledging the presence of the allusion to the sacrifice on Sinai can we truly understand these passages.

Since some of Girard's followers have left the larger biblical narrative of God's covenant relationship with Israel to the side, the next chapter will sketch briefly the Old Testament's account of YHWH in covenant with Israel, Israel's failure to keep the covenant's stipulations, and the covenant's dissolution. In my view the Gospels, and hence the cross of Christ, can only be understood aright if we place them within this larger narrative framework that the biblical canon provides. As we will see, every soteriological understanding of Christ's death has a narrative framework, and this narrative framework does much to differentiate one version of soteriology from another.

3

Jesus as Savior in Which Story? (Part 1)
Israel's Hopes for Restoration

Introduction

MICHAEL ROOT HAS OBSERVED that every soteriology heralding Jesus as the redeemer situates him within a larger tripartite narrative structure. As he explains, every soteriology employs the same structural components: "Soteriology presumes two states of human existence, a state of deprivation (sin, corruption) and a state of release from that deprivation (salvation, liberation), and an event that produces a change from the first state to the second."[1] Within distinctively Christian soteriologies, Jesus is the figure who precipitates the transition from the "state of deprivation" to the "state of release."

Even though Christians have commonly agreed that Jesus Christ is the one who ushers in the "state of release," there has been little agreement on what it means for Christ to accomplish salvation. To put it simply, there is agreement *that* Christ provides salvation, but no consensus on *how* he provides it. The many disagreements between various Christian soteriologies

---

1. See Root, "The Narrative Structure of Soteriology," 145. The one place where I disagree with Root is his assertion that atonement theories "are not theoretical" (ibid., 155). He is followed here by others who conclude that narrative theology is non-theoretical. E.g., van den Brink, "Narrative, Atonement, and the Christian Conception of the Good Life," 113–29, esp. 118–20. Just because a narrative structure can be discerned at the core of all atonement theories, it does not follow that they are un-theoretical. On the one hand, soteriologies can be expressed in a set of coherent propositions (i.e. human sin creates a debt between humans and God or Jesus' death deceives the devil). On the other hand, these same propositions can be translated into a narrative that embeds them within a larger plot structure. The fact that the narrative of Christian soteriology has frequently undergone revision in order to support new propositions (For example, Anselm thought it unbecoming of God for him to have to make a deal with a devil and therefore excised the devil from his soteriological narrative.) indicates that propositions drive narrative emendations as much as, if not more than, narratives determine theoretical implications.

usually originate in the different ways the respective soteriologies frame the "state of deprivation" facing humanity. For example, according to Gregory of Nyssa, humans became the property of the devil through human sin and need to be ransomed from his control. Anselm thought it unconscionable that God would have to barter with the devil, and so he articulated a different "state of deprivation" that eliminated the devil from the scheme. Christian history is replete with other examples where different conceptions of humanity's need for salvation alter the way in which Christ saves human beings. The point is that, however theologians construe the "state of deprivation," it dictates what Jesus Christ must accomplish in his life, death, and resurrection to be the savior of humankind.

In order to articulate the human need or the "state of deprivation," theologians have often drawn on various cultural or biblical resources. Anselm, for example, utilized the feudal structure of medieval Europe, which was readily available to him in the surrounding culture. For him, God resembled a divine feudal lord who needed to be honored at all times by his human subjects. When human sin besmirched this honor, they incurred a debt that they could never repay on their own. Only the incarnate God-man could perform a meritorious action that would restore the honor of the divine lord. In a similar manner, Christian theologians have drawn from a wealth of resources in order to explain why humans need liberation.

Girard's soteriology is no different. The solution that his soteriology must provide originates in his mimetic theory. According to mimetic theory, when mimesis escalates into a community-wide pogrom, it finds relief only when an innocent victim is murdered. As a result of the first murder, the scapegoat mechanism has imperceptibly tyrannized subsequent human culture, and the truth of human violence has been forever obfuscated through mythology, which condemns the victims and later apotheosizes them. In Girard's soteriology, this presupposed anthropology becomes the "state of deprivation" from which humans need emancipation. Only the Christ event can dismantle this sorry state of affairs when God undeniably reveals the inherent sinfulness of humanity. In the end, like a good many other thinkers, Girard has developed his notion of the human need for salvation before proceeding to Christ's death and resurrection as the means of salvation.[2]

---

2. Though individuals like James Alison might object to my way of framing Girard's development of soteriology, I will simply point out that the progress of Girard's research began with his mimetic theory before he ever ventured into the Gospels. His discovery of mimetic desire and its generation of violence among human beings was published in books like *Deceit, Desire, and the Novel* and *Violence and the Sacred*, which antedate his engagement with the Gospels. The problem was theoretically in place before the solution was identified as Christ. See Alison, *Being Wrong*, 3–11.

The only difference with Girard is the nature of the human need and his reliance upon modern ethnographic and literary research to support it.

Without denying the ongoing need to make the Christ event understandable to modern Christians, are theologians at liberty to substitute different notions of the human problem as long as Christ still provides the solution?[3] Can theologians utilize whatever cultural, philosophical, and theological resources lie at hand to articulate the human need for salvation? In a short but potent article on the atonement, Robert Jenson complains that Christian soteriology has often run amuck by ignoring the larger storyline in which the New Testament Gospels situate Jesus.[4] All too often theologians remove Jesus from the historical and canonical storyline that the Gospels presuppose in order to put him into an interpretative schema of their choosing. To return again to Anselm, Jesus is situated in the larger construct of feudalism and is the one who satisfies the lord's demands for honor. For Jenson, Anselm's feudalistic soteriology is foreign to the Gospels. Abelard, in a contrasting yet all too similar move, "imagined a universal divine moral pedagogy aimed at educating moral creatures in virtue."[5] As a result, Christ's death on the cross fosters love in human hearts, which enables them to fulfill the righteous demands of the law. While there are elements of both Anselm's and Abelard's soteriology present in the Gospels, several of the elements depart from the biblical storyline. Even though contemporary appropriation of Christ's salvation is necessary for every generation, Jenson fears that theologians often haphazardly extract Jesus from his historical and theological context in the Gospels and place him into a foreign story. When this is done, the Christ event takes on new and sometimes contradictory meanings because Christ is made the panacea for problems and issues that were not in purview in the Gospels.[6] While he does not say so, Jenson would likely fault Girard for doing a similar thing in his soteriology.

In light of the concerns that Jenson raises, one can argue that Girard's hermeneutical approach to the Gospels is problematic for several reasons. First, Girard no longer seeks to understand the cross and resurrection from within the narrative of the Gospels themselves because the Gospels have been inserted into the storyline of Girard's mimetic anthropology where

3. Root suggests this is the case. See Root, "Narrative Structure," 155.
4. Jenson, "Doctrine of Atonement," 100–108.
5. Ibid., 104.
6. Lindbeck, "Scripture, Consensus, and Community," 88. Lindbeck warned about precisely this very thing. He wrote, "the more a theology translates the scriptural message into an alien idiom (rather than vice versa) the more easily it can be construed as having captured the essence of the gospel, just as . . . Freud's psychoanalytic interpretation is often treated by Freudians as having captured the essence of *Oedipus Rex*."

Jesus subverts humanity's penchant for scapegoats. In Hans Frei's well-known book, *The Eclipse of the Biblical Narrative*, he observed a marked shift in the interpretation of the biblical texts. In pre-modern biblical exegesis, the biblical narrative defined the lives of the interpreters because the pre-critical interpreters saw the biblical story running from creation to eternity as the story that governed their personal lives.[7] Thus, the biblical story was the world they inhabited. However, with the rise of historical-critical exegesis, exegesis became governed by external corroboration. In sum, critical exegesis made the world outside of the text—the ability of archeology or other historical records to corroborate the biblical accounts—the controlling factor in determining the truth of the text. The irony that Frei constantly delights in noting is that both liberals and conservatives made the external world the determining factor of the biblical story. In an effort to substantiate their respective views of the Bible, both succeeded in forsaking the meaning of the biblical narrative itself.[8] According to Frei, the meaning of a text can only be located in its narrative.[9] In *The Identity of Jesus Christ*, Frei identifies more specifically how interpreters abandon the New Testament narratives in order to define Jesus. One way is "by adding a kind of depth dimension to the story's surface, which is actually a speculative *inference* from what is given in the story, rather than a part of it. This procedure enables us to write something like the story behind the story . . . ."[10] Unfortunately, the "story behind the story" most often governs what the narratives about Jesus mean, distorting them to fit external needs or desires.[11] For Frei, this is a faulty way of proceeding, even it if delivers attractive results. Rather, if we are going to understand Jesus and his mission, Frei asserts that Jesus' "identity is grasped only by means of the story told about him."[12] Thus, the Gospels and the narratives they tell provide the key to understanding Jesus and what he accomplished on the cross. Girard's presupposition of the scapegoat mechanism's control over human culture constitutes another example of what Frei terms "the story behind the story." Though Girard offers an attractive exposition of human culture, his version of the "state of deprivation" precedes his

---

7. Ibid., 77.

8. Frei, *The Eclipse of Biblical Narrative*, 307–8 and Lindbeck, "Scripture, Consensus, and Community," 83.

9. Frei, *Eclipse*, 270.

10. Frei, *The Identity of Jesus Christ*, 90.

11. Ibid. He explains the deleterious effects of the foreign narrative thusly, " . . . an independently derived notion of Jesus' identity really shapes the story to conform to that notion."

12. Ibid., 87.

engagement with the biblical text and ultimately determines the nature of salvation that Christ provides.

Second, Girard's hermeneutics places the entire collection of biblical texts in counterpoint to a foreign body of literature. Instead of inferring the meaning of the biblical texts by allowing the texts to speak on their own, Girard proceeds by a direct contrast between the biblical texts and mythology in order to discern the inherent meaning and purpose of the biblical texts.[13] For example, Girard contrasts the story of Joseph's unjust treatment with the myth of Oedipus, who is deemed worthy of the charges of incest and parricide.[14] Likewise, the dialogues of Job are also set in contrast to the Oedipus account. For Girard, the calumny of Job's friends against him indicates he is another innocent victim of the scapegoat mechanism.[15] Even the climactic point of God's revelation, the Christ event, is set in contrast with Apollonius of Tyana.[16] By contrasting the biblical stories with myths, Girard concludes that the Bible exclusively defends the innocence of the victims while the myths justify their executions. Now, let it be noted here. I do believe comparing and contrasting the biblical texts with mythology constitutes a worthwhile *apologetic* endeavor, and Girard has done excellent work in defense of the biblical texts in this regard. Nevertheless, Girard overextends the implications of this comparison between the Bible and mythology. Though it is fully legitimate to identify the chief differences between mythology and the biblical texts, it is quite another to insist that these differences constitute the quintessential point of the biblical storyline. In my view, it is highly suspect to allow the contrast between the Bible and myths to determine the sole meaning and import of the biblical stories themselves, including the Gospels, as Girard has done. The upshot of Girard's hermeneutic is that an external reference point, i.e. mythology, becomes the prism for identifying the salvific content revealed in the Bible and reduces the biblical storyline to the univocal agenda of deconstructing mythology. This is certainly a step away from Frei's approach of discovering Jesus' identity in the narratives told about him and for that reason means one is proceeding on questionable hermeneutical grounds.

Third, Girard's defense of the Bible's uniqueness vis-à-vis mythology, though, comes at a price. To make this the central storyline of the biblical canon, several dominant biblical motifs are under-utilized in understanding

---

13. While Girard says this is not the case with all biblical stories, it is true of the way he exegetes the story of Joseph. See Girard, *Evolution and Conversion*, 201. Cf. Girard, *Things Hidden*, 141–79 and Fleming, *René Girard*, 116–18.

14. Girard, *I See Satan*, 106–15.

15. Girard, *Job*, 33–40.

16. Girard, *I See Satan*, 49–61.

the larger trajectory of Scripture.[17] For Girard, the biblical narratives are telling one story, namely, the story of how God has been at work in revealing humanity's violence. In order to amass evidence of the Bible's unique defense of the victims, Girard unfortunately overlooks important theological emphases that span the biblical canon. One finds little to no development, for instance, of Israel's complicated experience of being in a covenant relationship with YHWH, which consistently emerges in both Old and New Testaments. Instead, according to Girard, the ultimate story in the Bible is not one of God's workings with the nation of Israel and his restoration of the world, but rather, the slow dismemberment of mythological thought. This is not to deny that portions of the Bible situate themselves over against the mythological views of the world of their time. In fact, if anything, one can argue that Girard's understanding of the Bible's subversion of mythology is not nearly as far-reaching as it should be.[18] Regardless, by making mythology the lens for identifying what is unique in the Bible, Girard limits himself to a very selective portion of the Bible. In the attempt to remove the biblical texts from criticism, one can contend that Girard ends up reading the Bible in light of mythological texts, rather than vice versa. The search for mythology's cipher ends up placing biblical interpretation under the control of its dialogue partner, mythology. As a result, the story that the biblical texts tell has, in my view, been marginalized in an effort to substantiate the unique biblical defense of the victims. To borrow the term, "hermeneutical violence" has been committed because Girard's hermeneutics can only survive at the expense of other themes and theological insights in the biblical texts or at least the understanding of these themes sketched out below.[19]

In light of the hermeneutical issues that confront Girard, a different narrative framework for the Gospels and the Bible is required. This chapter and the following will proceed inductively in an attempt to listen to the biblical texts, especially the Gospels, on their own terms, to observe how they establish Jesus as a saving figure. It will, consequently, sketch a different

17. Wallace, "Postmodern Biblicism," 321.

18. Within the creation accounts of Genesis 1–2 alone there are several ways in which the texts directly counter Ancient Near Eastern mythology. While the Genesis account of creation does not contain the foundational murder like the *Enuma Elish* does, which supports the anti-mythological bent that Girard identifies, there are many other polemical points made which show that the Bible has more to say against mythology than Girard identifies. See Hasel, "Genesis Cosmology," 81–102; Hasel, "Cosmology in Genesis 1," 1–20; Klein, "Reading Genesis 1," 32–33; Flanagan, *Salvation History*, 11; Anderson, *From Creation to New Creation*, 22–27; Hamilton, *The Book of Genesis*, 127–28; Maag, "Alttestamentliche Anthropogonie," 39; and Bird, "Male and Female," 345.

19. Putt, "Exemplary Atonement," 41.

story of salvation history than the one that is found in Girard's writings. Of course, this is my understanding and articulation of salvation history, but I would contend that it is preferable to Girard's account for several reasons. First, the account of salvation history sketched below is based upon one of the biblical themes ignored in Girard's version, namely, Israel's covenant with YHWH that is capable of either assimilating or existing alongside of a number of other motifs. Second, I believe the nature of the Gospels' intertextuality, as plotted out in these two chapters, can claim much more widespread textual support from the Gospels. At the same time, it should be noted that Girard and I both agree that the Gospels are intertextual documents. We disagree, however, on the nature of that intertextuality. For Girard, the Gospels are polemically engaged in mythology. In my view, the Gospels' frequent allusions to and citations of Israel's prophetic hopes indicate that the intertextuality is not primarily mythology but Israel's theological traditions. Finally, by exploring some of the correlative themes in the intertestamental literature, we will have stronger historical and cultural precedent for choosing the following way of framing the Gospels than the one Girard adopts. Thus, I adopt the following account of salvation history because it can better account for the explicit elements of Israel's covenant relationship with YHWH, the Gospels' intertextual allusions, and the historical and cultural context in which the Gospels were composed.

As noted at the outset of the chapter, every soteriology requires a "state of deprivation," and this is something provided by one's account of salvation history. As Michael Root has rightly argued, the Gospels are not "uninterpreted data" but texts which possess "at least the seeds of interpretations in [their] descriptions of events and the patterns that organize those events into a narrative."[20] Unfortunately, Root never identifies what these "seeds of interpretations" are or what parameters the biblical narratives establish for soteriology. In order to fill in this lacuna, this chapter and its sequel will identify "the seeds of interpretations" latent in the Gospels, which should inform current soteriological reflection. In fact, the Gospels provide us with a good deal more than simply "the seeds of interpretations." The thesis of these next two chapters is that the Gospels, when read in light of the biblical canon, presuppose a particular "state of deprivation" instead of giving us a solution in search of a human problem. To put it another way, the Gospels come preloaded with a particular articulation of the human need for salvation that determines the manner in which Jesus functions as a saving figure. This preloaded articulation of the human need is not of the Gospel

---

20. Root, "Narrative Structure," 154.

writers' own creation but one they inherited from Israel's history of being in covenant with YHWH.

In what follows, I argue that the Gospels, despite being narratives in their own right, situate Jesus within a larger narrative that contains its own particular "state of deprivation." This is not the story of humanity bound in mythological deception or in debt to a feudal lord, but rather the story of Israel awaiting her restoration at the hand of YHWH.[21] This is the story that informs the Synoptic understanding of Jesus, which is revealed by the role that the Old Testament plays in identifying the importance of Jesus, explicating his proclamation of God's kingdom, and explaining the meaning of the symbolic actions he undertakes during his ministry. It is my contention that the Gospels already presuppose a certain "state of deprivation" that was elucidated in Israel's story in the biblical texts, namely, her experience of exile and punishment for breaking the covenant. For the Gospel writers, Jesus is first and foremost the savior in this larger narrative, for it is in this more encompassing story (i.e. salvation history) that they situate their own individual narratives about Jesus.

In order to demonstrate that the Gospels presuppose the storyline of Israel in relationship with God as definitive of the "state of deprivation," I will identify the key elements of Israel's own story and explain how the covenant was central to Israel's understanding of herself but also of her experience under exile. Despite suffering defeat and exile, Israel retained hope that God would restore her fortunes. These expectations and hopes, which reverberated throughout Jewish culture during the Second Temple period in variegated forms, provided the theological resources used to identify Jesus as a saving figure.[22]

---

21. The Gospels situate Jesus in the larger story of Israel because this is most likely how he understood himself. See Sanders, "Jesus and the Kingdom," 225–39.

22. Citing these other texts, especially the intertestamental literature, might seem questionable to some as if it were once again using external material to construct the "story behind the story." The intention behind using the intertestamental literature is twofold. On the one hand, it informs our understanding of how terms like "kingdom of God" were used in the first century. It is thus a way of enhancing our understanding and demonstrating whether particular interpretations and expectations were probable within the first century. After all, many interpretations are *possible*, but the real question is whether a particular interpretation was *probably* the case. Second, it also demonstrates continuity. When Old Testament expectations carry through the intertestamental literature into the New Testament with little variation, there is good reason to believe that the New Testament writers are reading the Old Testament in a similar way. As a result, incorporating the Jewish texts in this chapter is not to write a different "story behind the story," but to corroborate the interpretations taken here with external sources.

Israel's Theological Interpretation of Her History—an Abridged Version

Israel—YHWH's Covenant Partner

Israel's canonical history begins in Genesis with a brief overview of the primordial past. God the Creator had infused the world with goodness and blessing. However, the harmony and goodness of the created order was disrupted by human sin and disobedience, resulting in the curse and exile from the sacred presence of Eden (Gen 3:14–22). In Genesis 3–11, it seems as if sin and evil have gained the upper hand. Creation itself unravels as death becomes the final experience of every human being. In response to this state of affairs, God does not remain idle but chooses Abraham and his family as the vehicles through which God would return his creational beneficence to the world. The language of blessing in God's promise to Abraham should not be overlooked, for God promises Abraham, "I will make of you a great nation, and I will bless you, and make your name great, so that you will be a blessing. I will bless those who bless you, and the one who curses you I will curse; and in you all the families of the earth shall be blessed" (Gen 12:2–3). God's election of Abraham and his family, the Israelites, was ultimately for the purpose of blessing "all the families of the earth." From the viewpoint of Genesis, Israel was to be God's means of restoring creation to its original goodness and undoing the curse of sin and evil.[23]

A couple hundred years passed, and Abraham's family grew. However, instead of being free people in their own land, Abraham's descendants were subjugated to slavery by the Egyptians. YHWH, however, heard the plight of his people and came to their rescue. In the Exodus, God delivered his people from Pharaoh's tyrannous grip through a series of miraculous interventions. En route to the land God had promised the patriarchs, Israel entered into a formalized covenant relationship with God at Mt. Sinai. Through the covenant relationship, Israel became YHWH's "treasured possession" and "a priestly kingdom and a holy nation" (Exod 19:5–6).[24] The covenant designated Israel as God's peculiar people among the nations and his means of bringing blessing to the world.

There are few theological concepts that have shaped Old Testament theology more than the notion of God being in a covenant with Israel.[25]

---

23. Wolff, "The Kerygma of the Yahwist," 131–58, esp. 137–48.

24. On being a "priestly kingdom," see Propp, *Exodus 19—40*, 157–60.

25. The origins of this belief are indeed early as noted by several. See Levenson, *Sinai and Zion*, 36 and Eichrodt, *Theology of the Old Testament*, 1:36. Covenantal relationships often constituted kinship bonds between parties in the Ancient Near East. See McCarthy, *Old Testament Covenant*, 32–33.

The covenant established the boundaries and the expectations for the relationship between YHWH and his people. First of all, the covenant with YHWH, as any other covenant in the Ancient Near East, required loyalty and exclusivity. In fact, Jon Levenson believes that the emergence of monotheism in the Old Testament can be traced to the notion of a covenant between YHWH and Israel.[26] As Levenson observes, covenantal arrangements were exclusory by nature and mandated loyalty, as does a monotheistic worldview. That the covenant with YHWH expected no less from its constituents can be seen in the very first stipulation, the first of the Ten Commandments: "you shall have no other gods before me" (Exod 20:3). By contrast, other Ancient Near Eastern religions were much more inclusive and adopted other deities more readily. This noticeable difference suggests that the monotheism of ancient Israel derives from the understanding that she existed in a relationship with YHWH that excluded her from entertaining other partners (i.e. gods).

Not only did the covenant desire loyalty from YHWH's covenant partner, but it also included ethical norms for how to relate to one's neighbor.[27] Since the covenant established a relationship between YHWH and the covenant partners, it also created solidarity with other participants in the covenant. Because the individual participated in the covenantal relationship with other individuals, YHWH's ethical norms also mediated one's relationships with fellow human beings.[28] Thus, being in relationship with YHWH mandated ethical treatment of one's neighbor too. These stipulations are summarized in the latter portion of the Ten Commandments with prohibitions against murder, theft, slander, adultery, and envy (Exod 20:13–17).

As with any relationship, though, there are consequences if the expectations are not fulfilled. The stipulations of the Sinai covenant are repeated in Deuteronomy, an updated form of the covenant. There Moses, speaking on behalf of God, informs his audience of the potential results of being in covenant:

> See I have set before you today life and prosperity, death and adversity. If you obey the commandments of the Lord your God that I am commanding you today, by loving the Lord your God, walking in his ways, and observing his commandments, decrees, and ordinances, then you shall live and become numerous, and the Lord your God will bless you in the land that you are entering to possess. But if your heart turns away and you do

---

26. Levenson, *Sinai and Zion*, 56–70.
27. Boda, *A Severe Mercy*, 120; cf. 185, 517.
28. Levenson, *Sinai and Zion*, 53.

not hear, but are led astray to bow down to other gods and serve them, I declare to you today that you shall perish; you shall not live long in the land that you are crossing the Jordan to enter and possess (Deut 30:16–18).

In sum, Israel's continued residency in the promised land was contingent upon her faithfulness to the covenantal relationship.[29] Obedience would result in blessing and flourishing, while disobedience would bring exile and defeat at the hand of foreign powers.

The Monarchy and its Demise

After the Exodus, the Israelites settle in the promised land of Canaan. Eventually the tribal federation of the Exodus is consolidated into a single kingdom under King Saul. Saul, despite his great potential, disobeys God on several occasions and eventually dies at the hands of foreign enemies. His successor, David, is regarded as a man after God's heart (1 Sam 13:14) and becomes the model for the ideal king. As a result, God establishes another covenant specifically with David and his family. In it, he promises that David's dynasty would continue to rule over God's people (2 Sam 7:12–16). Moreover, God would regard David's descendants as his own sons, punishing them when they disobey, but never removing his line from the throne.

David's son Solomon succeeds him and augments the kingdom to its largest size. In addition, Solomon also builds the first Jerusalem temple, which becomes a central symbol in the life of ancient Israel. Solomon, though, is the last ruler over the united kingdom. Under his son's reign, the kingdom divides into the Northern Kingdom (Israel) and Southern Kingdom (Judah) around 922 BCE.

The story of the Northern Kingdom, as recounted in the biblical texts, is one of apostasy and idolatry. The first king of the Northern Kingdom, Jereboam, erects two altars to golden calves in order to preclude his people from going to worship in Jerusalem. This move cemented his political power since his people would be less likely to desert to the Southern Kingdom without a need to travel there to worship. While the altar to the golden calves likely continues YHWH worship, it does so by transgressing the prohibitions against making images of YHWH. As one might expect, the biblical texts view Jereboam's golden calves as disobeying the covenantal

---

29. While the demands of the covenant might seem like an imposition on Israel, there are many places where God is persuading not coercing them to enter into the covenant. See McCarthy, *Old Testament Covenant*, 55 and Brueggemann, *Theology of the Old Testament*, 417.

expectations (1 Kgs 13:1–4, 33–34). Eventually, the succeeding kings openly defect from YHWH worship altogether. The religious life of the Northern Kingdom reaches one of its nadirs when King Ahab erects a temple to Baal, a Canaanite god, in the center of the capital (1 Kgs 16:32). The legacy of the Northern Kingdom, from the view of the biblical writers, is certainly not a positive one. None of the kings are described as "good kings" because they fail to initiate moral and religious reform. Instead, they follow in the "sins of Jeroboam son of Nebat."[30] Thus, the fidelity expected in the covenant with YHWH had been repeatedly shattered with little intention of restoring it by any of the kings of the Northern Kingdom.

In 722 BCE, a mere two centuries after the Northern Kingdom's separation from the united monarchy, the Assyrian empire vanquishes it, taking its inhabitants into exile. The theological reasons behind this unfortunate state of affairs are articulated quite plainly in 1 Kings:

> This occurred because the people of Israel had sinned against the Lord their God, who had brought them up out of the land of Egypt from under the hand of Pharaoh king of Egypt. They had worshiped other gods and walked in the customs of the nations whom the Lord drove out before the people of Israel, and in the customs that the kings of Israel had introduced . . . . They despised his statutes, and his covenant that he made with their ancestors, and the warnings that he gave them. They went after false idols and became false; they followed the nations that were around them, concerning whom the Lord had commanded them that they should not do as they did (2 Kgs 17:7–8,15).

To put it simply, the Northern Kingdom suffers exile because they failed to observe the covenant faithfully. In defecting from YHWH and worshipping other gods, they had violated the expectations set forth in the covenant. As a result, they were on the receiving end of the covenant curses, which were death and exile from the land.

The Southern Kingdom's history plays out a bit differently, though it shares a similar fate. In contrast to the Northern Kingdom that had no "good kings," the Southern Kingdom had intermittent "good kings" who led the country in religious reform, even though they too had their share of immoral kings. In fact, the Southern Kingdom narrowly escaped the onslaught of the Assyrian superpower because it had King Hezekiah at its helm who had introduced religious reforms that promoted YHWH worship (1 Kgs 18:1—19:37; Isa 36–39). However, after Hezekiah, there were several series of evil kings who despised the covenant and promoted wanton

---

30. 1 Kgs 16:26, 31; 2 Kgs 10:29; 13:2, 11; 14:24; 15:9, 18, 24, 28.

idolatry—Manasseh was particularly noteworthy in this regard. The situation became irreparable, and, like the Northern Kingdom, the Southern Kingdom also suffered punishment for departing from the covenant. Through a series of invasions and deportations, which finally leveled Jerusalem in 586 BCE, the neo-Babylonian empire laid waste the Southern Kingdom and its temple. Again, the theological rationale for this political experience connects the Babylonian invasion with the sins of their bad kings. When the biblical record explains why this occurs, it says:

> Surely this came upon Judah at the command of the Lord, to remove them out of his sight, for the sins of Manasseh, for all that he had committed, and also for the innocent blood that he had shed; for he filled Jerusalem with innocent blood, and the Lord was not willing to pardon (2 Kgs 24:3–4; cf. 2 Chr 36:5–16).

Thus, although the covenant with YHWH held out the potential for blessing and life, both the Northern and Southern Kingdoms reap the opposite, cursing and exile, because they forsook the covenant.

Hopes for Restoration

With the Northern Kingdom's defeat and exile at the hand of the Assyrians and the Southern Kingdom's defeat by the Babylonians, the promised threats of the covenant had been enacted. While one might expect that this would sound the death knell for the Israelites and their religion, the experience of exile actually produces the opposite.[31] Under the shadow of foreign empires, the Israelites flourish. This was in large part due to the fact that, though they had experienced desolation at the hands of their conquerors, they anticipated a future wherein God would restore their fortunes.

Hopes for a restored Israel were not hard to find. The very prophets who had heralded the coming desolation of Israel and Judah had also prophesied that Israel's covenant God would not let her languish in exile forever. Consequently, the prophetic oracles fostered hopes for a restored Israel, which pervades many of the extant Jewish writings dating from the post-exilic times and into the Christian era.[32]

In what follows, I summarize several of the specific hopes for restoration after the exile. It reveals that, for Israel, her story was not simply locked away in the canonized past. Rather, it was a story in which the script was still being written, and the divine author had already hinted at what was about to

---

31. See Smith-Christopher, *Theology of Exile*.
32. Nickelsburg, *Jewish Literature*, 9–18.

transpire. While the Jewish people looked to the past and identified ways in which God had worked in her history (i.e. the exodus), they also looked to the future, anticipating a forthcoming work by her covenant redeemer. The following material encapsulates the story of Israel's experience of exile and hoped for return that the Gospel writers utilize to situate the life of Jesus.[33]

New Exodus

One of the hopes present in the prophets and intertestamental literature is the hope for a "new exodus." During the Babylonian and Assyrian invasions, portions of the Jewish population were removed from the land of promise. Like the original Exodus where the Jews had been enslaved to a neighboring power, the Assyrians and Babylonians had removed some of the Israelites from their homeland to serve foreign empires. The hope for a new exodus was that God would repeat what he had done in the first exodus where he had intervened and rescued Israel from an oppressive regime, bringing her to the land of promise. Using the first exodus as a type for what God was going to do on behalf of his exiled people, the prophets announced a message of hope and liberation: Israel would return from exile in a new exodus. This time, however, the people would come from Mesopotamia instead of Egypt.

Jeremiah, for example, ministering during the Babylonian invasions, utters the following oracle:

> Therefore, days are surely coming, says the Lord, when it shall no longer be said, "As the Lord lives who brought the people of Israel up out of the land of Egypt," but "as the Lord lives who brought out and led the offspring of the house of Israel out of the land of the north and out of the all the lands where he had driven them." Then they shall live in their own land (Jer 23:7–8).

Here the expected future act of bringing the covenant people back from exile is set in relief against the former exodus from Egypt. When God acted to bring them back from exile, it would be comparable to the original exodus, even superseding it in their communal consciousness.

With a similar expectation, Ezekiel prophesies the future re-gathering of Israel, "Therefore say: Thus says the Lord God: I will gather you from the peoples, and assemble you out of the countries where you have been scattered, and I will give you the land of Israel" (Ezek 11:17). In another passage, he utters a similar oracle: "I will bring you out from the peoples and gather

---

33. Sanders, *Jesus and Judaism*, 118. "What we know with almost complete assurance—on the basis of facts—is that *Jesus is to be positively connected with the hope for Jewish restoration.*" The emphasis is his.

you out of the countries where you are scattered..." (Ezek 20:34a). Similar refrains and expectations occur throughout the book of Ezekiel, revealing that the exile would end with a re-gathering of Israel to her homeland.[34]

Second Isaiah possesses a dense cluster of passages, which likewise anticipate a new exodus.[35] The opening verses of Second Isaiah contain the famous lines: "A voice cries out: 'In the wilderness prepare the way of the Lord, make straight in the desert a highway for our God. Every valley shall be lifted up, and every mountain and hill be made low; and uneven ground shall become level, and the rough places a plain" (Isa 40:3–4). The leveling of the mountains is later identified as the making of a road, which will allow the exiles to return: "And I will turn all my mountains into a road, and my highways shall be raised up" (Isa 49:11). Though the language here speaks of geological renovation, the imagery symbolizes God's creative work in returning the exiles to the land.[36]

The post-exilic Jewish literature frequently reiterates these same hopes and expectations that have their foundation in the prophetic texts above. The following texts demonstrate that the hope for a new exodus continued well into the intertestamental era. Some of these depict a future event while others are prayers to God, which reveal that, from the vantage point of the author, the new exodus still lies in the future. For example, the author of Baruch writes, "Arise, O Jerusalem, stand upon the height; look toward the east, and see your children gathered from west and east at the word of the Holy One, rejoicing that God has remembered them. For they went out from you on foot, led away by their enemies; but God will bring them back to you..." (Bar 5:5–6b). In this same vein, Sirach also possesses a similar expectation despite its sapiential and non-apocalyptic character: "Gather all the tribes of Jacob, and give them their inheritance, as at the beginning" (Sir 36:13–16).[37] 2 Maccabees likewise suggests that an imminent gathering was about to take place through the voice of one its protagonists: "We have hope

---

34. See also Ezek 28:25; 34:11–13; 36:24, 28; 39:26–28.

35. E.g. Isa 43:5–7, 18–19; 48:20–21; 49:7–12. Second Isaiah is usually dated from anywhere shortly before the return under Cyrus until well into the post-exilic era. Seitz dates Second Isaiah shortly before or shortly after the return under Cyrus. See Seitz, "Book of Isaiah," 6:318–19. Others date it much later. For example, Baltzer prefers 450–400 BCE. Baltzer, *Deutero-Isaiah*, 30–31.

36. Westermann, *Isaiah 40—66*, 37–39. Girard, in my opinion, works too hard to force the New Testament quotation of the verse into his soteriological framework and misses the more probable meaning of the verse. See Girard, *I See Satan*, 28–29. Contrary to Girard, ancient exegesis took the passage in the way I suggested above. See Bar 5:5–9 and *Pss. Solomon* 11:4.

37. Sirach 48:10 also contains the following: "At the appointed time, it is written, you are destined... to restore the tribes of Jacob."

in God that he will soon have mercy on us and will gather us from everywhere under heaven into his holy place . . . " (2 Macc 2:18b).[38] Finally, the *Psalms of Solomon* also expect a future return of the people: "Stand on a high place, Jerusalem, and look at your children, from the east and the west assembled together by the Lord. From the north they come in the joy of their God; from far distant islands God has assembled them" (*Pss. Sol.* 11:2–3).[39]

The above texts demonstrate that one of the pervasive hopes for restoration expected God to reassemble the twelve tribes that had been scattered during the exile. God, who had rescued Israel from Egypt's domination in the past, would emancipate the exiles and bring them back to dwell in their own land. Moreover, this hope for restoration appears in a wide array of literature, ranging from the wisdom literature like Sirach to the narratives of 2 Maccabees and the more apocalyptic *Psalms of Solomon*.[40] This was not just an expectation of certain apocalyptic authors, but a hope that many shared. For them, at some point in the future, the exile would be reversed, and God would bring Zion's children streaming back to her.[41]

New Covenant

From the view of the biblical writers, Israel's experience of exile was inherently intertwined with the covenant. Her infidelity to the covenant had warranted the exile in the first place. Only because Israel had transgressed the stipulations of the covenant, had YHWH dissolved the relationship by enacting the curses of the covenant. It would therefore follow that if YHWH

---

38. See also the important prayer offered earlier in the book, which views the return under Nehemiah as incomplete during the time of the Maccabees: "Gather together our scattered people, set free those who are slaves among the Gentiles, look on those who are rejected and despised, and let the Gentiles know that you are our God" (2 Macc 1:27).

39. A later section of the *Psalms* also speaks to this same expectation: "He will distribute them upon the land according to their tribes; the alien and the foreigner will no longer live near them" (*Pss. Sol.* 17:28). For evidence from Qumran, see 1QM 2.2–3 and 11QT 18.14–16.

40. There is some question regarding the authenticity of Sirach 36. Even if the text is a later interpolation, it simply means that the hopes for a new exodus were not original to this sapiential text, but it still would provide evidence that Jewish authors during this time anticipated the reconstitution of Israel. For dating the composite sections, see Gilbert, "Wisdom Literature," 298–99.

41. It is essential to understand the Deuteronomic viewpoint that the exile resulted from Israel's failure to keep the covenant. Schwager, who follows Girard quite closely, is able to talk about Jesus regathering Israel, but he lacks the theological presupposition that Israel's sin was a reason for the exile, which allows him to discredit any notion of God actually punishing sin. See Schwager, "Christ's Death," 111–13.

were to bring his people back from exile, he would enter again into a covenant relationship with them. In other words, the ruptured covenantal relationship would need to be resumed if Israel were to be reconstituted, and this is precisely what one finds in the prophetic texts of the Old Testament.

The well-known text from Jeremiah most explicitly displays the hope for a new covenant between YHWH and his people. As a result, it is worth quoting *in toto*.

> The days are surely coming, says the Lord, when I will make a new covenant with the house of Israel and the house of Judah. It will not be like the covenant that I made with their ancestors when I took them by the hand to bring them out of the land of Egypt—a covenant that they broke, though I was their husband, says the Lord. But this is the covenant that I will make with the house of Israel after those days, says the Lord: I will put my law within them, and I will write it on their hearts; and I will be their God, and they shall be my people. No longer shall they teach one another, or say to each other, 'Know the Lord,' for they shall all know me, from the least of them to the greatest, says the Lord; for I will forgive their iniquity, and remember their sin no more (Jer 31:31–34).

To begin, the promise of a new covenant expects the reconstitution of the covenantal relationship between YHWH and his people.[42] In the new covenant, he "will be their God" and Israel would be his "people," which is the covenantal formula that appears throughout Scripture.[43] At the same time, there is a disjunction that separates this covenant with the previous one ratified at Sinai. In the new covenant, God assumes a more active role in crafting the obedient covenant partner he desires so that they would obey his law.[44] Writing this law upon their hearts provided a more durable substance for the covenant than the former tablets of stone that Moses had broken on the mountain.[45] Nor could it be misplaced or lost like the book of the law found under Josiah's reign (2 Kgs 22:8). Nevertheless, it was the same law, which reveals that there is continuity between the old and new covenants.[46]

---

42. The promise of the new covenant presages the restoration of the people of Israel as a whole since the covenant is made with both the Northern and Southern Kingdoms.

43. E.g. Exod 6:7; Lev 26:12; Ruth 1:16; Jer 11:4; 30:22; 32:28; Ezek. 36:28; 37:27 among others. For a more thorough analysis on the covenant formula in Scripture, see Baltzer, *The Covenant Formulary*.

44. Ezekiel's depiction of God's restoration includes God taking a more active role in transforming the human partner. See Miller, *The Book of Jeremiah*, 6:812.

45. Keown, Scalise, and Smothers, *Jeremiah 26–52*, 133.

46. Hafemann, "The 'Temple of the Spirit,'" 29–42.

The divine expectations for the covenant partner had not changed. Instead, the change was to be found in the covenant partner's new ability to fulfill the covenant. Finally, YHWH promises to forgive their sins. This promise of forgiveness should be viewed in light of the belief that the exile was a direct punishment for sin. When God forgave Israel, her punishment for sin—the exile—would end. Consequently, the forgiveness of sin would signal the end of Israel's exile. Elsewhere, Jeremiah refers to this covenant as an "everlasting covenant" (Jer 50:5). The added quality of permanence relies, on the one hand, with God's established commitment to Israel in spite of her moral and relational failings. On the other hand, Israel is expected to be a different kind of covenant partner that will no longer forsake her passionate lover.[47]

Similarly, Ezekiel expects the ruptured covenant relationship to be renewed by one that surpasses the first covenant:

> Yes, thus says the Lord God: I will deal with you as you have done, you who have despised the oath, breaking the covenant; yet I will remember my covenant with you in the days of your youth, and I will establish with you an everlasting covenant. Then you will remember your ways, and be ashamed when I take your sisters, both your elder and your younger, and give them to you as daughters, but not on account of my covenant with you. I will establish my covenant with you and you shall know that I am the Lord, in order that you may remember and be confounded, and never open your mouth again because of your shame, when I forgive (בכפר) you all that you have done, says the Lord God (Ezek 16:59–63).

Again, we see the coalescence of several themes that were present in Jeremiah. The re-establishment of the covenant correlates with the forgiveness of Israel. The sin that had ruptured the relationship would be absolved, and God himself would be the one who atoned for their sin.[48] Moreover, there is an enduring permanence in the new covenant since it will be an "everlasting covenant" as God's covenants with Noah, the patriarchs, and David had been (Ezek 16:60; 37:26).[49] Like Jeremiah, the only reason the covenant

---

47. Jeremiah 32:40, "I will make an everlasting covenant with them, never to draw back from doing good to them; and I will put the fear of me in their hearts, so that they may not turn from me."

48. Gowan, *Theology of the Prophetic Books*, 136. Gowan notes that, in this passage, we see a unique progression. Rather than granting forgiveness *after* Israel realizes its sin, it seems Israel can only realize her sin after being offered forgiveness first. See also Zimmerli, *Ezekiel 1*, 353.

49. For other uses of "everlasting covenant," in the Bible see Gen 9:16; 17:7, 13, 19; 2 Sam 23:5; 1 Chron 16:17; Ps 105:10.

could be expected to last forever lies in the new heart and the new spirit that God would impart, which will be developed more in the following hope for restoration.[50] Riddled throughout Ezekiel are expectations that God will ratify the covenant with Israel once again. Sometimes he calls it the "covenant of peace" (Ezek 34:25; 37:26), which captures the return of creational blessing to the world, the original intent of the covenant with Abraham. At other points, he speaks of bringing Israel into "the bond of the covenant" (Ezek 20:37), which emphasizes reconciliation between two estranged parties. Together these passages indicate that, though Israel had broken the covenant and was currently suffering her just deserts in exile, things would not always lie in a state of disrepair. When God acted on Israel's behalf, he would reinstate the covenantal relationship with his people.

In a similar vein, several Isaianic texts affirm the enduring nature of God's renewed covenant with Israel: "For the mountains may depart and the hills be removed, but my steadfast love shall not depart from you, and my covenant of peace shall not be removed, says the Lord, who has compassion on you" (Isa 54:10). In this passage, YHWH's "steadfast love" ensures that the covenant with his people will never come to an end.[51] Other passages affirm the permanence of the covenant by indicating that, although God will give Israel justice and allow her to be punished, afterward he will establish "an everlasting covenant with them" (Isa 61:8; cf. 55:3). While some passages in Isaiah corroborate aspects of the new covenant hope that were identified in Jeremiah and Ezekiel, there are some sections that add to the developing picture. For example, YHWH's servant becomes a "covenant to the people" (Isa 42:6; 49:8), which quite possibly alludes to an extension of God's covenant to those beyond Israel's borders since the "people" are likely Gentiles.[52] If so, the covenant is not exclusively directed at Israel but returns benefits to those normally deemed outside of the covenant community. Moreover, whereas Moses was the mediator of the covenant at Sinai, here YHWH's servant actually becomes the covenant. Though the phrasing is odd, it suggests the servant "is the concrete means by which God's relationship with Israel is embodied and manifested."[53] In other words, the servant would inaugurate the covenantal relationship anew.

---

50. Brownlee, *Ezekiel 1—19*, 251.

51. Some suggest that this "covenant of peace" mirrors God's covenant with Noah after the flood. If so, then the author sees the inauguration of this covenant as the commencement of a new age. See Baltzer, *Deutero-Isaiah*, 446–47.

52. So Childs, *Isaiah*, 326. Baltzer leans in this direction but remains noncommittal. Baltzer, *Deutero-Isaiah*, 131–32.

53. Seitz, "Book of Isaiah," 6:430.

The major prophets of the biblical canon all attest, in various ways, to the expected hope that Israel's restoration would include the resumption of the covenantal relationship. Only this time, the covenant would be an eternal one. Exactly how widespread the hope for a new covenant was in the intertestamental era is difficult to ascertain. Certainly, it is not as well attested as many of the other hopes for restoration, which has led some people to suggest that covenantal theology was not as thoroughgoing as one might expect.[54] Still, the hope for a new covenant emerges in several prominent Second Temple Jewish texts, which demonstrates the hope still retained its force for at least some of the Jews during this time. For example, in the book of *Jubilees*, Abraham's blessing to Jacob, collocates the hope for Israel's renewal of the covenant and the forgiveness of her sins:

> May he cleanse you from all sin and defilement, so that he might forgive all your transgressions, and your erring through ignorance.... And may he renew his covenant with you, so that you might be a people for him, belonging to his inheritance forever. And he will be God for you and for your seed in truth and righteousness throughout all the days of the earth (*Jubilees* 22:14–15; cf. 22:30; OTP 2:98).

The pattern of covenant renewal has become the paradigm for Israel's historicized relationship with her covenant-keeping God. Another important text, Baruch 2:35, sounds much like the prophetic literature with its promise of an eternal covenant: "I will make an everlasting covenant with them to be their God and they shall be my people; and I will never again remove my people Israel from the land that I have given them."[55] The repeated theme of return and covenant occur together, indicating that the new exodus and reconstitution of Israel coincide with the institution of the "everlasting covenant."

No other group of texts during the Second Temple period references the covenant as frequently as the Qumran scrolls. This is due to the fact that the Qumran community understood themselves as having entered into a covenantal pact. Everyone who entered their community and submitted to the injunctions of *The Community Rule* submitted themselves to "the

---

54. Grabbe, "Did all Jews Think Alike," 264. While I appreciate the author's caution here, it is not apparent that the silence of many ancient Jewish authors regarding Israel as God's covenant people insinuates they lacked such a self-understanding.

55. Dating the book of Baruch is particularly difficult. Portions of the book (Bar 1:1—3:8) were translated along with the rest of Jeremiah in 116 BCE, which suggests part of the book was written prior to this time. As a result, a date in the second century BCE seems well founded. See Nickelsburg, "Bible Rewritten," 140–46.

Covenant before God."⁵⁶ Thus, they viewed their community's rules as a covenant with God. Moreover, in multiple instances, the *Damascus Document* refers to a time in the community's past when they had established a "New Covenant" in Damascus.⁵⁷ It is safe to say, the Qumran community understood themselves as a covenant community focused on being faithful to God.

In appropriating language of the new covenant to define themselves, the question arises whether the Qumran community saw themselves as heir to Jeremiah's new covenant or whether they understood their covenant differently. Unfortunately, the word "new" (חדש) is ambiguous in this application because it can mean "new" as in brand new, or it can mean something like "renew." In what sense did the Qumran community believe their community had entered a "new" covenant? Most scholars have concluded that the Qumran community understood their covenant as a renewed covenant rather than Jeremiah's new covenant for several reasons.⁵⁸ First, the covenant being renewed is the Sinai covenant. When a person joined the community, he undertook "a binding oath to return with all his heart and soul to every commandment of the Law of Moses."⁵⁹ In the scrolls, the disjunction that Jeremiah envisions between the old and new covenants is absent since it is precisely the covenant with Moses that is being renewed.⁶⁰ Second, Jeremiah's expectation that God's role would be more pronounced in the new covenant age is also lacking in Qumran. Instead, one finds an increased emphasis upon human effort. Consider the following passage from the *Rule of the Community*:

> No man shall walk in the stubbornness of his heart so that he strays after his heart and eyes and evil inclination, but he shall circumcise in the Community the foreskin of evil inclination and of stiffness of neck that they may lay a foundation of truth for Israel, for the Community of the everlasting Covenant (1QS 5.4–6, trans. Vermes).

---

56. 1QS 1.16–26 (trans. Vermes). See also CD 2.2.

57. CD 8.20–1; 6.19; 19.33; and 20.10b–12; cf. 1QpHab2.3–6.

58. Talmon, "The Community of the Renewed Covenant," 2–5; Freedman and Miano, "People of the New Covenant," 22–26; and Evans, "Covenant in the Qumran Literature," 55.

59. 1QS 5.8–9 (trans. Vermes).

60. Evans, "Qumran Literature," 59, 79 and Abegg, "The Concept of the Qumran Sectarians," 84. If there is anything "new" being imparted in the Qumran covenant, it resides in the "hidden things," or their authoritative interpretation of Torah. See Ibid., 85–88.

In the Qumran scrolls, Jeremiah's emphasis on God's transformation of the covenant partner has receded before a burgeoning emphasis on the human partner.[61] As a result, scholars have concluded that the Qumran community did not believe that they were living in the age of fulfillment, but were rather the faithful remnant that was fulfilling God's original covenant with Moses.[62] Their fidelity and loyalty to the covenant would eventually precipitate the final eschatological age where God would restore the faithful in Israel.

While one does not find expectations of a future covenant that surpasses the one from Sinai as in the prophets, the Qumran texts reveal that Israel's history is one of covenant renewal.[63] When Israel's sin ruptures the covenant, God is willing to renew the covenant when Israel responds in repentance and humility. The community continued this pattern and saw themselves as the part of Israel that was serious about being faithful to God's covenant. The prophetic texts and several of the other texts from the intertestamental time period anticipated a new covenant being made in the eschatological era. It would be an eternal, unbreakable covenant wherein YHWH would transform his covenant partners. Though this eschatological covenant would surpass the previous covenants, it continued Israel's pattern of repeated covenanting with God.

Impartation of the Divine Spirit

Israel's history of breaking the covenant throughout her history implied that Israel on her own was impotent to produce the new obedience anticipated in the new covenant. As a result, Israel's prophets anticipated a future work of divine transformation that would produce the heightened obedience. In order for this to happen, YHWH would have to become more directly involved with the transformation of his covenant partner. Ezekiel, for instance, looked forward to a time when YHWH would take on a more active role by fulfilling the following promise: "I will sprinkle clean water upon you, and you shall be clean from all your uncleannesses, and from all your idols I will cleanse you. A new heart I will give you, and a new spirit (רוח) I

---

61. Freedman and Miano, "New Covenant," 22.

62. Vermes, *Dead Sea Scrolls*, 67–72.

63. Some have argued that Jeremiah's covenant was never understood as a radical break with the former one since every covenant renewal had elements of continuity and discontinuity. If this is the case, then the Qumran community could lay claim to being inheritors of Jeremiah's covenant. However, even Tan who suggests this possibility still admits that the Qumran community *never* appropriated the language of Jeremiah and still expected a future renewal of the covenant during the eschatological age. See Tan, *The Zion Traditions*, 209–15.

will put within you; and I will remove from your body the heart of stone and give you a heart of flesh" (Ezek 36:25–6). In this passage, YHWH promises to change the object of Israel's affections by giving them a new spirit and a new heart. In the context of Ezekiel the removal of the "heart of stone" symbolizes the cessation of idolatry. Elsewhere, Ezekiel describes Israel as worshipping gods of "wood and stone" (Ezek 20:32) and as having taken "idols into their hearts" (Ezek 14:4).[64] Speaking metaphorically, Israel's heart had turned into the object of its affection: stone idols.[65] Only a work of divine transformation could alter what their hearts had become. Moreover, only a living God who has "breath" or "spirit"—something the idols lacked—could reverse Israel's ossified spiritual condition.[66] For Ezekiel, the impartation of the divine "spirit" or "breath" would transform God's covenant partner, so they would fulfill the covenantal expectations.

Perhaps one of the most vivid prophesies about Israel's future restoration and the impartation of the divine spirit can be found in Ezekiel's vision of the valley of the dry bones. In this vision, the seer is brought before a valley of desiccated skeletons and asked, "Mortal, can these bones live?" (Ezek 37:3). The seer is then instructed to prophesy to the bones, telling them that God would impart his "breath (רוח)" to them (Ezek 37:5) and quicken them. As he watches, sinews attach to the bones, then flesh and skin cover the skeletons, and finally the divine breath revivifies them. The text interprets the vision in the following commentary:

> Then he said to me, "Mortal, these bones are the whole house of Israel. They say, 'Our bones are dried up, and our hope is lost; we are cut off completely.' Therefore prophesy, and say to them, Thus says the Lord God: I am going to open your graves, and bring you up from your graves, O my people; and I will bring you back to the land of Israel. And you shall know that I am the Lord, when I open your graves, and bring you up from your graves, O my people. I will put my spirit within you, and you shall live, and I will place you on your soil; then you shall know that I, the Lord, have spoken and will act, says the Lord" (Ezek 37:11–14).

In the light of the larger collection of oracles in Ezekiel, this vision is important for it inverts the earlier prophecy of doom against Israel where YHWH promised: "I will lay the corpses of the people of Israel in front of their idols;

---

64. Kutsko, *Heaven and Earth*, 128–29.

65. An excellent study on the biblical understanding of how worshipping idols adversely affects the worshipper is Beale, *We Become What We Worship*.

66. Kutsko, *Heaven and Earth*, 136. For the "breathlessness" of idols, see Jer 10:14.

and I will scatter your bones around your altars" (Ezek 6:5). The idols had failed to save them from the exilic punishment, leaving them in the despair of death and exile. YHWH alone possessed the power of restoring them to their homeland, which is captured in the metaphor of resurrection.

While the prophecy of Ezekiel 36 simply spoke of a "new spirit" being given to Israel, Ezekiel 37 clearly identifies this spirit as YHWH's when he promises: "I will put my spirit (רוחי) within you" (Ezek 37:14a). The presence of the divine spirit and its role in restoring life to the dead evokes the creation accounts where the Spirit of God hovers over the primordial waters (Gen 1:2) and breathes life into Adam (Gen 2:7).[67] In a similar fashion, Israel's restoration would constitute an act of God's creative power as he created her anew. The experience of exile and restoration utilized the metaphor of resurrection to capture God's intervention on Israel's behalf. Israel's death in the exile would be overturned in her resurrection when God restored Israel to the land of promise (Ezek 37:12). Through the impartation of his Spirit, YHWH would root out the love for idols in Israel's hearts and breathe life into his people once more.

In the minor prophet Joel one finds a similar expectation. After God restores his people, YHWH promises, "Then afterward I will pour out my spirit on all flesh; your sons and your daughters shall prophesy, your old men shall dream dreams, and your young men shall see visions. Even on the male and female slaves, in those days, I will pour out my spirit" (Joel 2:28–29). Whereas Ezekiel emphasizes the divine spirit's transforming work, Joel emphasizes the role that the divine spirit played in prophesy. Nevertheless, both Joel and Ezekiel foretell of an increased role of the divine spirit in the age of Israel's restoration when YHWH would impart his spirit to his people.

New Temple

The Jerusalem temple, the central symbol of Jewish religious life, was not immune to the destruction of the invading armies. When the Babylonians invaded the Southern Kingdom for the final time, they pillaged the temple, stripped it of its gold, and left it in a pile of ruins. This state of affairs would not continue indefinitely, and the prophets, along with a host of post-exilic writers, expected the Jerusalem temple to be rebuilt when God restored his people to their land. Probably the most expansive example of the hope for a new temple can be found in Ezekiel's vision of the new temple (Ezek 40:1—44:3) with its extremely precise measurements for every component of the

---

67. Levenson, *Resurrection and the Restoration*, 159.

temple. Ezekiel, however, was not alone as a wide array of texts exemplifies an expectation that the temple itself would be rebuilt in splendor.

The later portions of Isaiah record several oracles anticipating the temple's rebuilding. For example, Isaiah 44:28 reads: "Thus says the Lord, your Redeemer, who formed you in the womb . . . who says of Jerusalem, 'It shall be rebuilt,' and of the temple, 'Your foundation shall be laid'" (Isa 44:28).[68] Interestingly, those outside the covenant would also be able to worship in the new temple. It was to be a "house of prayer for all peoples" (Isa 56:7)[69] and "the flocks of Kedar" and the "rams of Nebaioth"—the animals belonging to the people of Ishmael—"shall be acceptable on my altar" (Isaiah 60:7). Micah also has a similar expectation: "In days to come the mountain of the Lord's house shall be established as the highest of the mountains, and shall be raised up above the hills. Peoples shall stream to it, and many nations shall come . . . " (Micah 4:1–2a). Thus, the prophetic texts anticipate a time when the temple, though toppled by the Babylonians, would be rebuilt into an edifice where Israel and the nations could worship YHWH.

The intertestamental literature continues to resound with various permutations of this expectation as well. Tobit, for instance, anticipates a future rebuilding during the time of restoration:

> But God will again have mercy on them . . . and they will rebuild the temple of God, but not like the first one until the period when the times of fulfillment shall come. After this they all will return from their exile and will rebuild Jerusalem in splendor; and in it the temple of God will be rebuilt, just as the prophets of Israel have said concerning it. Then the nations in the whole world will all be converted and worship God in truth. They will all abandon their idols, which deceitfully have led them into their error; and in righteousness they will praise the eternal God (Tob 14:5–7a).

Tobit pictures the restoration of Israel, the time of "mercy," as coterminous with the rebuilding of the temple. The seer of 1 *Enoch* also envisions "that ancient house being transformed" and the edification of "a new house, greater and loftier than the first one," which will be built "in the first location which had been covered up—all its pillars were new, the columns new; and the ornaments new as well as greater than those of the first, (that is) the old (house) which was gone" (1 *En.* 90:28–29; OTP 1:71).[70] The *Sibylline Oracles*

---

68. In addition to these passages, see Isa 56:1–6; 60:13, 20.

69. Deuteronomy 23:1–8 forbids eunuchs and certain foreigners from entering the temple. This text in Isaiah undoes the earlier prohibition and possibly revolutionizes the idea of God's people. Westermann, *Isaiah*, 305.

70. See also 1 *En.* 91:13.

also possess a dream where "the temple will again be as it was before" (*Sib. Or.* 3.294; OTP 1:368).[71]

The expectation of a new temple appears in a myriad of texts, indicating it was widespread during the era. For some, the temple is simply rebuilt, but many of them believe the new temple will be more glorious than the former. Moreover, in some of the texts, the eschatological temple is no longer simply for the Jewish people. Instead, the temple welcomes "foreigners" and other "peoples" into its courts (Isa 56:7; Mic 4:1-2). When some of these texts include the Gentiles in their eschatological vision, we see the promise to Abraham—by whom God would bring blessing to all the nations—returning to a prominent place in Israel's story. Her vocation as God's means of blessing the world would occur when God acted to vindicate his name and rebuild the temple so humanity could be united in the worship of Israel's God. Finally, a point worth mentioning in light of the theological questions to which we will return shortly, the fact that some of the prophets envisioned sacrifices being offered in the eschatological temple indicates that, whatever one does with the prophetic critique of sacrifice, it cannot be taken as a wholesale indictment and annulment of the sacrificial system.

Eschatological Ruler[72]

If God were to restore the exiles to their homeland in order to inhabit the land freely, then there would have to be a political structure to safeguard the peace of Israel and Judah. Thus, the hope that God would raise up a righteous ruler in the coming renewal of Israel is logically integrated with the other hopes for restoration. Moreover, if Israel had suffered the exile because their leadership abrogated the covenant, then the eschatological reconstitution would need a righteous ruler who would not only defend the people from their enemies but foster faithfulness to YHWH.

The Old Testament affirmed that God had chosen a particular dynasty to lead his people, and the origins of an expectation for an eschatological ruler likely have their foundation in YHWH's covenant with David. In 2 Samuel 7, YHWH makes a personal covenant with David saying,

---

71. Other exemplary texts are *Jubilees* 1:15a, 17 and 11QT 19.10.

72. Because the language of "Messiah" can be restrictive when texts not using the term are excluded or too ambiguous since the word can refer to multiple roles and offices in ancient Israel, I have adopted the language of "eschatological ruler" to capture more accurately the essence of this particular hope for restoration. Regarding the pluriform nature of messianic expectation in Second Temple Judaism, see Collins, *Scepter and the Star*, 18. He identifies four different messianic paradigms that appear during this time: "king, priest, prophet, and heavenly messiah."

> When your days are fulfilled and you lie down with your ancestors, I will raise up your offspring after you, who shall come forth from your body, and I will establish his kingdom. He shall build a house for my name, and I will establish the throne of his kingdom forever. I will be a father to him, and he shall be a son to me. When he commits iniquity, I will punish him with a rod such as mortals use, with blows inflicted by human beings. But I will not take my steadfast love from him, as I took it from Saul, whom I put away from before you. Your house and your kingdom shall be made sure forever before me; your throne shall be established forever (2 Sam 7:12-16).[73]

The covenant with David affirms several things: 1) David's royal descendants possess a filial relationship with God; 2) the construction of the temple (i.e. a house for God) is the responsibility of David's descendent; 3) when David's son disobeys, he will be subject to divine discipline; and 4) regardless of how much discipline might be needed, David's dynasty would remain. The latter point probably proved to be generative of the hope that God would raise up an eschatological ruler for his people, for if David's dynasty were to remain in spite of discipline, it would be resumed after the exile.

In light of the covenantal promises made to David, it only seems reasonable that, when God acted to restore his people to their homeland in freedom, then God would also reinstate the Davidic dynasty over them.[74] This is precisely what one finds in a host of texts starting with the prophets and continuing on into the later portions of the Second Temple era. The Isaianic oracles speak of the future coming of the "root of Jesse" (Isa 11:10)[75] or the day when "[a] shoot shall come out from the stump of Jesse ... " (Isa 11:1a). This future descendant of David will come in the era of restoration: "When the oppressor is no more, and destruction has ceased, and marauders have vanished from the land, then a throne shall be established in steadfast love in the tent of David, and on it shall sit in faithfulness a ruler who seeks justice and is swift to do what is right" (Isaiah 16:4b-5). Jeremiah

---

73. References to the Davidic covenant reverberate throughout the rest of the Old Testament: Ps 89 and 132:8-18.

74. Some, in my view, are far too restrictive in their use of messianic language. E.g. Fitzmyer, *The One Who is to Come*, 47-48. Fitzmyer does not think the exilic hope for a new Davidic king is messianic simply because texts like Jer 30:8-9 do not describe David's coming descendant as a "Messiah." Unfortunately, this overlooks the fact that kings were anointed. As a result, it seems counter-intuitive to argue that a coming Davidic king could not be considered a "Messiah" just because the exact term is absent.

75. Though some interpreters have understood this text as anticipating a post-exilic community, the evidence suggests that it should be taken as a kingly figure. See Stromberg, "The 'Root of Jesse,'" 655-69.

anticipates the future coming of the "Branch," someone from David's line (e.g. Jer 33:15).[76] This coming king would reign righteously: "The days are surely coming, says the Lord, when I will raise up for David a righteous Branch, and he shall reign as king and deal wisely, and shall execute justice and righteousness in the land . . . . And this is the name by which he will be called: 'The Lord is our righteousness'" (Jeremiah 23:5–6).[77] For Ezekiel, David would again "shepherd" the people and be the "prince" of Israel (Ezek 34:23–24; 37:24–25). The minor prophets also look forward to God's restoration of "the booth of David" (Amos 9:11), the installment of "David their king" (Hosea 3:5), and the birth of the ruler in Bethlehem, David's hometown (Mic 5:2). Thus, the hope for the coming eschatological ruler, especially a Davidic ruler, is quite prominent in the prophetic corpus.

The intertestamental literature reiterates this hope in a number of places. The *Psalms of Solomon* expect a day when the "Messiah will reign" (*Pss. Sol.* 18.5; OTP 2:669) and when God would "raise up for them their king, the son of David . . . . And he will be a righteous king over them . . . and their king shall be the Lord Messiah" (*Pss. Sol.* 17.21–22, 32; OTP 2:667). The *Testament of Judah*, enlisting language reminiscent of the biblical prophets, believes "the Shoot of God Most High" will arise from the tribe of Judah (*T. Jud.* 24.4; OTP 1:801).[78] The *Sibylline Oracles* do not provide the lineage of the future king but simply say that "then God will send a King from the sun who will stop the entire earth from evil war, killing some, imposing oaths of loyalty on others; and he will not do all these things by his private plans but in obedience to the noble teachings of the great God" (*Sib. Or.* 3.652–56; OTP 1:376). *2 Baruch* also expects an "Anointed One" who will mete out justice upon evildoers (*2 Bar* 40:1–2; OTP 1:633).[79] The explicitly Davidic lineage of the coming "Messiah" is again present in *4 Ezra*: " . . . this is the Messiah whom the Most High has kept until the end of days, who will arise from the posterity of David, and will come and speak to them; he will denounce them for their ungodliness and for their wickedness, and will cast up before them their contemptuous dealings" (*4 Ezra* 12:32; OTP 1:550). Thus, many of the intertestamental books continue to preserve a hope for an eschatological ruler, and many of them expect the monarch to possess Davidic lineage.

76. In the context of Jeremiah 33:15, the reason for expecting a future Davidic king lies in the Davidic covenant (Jer 33:17, 21).

77. Bird, *Are You the One*, 39. Here the "righteous Branch" is contrasted with Zedekiah's failure to promote righteousness as the meaning of his name would suggest ("Righteousness of Yahweh").

78. Scholars have long noted that the text, as we have it, appears to be a later Christian redaction of the document.

79. Other allusions to the Messiah in *2 Baruch* are: *2 Bar* 29:3; 39:7; 70:9; 72:1–6.

The messianic expectation at Qumran is a bit more complicated, for it seems that there was a hope for a political figure alongside of a priestly one. This twofold nature of their messianic expectation trades upon the ambiguity of the Hebrew word for Messiah (משיח), which simply designates someone who is anointed, something true of priests, kings, and prophets. The Qumran community's expectation of two Messiahs can be seen in the *Rule of the Community*'s anticipation of "the Prophet and the Messiahs of Aaron and Israel."[80] The two figures, though different people, would serve different roles in Israel's restoration. The "Messiah of Aaron" would be a new high priest who would lead religious reforms, and the "Messiah of Israel" would be a royal, political figure.[81] While some Qumran texts simply talk about a messianic figure, others emphasize the Davidic lineage of the eschatological ruler by utilizing the terminology of the prophets, "Branch of David."[82] One of the most explicit texts on the subject affirms the Davidic covenant and anticipates a Messiah from David's line:

> The scepter [shall not] depart from the tribe of Judah ... [xlix, 10]. Whenever Israel rules, there shall [not] fail to be a descendant of David upon the throne (Jer. xxxiii, 17). For the ruler's staff (xlix, 10) is the Covenant of kingship, [and the clans] of Israel are the divisions, until the Messiah of Righteousness comes, the Branch of David (4Q252 fr. 1, 5.1–6, trans. Vermes).

Other texts simply allude to a "Messiah" that will inaugurate the eschatological renewal by the power of the divine spirit, without specifying his lineage.[83] Sometimes, there is no mention of a "Messiah" but simply an allusion to a future political ruler.[84] Despite the twofold nature of Qumran's messianic expectation, the authors—as many others during the late Second Temple era—still anticipated an eschatological ruler from the Davidic dynasty who would defeat Israel's enemies and lead his people to serve God in righteousness.[85]

Josephus also reminds us that messianic hopes were alive and active in the first century. Part of what precipitated the Jewish revolt against the

---

80. 1QS IX, 11 (trans. Vermes); Cf. 1QSa II, 11–21. The expectation of two separate figures is not present in all texts like the *Damascus Document*, which expects only "the Messiah of Aaron" (CD 12.22).

81. Liver, "The Doctrine of the Two Messiahs," 155–56.

82. 4Q174 I, 11–12; 4Q285, fr. 7; 4Q161, frs. 8–10.

83. 4Q521.

84. 1Q28b(1QSb), 5 speaks of a future "Prince of the Congregation" that will establish the covenant and rule in righteousness. Likewise CD 7.19 alludes to the "Prince of the whole congregation."

85. Wolters, "Qumran Documents," 77.

Romans in 66 CE was "an ambiguous oracle that was also found in their sacred writings, how, 'about that time, one from their country should become governor of the habitable earth.'"[86] In addition, Josephus mentions a number of insurrectionists who led unsuccessful rebellions against the Romans who seem to conduct themselves as the expected political ruler. Theudas, whom Josephus calls a "magician," took his people to the Jordan River and, in the manner of Moses and Joshua, promised to divide the river.[87] However, before he could carry out his intentions, the procurator decapitated him. There was also the anonymous Jew from Egypt who claimed to be a prophet capable of felling the walls of Jerusalem and conquering the Roman garrison whom the Romans also brought to a swift end.[88] In a similar fashion, Athronges assumed political authority for a time, even though he mainly waged guerilla warfare on the occupying Roman force.[89] Other figures like Menahem and Simon bar Giora also arose and asserted political authority as a result of their short-lived victories and postured themselves as delivering kings.[90] While we do not possess evidence that these figures claimed to be a Messiah, the promise of disassembling the walls of Jerusalem and dividing the Jordan river evoke images of Joshua's conquest of Canaan and suggest some of these individuals believed they were going to fulfill the hopes for a new exodus by leading a "new conquest of the land" as a political leader.[91]

The above texts indicate that there was a widespread expectation that God's restoration of Israel would occur under the leadership of a Messianic figure who was often, though not always, understood to be a descendent of David.[92] This figure would deliver Israel by conquering her enemies and

---

86. Josephus, *J.W.*, 6.312, trans. Whiston. For an interesting interpretation of the passage, see Wright, *New Testament*, 312–14.

87. Josephus, *Ant.*, 20.97–99. The violent response of the procurator suggests that this gathering was not simply a demonstration of his power but also had overtones of a revolution.

88. Josephus, *Ant.*, 20.169–70; Josephus, *J.W.*, 2.261–62.

89. Josephus, *Ant.*, 17.278–84; Josephus, *J.W.*, 2.60–65.

90. For Menahem, see Josephus, *J.W.* 2.433–34, 444. For Simon bar Giora, see Ibid., 4.503–10.

91. Evans, "Aspects of Exile and Restoration," 302–5. It is possible that these individuals never made any messianic claim, despite their symbolic actions. The only person Josephus identifies as "Messiah" is Jesus. See Josephus, *Ant.*, 18.63, which is possibly a Christian redaction. However, he obliquely alludes to Jesus being the Messiah in *Ant.*, 20.200 as well, which further substantiates the title in Josephus' work.

92. Some scholars suggest that messianic expectation waned between the "early fifth to the late second century BCE" (Collins, *Scepter and the Star*, 51). Fitzmyer argues it really only emerges in the second century BCE within the book of Daniel (Fitzmyer,

ruling in righteousness. At the same time, we need to refrain from supposing that all Jews in the Second Temple period expected a Davidic king or shared a similar understanding of the coming Messiah. The belief, for example, seems conspicuously absent from some post-exilic texts like Ezra-Nehemiah.[93] Likewise, the evidence of a belief in two Messianic deliverers at Qumran indicates that the Messianic expectation existed in different permutations. To be safe, we should abstain from assuming the hopes for a messianic deliverer were a monolithic whole that unequivocally describes all Jews during this time period.[94] With this caveat in place, though, one can still say that such a belief was apparently well known and pervaded much of the Jewish world of the first century. As Collins concludes, there was a "common core" to the messianic expectation that saw "the Davidic messiah as the warrior king who would destroy the enemies of Israel and institute an era of unending peace...."[95]

The Enduring Exile

The above texts have identified how various biblical and intertestamental authors anticipated God's future restoration from exile. While it is difficult to determine the degree to which the average person held these beliefs, the widespread occurrence of these beliefs in diverse texts and genres suggests the above examples do not represent isolated phenomena but a tradition representative of a wider portion of the people. To summarize, they expected God to bring them back from exile in a new exodus and raise up an eschatological ruler to procure political peace. In addition to a renewed political situation, God would also re-establish his relationship with them by

---

One Who is to Come, 62). However, as Collins notes, there is very little evidence coming from this time period to give us an accurate picture of what beliefs were commonly held (Collins, *Scepter and the Star*, 40). In fact, the little evidence that there is Collins must explain away as a later insertion to maintain his thesis. While his assessment of Sirach is convincing, his analysis of the *Sibylline Oracles* is not. His equation of the "King from the sun" (*Sib. Or.* 3.652) with one of the Egyptian kings overlooks the association with Jerusalem that is present in the surrounding context, especially with an anticipated assault on the Jerusalem Temple (Collins, *Scepter and the Star*, 46–49). Even if the text mirrors the *Potter's Oracle* as Collins observes, this does not preclude the author from adopting such language in order to situate his expectation of a future Jewish king. Due to the fact that contrary evidence must be explained away and because sufficient evidence is lacking in order for us to make solid assertions here, arguing that messianic expectation fell into disuse during this time is tenuous, though not impossible.

93. Goswell, "Davidic Hope in Ezra-Nehemiah," 19–31 and Goldstein, "Authors of 1 and 2 Maccabees," 69–96.

94. Wright, *New Testament*, 308.

95. Collins, *Scepter and the Star*, 78.

inaugurating a new covenant, imparting his Spirit into them so they would fulfill the covenantal stipulations and rebuilding the temple so the worship of YHWH as prescribed in Torah could be resumed.

Historically speaking, the exile of the Southern Kingdom did not last long. When the neo-Babylonian empire was overrun by the Persians in 539 BCE, Cyrus the Persian king issued a decree sending the Jewish exiles back to their homeland to rebuild the temple.[96] Certainly, Cyrus' release of the exiles was a reversal of the exile, but did this return to the homeland constitute a complete fulfillment of the hopes for Israel's restoration? Did the state of exile end when Cyrus utters his decree for the Jews to return?

While it can be said that aspects of the hopes for restoration came true with the return under Cyrus, I contend there is enough post-exilic evidence to conclude that the Jewish people believed the exilic state continued and that restoration had not been completely fulfilled even after they had returned and had begun rebuilding their land and temple under the Persians. To put it another way, though the Jewish people enjoyed a modicum of freedom under the Persians and subsequent empires, they did not believe they had entered into the era of the promised deliverance. This thesis is not original with me, but has been advanced already by N. T. Wright who makes it the basis of his provocative reconstruction of Jesus' ministry.[97] Since some scholars have questioned Wright's presupposition that many Jews of the first century viewed themselves as still being in "exile," it is worth reviewing the evidence in favor of it here since it impacts the reading of the Gospels offered in the following chapters.[98]

The best evidence for Wright's notion of a continuing exile come from postexilic sources, namely, those written *after* Cyrus' decree to return to the land. For example, Ezra categorizes the Jewish people as "slaves" since, though they had returned to the ancestral lands, they still were subjected to foreign powers (Ezra 9:9). A similar affirmation is made in Nehemiah when Ezra describes his people *after the return*: "Here we are, slaves to this day—slaves in the land that you gave to our ancestors to enjoy its fruit and its good gifts" (Neh 9:36).[99] These passages reveal that, even though they

---

96. Ezra 1:1–4.

97. Wright, *New Testament*, 268–72, 299–301; Wright, *Jesus and the Victory of God*, 126–27, 203–9, 268–74.

98. For some of the critiques, see Jones, "Disputed Questions in Biblical Studies," 400–5; Casey, "Where Wright is Wrong," 95–103; Dunn, "Jesus and the Kingdom," 3–36; and Dunn, 'Review of *Jesus and the Victory of God*," 727–34, esp. 730–31.

99. This same view of a continuing exile is reflected in 1 Esdras, a text written in the late second century BCE, where Ezra prays similarly: "O Lord, I am ashamed and confused before your face. For our sins have risen higher than our heads, and our mistakes

had physically returned to the land, their physical return was at best only a partial fulfillment of the promises for restoration. Because the Persians retained political authority, they were simply slaves. The viewpoint of Ezra and Nehemiah suggests that the exilic state of affairs could be experienced as a slave in one's own land.

Similarly, the book of Tobit, a story set in the Assyrian exile, utilizes the familiar trope of Jews being faithful to YHWH in exile in order to speak to the existential situation of Jews living hundreds of years later. The book itself is usually dated between 225–175 BCE.[100] The fact that it addresses a post-exilic community suggests a presupposed elongation of the exile, for it borrows on the metaphor of exile in order to encourage Jews living under foreign domination. In the book, there are numerous references to a future change of fortunes when YHWH "will again show mercy" on his people (Tob 13:5). Probably the most explicit is Tobit 14:5 where Tobit prophesies:

> But God will again have mercy on them [Israel and Judah], and God will bring them back into the land of Israel; and they will rebuild the temple of God, but not like the first one until the period when the times of fulfillment shall come. After this they all will return from exile and will rebuild Jerusalem in splendor; and in it the temple of God will be rebuilt, just as the prophets of Israel have said concerning it.

Here the author, who is situated several centuries after the initial return to the land, still anticipates a future fulfillment of the prophets' message.[101]

In addition, Daniel 9 also demonstrates a belief that the exile continues past the return under Cyrus. The chapter begins with Daniel contemplating the words of Jeremiah that promised seventy years of exile (Dan 9:1–2).[102]

---

have mounted up to heaven from the times of our ancestors, and we are in great sin to this day. Because of our sins and the sins of our ancestors, we with our kindred and our kings and our priests were given over to the kings of the earth, to the sword and exile and plundering, in shame to this day" (1 Esdras 8:74b–77). For the date, see Attridge, "Historiography," 158–59. See also 2 Macc 1:27 and its view of the return under Ezra and Nehemiah.

100. Fitzmyer, *Tobit*, 50–51. Nickelsburg suggests it could be before 200 BCE. See Nickelsburg, "Biblical and Post-Biblical Times," 45.

101. The book of Tobit emphasizes the exilic state of being outside of the land. As a result, even though one can emphasize its post-exilic origins, it seems likely that the texts here describe those outside the land after the original return rather than those who had returned and were living in the land. On this points, see Weitzman, "Allusion, Artifice, and Exile," 49–61. If this caveat is warranted, then we see something different than the slave-in-one's-own-land idea that was present in Ezra and Nehemiah since it is addressing those displaced from the land.

102. The prophecies in view are Jeremiah 25:11–12 and 29:10.

In the middle of confessing the sins of his people, Daniel is informed that the exile is not simply seventy years but "Seventy weeks are decreed for your people and your holy city: to finish the transgression, to put an end to sin, and to atone for iniquity, to bring in everlasting righteousness, to seal both vision and prophet, and to anoint a most holy place" (Dan 9:24). While the text ambiguously fails to identify whether these seventy weeks are days, months, or years, the most persuasive explanation sees them as years.[103] As a result, the revelation to Daniel indicates the exile will last four hundred ninety years, which is long after the return to the land. In fact, the revelation given to Daniel only begins its reckoning of the four hundred ninety "from the time that the word went out to restore and rebuild Jerusalem" (Dan 9:25b), which would certainly indicate the exile did not terminate with the return under Cyrus. Thus, Daniel's elongation of the time period and his dating from the return to the land indicate that the exilic state endured past the return under Cyrus and well into what many typically consider the "post-exilic" era.[104]

Baruch represents another non-canonical work that, like Tobit, was composed or reached its final form well after the return under Cyrus yet continues to use the setting of the literal Babylonian exile to speak to the existential situation currently facing the Jewish people in the author's day.[105] In a penitential prayer that the Jewish people were supposed to utter nationally, they confess "we are today in our exile where you have scattered us, to be reproached and cursed and punished for all the iniquities of our ancestors, who forsook the Lord our God" (Bar 3:8). While the expression that "we are today in our exile" is certainly true for the fictive setting during the Babylonian exile, it is suggestive that a later author would include the prayer as a model for penance in his own day.

While it seems clear that several texts do not see the return under Cyrus as the fulfillment of Israel's hoped for restoration or as the end of the exile, one could posit that the period of independence won by the Maccabees would constitute a time of such fulfillment. Perhaps the best case for defending the notion of an enduring exile comes from those texts written during and after the Hasmonean era.[106] One of the most explicit support-

---

103. Miller, *Daniel*, 257–58.

104. Halvorson-Taylor, *Enduring Exile*, 201.

105. For a probable dating in 164 BCE, see Nickelsburg, "Bible Rewritten," 145–46. The book of Baruch is notoriously difficult to date for there may have been portions of the book written at different intervals. For dating some of the respective parts of Baruch, see Moore, "Book of Baruch," 312–20.

106. VanderKam, "Exile," 89–109. Judith, which was completed during the Hasmonean era, also suggests that the Jewish people could endure slavery in various places.

ing texts is the book of 2 Maccabees.[107] In 2 Maccabees 2:1-8, the author records one of the traditions regarding the ark of the covenant. According to this particular tradition, Jeremiah hid the ark of the covenant and other temple utensils when the Babylonians were invading Judea. Purportedly, these temple instruments would remain hidden "until God gathers his people together again and shows his mercy" (2 Macc 2:7), which indicates that the period of Jewish independence under the Hasmoneans did not fulfill the hopes for a new exodus or a complete return from exile.

Although the Maccabees do gain independence and purify the temple, there is never an argument in the text for the recovery of the temple artifacts interred by Jeremiah, nor are they used during the purification of the temple (2 Macc 10:1-8). In the letter to the other Jews, inviting them to celebrate the purification of the temple (i.e. Hanukkah), there is more evidence that the fullness of restoration lays in the future from the vantage point of the author:

> It is God who has saved all his people, and has returned the inheritance to all, and the kingship and the priesthood and the consecration, as he promised through the law. We have hope in God that he will soon have mercy on us and will gather us from everywhere under heaven into his holy place, for he has rescued us from great evils and has purified the place (2 Macc 2:17-18).

This text is important for realizing that, though the Jews had won their independence and resumed worship at the temple, the author does not believe they had yet entered into the period of restoration. God had yet to give them "mercy" and the new exodus, God's ingathering of all exiles, had not happened even though they appear to be on the cusp of such a great event.

The Dead Sea Scrolls which have provided significant evidence for the continuation of the Jewish hopes for restoration in the previous portion of

---

Judith 8:22 says, "The slaughter of our kindred and the captivity of the land and the desolation of our inheritance—all this he will bring on our heads among the Gentiles, wherever we serve as slaves; and we shall be an offense and a disgrace in the eyes of those who acquire us." In fact, Judith might have an intentionally anti-Hasmonean agenda further supporting the argument that, at least some, did not believe the Hasmoneans brought the end to the exilic state of affairs. See Eckhardt, "Reclaiming Tradition," 243-63.

107. 2 Maccabees has been dated variously. Schwartz argues for an early date of 143-42 BCE. Schwartz, *2 Maccabees*, 3-15. However, the final form of the book has assimilated various pieces dating to different time periods, which leads some to conclude that the final redactor is a little later, though he likely used earlier sources. As a result, some have given a range from 77 BCE to the time of Nero for the date of the final form. See Attridge, "Historiography," 176-78.

this chapter can be also safely located "between 200 BCE and 70 CE."[108] In fact, it is unsurprising that the Qumran community did not believe the time of restoration had arrived during the Hasmoneans, for the sect was generated by the opposition between their founder, the Teacher of Righteousness, and the Hasmoneans who were purportedly meddling in the religious affairs of the temple and the priesthood.[109] Still, the scrolls provide evidence of another group of Jewish people that did not identify the period of Jewish independence as a fulfillment of Israel's hopes for restoration.[110]

One can also marshal support from some of the prevailing ideologies that arise during the Hasmonean era, particularly the fervent increase in messianism that pervades the period.[111] Though I remain doubtful whether we can confidently say that messianism only emerged at this time, the fact that evidence for messianism abounds after the Jews regain control of the land suggests that they still anticipated a future deliverance at the hands of the Messiah even though they had gained political freedom through the Hasmoneans.

When the Romans overthrow the fragile Jewish state in 63 BCE, one would expect the Jewish people to re-appropriate the thoughts and beliefs about their existential situation that were typical of the period under the Persians because they would once again be slaves in their own land. Such is, in fact, what one finds. In Josephus' imploring speech, begging the last holdouts of the Jewish revolt against the Romans (66–70 CE) to surrender, he tells his audience that the Romans only gained control over Palestine because the former Jewish political rulers had sinned and thereby brought Roman hegemony upon the people.[112] In other words, Pompey's invasion

---

108. Vermes, *Dead Sea Scrolls*, 14. For a more specific dating of the community's existence, which has them, at best, continuing in a moribund existence in the first century, see Wise, "The Origins and History of the Teacher's Movement."

109. Vermes, *Dead Sea Scrolls*, 54–66 and Collins, *Scepter and the Star*, 9–10.

110. Neusner suggests that the Hasmonean dynasty could not be considered the fullness of restoration because it did not fulfill the expectations in Scripture. Neusner, *Self-Fulfilling Prophecy*, 59.

111. Fitzmyer, *One Who is to Come*, 82–133. I personally believe Fitzmyer has been too cautious in limiting the genesis of messianism to the second century BCE. However, Fitzmyer can make his argument because messianic expectations begin flourishing after the Jews win their independence from the Seleucids.

112. He specifically faults Aristobulus and Hyrcanus here for the demise of Israelite independence. However, Josephus also thinks that the new revolutionaries have sinned so egregiously that God now supports their enemies instead of them. See Josephus, *J.W.*, 5.395–419. Bryan, however, misses the import of this passage when he says that the passage, rather than being "proof" of a continuing exile under the Romans, is simply talking about the origins of Roman domination. See Bryan, *Israel's Traditions*, 15. Bryan fails to acknowledge that Josephus compares the revolutionaries of his present

(63 BCE) inaugurated a new form of exilic punishment where Israel was receiving her just deserts, even if they remained in the land. From Josephus' point of view, the Jews of Pompey's day had sinned and, therefore, were again subjugated to a foreign power. The rebels of his day were running the same risks and would likely face the same result. In addition, Josephus also tells us that some of the revolutionaries during the period of Roman control still equated Roman taxation with slavery.[113] Despite the fact that the Romans periodically permitted Palestine semi-autonomous rule under various client kings, levying taxes to fund a foreign power could still be seen, as it ostensibly was under Ezra and Nehemiah, as tantamount to being serfs in the homeland.

One can also point to *4 Ezra*, which dates to the end of the first century.[114] In *4 Ezra* 13:40–47 the author speaks of the existence of the ten northern tribes, which had been exiled under the Assyrians. Historically, these exiles had never returned to the land unlike portions of the two southern tribes under Cyrus of Persia. According to the author of *4 Ezra*, the ten northern tribes existed in a land called Arzareth, a place beyond the Euphrates River. At some point in the future, "the Most High will stop the channels of the river again, so that they may be able to pass over" (*4 Ezra* 14:47; OTP 1:553). The return of the northern tribes, as described in this text, mirrors the splitting of the Red Sea by Moses and the crossing of the Jordan River by Joshua. The imagery anticipates a future new exodus where God will bring his people back to the land. Moreover, though some of the Jewish people return under Cyrus the Persian, even well into the first century, some Jews believed that the exile was still *a current literal and historical experience* for the ten northern tribes.[115]

---

day to the generation of the Babylonian siege and says "the Jews of that age were not so impious as you are. Wherefore I cannot but suppose that God is fled out of his sanctuary, and stands on the side of those against whom you fight" (Josephus, *J.W.*, 5.411–12). Josephus is clearly invoking Deuteronomic theology, which threatened exile and defeat as punishment for sin, and is applying it to his current context. The paradigm of sin and punishment (as exile) is operative under the Romans as much as it was under the Babylonians. While I will concede that Josephus never identifies Roman subjugation as an experience of "exile," the same interpretive paradigms are operative here in Josephus to explain the political situation under the Romans.

113. Josephus, *Ant.*, 18.4: "[Y]et there was one Judas, a Gaulonite, of a city whose name was Gamala, who, taking with him Sadduc, a Pharisee, became zealous to draw them to a revolt, who both said that this taxation was no better than an introduction to slavery . . . " (trans. Whiston).

114. Date for this book is c. 100 CE. See OTP 1:520 and Stone, "Apocalyptic Literature," 412.

115. To this can be added evidence from Philo who, despite his strong penchant for allegory, exhibits the same expectation in the first century that the restoration of Israel lay in the future. Philo, *De Praemiis et Poenis*, 165–68.

At this point, we are in a position to reassess the various claims being made about the notions of an "enduring exile" within the Jewish worldview of the Second Temple era. The notion has been challenged on several grounds. For one, the Jews did, in fact, return to the land of promise and worshipped at a reconstructed temple, so some critics have questioned how Jews living in the land could conceive of themselves as still in exile.[116] Despite these observations, Wright's notion of an enduring exile cannot be quickly discounted. Several people who adopt Wright's notion of an enduring exile point out one can still speak of the exile continuing in a literal sense as long as it is used to refer to the ten tribes of the Northern Kingdom who had not returned from exile.[117] Yes, the exiles from the Southern Kingdom had returned to the land after being taken into exile by the Babylonians. Nevertheless, the exiles of the Northern Kingdom who had been exiled during the Assyrian conquest had yet to return.[118] Since the exiles from the Northern Kingdom had never returned, one can legitimately argue that Jews in the first century would have viewed portions of their people as still literally residing in exile, even if that was not indicative of their personal experience.[119] The evidence from 2 Maccabees and *4 Ezra* suggests that at least some of the Jewish people believed this was an ongoing state for them as a people group during and after their political independence.

Other critics of Wright's thesis have contended that the metaphor of exile loses its ability to capture the Jewish understanding of their historical situation after the return under Cyrus. Such critics contend that, though Wright is correct that Jewish writers continue to speak of their restoration as a future event, the metaphor of exile loses its potency as time goes on.[120] For such critics, it is better to speak of a state of "non-restoration" rather than an ongoing exile. Though I agree that it is more encompassing and more accurate to describe the Jewish outlook in the first century as one of "non-restoration," it is wrong to conclude that Jews in this time period "did

---

116. Casey, "Where Wright is Wrong," 99–100; Dunn, "Jesus and the Kingdom," 21–25; and Bryan, *Israel's Traditions*, 13–14.

117. Pitre, *Jesus, the Tribulation, and the End of the Exile*, 32–39. A similar point is made in Dennis, *Jesus' Death and the Gathering of True Israel*, 84.

118. One can also note that some of the Jewish people were never exiled, and yet the exile of the few became an existential paradigm for later Jewish people. See Neusner, *Self-Fulfilling Prophecy*, 31 and Neusner, "Exile and Return," 224.

119. Moreover, if we proceed with the understanding that the Jewish people of their time had a group-oriented consciousness where the individual's experience was integrated into the experience of the community as a whole, it is not difficult to suppose that even those residing in the land would continue to think of their people, and hence themselves, as still experiencing exile. See Cohen, *Maccabees to the Mishnah*, 10–14.

120. Bryan, *Israel's Traditions*, 19.

not often *describe* their situation" as an "ongoing exile."[121] All of the texts mentioned above that anticipated the re-gathering of God's people certainly indicate a belief that portions of the Jewish people were still at large, having yet to return. In addition, if we follow Halvorson-Taylor in expanding the metaphor of exile to include "political disenfranchisement" and "a feeling of separation from God,"[122] as Ezra-Nehemiah and some of the evidence from Josephus allows, then one does seem justified in broadening the metaphor of exile to include the situation under the Romans where they were again slaves in their own land. Though the metaphor of exile is not comprehensive enough to capture all that God would remedy in the age to come, it remains a valid one into the first century. The range of textual evidence supports the affirmation that throughout the Second Temple period, even though several elements of the hopes for restoration had partially come to fruition, many of those promises had yet to be fulfilled and some of the ones that had been fulfilled were still incomplete. Among those incomplete promises was the full return from exile, which remains a valid metaphor among a matrix of other hopes for restoration that were, at the most, partially fulfilled.[123] Perhaps instead of using the metaphor of "exile," one is better suited in simply saying that, in the first century, Israel awaited the completion and fulfillment of its restoration.[124] This hoped-for state of affairs can be described in various ways and with various metaphors, one of which is the return from exile, the new exodus.

121. Ibid., 13 (emphasis is his).

122. Halvorson-Taylor, *Enduring Exile*, 1; cf. 203–4. Perhaps the most powerful criticism of the metaphorical use can be found in Bryan's conclusion that the notion of exile was not expanded to include other hopes for restoration but was instead minimized as a more complex understanding for the hopes for restoration was born. See Bryan, *Israel's Traditions*, 12–20. Still, since the literal sense of the term is valid as argued by Pitre and Dennis, then it seems that the return from exile still remains a valid metaphor into the first century.

123. According to Neusner, the pattern of exile and return became paradigmatic of all Judaisms since the experience of the exile was stamped across Israel's sacred texts. If Neusner's assertion is correct, that the experience of exile was not simply experienced but generated a consciousness adopted by others who never endured exile, then there is reason to apply the awareness of "exile" to those who had never experienced it literally for themselves. See Neusner, *Self-Fulfilling Prophecy*, 1–8.

124. Thus, my conclusion bears much affinity with N. T. Wright and those who have followed him on this point: Evans, "Jesus and the Continuing Exile of Israel," 77–100; Evans, "Exile and Restoration," 299–328; Bauckham, "The Restoration of Israel in Luke-Acts," 436; Snodgrass, "Reading & Overreading the Parables," 62; and Halvorson-Taylor, *Enduring Exile*. With qualifications to the thesis, but still expressing general agreement: Dennis, *Gathering of True Israel*, 81–116; Scott, "Restoration of Israel," 796–805, esp. 796–99; Hatina, "Exile," 348–51; Gowan, *Prophetic Books*, 195–98; and Tan, *Zion Traditions*, 233.

Conclusion

This chapter began with the realization that every soteriology has a particular narrative structure that explains humanity's need and how Jesus saves humanity from this plight. Sketching an account of salvation history through the Old Testament that is notably different from Girard's, we saw how Israel's story of being in covenant with YHWH was central to the storyline of the biblical canon. Not only did it explain the exile, it also provided hopes for Israel's anticipated restoration, when the faithful covenant partner would again pursue his wayward people. As we observed with each of the hopes, the intertestamental literature continues to reiterate the same expectations for restoration that pervade the biblical prophets, leading us to the conclusion that this was a common Jewish theological framework at the time of Jesus. While the reading of the Gospels and the Last Supper sayings offered in subsequent chapters is not wholly contingent upon Wright's thesis of a continuing state of exile (or non-restoration), I believe that reading the Gospels from this vantage point delivers an understanding of the texts that is better attested canonically and historically. If the Gospels are writings conversant with the theological hopes and ideas of their time, we should not be surprised to see the same themes and hopes re-emerge there. In fact, that is what we do find, as the next chapter demonstrates.

4

Jesus as Savior in Which Story? (Part 2)

The Restoration of Israel as the Leitmotif in the Gospels

WHILE NOT ALL JEWS in the first century would have necessarily embraced the hopes for restoration, it is likely that a large number of the Jewish population would be waiting for God's restoration of his people, even if they differed on the exact nature of how this restoration would play out. In this section, I argue that the Gospel writers draw upon Israel's experience of exile and waiting for God's restoration in order to define the "state of deprivation," which Jesus remedies. When the Gospel writers identify Jesus as a saving figure, they do so by locating him within Israel's larger narrative of waiting for restoration. As we will see, each of the Synoptics explicitly connects Jesus to the various hopes for restoration. For them, the story of Israel had entered a new era wherein her covenant God was making good on his promises. For them, Jesus is a saving figure because he releases Israel from her "state of deprivation." As a result, Jesus is the climax and the culmination of a much longer story, one that the Gospel writers presume as the backdrop for their own particular narratives.

The following account is by no means meant to be exhaustive. There are many other allusions to restoration theology tucked away in various pericopes that go unmentioned here. The data that follows has been selected because it best identifies the most salient points of contact between the Synoptic presentation of Jesus and restoration theology. More of course can be said and written on the topic, but what is stated below sufficiently demonstrates that the Synoptic writers see Jesus as a savior in light of the Jewish hopes for restoration. Our journey, as any good journey should, starts at the beginning of the accounts.

Infancy Narratives

Of the Synoptics, only Matthew and Luke provide information regarding Jesus' life before the beginning of his ministry. While these stories are often rehearsed during the Christmas season, the accounts provide much more than a heartwarming story of Jesus' birth. In fact, they set the tone for the rest of their narratives by firmly situating the infant Jesus within the larger story of Israel.

Matthew's Genealogy

Matthew's Gospel opens with the genealogy of Jesus, which he finds essential for informing his reader of Jesus' significance. It takes little time for Matthew to declare Jesus is "the Messiah, the son of David" (Matt 1:1b), which maps him onto Jewish messianic expectations. When Matthew records Jesus' ancestry, he is not simply concerned with establishing Davidic lineage but also with identifying Jesus as a key figure in God's restoration of Israel. As he transcribes the ancestors from Abraham to Jesus, he identifies three series of fourteen generations that resonate with a familiar theme: "So all the generations from Abraham to David are fourteen generations; and from David to the deportation to Babylon, fourteen generations; and from the deportation to Babylon to the Messiah, fourteen generations" (Matt 1:17). This segmentation, despite omitting several names at various points, demarcates three primary epochs in the course of Israel. The first section of fourteen begins with Abraham and ends with the monarch, "King David" (Matt 1:6). The second segment goes from the united monarchy to the Babylonian exile. With the passing of another set of fourteen generations after the exile, the evangelist believes the next part of God's divine activity, namely, the restoration of Israel through his Messiah has come to pass.[1] In all of this, the author is making the point that those who have been waiting for the restoration of Israel should expect the final person in the list, Jesus, to fulfill Israel's hopes for restoration and introduce the next era in Israel's story. It also seems highly likely that Matthew's emphasis upon fourteen, which seems arbitrarily imposed upon the genealogy at points, is one more pointer to Jesus' Davidic lineage.[2]

---

1. Davies and Allison, *Matthew*, 1:180.

2 When the Hebrew letters of David's name (דוד) are added together, they total fourteen. See Davies and Allison, *Matthew*, 1:63–65. Not all agree with this proposal, but it seems likely enough. For a different view, see Waetjen, "Genealogy as the Key," 205–30.

Matthew's genealogy shows us several things. First, it reveals a belief that, with the arrival of Jesus, the larger story of Israel has advanced to the next stage. The age of the exile has passed, and God's time of restoration has now begun with Jesus as its central figure.[3] Second, the repeated affirmation of Jesus' connection to David reveals that Jesus bears the ancestry required to fulfill the expectation for a new Davidic king and Israel's hope for an eschatological ruler. He is from the beginning of the Gospel, the Messiah.

Flight to Egypt

Nestled within the Matthean infancy narratives lies the escape to Egypt that results from Herod's decision to annihilate the male children who could potentially threaten his kingdom (Matt 2:13–23). Upon being warned in a dream, Joseph takes his fledgling family to Egypt and returns to the homeland once Herod dies. By recounting this story, the evangelist is highlighting similarities between Jesus and another prominent figure in Israel's history, Moses. Like Jesus, Moses' life was endangered because Pharaoh desired to kill all the baby boys in order to solidify political power (Exod 1:15–22). As a result, his parents were forced to hide him. Later in life, Moses flees Egypt to save his life. The similarities here are not coincidental for the evangelist wants us to see a similarity between Jesus and Moses.[4] Other comparisons between Jesus and Moses abound in Matthew, which have been summarized thoroughly in Dale Allison's work, *The New Moses*.[5] The comparison with Moses serves the evangelist's desire to posture Jesus as the fulfillment of Old Testament prophecies. In Deuteronomy 18:15, Moses himself indicates that God would someday raise up someone like Moses: "The Lord your God will raise up for you a prophet like me from among your own people; you shall heed such a prophet." Interestingly, Deuteronomy ends with a solemn observation: "Never since has there arisen a prophet in Israel like Moses, whom the Lord knew face to face" (Deut 34:10). Thus, although Deuteronomy expresses a hope for a future prophet like Moses, it affirms that there had not been such a prophet again. It is hardly surprising that the

---

3. Eubank, *Wages of Cross-Bearing*, 109–21.

4. Allison, *New Moses*, 140–64.

5. Ibid. Another persuasive parallel occurs in the Sermon on the Mount. In Matthew 5:1, Jesus "went up the mountain" prior to giving a revolutionary sermon that heightened the commands of the Mosaic Law. It is no coincidence that Moses likewise ascended a mountain in order to receive the Law from God. See Ibid., 174–80. Another author who emphasizes the Moses-Joshua typology in order to categorize the kind of salvation Jesus brings is van Aarde, "ΙΗΣΟΥΣ," 7–31.

evangelist seizes upon this unfulfilled prophecy in order to show another way in which Jesus fulfills the Old Testament.

In light of this, the parallels with Moses suggest Matthew finds more behind the similarities. Moses, after all, was the person who led his people to liberation in the original Exodus. If we can presume that the people of Jesus' day possessed a consciousness that they were still waiting for a similar experience of salvation, as N. T. Wright and others do, then we can conclude that Moses and Jesus share a similar role of leading God's covenant people to redemption. Allison, after analyzing all of the various ways Moses typology is present in Matthew, concludes that Matthew is intentionally casting Jesus as a new savior figure who will likewise lead his people to freedom. As he puts it, "... the story of Jesus is the story of a new exodus."[6] As a result, Jesus is the figure who stands at the climax of Israel's story, for he is the one who fulfills their hopes and expectations, and this picture of Jesus as the new Moses begins its development in the infancy narrative of Matthew.[7]

Luke's Infancy Narratives

Similar and yet distinct from Matthew, the opening chapters of Luke are steeped with the hopes for restoration and the larger story of Israel.[8] The opening angelic birth announcement to Mary identifies Jesus as "the son of the Most High" to whom God would give "the throne of his ancestor David" (Luke 1:32), establishing him as the Messianic redeemer in the line of David. In addition, the final line of Mary's *Magnificat* extols God for being merciful to Israel "according to the promise he made to our ancestors, to Abraham and his descendants forever" (Luke 1:55). This commentary indicates the birth of Jesus fulfills the Abrahamic covenant that anticipated God's creational blessing flowing to the Gentiles, a group that becomes specifically designated as a recipient of these blessings later in Acts.[9] Likewise, Zechariah, the father of John the Baptist, exclaims "Blessed be the Lord God of Israel, for he has looked favorably on his people and redeemed them. He has raised up a mighty savior for us in the house of his servant David" (Luke 1:68–69). Again the connection between Jesus and David is mentioned, solidifying Jesus' identity as the messianic leader of Davidic descent and the

---

6. Allison, *New Moses*, 196.

7. Ibid., 272–74.

8. Pao and Schnabel, "Luke," 256–75 and Marshall, *Luke*, 96–97.

9. In Acts 3:25 the promise to Abraham is referenced again with special emphasis on the blessing of the Gentiles. This does not insinuate the replacement of Israel but that the blessing of Israel would extend to the Gentiles. See Tannenhill, "Lukan Narrative," 327–28.

one who is to bring the redemption of God's people. Like Mary, Zechariah also affirms that God "has remembered his holy covenant, the oath that he swore to our ancestor Abraham" (Luke 1:72b–73a).[10] Moreover, when Zechariah speaks of his son's role in God's eschatological program, he says "you will go before the Lord to prepare his ways, to give knowledge of salvation to his people by the forgiveness of their sins" (Luke 1:76b–77). While this picks up the language of Isaiah 40:3 that will be used to introduce John the Baptist later, it also ends with an allusion to the forgiveness of sins, which evokes the promises of the new covenant. This new era of salvation is when "... the dawn from on high will break upon us, to give light to those who sit in darkness and in the shadow of death, to guide our feet into the way of peace" (Luke 1:78b–79), which alludes to several passages from Isaiah that anticipate the coming restoration.[11] Through the various monologues concerning Jesus and John the Baptist in the first chapter of Luke, the author affirms that Jesus and his predecessor John usher in the era of restoration.

As Luke continues, there are repeated points of contact with restoration theology in the infancy narratives. When the angels announce Jesus' birth to the shepherds, they identify him as "the Messiah, the Lord" (Luke 2:11), again affirming his messianic role. When Mary and Joseph take Jesus to the temple to be purified according to Mosaic law, they are greeted by Simeon who is "looking forward to the consolation (παράκλησιν) of Israel" (Luke 2:25). The "consolation of Israel" most certainly constitutes a euphemism for Israel's restoration since the verb form παρακαλέω is found throughout Isaiah and signifies "the arrival of the eschatological era when God fulfills his promises to Israel ...."[12] Moreover, Simeon had been informed he was not to die until he had met the Messiah (Luke 2:26). After meeting the child, Simeon utters a brief monologue, which indicates all the things he had been waiting for were fulfilled by the infant Jesus: "Master, now you are dismissing your servant in peace, according to your word; for my eyes have seen your salvation, which you have prepared in the presence of all peoples, a light for revelation to the Gentiles and for glory to your people Israel" (Luke 2:29–32). God's salvation had arrived in the person of Jesus, and like the

---

10. For insights on the alternations between male and female, see Bailey, *Jesus Through Middle Eastern Eyes*, 59–60.

11. The likely allusions are to Isaiah 9:2, "The people who walked in darkness have seen a great light; those who lived in a land of deep darkness—on them light has shined" and Isaiah 42:6c–7, "I have given you as a covenant to the people, a light to the nations, to open the eyes that are blind, to bring out the prisoners from the dungeon, from the prison those who sit in darkness."

12. Pao and Schnabel, "Luke," 271.

universal vision of many Second Temple texts, this salvation was not isolated to Israel but would encompass the Gentiles as well.[13]

After the encounter with Simeon, the author introduces Anna, a prophetess from Asher, who is elated about meeting the newborn Jesus and begins "to speak about the child to all who were looking for the redemption of Jerusalem" (Luke 2:38). The word "redemption" had overtones of restoration as well. Coins minted during the Jewish revolts bore the term as an expression of the hoped for liberation of their people.[14] It is also likely that Anna's tribe of Asher is significant since this was one of the northern tribes that had not returned from exile.[15] If so, this is just one more way in which the author of Luke opens his narrative about Jesus by recalling several of the eschatological hopes of Israel, particularly the hopes for a new Davidic king, the anticipated forgiveness of the new covenant, and the inclusion of Gentiles as beneficiaries of Israel's restoration.

Summary

The infancy narratives of Matthew and Luke establish the trajectory that their particular narratives about Jesus will take. Most importantly, though, Matthew and Luke both see their narratives about Jesus as the most recent chapter in God's ongoing saga with Israel. Matthew and Luke do not stand on their own but rest upon the antecedent chapters that had been written in Israel's canonical history. For Matthew, the promises to David and the subsequent exile form the background for his expectation that the fourteenth generation would give rise to a new era in which David's line would resume its kingly authority. Moreover, just as Moses had led his people from bondage to freedom, even so Jesus performed the role of a new Moses who would also lead his people on the long expected new exodus. For Luke, God's promises to Abraham meant he would act to restore his people and to raise up a new Davidic king who would bring God's salvation to the world

---

13. The temple setting seems significant. Many of the texts expecting a reconstructed and glorified temple believed the Gentiles would come to worship Israel's God. The reference to the inclusion of the Gentiles in the temple provenance likely indicates Jesus fulfills the eschatological role of the temple.

14. Bauckham, "Restoration," 451. Some of the coins bore the date corresponding to the year of the revolution in which they were minted being stamped with "First year of the redemption of Israel." See Madden, *Jewish Coinage*, 162 and 164. During the Maccabean revolt they also struck the word "redemption" on their coins (ibid., 47). See also Wacks, *Biblical Numismatics*.

15. See Bauckham, "Restoration," 458.

for Jews and Gentiles alike. With Jesus, the "consolation" and "redemption" of Israel had begun.

The Calling of the "Twelve"

The belief that Jesus had a group of twelve disciples is widespread in early Christianity, appearing in the Gospels and a myriad of other texts. The Gospels, though attesting to other followers of Jesus, unequivocally affirm that Jesus had twelve specific followers designated as disciples.[16] In addition, the creed which Paul relays in 1 Corinthians 15:3-6 indicates that there was a group known among early Christians as "the twelve." While some have questioned the historicity of this number, many scholars have persuasively argued for its authenticity.[17] More importantly, this number appears to have had great significance for Jesus' followers. Shortly after Judas' suicide, the disciples felt compelled to pick a twelfth person to serve alongside of them, Matthias (Acts 1:15-26). As C. K. Barrett notes, "The NT is more interested in the fact that the Twelve existed than in what they did."[18] Thankfully, the Gospels hint at the rationale for ensuring there were twelve disciples. The most revealing statement in the Synoptics is the Q saying where Jesus responds to Peter's exclamation that they had forsaken everything to follow Jesus. Jesus replies to Peter, "Truly I tell you, at the renewal (παλιγγενεσίᾳ) of all things, when the Son of Man is seated on the throne of his glory, you who have followed me will also sit on twelve thrones, judging the twelve tribes of Israel" (Matt 19:28; cf. Luke 22:29-30). Here the logic behind the twelve disciples becomes apparent. The twelve disciples symbolize the twelve tribes of Israel.[19] Many scholars rightly contend that when he chose twelve disciples, Jesus was intentionally demonstrating that his ministry was focused on reconstituting Israel and inaugurating the age of restoration.[20]

16. Matt 10:1-5; 11:1; 19:28; 20:17; 26:14, 20, 47; Mark 3:16; 4:10; 6:7; 9:35; 10:32.

17. E.g. Meier, "The Circle of the Twelve" 635-72; McKnight, "Jesus and the Twelve," 203-31; and Allison, *Constructing Jesus*, 67-76.

18. Barrett, *Acts of the Apostles*, 14.

19. In the *Testaments of the Twelve Patriarchs* the patriarchs are supposed to rule over their respective tribes (*T. Jud.* 25:1-2). 4Q164 also equates a group of twelve as the leaders of the tribes of Israel. The relevant Jewish literature shows that a group of twelve were anticipated to rule over Israel and Jesus appears to have placed this authority on his disciples. Early Christian exegetes also adopted this understanding. See Theophylact, *Comm. Matt.* on Matt 10:1.

20. Meier, "Twelve," 656-58; Wright, *Jesus and the Victory of God*, 300, 532; Allison, *Constructing Jesus*, 71, 232-33; and Sanders, *Jesus and Judaism*, 98, 233. Josephus also uses the term παλιγγενεσίᾳ in reference to the restoration of Israel in *Ant.* 11.66. For Josephus' use of the word, see Geyser, "Jesus, the Twelve and the Twelve Tribes," 16.

Of course, this is not a literal fulfillment, but a symbolic demonstration that the nation composed of twelve tribes was being restored.[21] Though the nature of this fulfillment is symbolic, it is nevertheless evocative of the hope for a new exodus and should be seen as such.

Jesus, Isaiah, and the Proclamation of the "Gospel"

The Gospels bear the impressions of Isaiah in a number of ways. In particular, the Synoptic presentation of Jesus' proclamation of the "good news" or "gospel" bears striking affinity with the Isaianic prophecies.[22] In fact, the very title, "gospel," likely derives from Isaiah. Mark begins his work by labeling it the "good news (εὐαγγελίου)" of Jesus Christ (Mark 1:1).[23] Matthew, likewise, uses the word to capture the essence of Jesus' message: "Jesus went throughout Galilee, teaching in their synagogues and proclaiming the good news (εὐαγγέλιον) of the kingdom" (Matt 4:23).[24] In Luke, Jesus describes his mission as preaching the good news of the kingdom saying, "I must proclaim the good news (εὐαγγελίσασθαί) of the kingdom of God to the other cities also; for I was sent for this purpose" (Luke 4:43).[25] The Synoptics use "good news" or "gospel" in both noun and verb forms to summarize their narratives about Jesus—in the case of Mark—and to encapsulate what Jesus taught about God becoming king—in the case of Matthew and Luke. While the LXX version of Second Isaiah only uses the verb form of the εὐαγγελ- root, the Gospels' usage is redolent of Isaiah. The LXX version of Second Isaiah only uses the verb form of the word, but whenever it does, it is describing God's saving activity on behalf of his people.[26] In Isaiah 52:7 the proclamation of good news is wed to the declaration that Israel's God was king: "How beautiful upon the mountains are the feet of the messenger who announces peace, who brings good news (εὐαγγελιζόμενος ἀγαθὰ), who announces salvation, who says to Zion, 'Your God reigns.'" One should not overlook the fact that Isaiah and the Synoptics share the same matrix

21. McKnight, "Jesus and the Twelve," 228.

22. A collection of the allusions to Isaiah in the Gospels can be found in Evans, "From Gospel to Gospel," 667–70.

23. Mark uses the term frequently: Mark 1:14–15; 8:35; 10:29; 13:10; 14:9; 16:15. Regarding its connections to Isaiah, see Evans, "Isaiah in the New Testament," 653, 674–77 and Hooker, *Jesus and the Servant*, 65–67.

24. Matthew 9:35; 11:5; 24:14; 26:13.

25. Luke 1:19; 2:10; 4:18 (quotation from Isaiah); 7:22; 8:1; 9:6; 16:16; 20:1; Acts 5:42; 8:4, 12; 10:36; 11:20; 13:32; 14:7; 14:15; 14:21; 15:7; 15:35; 16:10; 20:24.

26. See the following: Isa 40:9; 52:7; 60:6; 61:1.

of kingdom, salvation, and good news. Because the LXX version of Second Isaiah contains a dense cluster of the εὐαγγελ- word group and uses it in a similar fashion as the Gospels do, scholars have concluded that the use of "good news" or "gospel" in the New Testament Gospels, ultimately has its roots in Isaiah.[27] To put this another way, since the Gospels share this terminological similarity with Isaiah, the Gospel writers are suggesting to their readers that the "good news" expected in Isaiah is coming to pass in the ministry of Jesus.

Nevertheless, there is more reason to believe that the Gospels are placing their narratives about Jesus against the backdrop of Isaiah's oracles than lexical similarities. When the Synoptics begin their presentation of the ministries of Jesus and John the Baptist—the one they clearly designate as Jesus' forerunner—they explicitly cite significant verses from Isaiah. Mark, the earliest of the Synoptics, opens his Gospel by writing in the second verse, "As it is written in the prophet Isaiah, 'See I am sending my messenger ahead of you, who will prepare your way; the voice of one crying out in the wilderness: 'Prepare the way of the Lord, make his paths straight'" (Mark 1:2–3). Despite attributing the entire citation in Mark 1:2 to Isaiah, only Mark 1:3 is directly from Isaiah 40:3.[28] The citation only differs from the LXX of Isaiah 40:3 with the substitution of "his" (αὐτοῦ) in the place of "our God" (τοῦ

---

27. Broyles, "Gospel (Good News)," 282–86, esp. 285 and Hooker, *Jesus and the Servant*, 66.

28. The first part of the quotation, "See, I am sending my messenger ahead of you," corresponds exactly to the LXX of Exodus 23:20 that introduces a section in which YHWH affirms that his messenger will lead the Israelites into the land of promise. Within the literary context of Exodus, the passage regarding the messenger concludes the Book of the Covenant and is situated before the covenant's ratification in Exodus 24 (Childs, *Exodus*, 486). Mark, curiously, never explicitly identifies the "messenger" with John the Baptist like some of the other Gospels, which means that it could ostensibly refer to Jesus instead. For such a view, see Watts, *Isaiah's New Exodus*, 87. However, scholarly consensus appears to follow the other Gospels and identify John the Baptist as the messenger in Mark. See Collins, *Mark*, 136–37.

The second portion of the quotation, which identifies the messenger as the one "who will prepare your way," reflects the Hebrew text of Malachi 3:1. While it is difficult to know how much of Malachi's original context Mark would assume for his readers, the entire verse identifies the coming messenger as the mediator of the covenant: "See, I am sending my messenger to prepare the way before me, and the Lord whom you seek will suddenly come to his temple. The messenger of the covenant in whom you delight—indeed, he is coming, says the Lord of hosts" (Mal. 3:1). It is tempting to press the connection with the covenant present in the context of Exodus 23 and Malachi 3 to conclude that Mark believed the messenger would inaugurate a new covenant. However, since διαθήκη appears only once in the Gospel (Mark 14:24), the connection should not be overextended.

θεοῦ ἡμῶν).²⁹ Although the first two chapters of Matthew and Luke contain the genealogies and infancy narratives, when their storylines transition to John the Baptist's ministry as a forerunner of Jesus, they also insert the same citation of Isaiah 40:3, following Mark's emendations verbatim.³⁰ The Synoptics' paradigmatic use of Isaiah 40 indicates that the Synoptics are situating John the Baptist and Jesus within the larger story of Israel's restoration.

These verses from Isaiah 40 are in all actuality quite significant in the larger book of Isaiah.³¹ In fact, they mark a distinctive shift from Isaiah 1–39 to the second half of the book, Isaiah 40–66. Old Testament scholars have long observed that Isaiah 40–66 possesses a more exuberant hope for the immediate future than one sees in Isaiah 1–39.³² Isaiah 39 ends with King Hezekiah being forewarned of the coming Babylonian exile (Isa 39:5–8), whereas Isaiah 40 presupposes the Babylonian exile has occurred, and Babylon itself has either faced or soon will experience its demise.³³ The second half of Isaiah, often called Second or Deutero-Isaiah, anticipates God's imminent restoration of his people in glorious fashion. The opening verses of Isaiah 40 demonstrate this distinctive shift to the hope of a return from exile:

> Comfort, O comfort my people, says your God. Speak tenderly to Jerusalem, and cry to her that she has served her term, that her penalty is paid, that she has received from the Lord's hand double for all her sins. A voice cries out: "In the wilderness prepare the way of the Lord, make straight in the desert a highway for our God. Every valley shall be lifted up, and every mountain and hill be made low; the uneven ground shall become level,

---

29. Isaiah 40:3, "A voice cries out: 'In the wilderness prepare the way of the Lord, make straight in the desert a highway for our God.'"

30. See Matthew 3:3, Luke 3:4–6, and John 1:23. Luke, it should be noted, cites more than Isaiah 40:3, though his alterations suggest he follows Mark.

31. In interpreting Old Testament citations, one can err by giving too much weight to the original context (here Isaiah, Exodus, and Malachi) of the citation or by privileging the new context (here Mark, Matthew, and Luke) at the expense of the original one. See Moyise, "Wilderness Quotation," 78–87. Given the other parallels with restoration theology in the Gospels, we have good reason to see the larger context of Isaiah influencing these citations.

32. Because of this marked distinction, scholars generally assume there is a different prophet responsible for the oracles and messages contained within the latter portion of the book. Moreover, many also designate Isaiah 56–66 as Third or Trito-Isaiah, though people like Westermann still see the latter portion as ideologically dependent upon the prophet "Deutero-Isaiah." See Westermann, *Isaiah*, 3–29. However, such rigid demarcations in Isaiah can no longer be wholly maintained without qualifications. See Seitz, "Book of Isaiah," 6:314.

33. Ibid., 6:316.

and the rough places a plain. Then the glory of the Lord shall be revealed, and all people shall see it together, for the mouth of the Lord has spoken" (Isaiah 40:1–5).[34]

These initial verses of the latter portion of Isaiah indicate the former promises of judgment have run their course, and promises of comfort have supplanted the former oracles of destruction. In other words, the sins that led to the punishment of exile have been "paid." As the prophet said, "she has served her term." Moreover, God appears to be reconciled with his faithless covenant partner. The opening line of this passage identifies Israel as "my people" and YHWH as "your God," which is an abbreviated version of the covenant formula.[35] Thus, God's physical and political reconstitution of Israel after the exile coincides with a re-establishment of the covenantal relationship between God and Israel.

The ending portion of the passage (Isa 40:3–5) speaks of forming a highway in the desert for God. This redeploys the "highway" language used earlier in the book to signify the return of the exiles (Isa 35:8–10).[36] While there are debates over whether the wilderness and desert are to be interpreted literally as the desert that separated the exiles in Babylon from their homeland[37] or metaphorically as the spiritual condition of Israel,[38] or both,[39] Old Testament scholars agree that the language of flattening the mountains depicts the return from exile. Clearly, the opening verses of Isaiah 40 anticipate God's intervention on Israel's behalf in the New Exodus.

What are the Synoptic writers trying to convey when they conspicuously cite the opening verses of Isaiah 40 as they seek to explain the importance of the movement begun by John the Baptist and fulfilled by Jesus? Watts puts it well: citing Isaiah 40 at the commencement of the Gospels "indicates that the primary horizon is Israel's narrative and in particular

---

34. For the significance of this passage at Qumran, see 1QS 8.12–16.

35. Baltzer, *Deutero-Isaiah*, 49. The longer version is: "And you shall be my people, and I will be your God" (Jer 30:22; cf. Exod 6:7; Lev 26:12; Ruth 1:16; Jer 11:4; 32:28; Ezek. 36:28; 37:27). For more on the covenant formula throughout Scripture, see Baltzer, *Covenant Formulary*.

36. Isaiah 35:8, 10: "A highway shall be there, and it shall be called the Holy Way; the unclean shall not travel on it, but it shall be for God's people; no traveler, not even fools, shall go astray ... and the ransomed of the Lord shall return, and come to Zion with singing; everlasting joy shall be upon their heads; they shall obtain joy and gladness, and sorrow and sighing shall flee away." See Childs, *Isaiah*, 299.

37. Westermann, *Isaiah*, 37–39.

38. For a rejection of Westermann's view in favor of a metaphorical interpretation, see Seitz, "Book of Isaiah," 6:335.

39. Baltzer, *Deutero-Isaiah*, 53–54.

Isaiah's prophetic hopes of restoration . . . ."[40] Morna Hooker concurs, commenting that when the Gospel of Mark opens with this citation from Isaiah, "the key to understanding what this 'Gospel'—or 'Good News'—might be is to be found in the book of Isaiah."[41] In other words, Mark—Matthew and Luke follow him on this point—situates the story of Jesus' ministry, death, and resurrection within Second Isaiah's expected restoration in order to show that such hopes were coming to pass in and through the events recorded in the Gospels. The return from exile and the time of restoration were finding their fulfillment in and through the ministry of Jesus. As a result, the Gospels are drawing upon the prophetic expectations in order to inform their readers about the importance of Jesus' ministry. The key point, however, is that the Synoptics place Jesus' ministry into a larger story and this larger story is of Israel's exile and restoration.

The Baptism

The presence of restoration theology, however, is not only to be found in Old Testament allusions and citations. It is also found in some of the significant events the Gospels record, like the baptism of Jesus. The Synoptics similarly introduce the ministry of Jesus with his predecessor, John the Baptist, who calls the Jewish people to repentance, baptizing those who repent in the Jordan River. In Mark's Gospel, John the Baptist identifies himself as the harbinger of a more powerful baptizer: "I have baptized you with water; but he will baptize you with the Holy Spirit" (Mark 1:8). Matthew and Luke both record John uttering similar affirmations that the coming one would baptize with the Holy Spirit (Matt 3:11; Luke 3:16). By contrasting John the Baptist and Jesus in this way, the Gospels identify a qualitative difference between John the Baptist and Jesus. Though John possesses the significant role of preparing "the way," Jesus is the one who brings the eschatological promise of the Spirit. This is most fully developed in Luke-Acts during the feast of Pentecost when the Spirit of God falls palpably upon the followers of Jesus (Acts 2:1–21). Nevertheless, the affirmation that Jesus baptizes with the Spirit reveals that the anticipated impartation of the divine spirit has arrived with Jesus.

Contrary to what one might expect, John the Baptist is the one who baptizes Jesus in the Jordan River, rather than vice versa. During the baptism of Jesus, Mark records the following events: "And just as he was coming up

---

40. Watts, "Mark," 113.

41. Hooker, "Isaiah in Mark's Gospel," 35. This is corroborated in Combrink, "Salvation in Mark," 38.

out of the water, he saw the heavens torn apart (σχιζομένους) and the Spirit descending like a dove on him. And a voice came from heaven, 'You are my Son, the Beloved; with you I am well pleased'" (Mark 1:10–11).[42] The divine voice at the baptism—which Luke and Matthew adopt with little substantial change[43]—contains allusions to several key Old Testament texts, confirming Jesus' eschatological roles as Israel's king and YHWH's servant.[44] The first Scriptural allusion in the divine pronouncement comes from Psalm 2:7 LXX: "You are my son (υἱός μου εἶ σύ)."[45] Psalm 2 was an enthronement Psalm that celebrated the coronation of a Davidic king. In fact, the Psalm itself contains other Scriptural allusions, namely, that of 2 Samuel 7:14 where God covenants with David, pledging that he will be "a father" and David's progeny would be God's "son." The allusion to Psalm 2:7 at the baptism plants Jesus firmly within the eschatological hopes of Israel, specifically their hope for a Davidic king that would lead his people in righteousness.[46]

The second part of the pronouncement at the baptism, "with you I am well pleased (ἐν σοὶ εὐδκόησα)," mirrors the description of YHWH's servant in Isaiah 42:1a: "Here is my servant, whom I uphold, my chosen,

---

42. The tearing of the heavens possibly echoes Isaiah 64:1: "O that you would tear open (ἀνοίξῃς) the heavens and come down . . . " suggesting further connections between Isaiah and Mark. See Hooker, "Mark's Gospel," 45. The differences in the Greek texts, however, do not make the issue conclusive.

43. The divine voice differs only moderately in Matthew with a switch from the second to the third person. Mark 1:11 is in the second person: "Σὺ εἶ ὁ υἱός μου ὁ ἀγαπητός, ἐν σοὶ εὐδόκησα."
Matthew 3:17 is in the third person: "Οὗτός ἐστιν ὁ υἱός μου ὁ ἀγαπητός, ἐν ᾧ εὐδόκησα."
Luke 3:22 follows Mark by putting the voice in the second person: "Σὺ εἶ ὁ υἱός μου ὁ ἀγαπητός, ἐν σοὶ εὐδόκησα."

44. Despite Hatina's warning that we should not become myopic in exegeting embedded Scriptural allusions, I find the connection that some make between (ἀγαπητός) and the beloved son of passages like Gen 22:2, 12, and 16, to be strained, though not impossible. The reason for my reluctance here is the presence of ἀγαπητός in Matt 12:18's quotation of Isa 42:1, which could possibly attest to a textual tradition which we no longer have. If so, there would be no need to posit another text behind the allusions here. See Hatina, "Embedded Scripture Texts," 81–99.

45. Against those who would discredit the allusion to Psalm 2:7 and attribute most of the wording here to Isaiah, see Marshall, "A Son of God," 326–36.

46. Some scholars are much too cautious and refuse to see this as an affirmation of Jesus' messianic role based upon the fact that "son of God" was not a messianic title in Judaism before the emergence of Christianity. Mark's language of anointing by the Spirit coupled with the fact that the Davidic kings were God's metaphorical "sons" suggests that we can safely assume the allusion to Psalm 2:7 would be regarded as Messianic, which is the case in other Qumran scrolls like 4Q174. Thus, I take a different position than the following: Fitzmyer, *Gospel according to Luke*, 1:479–85 and Hooker, *Servant*, 68–69.

in whom my soul delights."[47] In the quotation in Mark 1:11, the text resembles the MT rather than the LXX.[48] While some have been reluctant to embrace an allusion to Isaiah 42:1 based on the dissimilarity between the LXX and Mark 1:11,[49] the allusion cannot be so easily dismissed. In Isaiah 42:1, YHWH not only delights in his servant, but he also puts his Spirit upon him,[50] which is precisely what occurs in the baptismal scene. Thus, even if the linguistic connections are not exact, there is certainly enough conceptual contact between the two passages to conclude that an allusion to Deutero-Isaiah's servant is present.

The Synoptic account of the baptism once again paints Jesus on the eschatological canvas of Second Temple Judaism, weaving several of the hopes for restoration into one dense episode. Jesus' relationship with God mirrors that of the Davidic king, endowing him with the mantle of the eschatological ruler. In addition, Jesus assumes the role of YHWH's servant, further demonstrating the influence of Second Isaiah's restoration theology upon the Gospels and Jesus' ministry.[51] Finally, the Spirit descends upon Jesus at the baptism, giving him the ability to baptize others in the Spirit, the very means by which God would transform his faithless covenant partners into obedient participants. Thus, the baptism of Jesus combines several strands of restoration theology and connects them with the person and ministry of Jesus of Nazareth.

Jesus as YHWH's Servant

The Synoptics, however, contain more than a subtle allusion to Jesus as YHWH's servant at the baptism. In the case of Matthew and perhaps Luke,

---

47. Watts, *Isaiah's New Exodus*, 114–5 and Guelich, *Mark 1–8:26*, 34.

48. While the allusion in the baptismal formula departs from the LXX, Matthew has not assimilated the allusion to Isa 42:1 in Matt 3:17 to his citation of the same verse in Matt 12:18. The most likely explanation is that Matthew is trying to maintain affinity with Mark in Matt 3:17 more than Isa 42:1. So Luz, *Matthew 1–7*, 180.

49. Hooker, for example, originally thought an allusion to Isa 42:1 was probable but suggests this was not to put Jesus in the role of the servant (at least as an individual), but simply to associate him with the eschatology of Second Isaiah (Hooker, *Servant*, 68–73, 148–50). More recently, she has been more forceful and repudiated any connection with Isaiah 42:1, saying "there is little to indicate that Mark had Isa 42:1 in mind" (Hooker, "Mark's Gospel," 46). In my opinion, she unnecessarily dismisses likely connections to the servant here. The connection with the Spirit and the conceptual similarities, though possessing linguistic differences, provide enough evidence to posit a very likely allusion to Isa 42:1, in my opinion.

50. Isaiah 42:1, "Here is my servant, whom I uphold, my chosen, in whom my soul delights; I have put my spirit upon him; he will bring forth justice to the nations."

51. Davies and Allison, *Matthew*, 1:342–43.

Jesus is placed more soundly within the eschatological expectations of Isaiah's prophecies by identifying him as YHWH's servant.[52] In the book of Isaiah, Old Testament scholars have traditionally identified four distinct poems or songs about YHWH's servant embedded in the second portion of Isaiah: Isaiah 42:1–4; 49:1–6; 50:4–9; and 52:13—53:12.[53] Though ancient readers would not have read them as a distinct group, the texts are relevant to the Gospels since the Gospels use the servant songs on several occasions in order to explain Jesus' mission and identity. We have already had the occasion to observe the allusion to YHWH's servant at the baptism of Christ, but there are several others.

One of the most extensive citations from the first servant song (Isa 42:1–4) is to be found in Matthew's Gospel. Matthew 12 opens with Jesus and the Pharisees debating the legality of plucking grain on the Sabbath. The next pericope has Jesus healing a man on the Sabbath, further infuriating the Pharisees (Matt 12:9–14). With conflict seeming imminent, Jesus withdraws from the scene and continues to heal people, forbidding them "not to make him known" (Matt 12:16). These events, especially the withdrawal from the imminent conflict, are taken to be a direct fulfillment of Isaiah 42:1–4 and Matthew quotes the passage extensively (Matt 12:18–21).[54] By doing so, Matthew identifies Jesus as YHWH's spirit-endowed servant "who will proclaim justice to the Gentiles" (Matt 12:18). While it is not entirely apparent how Matthew thinks Jesus takes upon himself the characteristics of Isaiah's servant, the context suggests a few things. First, Jesus has just withdrawn from a situation that could potentially escalate into conflict. Thus, the servant's gentle and humble approach—"He will not wrangle or cry aloud, nor will anyone hear his voice in the streets" (Matt 12:19)—has been exhibited in Jesus' choice to de-escalate a conflict.[55] Second, the quotation from Isaiah twice mentions the servant's relationship to the Gentiles, for the servant "will proclaim justice to the Gentiles" and "in his name the Gentiles will hope" (Matt 12:18, 21). One could suggest that the preceding discussions about Sabbath observance might be insinuate that Sabbath observance should not be as fastidious for the Gentiles as some of the Jewish sects made it. Even if there is not a subtle allusion to lessening the Sabbath requirements for specifically Gentile followers, the full quotation of Isaiah

52. For the scholarly debate on this issue, see some of the essays in Bellinger and Farmer, *Suffering Servant*.

53. Distinguishing four servant songs in the latter half of Isaiah has its origins in an old, but distinguished work on Isaiah, Duhm, *Das Buch Jesaja*.

54. The *Isaiah Targum* does interpret the servant figure messianically. See *Isa. Tar.* 42:1 and 52:13.

55. Blomberg, "Matthew," 44.

42:1–4 indicates the mission of Jesus has a universal thrust and is not limited to the confines of the Jewish people.[56]

There are also allusions in the Gospels to the final servant song (Isa 52:13—53:12) in order to explicate the person and mission of Jesus. In Matthew 8, the author lists a series of miracles wherein Jesus heals a leper, the centurion's servant, and many others at Peter's house. At the end of this series, Matthew writes, "This was to fulfill what had been spoke through the prophet Isaiah, 'He took our infirmities and bore our diseases'" (Matt 8:17). Here he cites a small segment from the final servant song, Isaiah 53:4, in order to show Jesus as the fulfillment of Isaiah's prophecies. The quotation of the verse indicates that Jesus fulfills his eschatological role through healing the infirmities and diseases of others.[57] Interestingly, Matthew and Mark never use the final servant song to explain the death of Jesus. If they do it only seems to be in the possible—and very subtle—allusions in the ransom and Last Supper sayings.[58]

Luke, however, does use the final servant song to explain that Jesus' ignominious demise was part of God's plan. In Luke 22, shortly before the events that precipitate his death, Jesus says " . . . this scripture must be fulfilled in me, 'And he was counted among the lawless'; and indeed what is written about me is being fulfilled'" (Luke 22:37). The Scriptural allusion comes from Isaiah 53:12, which indicates that Jesus' death in Jerusalem between two thieves mirrors the suffering servant.[59] While there has been contentious debate over whether Luke-Acts alludes to the final servant song in order to imply Jesus' death shares the atoning value attributed to the servant, what can certainly be said is that Luke drew a direct parallel between the death of YHWH's servant and Jesus, again situating the events of Jesus' life in the context of Second Isaiah.[60]

---

56. Schnackenburg, *Matthew*, 113–14; Harrington, *Matthew*, 181; and Nolland, *Matthew*, 495. The author of Matthew also presumes the presence of the Gentile mission. See Matt 28:19–20.

57. Blomberg, "Matthew," 33.

58. It is possible that Jesus' ransom sayings which describe him serving others and being a ransom "for many" (Matt 20:28//Mark 10:45) has points of contact with the final servant song. See Watts, "Jesus' Death," 125–51.

59. For a typological connection between Jesus and the servant, see Koet, "Isaiah in Luke-Acts," 87–89.

60. The issue depends upon the amount of Isaiah's original context Luke presumed for his readers. Some conclude that the allusion would infer the larger context and thus describe Jesus' death as a vicarious atonement, like the servant's (e.g. Pao and Schnabel, "Luke," 388–89). Luke was very much aware of the larger servant song since he cites a much larger portion in Acts 8:26–40. Perhaps Luke's failure to provide proof texts that predict the Messiah's death when he alludes to such passages in the Old

The use of servant imagery to describe Jesus buttresses a former conclusion. In short, the eschatological hopes contained within Isaiah inform the Gospel writers' understanding of Jesus. Just as the servant possessed a role in YHWH's eschatological program, even so the Gospel writers indicate at important junctures that Jesus is bringing these expectations to fulfillment. Jesus has therefore donned the mantle of YHWH's servant.

Preaching of the Kingdom of God

Thus far, it seems clear that the Gospel writers situate Jesus' activity within the larger hopes and expectations for Israel's renewal, especially those found in Isaiah. Does the same thing hold true for Jesus' main message, the arrival of the kingdom of God? New Testament scholarship has been unified around the assertion that the Kingdom of God was the central message of Jesus' ministry. Unfortunately, there has been little agreement on what Jesus meant when he proclaimed the kingdom's arrival.[61] Despite the contentions of some who have sought to strip Jesus' notion of the kingdom of its eschatological and apocalyptic trappings,[62] the argument that Jesus' view of the kingdom would have been colored with the eschatological elements typical of his day and age still seems persuasive.[63] Even those who dismiss apocalyptic thought in Jesus are forced to acknowledge the widespread

Testament (Luke 24:46; Acts 13:29) is because he includes the key texts elsewhere in his two-volume set, namely, in Acts 8. However, Hooker notes that even with the fuller citation in Acts 8, the author of Luke-Acts never quotes the portions of the final servant song that indicate his death was a vicarious atonement. See Hooker, *Servant*, 114 and Hooker, "Isaiah 3," 91–92. Instead, the emphasis is always on the kind of death and humiliation that both figures encounter. In light of this, one cannot definitively assert that the author of Luke-Acts utilized Isaiah 53 to indicate that, like the servant, Jesus' death was a vicarious atonement for others, though it is not beyond the realm of possibility. The most persuasive argument for seeing an overt connection between Isaiah's suffering servant and Jesus is found in the way the Gospels use "baptism" as a euphemism for Christ's death (e.g. Mark 10:38–39; Luke 12:50). If the baptism is the point at which Jesus takes on the role of the Isaianic servant, it is at least suggestive that the use of "baptism" to refer to his imminent death implies that the Gospel writers saw Jesus as assuming the role of Isaiah's suffering servant at his baptism. See Legault, "Le baptême de Jésus," 147–66.

61. There has been debate over whether the kingdom is a future, supra-temporal reality (Schweitzer) or whether it is an imminent experience of God realized in Jesus' ministry (Dodd). For their respective views, see Schweitzer, *Mystery of the Kingdom* and Dodd, *Parables of the Kingdom*.

62. Crossan, *The Historical Jesus*, 421–22. He ends his summary of the kingdom with the now well-worn phrase concerning Jesus: "He announced in other words, the brokerless kingdom of God" (ibid., 422). Cf. Evans, *Fabricating Jesus*, 103–22.

63. See Sanders, *Jesus and Judaism*, 91–95.

apocalyptic dimension of late Second Temple Judaism,[64] which most likely influenced Jesus as well.

In attempting to describe the nature of the "kingdom of God," Norman Perrin helpfully reminds scholars that the kingdom of God functions as a symbol. As a symbol, it captures Israel's past history in which God had demonstrated himself as king. As Perrin observes, the worldview underlying the Old Testament understood "the world as being under the direct control of the God who had acted as a king on their behalf *and would continue to do so*."[65] Thus, on the one hand, the symbol of the kingdom was rooted and grounded in the antecedent history of the Jewish people. On the other hand, it was poised for the future, anticipating God's work on behalf of Israel. As a result, the symbol of God's kingdom encapsulated the meta-narrative of the Jewish people, reminding them of their past and informing their expectations of the future.[66]

The Old Testament possesses manifold texts that point to the belief that God was Israel's king specifically and, more globally, the world.[67] For example, in the book of Numbers, Balaam states: "The Lord their God is with them, acclaimed as a king among them" (Num 23:21). It was the belief that God was the true king of Israel which made Israel's request for a human

---

64. Even Crossan concedes the overwhelming influence of apocalyptic thought in the kingdom of God language during the turning of the eras. In order to separate Jesus from the apocalyptic types, he has to distinguish a "sapiential kingdom" from the apocalyptic one. Crossan, *Historical Jesus*, 284–91. Such a clean-cut separation seems unlikely. It seems more likely that a pluripotent symbol like the kingdom of God could connote both the notion that God would return in judgment and that he was the moral lawgiver of the world. Moreover, comparing Jesus' beatitudes with those in 4Q525 reveals that Jesus' beatitudes are eschatological while those in 4Q525 are sapiential, demonstrating that Jesus exhibited an eschatological outlook instead of a purely sapiential one. See VanderKam and Flint, *Dead Sea Scrolls*, 336–38.

65. Perrin, *Language of the Kingdom*, 23. Perrin demarcates between a steno-symbol and a tensive symbol. A steno-symbol has only one referent in a given context, whereas a tensive symbol can never be equated with any individual referent and, thus, can never be fully "exhausted" by the things signified (ibid., 30). According to him, Jesus uses the kingdom "as a tensive symbol" (ibid., 56).

66. Perrin, *Language of the Kingdom*, 33. While categorizing the "kingdom of God" as a symbol is helpful, Perrin goes too far when he says that Kingdom is "not an *idea* or a *conception*." While Perrin's view helpfully shows why the phrase has such ambiguity on the lips of Jesus, it is going too far to suggest that understanding the kingdom of God as a symbol voids it of concepts or ideas. Here Sanders' incisive rejoinder is helpful. Just because the kingdom is a symbol capable of various interpretations, this does not mean it has no concepts associated with it or that we cannot identify a core range of meaning within the Gospels. See Sanders, *Jesus and Judaism*, 125–27.

67. 1 Chron 16:31; 28:5; 2 Chron 13:8; Pss 10:16; 22:28; 24:8–10; 47:2; 93:1; 95:3; 96:10; 97:1; 99:1–4; 145:11–13; 103:19; Isa 6:5; Jer 8:19; 10:10; 48:15; 51:57; Mal 1:14.

king in 1 Samuel 8:7 problematic.[68] Of course, being king over Zion did not preclude God from being king over the world either. In fact, because YHWH had connected himself with a particular people, this allowed him to establish his hegemony over the world. Psalm 47:8 manifests God's authority over global geopolitics: "God reigns over the nations; God sits on his holy throne." When the prophetic texts announce God's restoration of his people, they appeal to the belief that God is king over the nations in order to ground their eschatological hopes. In Jeremiah 44, the oracle affirms YHWH's kingship over Egypt: "As I live, says the King, whose name is the Lord of hosts, one is coming like Tabor among the mountains, and like Carmel by the sea. Pack your bags for exile, sheltered daughter Egypt! For Memphis shall become a waste, a ruin, without inhabitant" (Jer 44:18–19). Though Egypt will experience exile, God's primacy means he can bring his own people back from exile:

> But as for you, have no fear, my servant Jacob, and do not be dismayed, O Israel; for I am going to save you from far away, and your offspring from the land of their captivity. Jacob shall return and have quiet and ease, and no one shall make him afraid. As for you, have no fear, my servant Jacob, says the Lord, for I am with you (Jer 44:27–28).

God's rule over the world means he can mete out justice on the persecuting nations and redeem his people from exile. Like Jeremiah, Second Isaiah also correlates God's kingdom with his ability and choice to save and redeem his people.[69] Isaiah 44:6 reads, "Thus says the Lord, the King of Israel, and his Redeemer, the Lord of hosts: I am the first and I am the last; besides me there is no god." When the prophets speak of God being king, they are not simply making the metaphysical claim that God controls the world. Rather, the claim that God is king goes hand in hand with the expectation that God will act to save and redeem his people.[70]

Among the Old Testament books that would have influenced a first century Jew's understanding of the kingdom of God, few would surpass Daniel. In Daniel 2, King Nebuchadnezzar has a vexing vision about a statue composed of different metals. Its head was made of gold, the chest and arms of silver, the torso and thighs of bronze, the legs of iron, and its feet had

---

68. 1 Samuel 8:7 "And the Lord said to Samuel, 'Listen to the voice of the people in all that they say to you; for they have not rejected you, but they have rejected me from being king over them.'" Cf. 1 Sam 12:12–19.

69. Isa 33:22; 52:7.

70. God as king could refer to both God's rescue (Zeph 3:15) and punishment of Israel and Judah (Ezek 20:33).

a mixture of iron and clay (Dan 2:32–33). In the dream, a stone uncut by human hands demolishes the statue, and this stone turns into a mountain (Dan 2:35). Fortunately, the narrator interprets the vision for the reader and notes each of the respective metals stands for a respective kingdom or empire. Most relevant to the discussion here concerns the stone that pulverizes the statue, which is interpreted as the following: "And in the days of those kings the God of heaven will set up a kingdom that shall never be destroyed, nor shall this kingdom be left to another people. It shall crush all these kingdoms and bring them to an end, and it shall stand forever" (Dan 2:44).[71] Thus, the arrival of God's kingdom terminates the rule of the empires that have plagued God's people, liberating them from the bondage they had endured.

Daniel 7 reiterates the same succession of kingdoms that appears in Daniel 2. This time, however, the kingdoms are portrayed as grotesque beasts—a winged lion, a bear, a four-headed leopard, and one extremely terrifying beast with manifold horns. In the place of the stone, a different figure brings judgment on the kingdoms. The narrator describes the climax of the vision, the end of the persecuting empires, in the following manner:

> As I watched in the night visions, I saw one like a human being (υἱὸς ἀνθρώπου LXX) coming with the clouds of heaven. And he came to the Ancient One and was presented before him. To him was given dominion and glory and kingship, that all peoples, nations, and language should serve him. His dominion is an everlasting dominion that shall not pass away, and his kingship is one that shall never be destroyed (Dan 7:13–14).

In the vision, the Son of Man figure is equated with "the people of the holy ones of the Most High" (Dan 7:27). If read at face value, the vision suggests

---

71. Josephus conspicuously avoids discussing the nature of this stone that crushes the worldly kingdoms. In fact, he likely omits the interpretation of the stone because of its political ramifications: "Daniel did also declare the meaning of the stone to the king; but I do not think proper to relate it, since I have only undertaken to describe things past or things present, but not things that are future: yet if anyone be so very desirous of knowing truth, as not to waive such points of curiosity, and cannot curb his inclination for understanding the uncertainties of futurity, and whether they will happen or not, let him be diligent in reading the book of Daniel, which he will find among the sacred writings" (Josephus, *Ant.*, 10.10.4, trans. Whiston). If Josephus can be taken as a paradigm for how Daniel was read in the first century, it seems that the common Jewish person would have seen the Roman empire as the final kingdom in the succession since Josephus says he is only talking about realities that were currently present or in the past. The only thing that lay in the future, from Josephus' point of view, was the arrival of God's kingdom, which would sound the death knell for the Romans. Even though he was able to sound loyal to Roman occupation by citing Daniel's prophecy (Josephus, *Ant.*, 10.11.7), he was selective in the parts he chose to include.

that when God—here the Ancient of Days—establishes his kingdom, he will judge the foreign empires and liberate his people. The people in view would be Israel as a corporate entity. However, it is not difficult to see how a messianic reading of the Son of Man figure could emerge. Daniel 9 speaks of the arrival of a "prince" and "an anointed one" being cut off (Dan 9:26). If the Son of Man figure were equated with the "anointed one" of Daniel 9, then the hopes for God's redemption could be located on a particular individual, a Messiah. Whether Daniel 9 influenced the interpretation of the Son of Man figure or not, there are several ancient texts that do see the Son of Man figure as synonymous with a messianic ruler.[72] Regardless of how Daniel was interpreted or meant to be interpreted, there is an underlying expectation for the future and its relation to the kingdom of God. From the seer's point of view, the pagan human empires were presently being allowed to run their course. However, in due time, God would judge them too. When he did so, he would free his people from their oppression. Thus, the arrival of God's kingdom would emancipate his people from their enemies, which was essential for their complete restoration.

The non-canonical literature of the Second Temple era continues to connect the kingdom of God with the restoration of God's people. For instance, the third book of the *Sibylline Oracles* indicates that the Jerusalem temple will fulfill its eschatological function after the kingdom of God arrives:

> And then indeed he will raise up his kingdom for all ages among men, he who once gave the holy Law to pious men, to all of whom he promised to open the earth and the world and the gates of the blessed and all joys and immortal intellect and eternal cheer. From every land they shall bring incense and gifts to the house of the great God. There will be no other house among men, even for future generations to honor except the one which God gave to faithful men to honor (for mortals will invoke the son of the great God) (*Sib. Or.* 3:767–74; OTP 1:379).[73]

Here the inclusion of the Gentiles in the worship of God has come to pass, and God's rule extends over the nations from the temple itself. The

---

72. For example, in *4 Ezra*'s apocalyptic vision, the fourth kingdom—the one equated with Daniel's fourth kingdom (*4 Ezra* 12:11)—terminates with the roaring of the lion that symbolizes the Messiah (*4 Ezra* 12:31–32). *1 Enoch* 46:1–4 also interprets the Son of Man as a singular individual, most likely the Messiah, even though the text never explicitly states such. For a fuller development, see Wright, *New Testament*, 313–20 and Vermes, *Jesus the Jew*, 170–72.

73. The editors regard the portion in parentheses as a Christian interpolation.

Assumption of Moses likewise anticipates God's future kingdom and with it, God's judgment of evil nations:

> Then His kingdom will appear throughout his whole creation. Then the devil will have an end. Yea, sorrow will be led away with him.... For God Most High will surge forth, the Eternal One alone. In full view will he come to work vengeance on the nations. Yea, all their idols will he destroy. Then will you be happy, O Israel! And you will mount up above the necks and the wings of an eagle. Yea, all things will be fulfilled. And God will raise you to the heights. Yea, he will fix you firmly in the heaven of the stars, in the place of their habitations (*As. Mos.* 10.1, 7–9; OTP 1:931–32).[74]

Similarly, *The Testament of Dan* makes God's reign over Israel coterminous with Israel's restoration:

> And Jerusalem shall no longer undergo desolation, nor shall Israel be led into captivity, because the Lord will be in her midst [living among human beings]. The Holy One of Israel will rule over them in humility and poverty, and he who trusts in him shall reign in truth in the heavens (*T. Dan*, 5:13; OTP 1:810).

Again we can see a number of themes being consistently combined. The restoration of Israel often appears alongside of the assertion that Israel's God is king. This suggests that the symbol of God's kingdom is not simply an assertion regarding a metaphysical belief, but signifies God's ability to redeem his people and usher in the promised age of restoration.[75]

In light of this, when Jesus proclaimed the arrival of God's kingdom in first century Palestine, his listeners would likely have heard his message as heralding the anticipated age of restoration. N. T. Wright summarizes the point well: "If, then, someone were to speak to Jesus' contemporaries of YHWH's becoming king, we may safely assume that they would have in mind, in some form or other, this two-sided story concerning the double reality of exile. Israel would 'really' return from exile; YHWH would finally return to

---

74. Regarding the date: "the position that the work has its roots in the early 2d century B.C. but reached final form in the early 1st century A.D. appears the most likely. Actually, any theory that admits that the work as a whole would have been known in Palestine in the first part of the 1st century A.D. qualifies it for our consideration...." Meier, *Mentor, Message, and Miracles*, 255.

75. Ibid., 264. As Meier concludes, "the symbol of God ruling as king was alive and well in the 'intertestamental' period and was often connected with eschatological hopes (sometimes with apocalyptic elements) concerning the restoration of all Israel gathered around Mt. Zion or Jerusalem."

Zion."[76] Because the kingdom was widely associated with the restoration of Israel, one can expect that Jesus also operated with a similar understanding.[77] John P. Meier, who arrives at a similar conclusion regarding the understanding of God's kingdom, chides his critics: "If, as some critics have claimed, Jesus did not want his use of the symbol to embody eschatological hopes for the future, it would have been absolutely necessary for him—unless he did not care about being misunderstood—to make clear that he did not intend an eschatological dimension when he employed the symbol."[78] However, as Meier demonstrates, there are enough similarities between Jesus' descriptions of the kingdom and the dominant Jewish pattern that indicate Jesus equated the arrival of the kingdom with God's redemption of his people as understood within restoration theology. In light of these connections between the kingdom of God and Israel's restoration, we can assume that even Jesus' central message of the kingdom invoked Israel's ongoing chronicle of God's people awaiting restoration.

In addition, one is not left to posit the meaning of the kingdom in Jesus' proclamation simply by external literature. The Gospels themselves firmly establish a relationship between the kingdom's arrival and Israel's restoration. Matthew, for example, makes the association with restoration clear in the geographical setting where Jesus begins his ministry. When Jesus initiates his announcement of the kingdom in Matthew (Matt 4:17), we are told immediately before that Jesus

> left Nazareth and made his home in Capernaum by the sea, in the territory of Zebulun and Naphtali, so that what had been spoken through the prophet Isaiah might be fulfilled: "Land of Zebulun, land of Naphtali, on the road by the sea, across the Jordan, Galilee of the Gentiles—the people who sat in darkness have seen a great light, and for those who sat in the region and shadow of death light has dawned" (Matt 4:13b–16).

76. Wright, *Jesus and the Victory*, 206. See also, Wright, *New Testament*, 307; Meier, *Mentor, Message, and Miracles*, 269; and Combrink, "Salvation in Mark," 43.

77. Wright, *Jesus and the Victory*, 224. "The question is *not*, did 'kingdom of god,' for Jesus, still mean 'Israel's god, the creator, at last asserting his sovereign rule over his world,' with the connotation of the return from exile, the return of YHWH to Zion, the vindication of Israel by this covenant god, and the defeat of her enemies? That simply *was* its basic, irreducible meaning within first-century Palestine. The question is, *in what sense* did Jesus affirm this meaning, and how did he redefine the concept in such a way as to give rise to the meanings that emerge among his earliest followers?"

78. Meier, *Mentor, Message, and Miracles*, 269. After surveying several relevant kingdom sayings from Jesus, he concludes that "Jesus did understand the central symbol of the kingdom of God in terms of the definitive coming of God in the near future to bring the present state of things to an end and to establish his full and unimpeded rule over the world in general and Israel in particular" (ibid., 349).

By noting this geographical change, Matthew makes a theological point by citing Isaiah 9:1-2. Mentioning the tribes of Zebulun and Naphtali is significant because these are two of the northern tribes that remained in exile.[79] It seems quite likely that Matthew finds the geographical location significant because these are precisely the tribes waiting for their restoration. Thus, when Jesus begins his proclamation of the kingdom, which signified that God's restoration of his people was underway, he did so precisely in those regions that were in need of it.[80] Moreover, the expectation that Israel's restoration would affect the Gentiles also comes into play. By citing Isaiah 9:1-2, Matthew also draws attention to this region's moniker, "Galilee of the Gentiles," in order to show that the Gentiles are beneficiaries of the kingdom along with the beleaguered nation of Israel.[81] Therefore, when Jesus does begin his proclamation of the kingdom, it stands within the stream of the Jewish storyline that anticipated God's redemption of their people, which—according to some expectations—would flow past Palestine's borders to engulf the Gentiles as well.

When we evaluate Jesus' notion of the kingdom as presented in the Gospels more closely, not only is it recognizable that there are Old Testament antecedents for this symbol of the Jewish worldview, but we particularly find demonstrable similarities with the Old Testament book of Daniel. This is not to suggest that Jesus fails to add his own creative twists and nuances to the Jewish expectation but that he uses the eschatological terminology of Daniel as a vehicle to convey his own proclamation of the coming kingdom. What follows are some of the more persuasive parallels that can be established between Daniel and Jesus' proclamation of the kingdom in the Gospels.

The first of these is the fact that both Jesus and Daniel speak of a specific "time" being completed before the arrival of the kingdom, which Craig Evans terms a shared "language of imminence."[82] In Daniel 7:22, which interprets the Ancient One's judgment upon the beasts in Daniel's vision,

---

79. The *Isaiah Targum* interprets Isaiah 9:1-2 as a reference to the exile: "For none shall be weary who shall come to oppress them, as at the former time, when the people of the land of Zebulun, and the people of the land of Naphtali went into captivity: and those that were left, a mighty king led into captivity, because they did not remember the power of the Red Sea, neither the wonders of the Jordan, the war of the fortifications of the nations" (*Tg. Isa.* 9:1-2, trans. Pauli).

80. McComiskey, "Exile and Restoration," 675-79. Not all take this line of interpretation. Some argue that this citation reveals Jesus' movement as inclusive of Gentiles. E.g. Davies and Allison, *Matthew*, 1:379-85; Beaton, "Isaiah in Matthew's Gospel," 68; and Nolland, *Matthew*, 174.

81. Davies and Allison, *Matthew*, 1:383-85.

82. Evans, "Daniel in the New Testament," 511-12.

the text says: "Until the Ancient One came; then judgment was given for the holy ones of the Most High, and the time arrived when the holy ones gained possession of the kingdom." The Greek translations of this text bear remarkable resemblance to later statements of the Gospels and are listed here:

Daniel 7:22 LXX θ " ... <u>ὁ καιρὸς ἔφθασεν</u> καὶ <u>τὴν βασιλείαν</u> κατέσχον οἱ ἅγιοι."[83]

Daniel 7:22 LXX " ... <u>ὁ καιρὸς ἔφθασε</u>, καὶ <u>τὴν βασιλείαν</u> κατέσχον οἱ ἅγιοι."

At the end of the book, Daniel is instructed, "But you, Daniel, keep the words secret and the book sealed until the time (καιροῦ) of the end..." (Daniel 12:4 LXX). In both Daniel 7:22 and 12:4, there is a certain "time," that must elapse before the kingdom of God arrives.

Interestingly, this is precisely the terminology Jesus uses in his announcement of the kingdom. In Mark 1:15, Jesus says, "The time is fulfilled, and the kingdom of God has come near; repent, and believe in the good news." The Greek translation here mirrors the language of Daniel as noted in the underlined portions of the Greek text: "πεπλήρωται <u>ὁ καιρὸς</u> καὶ ἤγγικεν ἡ <u>βασιλεία</u> τοῦ θεοῦ·" (Mark 1:15). Matthew's version drops the reference to the time being completed, but still retains the imminence of the kingdom's arrival when Jesus utters the call: "Repent, for the kingdom of heaven has come near (μετανοῖετε ἤγγικεν γὰρ ἡ <u>βασιλεία</u> τῶν οὐρανῶν)" (Matt 3:2; 4:17). There is also the Q saying that speaks to the nearness of the kingdom as a result of Jesus' exorcisms as well. Jesus makes the assertion that if his exorcisms come from God's Spirit, "then the kingdom of God has come to you" (Matt 12:28b; Luke 11:20b). The Greek here again echoes the imminent language found in the Greek text of Daniel as well: "ἔφθασεν ἐφ' ὑμᾶς ἡ <u>βασιλεία</u> τοῦ θεοῦ." Thus, the anticipated arrival of the kingdom, the expiration of the "time" that Daniel expected, reveals the influence of Danielic eschatology upon Jesus' proclamation.

Second, Daniel 2, which reveals the sequence of human kingdoms ultimately fading before the kingdom of God in the vision of the metal statue, repeatedly describes the kingdom as a "mystery," which is also how the Gospels describe the kingdom.[84] Again, the similarities here do not seem

---

83. Though Theodotian's translation is later than the New Testament, it reflects closer affinity with the Hebrew and Aramaic text of Daniel.

84. Evans, "Daniel in the New Testament," 512–14. See also Collins, "The Influence of Daniel," 105–6. The same connection with "mystery" and the kingdom is also present in Tob 12:7–11.

coincidental since they appear in conjunction with a great deal of other similarities, which substantiates the literary connection.

> Daniel 2:19: "Then the mystery (τὸ μυστήριον) was revealed to Daniel . . ."[85]
>
> Daniel 2:27: "Daniel answered the king, 'No wise men, enchanters, magicians, or diviners can show to the king the mystery (τὸ μυστήριον) that the king is asking."
>
> Daniel 2:30a: "But as for me, this mystery (τὸ μυστήριον) has not been revealed to me because of any wisdom that I have more than any other living being . . . ."
>
> Daniel 2:47: "The king said to Daniel, 'Truly, your god is God of gods and Lord of kings and a revealer of mysteries, for you have been able to reveal this mystery (τὸ μυστήριον τοῦτο)!"
>
> Mark 4:11a: "And he said to them, 'To you has been given the secret (τὸ μυστήριον) of the kingdom of God (τῆς βασιλείας τοῦ θεοῦ) . . . ."
>
> Matt 13:11a: "He answered, 'To you it has been given to know the secrets of the kingdom of heaven (τὰ μυστήρια τῆς βασιλείας τῶν οὐρανῶν) . . . ."
>
> Luke 8:10a: "He said, 'To you it has been given to know the secrets of the kingdom of God (τὰ μυστήρια τῆς βασιλείας τοῦ θεοῦ) . . . ."

Both Daniel and the Gospels describe the kingdom as a μυστήριον that unaided human wisdom cannot penetrate. Only God's disclosure manifests the realities of the kingdom.

Third, another peculiar linguistic similarity can be found in Daniel 2 when the stone uncut by human hands crushes the statue of variegated metals.[86] In the interpretation, the seer says:

> And in the days of those kings the God of heaven will set up a kingdom that shall never be destroyed, nor shall the kingdom be left to another people. It shall break in pieces (λικμήσει) all these kingdoms and bring them to an end, and it shall stand forever, just as you saw that a stone was cut from a mountain by no human hand, and that it broke in pieces the iron, the bronze, the clay, the silver, and the gold (Dan 2:44–45a).[87]

85. For these passages from Daniel, the Greek comes from the LXX.
86. Collins, "Influence of Daniel," 106.
87. LXX Θ for the Greek. The English translation is from the Aramaic.

At the end of the Parable of the Wicked Tenants, Jesus gives a warning about the rejected cornerstone, and uses the same words to depict the effects of stumbling over the cornerstone as Daniel used of the stone pulverizing the statue. In Luke, Jesus says: "What then is this that is written: 'The stone that the builders rejected has become the cornerstone?' Everyone who falls on that stone will be broken to pieces, and when it falls on anyone, it will crush him (λικμήσει)" (Luke 20:17–18). Again, the connection between the texts occurs not just in the "crushing" but also in the fact that a "stone" does it in both texts, which strengthens the likeliness of an allusion here. Just like the kingdom of God will crush the opposing nations, even so those who reject Jesus will face a similar end.

Fourth, Jesus uses some of the same terminology to refer to eschatological figures or events that one finds in Daniel.[88] In the following texts, Jesus warns about a "desolating sacrilege," which is language used in Daniel to speak of the pagan overlords' pollution of the temple.

> Daniel 11:31 LXX: "Forces sent by him shall occupy and profane the temple and fortress. They shall abolish the regular burnt offering and set up the abomination that makes desolate (βδέλυγμα ἐρημώσεως)."

> Mark 13:14: "But when you see the desolating sacrilege (τὸ βδέλυγμα τῆς ἐρημώσεως) set up where it ought not to be (let the reader understand), then those in Judea must flee to the mountains;"

> Matthew 24:15: "So when you see the desolating sacrilege (τὸ βδέλυγμα τῆς ἐρημώσεως) standing in the holy place, as was spoken of by the prophet Daniel (let the reader understand) . . . ."

This does not mean that Daniel and Jesus necessarily have the same thing in mind when using this language, but it does show that Jesus adopted the language of Daniel as a means of referring to future pestilence in language that his audience would most likely associate with Daniel.

Fifth, Jesus' parable of the mustard seed resembles Nebuchadnezzar's dream in Daniel 4.[89] In Daniel 4, Nebuchadnezzar has a dream of a tree and explains it in the following way:

> Upon my bed this is what I saw; there was a tree at the center of the earth, and its height was great. The tree grew great and

---

88. Collins, "Influence of Daniel," 110.

89. Evans, "Daniel in the New Testament," 522. See also Collins, "Influence of Daniel," 107.

strong, its top reached to heaven, and it was visible to the ends of the whole earth. Its foliage was beautiful, its fruit abundant, and it provided food for all. The animals of the field found shade under it, the birds of the air nested in its branches, and from it all living beings were fed (Dan 4:10–12).

In the interpretation of this dream, Daniel identifies this great tree with Nebuchadnezzar and his kingdom (Dan 4:22). The tree thus symbolizes the protective effects of the Babylonian empire. If we skip forward to Jesus in the Gospels, Jesus' parable of the mustard seed borrows imagery from Nebuchadnezzar's dream of Daniel 4:

> He put before them another parable: "The kingdom of heaven is like a mustard seed that someone took and sowed in his field; it is the smallest of all the seeds, but when it has grown it is the greatest of shrubs and becomes a tree, so that the birds of the air come and make nests in its branches" (Matt 13:31–32; cf. Luke 13:18–19).

Commentators have often noted that mustard plants rarely become large enough to be considered a "tree" where birds build their nests, though they do grow rapidly.[90] This incongruity with real mustard plants should not cause undo discussion about the accuracy of Jesus' botanical knowledge, but should instead throw greater weight behind a likely allusion to Daniel 4. Just as Nebuchadnezzar's kingdom had grown large and had become a nesting place for the peoples of the world, even so the kingdom of God, despite its humble beginnings, would likewise impact the world scene.

Finally, the Gospels utilize the enigmatic figure of Daniel 7:13 who is "like a son of man (LXX: υἱὸς ἀνθρώπου)" to explicate Jesus and his mission. In Daniel's vision, the one "like a son of man" receives the kingdoms of the world after the Ancient One defeats the beasts. In the Gospels, the phrase "Son of Man (ὁ υἱὸς τοῦ ἀνθρώπου)" is almost ubiquitously found on the lips of Jesus in the Gospels, with the only exception being John 12:34 where the people are interrogatively quoting Jesus' own words.[91] Biblical scholars have long debated how Jesus used the phrase "Son of Man," since its Aramaic equivalent could be used as a circumlocution for oneself as well. Certainly several of the Son of Man sayings fit into this category. However, there are a number of sayings that clearly betray the influence of Daniel 7, which connect Jesus directly with the Son of Man figure in Daniel. At his trial before the religious leaders, Jesus is asked if he is the Christ. He

---

90. Davies and Allison, *Matthew*, 2:420.
91. Marshall, "Son of Man," 775–81.

responds, "I am; and you will see the Son of Man seated at the right hand of Power, and coming with the clouds of heaven" (Mark 14:62).[92] Though some argue that the connection between Jesus and the Son of Man in Daniel 7 was the creation of the early church, the fact that the church quickly discontinued use of the title suggests that this connection stems from Jesus himself.[93] For our purposes, it is sufficient to note that the Gospel writers make this connection, identifying Jesus as the Danielic Son of Man and the one who ushers in the kingdom that would judge evil and restore God's people.

The aforementioned influences of Daniel upon the Gospels reveal that Daniel's eschatological language permeates the Gospels, making it quite likely that they adopt some version of Daniel's chronology. In fact, we can likely assume that Daniel influenced Jesus' own understanding of himself

---

92. Other sayings also seem to allude to Daniel 7: Mark 8:30//Matt 16:27//Luke 9:26; Mark 13:26//Matt 24:30//Luke 21:27; Mark 14:62//Matt 26:64//Luke 22:67-69. Vermes argues these passages do not go back to Jesus, and one is forced to reckon with the fact that connecting Jesus with Daniel's Son of Man would be ripe for exploitation by Christian theologians. However, although Vermes' interpretation of the Son of Man sayings as a circumlocution for oneself can be verified in some cases, it is peculiar that only Jesus uses the phrase to speak of himself in the Gospels. If it were a common circumlocution, why are not others using it to speak of themselves too? When other characters do use the phrase "Son of Man" (John 12:34), it is always when people cite or refer to things that were first said by Jesus in the narratives. The oft-cited observation that, outside of Jesus' usage in the Gospels, there are only a few passages that equate Jesus with the Son of Man holds true (Acts 7:56; Heb 2:6; Rev 1:13; 14:14). If this phrase were an invention of the church, one is hard-pressed to explain why the Gospels consistently have Jesus as the one connecting himself to the Son of Man figure of Daniel while Paul (especially in 1 Thessalonians where it would have been entirely appropriate given the content) and some of the other writers of the New Testament never adopt it. The dearth of the Son of Man references in the rest of the New Testament, especially when it would have been expedient, does invoke the criterion of dissimilarity in its favor. Though Vermes is fully aware of this fact, he fails to acknowledge how it undermines his conclusion. See Vermes, *Jesus the Jew*, 160-86. Casey, who follows a position similar to Vermes is forced to posit a complicated origin of the association with Daniel but does not satisfactorily explain why such an association fails to influence other New Testament writings that anticipate the second coming as well. See Casey, *Son of Man*, 224-39. Thus, it seems preferable to follow those who contend that Jesus did connect himself to the ambiguous "Son of Man" figure in Daniel 7 on at least a few occasions. See Bauckham, "Son of Man," 23-33; Marshall, "Son of Man," 775-81; Allison, *Constructing Jesus*, 293-303; and Dunn, *Christology in the Making*, 86-87.

93. So Dunn, "Danielic Son of Man," 545-47 and Marshall, "Hope of a New Age," 11. Some have tried to see Jesus' reference to the "Son of Man" as an individual or an angel other than himself. E.g. Collins, "Influence of Daniel," 105 and Allison, *Constructing Jesus*, 296-303. This is where the use of "Son of Man" as a circumlocution for oneself is relevant. If Jesus uses the phrase as a circumlocution for himself in some instances, it seems likely that when he makes the connection with Daniel, he is making the affirmations about himself rather than another figure.

and what God was about to do for his people.[94] The apocalyptic imagery found in the dreams and visions of Daniel could be concretely connected with the ministry and events of Jesus' life. Probably the most prominent feature in the Gospels is identifying Jesus as God's agent, Daniel's Son of Man, that would usher in the kingdom of God. Because he served this role, Jesus could declare the "time" of the kingdom's arrival, and he could reveal to his followers the "mystery" of the kingdom. Those who stumbled over him would reap the effects of opposing the kingdom. All of these similarities reveal that the Gospel writers, and likely Jesus himself, adopted Daniel's eschatological expectations of God's future judgment on the foreign nations and the restoration of his people.

In summary, we have seen that Jesus' central message, the proclamation of God's kingdom, evoked the larger narrative of Israel that was still unfolding. The kingdom of God symbolized God's authority over the nations on the geopolitical scene. As a result of Israel's covenant infidelity, God had allowed certain pagan empires to dominate his people. However, when Israel's God chose to act, he would bring these nations to justice and rescue his faithful people from their plight. When Jesus announced the arrival of the kingdom of God, he proclaimed that God was acting or about to act to bring restoration to his people just as this larger prophetic vision expected. Thus, even Jesus' central message of the kingdom of God is rooted in the larger narrative of Israel and her hopes for restoration.

Cleansing the Temple

Other actions that Jesus performs orient his ministry in the world of Jewish restoration theology. In Jesus' final week before the crucifixion, he brazenly ventured into a central symbol of ancient Israel, the temple, and proceeded to chase out the moneychangers and those selling sacrifices in the temple courts (Mark 11:15–19; Matt 21:12–17; Luke 19:45–48). Though some scholars think the action was nondescript and likely went unnoticed, it is more likely that this event drew the ire of the Jerusalem leadership and catalyzed his death.

Regardless of its relation to his death several days later, what prompted Jesus to do it? What was wrong with the temple that elicited Jesus' response? It is difficult to defend the view that Jesus takes umbrage with the fact that the Israelites were not offering their own sacrifices but buying them from the merchants as Chilton, a biblical scholar influenced by Girard in some

---

94. Collins, "Influence of Daniel," 93.

ways, suggests.[95] Deuteronomy had long before sanctioned the buying and selling of sacrifices, particularly for those who had long commutes to the temple:

> But if, when the Lord your God has blessed you, the distance is so great that you are unable to transport [the tithes], because the place where the Lord your God will choose to set his name is too far away from you, then you may turn it into money. With the money secure in hand, go to the place that the Lord your God will choose; spend the money for whatever you wish—oxen, sheep, wine, strong drink, or whatever you desire. And you shall eat there in the presence of the Lord your God, you and your household rejoicing together (Deut 14:24–26).

Deuteronomy clearly condones buying one's sacrifices in the provenance of Jerusalem. Moreover, paying the required half-shekel tax to the temple would have required some kind of currency exchange for those living outside the region (Exod 30:11–16). Clearly selling sacrifices to the out-of-towners or exchanging their foreign currency for the local fare was hardly sacrilegious, and it is unlikely that Jesus objects to this.

The only explanation of Jesus' motives in the Gospels' abbreviated accounts are located in Jesus' words. In a short pastiche that combines sayings from Isaiah and Jeremiah, Jesus utters an indictment against the temple: "Is it not written, 'My house shall be called a house of prayer for all nations'? But you have made it a den of robbers" (Mark 11:17).[96] Although the saying reveals Jesus' alignment with the former prophets' indictment of the temple, it is not entirely clear what Jesus finds objectionable in the temple on the basis of these statements. Perhaps one clue can be found in Mark's longer description of the temple as "a house of prayer *for all nations.*"[97] Since the merchants had set up shop in the temple, the most likely locale was within the Court of the Gentiles.[98] Moreover, some scholars have suggested that selling sacrifices within the temple was a recent development occurring precisely around the time Jesus would have been there, which would make such a practice unprecedented.[99] If the exchange of sacrifices were set up in the

---

95. For this view, see Chilton, "Origin of the Eucharist," 17–28.

96. Citing here Isa 56:7 and Jer 7:11.

97. Emphasis is mine. See Marcus, *Mark 8–16*, 792. As Marcus observes, Mark's inclusion of Gentiles is at variance with other Jewish expectation of the temple's restoration, which would prohibit certain ethnicities. See 4Q174.

98. Witherington, *Mark*, 315.

99. Some have made the observation that this introduction of the merchants had only recently occurred under Caiaphas. E.g. Eppstein, "Cleansing of the Temple," 42–58 and Chilton, "Origin of the Eucharist," 24. If so, then the recent innovation could explain Jesus' visceral reaction.

Court of the Gentiles, it is possible that this particular venue precluded the Gentiles from being able to worship in the temple, which was the temple's eschatological function.[100]

In one of the more influential works on this subject, E. P. Sanders contends that the traditional interpretation of Jesus' temple action as cleansing or purifying the temple is unwarranted. In contrast, Sanders argues that the temple incident was a prophetic action meant to symbolize its future desolation. For him, the action in the temple should be interpreted not in light of its probable venue or the words on Jesus' lips, but on the basis of Jesus' other predictions of the temple's destruction and rebuilding.[101] He writes:

> On the hypothesis presented here the action and the saying form a unity. Jesus predicted (or threatened) the destruction of the temple and carried out an action symbolic of its destruction by demonstrating against the performance of the sacrifices. He did not wish to purify the temple, either of dishonest trading or of trading in contrast to 'pure' worship. Nor was he opposed to the temple sacrifices which God commanded to Israel. He intended, rather, to indicate that the end was at hand and that the temple would be destroyed, so that the new and perfect temple might arise.[102]

I think Sanders is right to see a foreboding warning about the temple's ominous future in Jesus' actions in the temple.[103]

If anything, the Markan "sandwich" of the cursed fig tree that bookends the temple incident certainly suggests that Jesus' actions presaged the temple's devastation. In the account of Mark, on Jesus' journey into Jerusalem on that day, he curses the fruitless tree saying, "May no one ever eat fruit from you again" (Mark 11:14). Immediately after uttering this judgment on the fig tree, Jesus enters the temple and chases out the money changers. The following pericope recounts the disciples walking past the cursed fig tree and noticing that it had withered "to its roots" (Mark 11:20). Since the cursing of the fig tree and its withering immediately surround the temple incident, Mark intends his readers to draw a connection between the fig tree and the temple incident. The tree's lack of fruitfulness that warrants judgment mirrors the temple's lack of fruitfulness, which will likewise result

---

100. For caution on this interpretation, see France, *Mark*, 445–46.
101. Sanders, *Jesus and Judaism*, 71–76. See also Bockmuehl, *This Jesus*, 92.
102. Sanders, *Jesus and Judaism*, 75.
103. Ibid., 76. He does, however, concede that there is no surety that the meaning of Jesus' action was "self-evident" to his contemporaries.

in its judgment.[104] Thus, Sanders is right to see the temple incident as a prophetic action that depicts the future judgment of the temple.

With that being said, I do not think this requires us to jettison the notion that Jesus desired a reform or cleansing of the temple as well.[105] It likely has both dimensions in view with the current practices in the temple precipitating its future judgment.[106] It very well could be that Jesus found the activities in the temple reprehensible and believed they were stymieing the temple from fulfilling its eschatological role of ushering the Gentiles into the worship of God and being a place designated for prayer.[107] Because the current temple regime had kept the temple from fulfilling its *raison d'être*, God would act in judgment.

Regardless of how one interprets the intention behind the action, the temple incident again helps us situate Jesus within the world of the first century. The temple was a central symbol of God's presence with his covenant people throughout Jewish history. It sat upon Mt. Zion, the place where God had chosen to make his name dwell. It was the place where God's glory had left during the exile,[108] and it was the center of hope for coming restoration. The expectation was that, when God restored his people, his glory would again come to dwell in the temple. When Jesus overturns the tables and chases out the livestock jockeys in the temple, it is not indicating that Jesus preferred a spiritualized form of religion over one performed through cultic rites and sacrifices. Rather, Jesus is performing a messianic action that clearly situates him within the larger world of Jewish eschatology and God's restoration of his people.[109] In several prominent texts anticipating a new and glorious temple, the Messiah is the agent who purifies or rebuilds it.[110] In this light, Meyer's words capture the significance of the event well: "It was at once a fulfillment event and a sign of the future, pledging the restoration of temple, Zion, and Jerusalem. Since these were symbol and synecdoche for the whole people of God, the cleansing of the temple pledged the perfect

---

104. Witherington, *Mark*, 312; see Marcus, *Mark 8–16*, 790–94.

105. In response to Sanders' conclusion that the Gospel writers softened Jesus' prophecy against the temple and make the issue about the temple's purity, Evans' counter-arguments are more compelling; see Evans, "Jesus' Action in the Temple," 237–70, esp. 238–40.

106. Witherington, *Mark*, 315–16.

107. McKelvey, *New Temple*, 64–65.

108. Ezekiel records the movements of God's glory as it leaves the Holy of Holies and eventually the city of Jerusalem altogether: Ezek 8:4; 9:3; 10:18–19; 11:22–25.

109. McKelvey, *New Temple*, 74.

110. *Sib. Or.* 5.414–33 and *Pss. Sol.* 17.21–32.

restoration of Israel."[111] Thus, like we have seen in several other texts, the cleansing of the temple is a symbolic gesture that hearkens to the larger narrative of Israel waiting for restoration, which is captured here when Jesus proceeds to call for reform of the central religious symbol in their world.

The Wicked Tenants and the Rejected Stone

While one would hesitate to call the parable of the wicked tenants and its closing quotation of Psalm 118:22–23 an essential piece of evidence that situates Jesus in the larger story of Israel, the emphasis that both Girard and Schwager place upon this passage warrants an extended treatment. Both of them find the identification of Jesus as the rejected stone essential to the gospel message, since it alludes to Jesus' future rejection by the masses in a way that also connotes mimetic rivalry.[112] While Schwager and Girard are correct in seeing the passage as an allusion to Christ's future victimization, they miss the true depth of how this passage evokes dimensions of restoration theology because they fail to read the Gospels in light of Israel's larger narrative.

In all three Gospels, the parable of the wicked tenants (Matt 21:33–44; Mark 12:1–11; Luke 20:9–18) occurs after Jesus' cleansing of the temple and the negative response the temple incident elicits from the Jerusalem leadership. In light of such a setting, the parable of the wicked tenants seeks to explain that, even though Jesus is the Messianic redeemer endowed with God's authority, he will still face rejection and death at the hands of the leadership.[113] In the parable, a landowner plants a vineyard and leases it to

---

111. Meyer, *Aims of Jesus*, 198.

112. Schwager, *Scapegoats*, 141; Girard, *Things Hidden*, 195; and Girard, *Evolution and Conversion*, 168.

113. For some, the parable of the wicked husbandmen contravenes the notion that the Son was sent to die since the purpose of his mission was to collect the produce of the vineyard. E.g. Finlan, *Options on Atonement*, 37–38. There are two things that can be said in response. First, this is asking the parables to be full-blown theological explanations when in fact they were told to make a specific point. The point in the context is not the meaning of the son's death, but what would happen if the leadership continued on its course of rejection. Second, in Mark's version of the story, which has some of the servants being killed, the father has to reckon with the possibility that his son would receive similar treatment. Many commentators have noted the naiveté of the father for believing that his son would be exempt from the brutality that the former servants had met. One might suggest the death of the son was a risk the father was willing to take. After all, the story is not one about being a cautious and protective parent but about YHWH's manifold, yet unsuccessful, attempts to woo Israel throughout her history. The most recent stage of this pursuit was in the person of Jesus who would have likely seen the very real possibility that he could face death like his predecessor, John the Baptist.

some tenants. At the time of harvest, he sends for his share of the produce. The servants he sends are turned away empty-handed after being brutalized. After seeing his servants severely rebuffed, the owner sends his son, hoping that he would be respected. However, the tenants conspire against this final courier too, knowing that he is the coming heir. They slay him upon arrival. Jesus then asks his audience what will happen when the owner comes to the vineyard. The ensuing answer anticipates that the owner will come and enact vengeance upon them.[114]

Most scholars observe the latent symbolism present in the parable. In Isaiah 5:1–7, Israel is depicted as YHWH's fruitless vineyard and is thereby threatened with punishment. Jesus' parable of the wicked tenants employs the same symbol, with an innovative wrinkle. As in Isaiah, Israel is the vineyard, and God is the planter. However, the addition of the other actors in the storyline adds a complexity to the allegory absent in Isaiah. The wicked tenants are the leadership that questions Jesus' authority and seeks his demise.[115] The son in the parable is most certainly Jesus,[116] which is confirmed by the way in which the language of sonship is applied to Jesus throughout the rest of the Gospels.[117] The parable thus anticipates the coming rejection of Jesus, which culminates in his execution on the cross.

The parable ends with the threat of punishment for those rejecting the son, at which point, the Synoptics cite Psalm 118:22–23: "The stone that the builders rejected has become the cornerstone; this was the Lord's doing and it is amazing in our eyes?" (Mark 12:10–11). The parable ends on the dismal note of the son's lynching, but the quotation of the Psalm indicates the son will be vindicated, which occurs at the resurrection of Christ.[118] While some have argued that the citation of Psalm 118 is a later addition

---

114. In Matthew, the people make this pronouncement (Matt 21:41) whereas Luke has Jesus saying this. For Girard, it is essential that Matthew has the crowds assuming God will return judgment upon the culprits since this distances Jesus from threats of divine violence. In Mark, however, the speaker is ambiguous, which explains why there is redaction on this point (Mark 12:9). Matthew and Luke both clear up the ambiguity, but do so in different directions. Matthew's difference can be explained as an attempt to assimilate the indictment of this parable with that of the previous one, the one about the two sons. In the previous parable, Jesus' interlocutors blissfully pronounce their own judgment (Matt 21:31), which is precisely what they do in Matt 21:41. Thus, although Girard is committed to seeing Matthew as original, it could in fact be an intentional redaction in light of its literary context. See Olmstead, *Matthew's Trilogy*, 114. Regardless, Luke's version is problematic for Girard.

115. Kingsbury, "Parable of the Wicked Husbandmen," 645.

116. Snodgrass, "Parable of the Wicked Tenants," 199–201.

117. See Breytenbach, "Das Markusevangelium," 218.

118. France, *Mark*, 462–64.

and that the parable was originally independent of the Psalm,[119] it must be acknowledged that the parable and citation are linguistically integrated in their current form, though it might be missed in English and Greek. The son of the parable (בן) linguistically connects with the following quotation about the stone (אבן), suggesting the quotation from the Psalm and the parable of the wicked tenants were meant to hang together as a unit.[120]

There are several elements in the text so far that indicate more is in view than simply the vindication of the rejected son/stone. First, the setting of the parable and the citation from Psalm 118 occur within the larger context of Jesus' cleansing of the temple and the questioning of his authority. In all likelihood, the evangelists see the parable and Psalm revealing the future plight of the temple as well. In fact, the later prediction of the temple's destruction in Luke 21:6, which speaks of "not one stone" being left on top of another, connects the usage of the word "stone" with the temple.[121] Second, the language of the "stone," though not always connected with the temple in the prophetic literature, often was. Zechariah 4 is typical in this regard:

> What are you, O great mountain? Before Zerubbabel you shall become a plain; and he shall bring out the top stone amid shouts of 'Grace, grace to it!' Moreover the word of the Lord came to me, saying, 'The hands of Zerubbabel have laid the foundation of this house; his hands shall also complete it (Zech 4:7–9a).[122]

In a similar vein, Isaiah prophesies:

> He [YHWH] will become a sanctuary, a stone one strikes against; for both houses of Israel he will become a rock one stumbles over—a trap and a snare for the inhabitants of Jerusalem. And many among them shall stumble; they shall fall and be broken; they shall be snared and taken (Isa 8:14–15).

In these passages the stone is essential in the temple edifice, and it is likely that the evangelists intended this allusion. In fact, the allusion to Isaiah 8:14 is made explicitly in Matthew and Luke with the additional description of these being the stone upon which people will stumble: "Everyone who falls on that stone will be broken to pieces; and it will crush anyone on whom it falls" (Luke 20:18).[123] Third, Isaiah's parable of the vineyard in Isaiah 5—the

---

119. Crossan, *Historical Jesus*, 351.

120. Kimball, "Jesus' Exposition of Scripture," 89.

121. Wagner, "Psalm 118," 172.

122. The *Targum Jonathan* interprets this messianically, expecting the revelation of the Messiah. See Churgin, *Targum Jonathan*, 124–25.

123. I use Luke's version here since it is more secure in the textual tradition. Matthew

subtext for the parable of the preceding wicked tenants—was connected with the temple in Jewish interpretation. The "watchtower" that the vineyard owner erects in Isaiah 5:2 is interpreted as the temple in the *Targum of Isaiah*.[124] Combining the parable's literary context with the way in which the prophetic literature used the terminology of the "stone" in conjunction with the temple's reconstruction, one can say the parable is about more than simply Jesus' rejection and vindication. It pronounces an indictment on the temple in Jesus' day.

The episode, therefore, advances at least two important things. First, the passage condemns those who oppose Jesus, particularly those upset about his recent actions in the temple. Jesus' comments in the passage rankle the leadership (Luke 20:19) and for good reason. They insinuate that "the present Temple and its present regime were regarded as part of the collection of the evil kingdoms."[125] Those who were plotting to lynch the son of the vineyard owner had set themselves up in opposition to the vineyard owner himself. Second, Jesus' statements suggest that he is forming a community or a movement that will essentially function as the temple's replacement.[126] When Jesus adopts the Psalm's use of the "cornerstone" to speak of himself and his movement, Jesus is doing something analogous to the Qumran community's application of this particular text. In the Scrolls, we find a peculiar instance where the Qumran community defined itself as a "precious cornerstone" and hence as a new "House of Holiness for Aaron."[127]

21:44, the corresponding verse in Matthew, still seems to warrant inclusion in the textual tradition. Only D, 33, several of the old Latin versions, the Sinaitic Syriac version, Irenaeus, Origen, and Eusebius omit the verse. The majority of manuscripts clearly favor the inclusion of the verse with support from several important manuscripts like: ℵ, B, C, L, W Z, Δ, Θ, 0102, 0233, family 1 and 13, and the Byzantine text type. Thus, the external evidence supports the inclusion. Moreover, the best explanation for a later entrance into the textual tradition would be a desire to harmonize the passage with Luke 20:18, which can be discounted because the wording in Luke and Matthew are significantly different. See Metzger, *Textual Commentary*, 47.

124. *Tg. Isa.* 5.2: "I sanctified them, and I made them glorious, I propped them up as a precious vine; and I built my sanctuary in the midst of them; and I gave also mine altar to make an atonement for their sins; and I thought that they should do good works before me, but they did evil works" (trans. Pauli).

125. Wright, *Jesus and the Victory of God*, 500-501. Cf. Olmstead, *Matthew's Trilogy*, 117.

126. In fact, the rending of the temple veil during Jesus' crucifixion in Mark 15:39 again points to the fact that Jesus functions as the replacement for the temple cult. See also Carroll and Green, *Death of Jesus*, 31-33.

127. 1QS VIII, 5-11 (Vermes). The atoning function of the community mentioned in this passage likewise corroborates the cultic function of the community, even in its isolation from the Jerusalem establishment. For another possible example along the same lines, see 4Q174.

In being a "cornerstone" they were functioning as a new temple, since their particular community rejected the Jerusalem temple because it had been commandeered by the wrong kinds of priests. Thus, there was a tendency within Second Temple Judaism to spiritualize the temple and locate it within the community that was following YHWH.[128] It seems entirely fitting to think that Jesus, in appropriating the cornerstone language about himself, is making a similar conclusion. In other words, when the Jerusalem leadership rejected the son, judgment would fall upon the leadership of Israel, which would result in the son's vindication. This vindication would also extend to those who followed Jesus because they would construct a "new people-temple."[129] In summary, the passage indicates that the expected eschatological temple would find its fulfillment in Jesus and his movement, rather than the edifice currently sitting on Mt. Zion.

Because of the latent replacement theology, the parable and the saying have been under pressure in recent decades to suppress any anti-Jewish content or meaning.[130] Though such efforts are understandable, such ideological agendas have distorted the parable's plain sense meaning.[131] This is not to say that the parable is anti-Semitic. After all, the vineyard of Isaiah (Israel) is not destroyed in the parable of the wicked tenants; the vineyard is kept and only the tenants (i.e. the leadership) are deposed in judgment.[132] Only in Matthew do we see an explicit mention of the transfer of the kingdom of God from the Jerusalem leadership to the ἔθνει (Matt 21:43) that performs the fruit of the kingdom. The reference to the ἔθνει indicates that a "*trans-ethnic* community of believers" will "replace the *nation* of Israel as subjects of the reign of God."[133] However, this does not mean that the Gentiles have supplanted the Jews in a supersessionistic state of affairs because Jews still make up part of this multi-ethnic group of believers.[134] Rather, just as Isaiah's

---

128. 4Q174 speaks of a "sanctuary of men" that will function as a temple offering sacrifices that are "the works of the Law." For further commentary on the subject, see McKelvey, *New Temple*, 46–53.

129. Watts, "Mark," 214. Cf. Moloney, *Mark*, 234 and Collins, *Mark*, 548.

130. E.g. Milavec, "Parable of the Wicked Husbandmen," 289–312 and Oldenhage, "Tainted Text," 165–76.

131. Snodgrass, "Wicked Tenants," 191–93.

132. Harrington, *Matthew*, 304–5.

133. Olmstead, *Matthew's Trilogy*, 117.

134. Ibid. He writes, "It will not do to identify this ἔθνος, on the one hand, merely as a new leadership group for Israel or, on the other, simply as the Gentiles who displace the Jews. This nation that God raises up in faithfulness to his promises to Abraham is defined along ethical—not ethnic lines, and . . . this ethical description of the new people functions both as an indictment of those now rejected and as a warning to those who would not be rejected."

warning implied that Israel could not presume her election would insulate her from the curses of the covenant, even so Jesus warns the leadership that their ethnicity was no guarantee of God's deliverance.[135] In view is the larger expectation that God's restoration of the world would bring in the Gentiles to worship Israel's God too. Thus, the passage again situates Jesus within the expectation that God would construct an eschatological temple, which has now become a spiritual reality in which both Jews and Gentiles participate.

Conclusion

While more could be said on the topic, this survey of how the Synoptics frame their individual narratives about Jesus and cast some of the significant events of his ministry reveals a significant point. The New Testament Gospels are not simply ready-made solutions in search of some kind of cultural or human problem to solve. They are narratives that presuppose the larger story of Israel and the problem or "state of deprivation" developed in that story. The previous chapter adumbrated Israel's canonical history, showing that she had been elected by YHWH to be his covenant partner. The covenant held out the hope of blessing should Israel maintain the covenant. Israel, however, abrogated the covenantal expectations, which resulted in exile under the Assyrians and Babylonians.

Despite the infidelity of his covenant partner, God promised to act on behalf of his people, to redeem them from their exilic plight. Israel's prophets spoke of a new age, an age wherein YHWH would bring his people back to the land in a new exodus. When he brought his people back to the land, he would renew the covenantal relationship with them when he forgave their sin, the divine spirit would be imparted to God's people to transform them, a new Davidic king would lead his people to righteousness and reign over God's kingdom, and the temple would be purified or rebuilt so the nations could come and worship Israel's God. While it is possible to say that the Babylonian exile technically terminated upon the return under Cyrus, I argued in the previous chapter that the Jewish people continued to expect a fuller restoration from their exilic conditions after the return under Cyrus. In other words, they still had not experienced full restoration from exile, though some of their sufferings were alleviated in periods of political autonomy or outright freedom in the centuries following the exile.

The story of Israel inheriting the land of promise, her exile from the land, and anticipated restoration form the prelude to the Synoptic Gospels, constituting the "state of deprivation" that needs to be remedied. As we saw

135. Evans, "Vineyard Parables," 82–86.

in this chapter, all the Synoptic evangelists take up Israel's hopes for restoration and direct them onto Jesus whom they identify as the central figure in God's program of restoration. The authors identify Jesus' ministry as the fulfillment of the restoration depicted in Second Isaiah, with Jesus as the central character. According to them, the very "good news" that Second Isaiah anticipated was coming to pass in the narratives the Gospels were telling about Jesus. Moreover, the Gospels inform us that Jesus' pedigree allows him to be the rightful heir to the Davidic covenant, and he can therefore fulfill the hope for an eschatological ruler who would conquer Israel's enemies and lead God's people in righteousness. At his baptism, Jesus is identified as the one who baptizes others with the divine Spirit and he assumes the Spirit-anointed role of the Son of God and God's servant. In addition, the main message of Jesus, namely that the kingdom of God had drawn near, likewise invoked the same story of Israel's hopes for restoration being fulfilled. Furthermore, Jesus' symbolic actions recalled these same hopes. Jesus' choice of twelve disciples symbolized the restoration of Israel's twelve tribes in a new exodus. His cleansing of the temple called Israel's central religious symbol to embody its eschatological role, which required its purification and welcoming of the Gentiles. Though more expressions of restoration are present within the Synoptics, what has been identified reveals that the Gospels are not narratives that stand on their own. They are narratives that presume the presence of Israel's larger story, and Jesus is a saving figure becomes he brings this story to its long awaited climax.[136]

This observation that the Synoptic Gospels presuppose an existing narrative, however imbedded in the Jewish worldview, is important for contemporary theology. It reveals that the Gospels are not solutions in search of a "state of deprivation" in order to make them complete or to establish Jesus as a saving figure. They already contain a presupposed "state of deprivation" wherein Jesus brings about the "state of release." For them, the "state of deprivation" is Israel's period of being under God's judgment during the exile and its lingering effects. Israel had yet to experience the restoration of its people, and this is the problem or "state of deprivation" that Jesus overcomes according to the Synoptics. The question for contemporary theology is whether their description of the "state of deprivation" is normative for current theological reflection or whether there is freedom to exchange it for another construct.

There are several reasons why subsequent interpretation of the Christ event should follow the path marked out by the evangelists. First, the Synoptic evangelists share this unified story despite the fact that they address

---

136. Tan, *Zion Traditions*, 219, 235.

various audiences. Matthew appears to be writing to a mixed audience of Jews and Gentiles, though the constituency seems to tilt toward a majority of Jewish folks since he sees no need to include Mark's explanations of Jewish customs.[137] Mark, however, must explain Jewish purity laws and other customs to his readers, which indicates his audience was mostly composed of Gentiles who were unfamiliar with such customs.[138] Luke ends his two-volume work with an indictment of Jewish obstinacy and hopes that the Gentiles would instead receive the Gospel. This rather pessimistic ending regarding the Jewish reception of the Gospel makes little sense if Luke's readers are Jewish, suggesting the intended recipients were Gentile.[139] Moreover, Luke's excision of issues like law-keeping that would have been important for Jewish readers corroborates the conclusion.[140] While the evangelists demonstrate freedom to shape their material in order to emphasize what was most relevant for their respective audiences, all of them find it necessary to situate Jesus within Israel's larger story. Certainly the predominantly Gentile settings were not without other possible "states of deprivation" that could have been constructed out of existential and theological material. Still, the Synoptic writers reveal a uniform conviction that Jesus is the savior within Israel's larger story of the world. This suggests that, even though the Gospel writers exhibit freedom to omit certain selections of Jesus' teaching or restructure it for the needs of their communities, they believed the larger story of Israel was essential for understanding the person and mission of Jesus, whether or not their readership had already adopted such a worldview as their own.

Second, there is a particular kind of privilege that should be afforded the Gospel writers along with others who propagated the early Christian *kerygma*. They were, after all, the first ones to proclaim Jesus as the savior. If modern Christians are going to stand with them and claim that Jesus is the savior, then it seems incumbent upon modern interpreters to ensure that their understanding of how Jesus saves at least coheres with those who first made the proclamation. If these original Christians had not identified and proclaimed Jesus as God's agent for restoring Israel, Jesus would simply be a name in Josephus' accounts of failed messianic imposters, and only

---

137. Brown, *New Testament*, 214–16. He suggests it was written to the church in Syrian Antioch. For a more predominantly Jewish audience, see Harrington, *Matthew*, 1–19.

138. Brown, *New Testament*, 161–63 and Witherington, *Mark*, 26–31.

139. More specifically, the audience could be a constituency of "god fearers" as argued in Nolland, *Luke 1–9:20*, xxxii–xxxiii. For an assertion of a more general Gentile audience, see Brown, *New Testament*, 269–71.

140. Evans, *Luke*, 3.

historians would know anything about him. It is only because Jesus could be identified as Israel's agent for restoration that the early Christians proclaimed that Jesus was God's savior. Only because of their testimony are people making the same claims today. If Jesus' story is not connected to any preceding history, but can be extracted and inserted into any soteriological construct of our choosing, then Jesus as a historically situated first century Jew no longer plays a necessarily central role in the divine drama. He could simply be interchanged with some other figure that speaks to the existential plight of humankind.

These considerations indicate that soteriology's task is not to find a "state of deprivation" that will make the Christ event relevant for our age. Rather, the task is to find a way of expanding the story that the Gospels tell so that it can be our story as well. This is not to deny interpreters the ability of utilizing modern advancements in human psychology or awareness of our existential deprivations, but instead to say that these cannot become the sum total of the human need for salvation. They can be utilized to extrapolate the human "state of deprivation" to the degree that it helps explain Israel's own plight waiting for God's restoration. The need for understanding how the story of Jesus is relevant to the twenty-first century will remain, but it does not give us freedom to revise that story in order create relevance. If Jesus is going to cease being the proverbial wax nose that is bent to justify every single theological program, then we must at least anchor Jesus within the historical context of his world, which was deeply informed by the larger story of God's dealings with Israel.[141]

With this in mind, we can return to our conversation with Girard. While Girard has constructed a compelling soteriological structure that puts Jesus at the transition point between humanity's "state of deprivation" and the "state of release," he can only do so by placing Jesus and the biblical texts within the larger story of the scapegoat mechanism and his account of human origins in the primordial past. The revelatory uniqueness of the Bible can only be discovered when Girard reads the biblical texts vis-à-vis mythological texts. Only when these other literary works are placed beside the biblical texts does the truth of the Bible emerge. Though Girard is able to identify allusions in the Gospels that might betray an awareness of the scapegoat mechanism—some of which can be downright uncanny—sometimes these identifications are unsatisfying or incomplete. What is more

---

141. Appeal to historical contexts has always been done to rein in the excesses of theological development. Johannes Weiss, for example, published *Jesus' Proclamation of the Kingdom of God* as a corrective to his own father-in-law's (Albrecht Ritschl) view of the kingdom. See Hiers and Holland, introduction to *Jesus' Proclamation of the Kingdom of God*, 1–54.

troubling, though, is the fact that Girard has little to say about a great deal of the restoration theology present in the Gospels. Most of it is ignored or reframed in support of his soteriology. One can at least wonder if Frei's fears have come true in Girard. The interpretive explanation found in the "story behind the story" has become enamoring to the point that the original story presupposed by the Gospels no longer appears essential to our understanding of them. While Girard is right to see Jesus as the focal point of God's revelation and that Jesus was an innocent victim on a Roman cross, I think he misses the fuller picture that the Gospels provide regarding Jesus' role in Israel's restoration.

If, in contrast to Girard, we follow the Gospels and see Jesus as the individual who inaugurated Israel's longed for restoration, then we are going to have to ask how his death and resurrection fit within this larger story. For example, does the death and resurrection of Jesus serve the more encompassing goal of restoring Israel? The next chapter will take up this very question by specifically investigating the most explicit set of passages where Jesus talks about the implications of his death with particular focus on the Last Supper sayings.

5

The Cross of Christ in Mark

UP TO THIS POINT, we have observed the fact that the Gospels situate Jesus within the larger narrative of Israel awaiting restoration. His ministry and proclamation of the kingdom coherently fit within this larger story. However, Jesus' life does not take the particular direction that one might expect for someone walking the dusty roads of Palestine proclaiming the imminent arrival of God's kingdom. He summons no major army and launches no political coup. To the contrary, Jesus meets his end on a Roman cross. Instead of wresting Palestine from Roman control, he dies at their hands. For some characters in the Gospels, this ends Jesus' bid to be Israel's messianic deliverer. However, the authors of the Gospels, along with his closest followers, continue to affirm that Jesus, in life *and* in death, is the one who restores Israel. What allows the authors of the Gospels to believe that Jesus, even as a dying Messiah, still remains the one to restore Israel, especially when his death might just as well be an abysmal failure?

The most clairvoyant answer to this question in the Gospels can be found in Jesus' words over the bread and the wine at the Last Supper. In each of the Synoptic Gospels, the Last Supper occurs in Jerusalem, hours before Jesus' arrest and crucifixion. Not only do these sayings immediately precede the crucifixion account, they also contain the densest and clearest articulation of the soteriological implications of Jesus' death. The next few chapters investigate how the Synoptic evangelists frame the saving significance of Jesus' death in the Last Supper accounts. Since these sayings record the speech of the Gospels' protagonist, they should be afforded the utmost weight for understanding how the Gospel writers—and most likely Jesus himself—understood how his death was part of Israel's restoration.[1] Following what is likely their chronological order—presuming Markan priority—we will analyze how each of the Synoptics records the Last Supper sayings, draw out the theological implications of the sayings, and then observe some of the ways in which the theological implications are present or operative in

---

1. Regarding the historicity of these sayings, see Meier, "The Eucharist," 335–51; Backhaus, "Hat Jesus," 343–56; and Pitre, *Last Supper*, 53-147.

other passages in the Gospels as well. As we will see, the Last Supper sayings are not isolated texts but the apexes of the theological implications present in the rest of the Gospel narratives.

Mark's Last Supper Account

As we turn our attention to the Gospel of Mark's Last Supper account, one can immediately observe that he introduces his account by framing it as a Passover celebration. The meal, as Mark describes it, occurred on "the first day of Unleavened Bread, when the Passover lamb is sacrificed" (Mark 14:12). The disciples who are aware of the date and the necessary preparations required for it ask Jesus: "Where do you want us to go and make the preparations for you to eat the Passover?" (Mark 14:12). Jesus then delegates the task of preparation to two of his disciples. That evening (Mark 14:17), Jesus arrived with his twelve disciples and eats with his disciples one last time.

Biblical scholars have long debated whether the Last Supper was in fact a Passover meal and if it actually fell on the day of the Passover feast. Some have balked at identifying the Last Supper meal as a Passover meal since some of the elements one would expect like the Passover lamb (the main course!), bitter herbs, and unleavened bread are never mentioned.[2] Moreover, the chronology of the events, especially the fact that Jesus dies on the following day, complicate the possibility that the Last Supper was a Passover feast because it would be unlikely for the Romans to execute Jesus during the festival.[3] In addition, Paul's account mentions nothing about the Passover, but simply talks of "the night when he was betrayed" (1 Cor 11:23). Probably the most difficult issue is that the Gospel of John presents an alternative chronology that departs from the Synoptics where Jesus dies on the day of preparation for the Passover rather than the day of Passover itself. In light of these considerations, some have discounted the Last Supper's historical association with the Passover altogether.

However, dissociating the Last Supper from the Passover celebration is unwarranted. Even if we concede the fact that later Jewish paschal traditions recorded in the Mishnah might not reflect its celebration in the first century,[4] there seems to be several peculiar parallels with later paschal traditions that

---

2. Delorme, "The Last Supper," 32–44. It is possible that such elements were dropped from the account since only the bread and wine were relevant for the church's observance of the Lord's Supper. In this regard, see Bornkamm, *Early Christian Experience*, 132–33 and Fuller, "Double Origin," 69.

3. Burkill, "The Last Supper," 161–77.

4. Bokser, "Last Supper," 24–33.

suggest the Last Supper was a Passover celebration of sorts.⁵ For example, the stipulations for Passover observance required one to eat the lamb in Jerusalem in the evening and remain within its environs for the night. All of this Jesus does, no longer returning to Bethany as he had done on previous nights.⁶ Moreover, the amount of preparation for the meal requiring the attention of two disciples would only be appropriate for the Passover or a celebration of similar importance. During the meal, the *paterfamilias* would preside over its various courses and interpret the various elements, which Jesus does for at least two of the elements, and it could be presumed that he did so for the others if they were present.⁷ In addition, they end the meal by singing a hymn (Mark 14:26), which was in accord with Passover tradition. Finally, even if Paul does not situate the Lord's Supper in the context of the Passover, he still refers to Jesus as the Passover lamb (1 Cor 5:7), which only makes sense if the Jesus tradition already had a reason to connect Jesus to this festival. For these reasons, the association between the Last Supper and the Passover cannot be dismissed as later projections upon the text, but as part of the context in which the meal occurred. Mark, at any rate, has certainly identified the meal as a Passover celebration in his account.⁸ As a result, many scholars suggest that, though the meal might have been celebrated early or at variance with usual custom, the meal was still Paschal in nature.⁹

5. See Jeremias, "Last Supper," 1–10 and Bahr, "Seder of Passover," 181–202.

6. Stein, *Jesus the Messiah*, 203–4.

7. Jeremias, *Eucharistic Words*, 41–84. Jeremias also argues that equating the Last Supper with Passover was at variance with early church tradition and therefore likely authentic. The only exception appears to be the Ebionites (ibid., 66). Others follow Jeremias in seeing the Last Supper as a Passover meal, e.g. Marshall, *Last Supper*, 58–62 and Nolland, *Luke 18:35–24:53*, 1055.

8. Casey, *Aramaic Sources*, 229. Against those who say this is a liturgical passage transposed into an institution narrative at the Passover, Casey writes, "This source was written by an Aramaic-speaking Jew from Israel, who was writing for people who shared *his* cultural assumptions. He thought he told us that this was a Passover meal in versus 12–16. He expected us to know what a Passover meal was like. Therefore he did *not* write an account of the meal. Rather, he narrated those aspects of the meal which enable us to understand how and why Jesus died" (ibid., 237; emphasis is his).

9. Witherington, *Mark*, 371; Marshall, *Last Supper*, 75; Wright, *Victory of God*, 555–56; and Bockmuehl, *This Jesus*, 93. Recently, Casey has argued that Rabbi Joshua's validation of Passover offerings sacrificed on Nisan 13 suggests that the great influx of pilgrims into Jerusalem required sacrifices to be performed a day early to accommodate everyone. For support, he cites *m. Zebaḥ.* 1:4. See Casey, *Aramaic Sources*, 226. In Neusner's version, the same saying is in *m. Zebaḥ.* 1:3: "The Passover which one slaughtered on the morning of the fourteenth [of Nisan] not for its own name ['under some other name']—R. Joshua declares valid, as if it were slaughtered on the thirteenth [of Nisan]." Adapted from Neusner, *Mishnah*, 699. The theory of different Jewish calendars

Without having to resolve the historical issues tidily, Mark's framing of the Last Supper within the Passover celebration has important theological implications. The Passover recalled Israel's historical past where God had miraculously intervened and rescued his people from slavery in Egypt. It is not surprising that Jesus uses this very festival that spoke of God's past intervention to signal once more that God's kingdom and rule was breaking into the world through the events about to transpire.[10] If, as I argued in the previous chapter, Jesus' story should be inlaid into the larger story of Israel, it should come as no surprise that Jesus, in the context of this festival, would draw upon Israel's past experience of salvation to declare that God was about to intervene once again.

"Take; this is my body"

Mark, in keeping with paschal tradition, notes that Jesus and the twelve came in the evening to eat the meal (Mark 14:17). After a short prediction that one of the twelve would betray him (Mark 14:18–21), Mark's account moves to some point in the middle of the meal—Mark says "while they were eating"—when Jesus "took a loaf of bread, and after blessing it he broke it, gave it to them, and said, 'Take; this is my body'" (Mark 14:22). The import of making an equation between the bread and Jesus is difficult to ascertain because Mark does not provide much detail or any explanatory phrases. In order to provide more explanation for the meaning of this phrase, some scholars have turned to a reconstructed rendition of the Aramaic. For such reconstructions, part of the issue hinges upon which Aramaic word was translated as σῶμά. Several options are possible. On the one hand, it could simply reflect an Aramaic idiom that was self-referential. In this case, the bread saying could simply be a reference to Jesus, meaning: "This is myself."[11] If the underlying Aramaic pointed toward Jesus' flesh or physical body rath-

---

with rival celebrations of the Passover was attractive to some, at least for a time: Jaubert, *Last Supper*; Gilmore, "Date and Significance," 256–69; Kodell, *The Eucharist*, 56, 66; and Kilmartin, *The Eucharist*, 37–48. There are, however, dissenters who conclude that Jesus had a farewell meal of some sort, but it was not in fact a Passover celebration. For this view, see Theissen and Merz, *The Historical Jesus*, 423–27. For a precise dating of the death of Jesus and its likely connection with the Passover chronology, see Brown, *Death of the Messiah*, 1350–78.

10. Jeremias, *Eucharistic Words*, 206. In subsequent years, traditions were recorded—whether these traditions were present in the first century cannot be proven—that expected the Messiah's return during the Passover. If current during the first century, Jesus' actions and words at the Last Supper would have contained a heightened sense of eschatological expectation.

11. Davies and Allison, *Matthew*, 3:471.

er than his person, there might be an interesting correlation with covenant ideology. Covenants extended kinship bonds to those who would not be privy to them normally. If Jesus equated his physical body with the bread, it is possible that Jesus is extending to his disciples the kinship established by the covenant that the words over the cup will make explicit.[12] Others have suggested that the reference to the bread implies that Jesus was a new Passover lamb, though this is not entirely persuasive.[13] If the Last Supper were a Passover celebration, then Jesus would have had a lamb at hand to use in reference to himself, and it would be likely that the tradition would have retained this as well had he said something along these lines. The absence of a saying over the lamb suggests that we are not to see the word over the bread as an identification of Jesus as the Passover lamb. Most likely the bread saying was self-referential, referring to Jesus' own self or body in some way. In addition, the bread saying likely assumes some of the Old Testament associations with it. Deuteronomy calls the Passover bread the "bread of affliction" (Deut 16:3), reflecting the painful process of leaving Egypt. This Old Testament connotation coupled with Jesus' action of breaking the bread suggests that the bread symbolizes the imminent suffering that Jesus was about to endure physically.[14] To put it simply, Jesus' words and actions over the bread emblematize his imminent suffering. Nevertheless, Jesus does not simply say that this will happen, he performs another symbolic sign, just as he did in the temple, that forever memorializes what is going to happen to him by breaking the physical bread in front of his disciples.[15]

"My Blood of the Covenant"

After speaking over the bread, Jesus takes a cup, blesses it, and has the disciples drink from it. The Passover meal as preserved in the Mishnah had a series of four cups, though whether the Mishnah reflects first-century

---

12. Cooke, "Eucharist as Covenant Sacrifice," 26–27. However, this is far from certain and other meanings are possible as well. See Casey, *Aramaic Sources*, 220, 239.

13. Koenig, *Feast of the World's Redemption*, 32. Jeremias suggests both sayings, "this is my body" and "this is my blood," designate Jesus as "the paschal lamb" (Jeremias, *Eucharistic Words*, 223). As the Passover lamb, Jesus secures redemption for others: "Jesus describes his death as this eschatological Passover sacrifice: *his vicarious . . . death brings into operation the final deliverance,* the new covenant of God" (ibid., 226). Jeremias overstepped the evidence for there is no suggestion that Jesus is making himself equivalent to the Passover lamb, even though Jeremias is correct regarding the eschatological and redemptive significance of the sayings.

14. Nolland, *Matthew*, 1075. Since Matthew follows Mark so closely here, Nolland's conclusions about Matthew's text are just as relevant to Mark.

15. Beck, "Last Supper," 192–98.

practice in this regard is unknown.¹⁶ If this particular meal followed the tradition of the four cup sequence, the readers are left ignorant of which cup it is, though some speculate that it was the third or fourth.¹⁷ The words over the cup are more explicative than those over the bread. Regarding the cup Jesus says, "This is my blood of the covenant (τὸ αἷμά μου τῆς διαθήκης), which is poured out for many" (Mark 14:24).

The statement is densely packed with allusions to several important Old Testament texts. On the one hand, Jesus equates the cup with "my blood of the covenant" which basically matches Exodus 24:8 in the LXX. In Exodus 24, Moses ratifies the covenant with YHWH and does so by offering sacrifices on Mt. Sinai. To inaugurate the covenant on Mt. Sinai, Moses takes the blood from the offerings and separates it into two portions. The first portion he dashes against the altar, but the second he sprinkles on the people and says, "See the blood of the covenant (τὸ αἷμα τῆς διαθήκης) that the Lord has made with you in accordance with all these words" (Exodus 24:8 LXX). Thus, when Jesus identifies the cup as his "blood of the covenant" there is a direct allusion back to the covenant-inaugurating sacrifice on Sinai.

What is the significance of making an allusion to the covenant sacrifice on Sinai? First, the allusion establishes the fact that Israel's expectation of a renewed covenantal relationship with YHWH is being fulfilled. Restoration theology, as discussed in the previous chapters, was not just an alteration in a political reality. It was also supposed to result in a new theological reality wherein Israel would be reunited to YHWH in a covenantal relationship. Jesus is saying that in the shedding of his blood, the moment of Israel's restoration was coming to fulfillment. Just like the former Passover from Egypt allowed Israel to enter into a covenant with God at Sinai, the Last Supper expected the covenantal relationship to be re-instantiated.¹⁸ As Cooke avers: "To a group of Jews gathered together for the paschal dinner that commemorated the Exodus, the words 'blood of the covenant' could not but recall the blood that Moses poured upon the altar and sprinkled over the people to signify and effect the divine-human brotherhood of the covenant."¹⁹

Second, the process of renewing the covenant often involved making atonement for the breach in the relationship. If the covenant had been broken by sin, then a means of atonement was essential in order to renew the relationship. I would contend that when the Last Supper sayings allude to

---

16. *m. Pesaḥ*, 10.2–7 (Neusner).

17. Nolland, *Matthew*, 1077. The third cup was a "cup of blessing . . . because the after-dinner grace came with it."

18. LaVerdiere, *Dining in the Kingdom*, 137.

19. Cooke, "Covenant Sacrifice," 33.

the sacrifice on Sinai, they are not simply stating that the covenant has been renewed, they are also indicating *how* this state of affairs comes about. To put it plainly, the allusion to the sacrifice on Sinai identifies Jesus' death as a means of atonement to repair the covenant. In other words, the allusion to Sinai "indicates that Jesus' death" effects a change "in the relationship between God and his people, Israel."[20] This fundamental change is the reason why the covenantal relationship with God can be re-forged.

This, however, is not the view of all. Some scholars and theologians, aware that the "blood of the covenant" alludes to Exodus 24:8, deny there is any implicit reference to atonement when it is taken up at the Last Supper. For example, James Alison believes the sacrificial allusion implies the subversion of sacrificial practices altogether, even though there is nothing in the text to support this, in my view.[21] Finlan attempts to avoid the overtones of atonement in the Last Supper sayings by asserting that Jesus' reference to "a new covenant ceremony" would bypass "any appeasing or substitutionary significance" because "the 'blood' image is not expiatory but enacts the community-creating function of a covenant sacrifice."[22] Likewise Koenig, who seems willing to say Jesus offers himself vicariously for others, still does not think that the allusion to Exodus 24:8 portrays Jesus as "a sacrifice for sin."[23] Following suit, Dowd and Malbon say the allusion simply means that "those whom God had liberated were in covenant relationship with God, not because their sins had been forgiven, but because God had liberated them. Their sins would have to be forgiven ... but that was not accomplished by the 'blood of the covenant.'"[24] Suffice it to say, these examples show that various scholars observe the allusion to the sacrifice on Sinai but do not believe the allusion indicates Jesus' death has atoning value.

If the covenant sacrifice of Exodus is only understood in light of the cultic practices of the Ancient Near East, the non-atoning view of the allusion at the Last Supper might be correct. Old Testament commentators have given various interpretations of the account of covenant sacrifice in Exodus. Many see the blood sprinkled on the people as a symbolic demonstration that covenants establish kinship between the parties involved.[25] In other

20. Casey, *Aramaic Sources*, 241.

21. Alison, *Being Wrong*, 172.

22. Finlan, *Options on Atonement*, 39. Cf. Léon-Dufour, *Sharing the Eucharistic Bread*, 144–46.

23. Koenig, *Feast*, 40. Koenig even says Jesus is "a ransom to free Israel from all forms of bondage," so there does not appear to be any theological motive for denying the sacrificial element in the passage.

24. Dowd and Malbon, "Jesus' Death in Mark," 292–93.

25. McCarthy, *Treaty and Covenant*, 162–63; Polak, "Covenant at Mount Sinai," 130–31; and Sarna, *Exodus*, 152.

words, the covenant begets a relationship between two formerly unrelated parties with the effect that they are related, as if by a biological bloodline. Others have suggested that the sprinkling of blood symbolizes the dire consequences of those who break the covenant.[26] In this view, anyone who breaks the covenant would be killed and have their blood shed just like the inaugurating sacrifice. For some authors, more than one interpretation is needed to make sense of the ritual of covenant sacrifice.[27] Unfortunately, Exodus does not interpret the meaning of the blood ritual on Sinai.[28] In the time period in which Exodus was written and edited, the sacrificial rite that inaugurated the covenant did not necessarily involve any overt atoning or expiatory effect, which means there is reason to consider the conclusions of Finlan, Koenig, and Dowd and Malbon.

Nevertheless, this does not conclude the matter. Ideas and interpretations change over time, and such is the case with the Jewish understanding of the sacrifice on Sinai. Because Exodus 24 lacks any kind of interpretive element explaining the importance of the ritual, later Jewish commentators felt compelled to clarify the meaning of the ritual, and they did so by explicitly imparting an atoning significance to it. For example, *Targum Onqelos* explicitly gives the sacrifice on Sinai atoning value by inserting the following explanatory phrases in italics into Exodus 24:8: "Whereupon Moses took the blood and sprinkled it *on the altar to atone for the people*, and he said, '*Here, this* is the blood of the covenant which the Lord has established with you in accordance with all these words.'" Likewise, *Targum Pseudo-Jonathan* follows suit: "Then Moses took *the half of* the blood *that was in the dashing-basins* and dashed (it) *against the altar to make atonement for* the people; and he said, 'Behold, this the blood of the covenant which the Lord has made with you in accordance with all these words.'" Both of these Targums have inserted explanatory phrases that explicitly make atonement the chief function of the covenant sacrifice. Thus, even if the ritual of covenant sacrifice was originally void of atoning significance, the diachronic history reveals that the covenant sacrifice eventually took on such connotations. Unfortunately, the current state of Targumic research does not permit us

---

26. Propp, *Exodus 19–40*, 308–9.

27. Hahn, *Kinship by Covenant*, 46–59. Nicholson takes a different tack and argues that blood was holy and therefore sanctified both the altar and the people whom it touched. Nicholson, "Covenant Ritual," 82–83. Hendel emphasizes the fact that the blood would serve as a communicative reminder of the covenant's reality, even though it would not delete other meanings like threat or atonement. Hendel, "Sacrifice as a Cultural System," 366–90. See also Hilber, "Theology of Worship," 182.

28. Childs comments, "for the Exodus narrative the importance lies with the effect of the rite and not with the theory behind it." Childs, *Exodus*, 506.

to conclude with absolute confidence that the Targums reflect first century interpretation on their basis alone.[29]

However, there is evidence that the understanding of the covenant sacrifice had taken on other connotations by the first century like purification and atonement.[30] Philo, though utilizing his trademark allegorical interpretation, describes some kind of purifying effect in the sacrifice on Sinai.[31] If the covenant blood originally signified a kinship bond or the punishment of breaking the covenant, it no longer had such meaning for Philo, even if he is not entirely in accord with the Targums. Philo at least demonstrates that the historical study of the ritual enacted in Exodus 24 cannot be used to limit its meaning in the first century.

Nevertheless, other evidence does prove that the Targumic interpretation of the atoning covenant sacrifice on Sinai was indeed present in the first century and current within first century Christian communities, the Epistle to the Hebrews.[32] Hebrews 9:18–20 recounts the sacrifice on Sinai in the following way:

> Hence not even the first covenant was inaugurated without blood. For when every commandment had been told to all the

---

29. In recent studies of Aramaic's evolution and the intertextual relationships between the Targums, Flesher and Chilton have persuasively argued that *Targum Onqelos*, at least its earliest form, was composed between 50 and 150 CE (*Targums*, 155). The earliest version of *Targum Onqelos* introduced a series of expansions that were later adopted by the other Targums like *Pseudo-Jonathan*. According to their analyses, *Pseudo-Jonathan* was completed by 400 CE (ibid., 157–59). Based upon the lack of loan words from Arabic, they argue that all of the Targums were completed before the Islamic period. It is troubling that *Targum Neofiti* fails to include the addition noted above, which should theoretically be present if the addition were a part of the earlier form that underlies *Targum Onqelos* and the Palestinian Targums. If Chilton and Flesher's chronology of Targumic origins is valid, this expansion in *Targum Onqelos* might come from the later stages of *Targum Onqelos*' composition. However, it should be noted that only a portion of the expansions of *Onqelos* make it into *Neofiti*, which means that this addition might still have been original to the earlier substratum of *Targum Onqelos* and simply not adopted by *Neofiti* for some unknown reason. On the partial inclusion of *Onqelos*' earlier expansions, see Flesher, "Targum Onqelos," 35–79. The absence of this particular verse from fragments of the Palestinian Targums prohibits us from ascertaining whether this addition was a part of the earliest stage of *Onqelos* or the later, though there is a possibility it was present in the earlier stage.

30. Brant Pitre suggests that Exodus 24:5–8 LXX and 4Q504 2.8–11 hint at developing notions of atoning blood. Personally, these two texts are too ambiguous to be cited positively as evidence. See Pitre, *Last Supper*, 111–12.

31. See Philo, *Her.*, 182–88.

32. Allison, *New Moses*, 258–59 and Davies and Allison, *Matthew*, 3:475. Interestingly, Hebrews is the biblical book that Girard, at least originally, believed did exhibit a "sacrificial interpretation" of the cross. Girard, *Things Hidden*, 224.

people by Moses in accordance with the law, he took the blood of calves and goats, with water and scarlet wool and hyssop and sprinkled both the scroll itself and all the people, saying, "This is the blood of the covenant that God has ordained for you."[33]

At this point, the author has basically recounted the Sinai sacrifice as recorded in Exodus 24.[34] The author then goes on to make the point—in an almost Targumic expansion—that the blood poured out on Sinai had an atoning function: "Indeed, under the law almost everything is purified with blood, and without the shedding of blood there is no forgiveness of sins" (Heb 9:22).[35] For the author of Hebrews, forgiveness and atonement can only be attained through the shedding of blood, and the sacrifice on Sinai attained atonement for Israel to enter into the covenant.[36] A few verses later, his attention turns from Moses' covenant sacrifice to the sacrifice of the new covenant. The author of Hebrews declares Jesus "has appeared once for all at the end of the age to remove sin by the sacrifice of himself" (Heb 9:26b). Not surprisingly, Hebrews possesses one of the strongest affirmations in the New Testament that the new covenant age has begun (Heb 8:1–13). For the author of Hebrews, the forgiveness of sins promised in the new covenant could only arrive if atonement were made first, which Jesus did on the cross. Thus, even if a person discounts the Targumic evidence as late, Hebrews reveals that the atoning interpretation of the Sinai sacrifice existed in the first century and that this same interpretation influenced at least one author of the New Testament.[37]

Now some might object to this dependence on Hebrews by citing Moffitt's recent argument that Hebrews assumes Jesus makes atonement by

---

33. There is a significant departure here from the LXX. Scholars debate whether Eucharistic traditions might have influenced Hebrews' composition. See Ellingworth, *Hebrews*, 469–70 and Johnson, *Hebrews*, 241.

34. There are, however, some differences that suggest conflation with other sacrificial rituals. See Koester, *Hebrews*, 419.

35. Dunnill writes, "Nonetheless, the covenant-sacrifice, as described here, has been subsumed into the dominant ideology of expiation, as a type of sin-offering, in line with a widespread intertestamental trend already described . . . ." Dunnill, *Covenant and Sacrifice*, 127; cf. 250–51. Hahn arrives at this same conclusion via a different route. Rather than arguing that the Sinai sacrifice had atoning significance, he takes the sacrifice as a "self-maledictory" ritual that had to be exacted before the covenant could be renewed. See Hahn, "Broken Covenant," 416–36.

36. Sanders also observes that first century belief regarded sacrifice as necessary for atonement and expanded atoning value to sacrificial practices that originally lacked it. See Sanders, *Judaism*, 252.

37. The date of Hebrews is debated, but usually still placed within the latter portion of the first century. For a dating before the fall of the temple, see Barton, "Hebrews," 195–207.

offering his resurrected life to God rather than dying on the cross.[38] Though he does see the death of Jesus as a necessary component of the process by which Jesus acquires atonement, it seems that Jesus' death is only a necessary precondition for Christ's resurrected life. In his concluding chapter he writes, "The logic of sacrifice in the biblical account is not a logic centered on slaughter, but a logic centered on the presentation of blood/life before God."[39] He further concludes that "Jesus' death" was not the effective cause of the atonement but rather "the necessary event that set into motion the sequence that resulted in the offering that effected the full atonement he obtained."[40] Thus, the event that acquired atonement was not the cross, though it was a necessary precursor, but rather Jesus' offering of himself as a resurrected high priest in the heavenly sanctuary.

However, for as helpful as Moffitt's study has been in refocusing attention on the implicit logic of resurrection in Hebrews, it is even more supportive for my argument that it is precisely when the author of Hebrews introduces the covenant sacrifice on Sinai into his more extensive reflection on Yom Kippur, as the author does in Hebrews 9:15-22, that Moffitt is forced to qualify his conclusions and retract the extent to which some of his claims can speak for the entirety of Hebrews. For example, when he comments on Hebrews 9:15-22 he concedes, " . . . the near context of Heb 9:15 presents other challenges to the larger argument of this study."[41] At this point, he acknowledges that one can no longer assert that the author of Hebrews always equated blood with Jesus' resurrected life and not his death on the cross. On the basis of the same passage, one can go even further than Moffitt does here and contend that it is questionable to claim that, in Hebrews, atonement and redemption are only acquired by the offering of Christ's resurrected life. Hebrews 9:15 indicates Jesus' death is also *an effective cause*—though Hebrews as a whole might not make it the only cause—of redemption and atonement: "For this reason he is the mediator of a new covenant, so that those who are called may receive the promised eternal inheritance, because a death has occurred that redeems them from the transgressions under the first covenant."[42] Thus, in my view, a close reading of Moffitt's study does not undermine but rather affirms the argument being made here on the basis of what he cannot claim in light of Hebrews 9:15-22.

---

38. Moffitt, *Atonement*.
39. Ibid., 299.
40. Ibid; Cf. pages 285-90 of the same work.
41. Ibid., 290.
42. For a supporting interpretation, see Attridge, *Hebrews*, 254-55.

I contend that the allusion to the Sinai sacrifice in Mark's Last Supper saying follows in the exegetical trajectory found in the book of Hebrews and the Targums. Finlan, Koenig, and Dowd and Malbon can only dismiss the atoning function of the covenant sacrifice because they anachronistically overlook the exegetical traditions that were current in the first century. Furthermore, in the next section we will see that Matthew—the earliest commentator on Mark, presuming the hypothesis of Markan priority is correct—certainly reads Mark in this particular way. If the evidence is assembled together—the fact that Jewish interpretation of the covenant sacrifice assumes atoning efficacy, that Hebrews explicitly locates this interpretation of Jesus' death in the first century, and that Matthew reads Mark in this particular way—we can conclude with a high degree of probability that Mark's allusion to the covenant sacrifice on Sinai implied Jesus' death atoned for sin as well.[43]

More, however, can be said. The phrase "my blood of the covenant" is allusive of other Old Testament texts as well. In Zechariah 9:11 YHWH says, "As for you also, because of the blood of my covenant (בְּדַם־בְּרִיתֵךְ) with you, I will set your prisoners free from the waterless pit." The NRSV has taken some interpretive liberties here since the first person possessive pronoun suffix "my" is not present in the Hebrew.[44] Regardless, the surrounding context is an oracle predicting the arrival of Jerusalem's humble king and YHWH's deliverance of Israel from her enemies. This particular verse weds the renewing of the covenant to other dimensions of Israel's restoration and it does so by introducing the presence of blood, quite possibly the means of renewing the covenant through atonement. When it comes to the allusions present in Mark's version of the Last Supper, we should not be forced to choose between Zechariah 9:11 and Exodus 24:8, since both are likely in view.[45] In fact, Zechariah 9:11 is likely an allusion to the covenant ceremony on Sinai as well since Jewish interpretation typically connected this oracle to the Exodus.[46] The one thing, however, that makes an allusion to Zechariah 9:11 likely is the fact that the context possesses a "redemptive" and

---

43. Pesch, *Das Abendmahl*, 95.

44. For a defense of the NRSV's rendering, see Mitchell, Smith, and Bewer, *Haggai, Zechariah, Malachi and Jonah*, 278.

45. Commenting on Matthew but still applicable here, see Moss, *The Zechariah Tradition*, 151–55.

46. Meyers and Meyers, *Zechariah 9–14*, 139–40. The *Targum of the Minor Prophets* also interpreted Zechariah 9:11 this way: "You also, *for whom* a covenant *was made* by blood, *I have delivered you from bondage to the Egyptians, I have supplied your needs in a wilderness desolate as an empty pit in which* there is no water." The italics represent the interpretive elements included in the reading of the text. Cited from Cathcart and Gordon, *Targum of the Minor Prophets*.

"eschatological" horizon that is similar to the Last Supper sayings, which Exodus 24 cannot claim, even though the Greek of Mark 14:24 matches that of Exodus 24:8.[47] In addition, the Isaianic figure of the servant also might be in view, which certainly comes into focus when we look at the later phrases of the cup saying. Though many fail to observe the Servant's role in establishing the covenant (Isa 42:6; 49:8), it is not impossible that the covenant-making role of Isaiah's servant or a similar eschatological expectation is also in view.[48] Some have also suggested that the new covenant promises of Jeremiah 31 are present in the covenantal allusions of Mark's text. The argument for this is based on the following verse where Jesus says, "Truly I tell you, I will never again drink of the fruit of the vine until that day when I drink it new (καινὸν) in the kingdom of God" (Mark 14:25). Those who argue for an allusion to Jeremiah's new covenant suggest that the use of "new" (καινὸν) signals the new covenant allusion too.[49] This, however, seems tendentious since the word "new" is never applied to the covenant but to the drinking of wine. Of the allusions present in the covenantal saying, the allusions to Exodus 24:8 and Zechariah 9:11 are the most probable because of the lexical similarity Mark's saying over the cup has with Exodus 24 and the eschatological similarity shared in conjunction with Zechariah 9.

"Which is Poured out for Many"

The sacrificial language that is present in the phrase "my blood of the covenant" is also present in the latter half of the cup saying where Jesus describes his blood as that "which is poured out for many" (Mark 14:24).[50] The reference to Jesus' blood being "poured out (ἐκχυννόμενον)" could allude to several things. It could, for instance, allude to a violent death at the hands of others, which is how the phraseology is utilized in several instances in the Septuagint (Lev 17:4; Num 35:33; Deut 19:10, 21:7, etc.). This is the view of Léon-Dufour who used the point to deny any reference to sacrifice in the

---

47. Lindars, *New Testament Apologetic*, 132–33.

48. One of the earlier few who emphasized the Servant's role in the renewing of the covenant is Kilmartin, *Eucharist*, 54–55. It is now heartily adopted in Pitre, *Last Supper*, 100–104.

49. So Combrink, "Salvation in Mark," 56. Others also posit a reference to the new covenant rather affirmatively: France, *Mark*, 570; Witherington, *Mark*, 374; Evans, *Mark 8:27—16:20*, 392–94; Pesch, *Das Abendmahl*, 95; and Moloney, *A Body Broken*, 54. I am still more inclined to follow Davies and Allison who remain skeptical of the connection with Jeremiah (*Matthew*, 3:473–74) without denying its possibility.

50. Casey writes of this verse, "The imagery is necessarily sacrificial, looking forward to the redemptive significance of Jesus' forthcoming death." Casey, *Aramaic Sources*, 241.

Last Supper sayings.[51] However, as we saw earlier, such cultic allusion is already present in the phrase, "my blood of the covenant." Thus, if the pouring out of Jesus' blood simply refers to a violent death, it cannot exclude a sacrificial allusion. In fact, the phrase could be a sacrificial allusion because the language of pouring out blood is used in Leviticus for expiatory sacrifices (Lev 4:7, 18, 25, 30, 34).[52] Consequently, it is possible that an intentional sacrificial allusion is present. In addition, the "pouring out" could also reflect the language of Isaiah's suffering servant who "poured out (הֶעֱרָה) himself to death" (Isa 53:12 MT).[53] What strengthens the possibility that the Isaianic servant might be in view is the following prepositional phrase, "for many (ὑπὲρ πολλῶν)" (Mark 14:24). Many scholars have concluded that this phrase constitutes an intentional allusion to Isaiah's final servant song since the Servant bears "the sin of many (πολλῶν)" (Isaiah 53:12 LXX).[54] If so, Jesus has been explicitly cast in the role of Isaiah's suffering servant who took on the transgressions and iniquities of others, which certainly fits with the interpretation taken above regarding the allusion to the sacrifice on Sinai. At the very least, the preposition ὑπέρ ("for") establishes Jesus' death as an event that will benefit others.[55] The former part of the cup saying has already identified what this benefit will be, namely, a reinstitution of the covenantal relationship with God. Here, it becomes clear that Jesus is willingly and sacrificially offering his life in order to bring others into the restored covenantal relationship with God.

---

51. So Léon-Dufour, *Eucharistic Bread*, 143. For him the cultic language is not in view in the entire saying.

52. Collins, "Mark's Interpretation," 550. See also Collins, *Mark*, 656; France, *Mark*, 570; Evans, *Mark 8:27–16:20*, 394; Kilmartin, *Eucharist*, 55; and Nolland, *Matthew*, 1079. Nolland suggests that the allusion to animal sacrifice is more prevalent here since crucifixion did not involve a great deal of spilled blood.

53. Evans, *Mark 8:27–16:20*, 393; Burkill, "Last Supper," 172; and Kodell, *Eucharist*, 65, 101. There is no apparent lexical dependence on the LXX at this point, but it possibly reflects the MT's reading of הֶעֱרָה.

54. Jeremias, *Eucharistic Words*, 226–27; Combrink, "Salvation in Mark," 52; France, *Mark*, 570–71; Marshall, *Last Supper*, 43, 89–91; Nolland, *Matthew*, 1081; Harrington, *Matthew*, 368; Carroll and Green, *Death of Jesus*, 44n17; Schnelle, *Theology of the New Testament*, 161; Schnackenburg, *Matthew*, 268; Meyer, "The Expiation Motif," 18–19; Perry, *Exploring the Evolution*, 24; Evans, *Mark 8:27–16:20*, 392; Benoit, "The Accounts of the Institution," 79–80; and Edwards, *Mark*, 427. There is no need to follow Pesch here and see the "many" as only Israel. In the context of the Gospels, it appears that the phrase "for many" would have in mind those outside of Israel's community as well. Contra Pesch, *Das Abendmahl*, 108, 122. Dunn, however, questions such certitude. See Dunn, *Jesus Remembered*, 815–16.

55. BDAG, 1030. It could in fact imply that Jesus' death was substitutionary or in the place of the "many." So Wallace, *Greek Grammar*, 383–89.

At this juncture, if we take a step back and ask how the words spoken over the bread and the wine make sense within the larger story of Israel, we find a remarkable coherence. The setting of the meal within the context of the Passover recalled Israel's story of being God's people whom he liberated from Pharaoh's oppressive rule in order to enter into covenant with them. That covenant had been broken by subsequent generations who had proven unfaithful. The previous chapter made the case that Jesus' ministry and proclamation of the kingdom are best understood against the backdrop of Israel's hopes for restoration, which had yet to dawn for the Jews of the first century.[56] One of these hopes for restoration was the reconstitution of the covenant relationship. At the Last Supper, Jesus establishes his death as the means by which the covenant with God is restored. This would imply that his death would be the means of atoning for Israel's transgression of the covenant and commence Israel's restoration.

All this comes to the fore in Jesus' last statement of the Last Supper in Mark where he says, "Truly I tell you, I will never again drink of the fruit of the vine until that day when I drink it new in the kingdom of God" (Mark 14:25). In light of what Jesus has said in the previous two verses about his death constituting the renewal of the covenant, his resolute expectation that the next great moment would be the arrival of the kingdom means his death would be one of the means by which Israel's restoration would arrive.[57]

Integration with the Rest of the Gospel

Though the Last Supper delivers Mark's most explicit statement on the soteriological implications of Christ's death, the sayings are of a piece with the larger flow of Mark's narrative. Mark's Gospel records several instances where Jesus predicts he would suffer and die, which are indicative of Mark's soteriology. Each prediction builds on the former and provides new insight into the meaning and causes behind his suffering. The first of these predictions occurs immediately after Peter's confession that Jesus is the Messiah (Mark 8:29). At this point, Jesus "began to teach them that the Son of Man must (δεῖ) undergo great suffering, and be rejected by the elders, the chief priests, and the scribes, and be killed, and after three days rise again" (Mark 8:31). The prediction imparts a particular necessity to

---

56. Nolland, *Matthew*, 1080.

57. Wright, *Victory of God*, 561–63 and Pitre, *End of the Exile*, 444–48. In my view, there is no need to create a false dichotomy where one is forced to choose between an "eschatological soteriology" wherein forgiveness is offered with the kingdom's arrival and a "staurological soteriology" whereby forgiveness is attained by the expiatory death of Jesus as Schwager does. See Schwager, "Christ's Death," 111.

the future suffering and resurrection with the insertion of the word δεῖ, suggesting that something within the divine will mandates this necessity.[58] Other passages in Mark suggest the necessity comes from the precedent outlined in the Scriptures (Mark 9:12; 14:21, 49). The agents who reject Jesus are clearly identified here as the Jewish leaders. At their behest, Jesus would suffer and die. What is particularly important about this prediction, especially in light of its context, is that it weds Jesus' future death and suffering with his messianic identity. Peter fails to understand how the messianic role would involve suffering (Mark 8:32), but this is precisely what Jesus embraces. Despite folding suffering into the messianic mission, suffering is not the end state, for the prediction culminates with the resurrection and vindication of the Messiah.

The second prediction occurs in the following chapter as Jesus and his disciples are passing through Galilee. On the way, Jesus says, "The Son of Man is to be betrayed into human hands (εἰς χεῖρας ἀνθρώπων), and they will kill him, and three days after being killed, he will rise again" (Mark 9:31). The content essentially matches the first prediction, but instead of identifying the instigators as the Jewish leaders like the first prediction, Jesus says he will fall "into human hands." The phrase does not simply broaden the list of culprits to the Romans nor clarify that the perpetrators are human. Quite significantly, it brings Israel's exilic punishment into view.

In the Septuagint, this expression is used in several ways that are likely informative for our understanding of the expression in Mark 9:31. In the first way, it signifies God's handing over of a nation to judgment by foreign powers, which was true of Israel in the exile. In Isaiah 19:4, YHWH says, "I will deliver the Egyptians into the hand of a hard master (LXX: εἰς χεῖρας ἀνθρώπων); a fierce king will rule over them, says the Sovereign, the Lord of hosts." The context of exile is also in view later when Isaiah warns the scroll might fall "εἰς χεῖρας ἀνθρώπου" when Israel is overwhelmed by her enemies in Isaiah 29:12. A couple of times it is used to refer to an alternate form of punishment and justice than what God would bring. When David has sinned and judgment is imminent, he prefers to fall into God's hands rather than "εἰς χεῖρας ἀνθρώπου" because God has mercy, unlike humans (2 Sam 24:14; 1 Chron 21:13).[59] In these passages, it likewise refers to a form of punishment. Finally, it could also mean given over to executioners, as in Jeremiah's case, where King Zedekiah swears to Jeremiah, "I will not put you to death or hand you over to these men (εἰς χεῖρας τῶν ἀνθρώπων) who

---

58. See Bolt, *From a Distance*, 49–50.

59. Sirach 2:18 expresses the same set of alternatives: "Let us fall into the hands of the Lord, but not into the hands of mortals; for equal to his majesty is his mercy, and equal to his name are his works."

seek your life" (Jer 38:16; LXX 45:16).⁶⁰ When it is utilized in Mark 9:31, Jesus' death is already in view, so the phrase is unlikely to be a redundant affirmation that Jesus will die. Instead, being betrayed "into human hands" likely implies that Jesus would share in Israel's exilic punishment.⁶¹

If Jesus' participation in Israel's exilic suffering is not in view in the second prediction, it certainly comes into focus in the third. On the way to Jerusalem, Jesus again says to his disciples, "See we are going up to Jerusalem, and the Son of Man will be handed over to the chief priests and the scribes, and they will condemn him to death; then they will hand him over to the Gentiles (παραδώσουσιν αὐτὸν τοῖς ἔθνεσιν); they will mock him, and spit upon him, and flog him, and kill him; and after three days he will rise again" (Mark 10:33–34). This prediction introduces all of the complicit parties and gives a far more detailed accounting of what will happen at his crucifixion like being mocked, flogged, and spat upon. Particularly noteworthy is that Jesus says the authorities will "hand him over to the Gentiles." The notion of being "handed over to the Gentiles" is a theologically significant phrase, which is allusive of Israel's exilic punishment. For instance, Psalm 105 speaks of God's response to Israel's unfaithfulness by invoking the phrase: " . . . he gave them into the hand of the nations (בְּיַד־גּוֹיִם), so that those who hated them ruled over them" (Ps 106:41; LXX 105:41).⁶² In the same manner, Hosea 8:10 LXX (not MT) also refers to the time of exile as the time when Israel was "παραδοθήσονται ἐν τοῖς ἔθνεσι." Ezekiel likewise pronounces judgment on Egypt by saying that YHWH "gave it into the hand of the prince of the nations (παρέδωκα αὐτὸν εἰς χεῖρας ἄρχοντος ἐθνῶν)" as a means of punishing them for their arrogance (Ezek 31:11; cf. 30:23, 26; 31:17).

Even a portion of the phrase, "among the nations/Gentiles," also referred to Israel's exilic punishment. The Pentateuch said that the punishment for breaking the covenant was that God would scatter Israel or let Israel perish "among [all] the nations" (Lev 26:33, 38; Deut 4:27). The prophetic texts similarly warn that God would "scatter them among the nations" in the imminent exilic punishment (Jer 9:16). Ezekiel uses the same language to captures Israel's exilic state:

> And they shall know that I am the Lord, when I disperse them among the nations (ἐν τοῖς ἔθνεσι) and scatter them through the countries. But I will let a few of them escape from the sword, from famine and pestilence, so that they may tell of their

---

60. In this regard, see also 1 Chron 21:13.
61. See also Bolt, *From a Distance*, 53–54.
62. The LXX has the following: "παρέδωκεν αὐτοὺς εἰς χεῖρας ἐχθρῶν."

abominations among the nations (ἐν τοῖς ἔθνεσι) where they go; then they shall know that I am the Lord (Ezek 12:15–16 LXX; cf. 4:13; 6:9; 20:23; 22:15).

Lamentations mourns the fact that "Judah has gone into exile with suffering and hard servitude; she lives now among the nations (ἐν ἔθνεσιν)" (Lam 1:3a. LXX; cf. 2:9; 4:20). Israel's cry in exile would later implore God to rescue them "from among the nations (ἐκ τῶν ἐθνῶν)" (1 Chron 16:35 LXX). The implication is that when Jesus is said to be handed over to the nations in this final Passion prediction, the text is mapping Jesus onto Israel's exilic experience. In other words, Jesus' imminent crucifixion would participate in Israel's exilic punishment, which is important for making sense of how Jesus' death brings restoration to Israel.[63] Like the former predictions, this one too anticipates Jesus' resurrection. In short, the prediction shows that what is about to happen to Jesus in his death and resurrection is a microcosm of Israel's experience of exile and restoration. As the Messiah, his suffering will participate in Israel's exilic punishment, which would serve to usher in the restoration.

This final prediction, moreover, is immediately followed by a pericope in which Jesus explicitly imparts soteriological significance to his death. The scene shifts to James and John lobbying Jesus for the privilege of sitting on his left and right in the kingdom. Jesus incredulously responds: "You do not know what you are asking. Are you able to drink the cup that I drink, or be baptized with the baptism that I am baptized with?" (Mark 10:38). It is interesting that the passage uses both drinking the cup and baptism as symbols of Christ's imminent death. The reference to the cup is significant in light of its appearance at the Last Supper and later in the Garden of Gethsemane. One might expect the Eucharistic cup to refer to Christ's death, but probably not his baptism. Nevertheless, the connection is here, which indicates that Jesus' Spirit-empowered mission inaugurated at the baptism, reaches its *telos* in the crucifixion.

The other disciples are enraged over James and John's audacious request. Instead of scolding only James and John, Jesus reveals that even the disciples who took offense at James and John's request were still operating with values antithetical to the kingdom. In response, Jesus reveals that the Kingdom of God functions differently. The greatest person is not the one who lords his greatness over another, but the one who is the "slave of all" (Mark 10:44). Then, to drive the point home, Jesus explains how he, the greatest in the kingdom, will serve others: "For the Son of Many came not to be served but to serve (διακονῆσαι), and to give his life a ransom (λύτρον)

---

63. Bolt, *From a Distance*, 56–58.

for many" (Mark 10:45). With this statement, Mark moves beyond simply describing events about to transpire and shifts to explaining the soteriological significance of Jesus' death.[64] This statement reveals that Jesus' death is not simply necessitated by Scriptural precedent. His death will accomplish something significant for redemption as a λύτρον.

In the common Greek usage, a ransom (λύτρον) was a payment made to procure the release or protection of something else.[65] Though some commentators point to the sacrifices of ancient Israel as the appropriate background for understanding the term, the legal texts of the Old Testament law codes also use λύτρον to refer to payments made in exchange for one's own life.[66] The word could draw its meaning from either the cultic or economic spheres, but both affirm the same notion that Jesus' death would be some form of exchange that liberates and saves the many.

Mark's ransom saying does bear several affinities with Isaiah 52:13–53:12 and quite likely draws upon the typology of the Suffering Servant of Isaiah, which sheds further light on the matter.[67] In Isaiah 53:11 LXX the servant is "the just one who serves many well (δίκαιον εὖ δουλεύοντα πολλοῖς)," which parallels the ransom sayings' "to serve," though different words are employed.[68] This lexical difference does not eliminate the connection since Mark utilizes both διακονέω and δουλεύω synonymously in the

---

64. Against the charge that this is a later creation of the early church, one can make the case that there is only one instance in the New Testament outside the Gospels of Jesus being called something close to a λύτρον. In 1 Timothy 2:6, Jesus is referred to as an "ἀντίλυτρον." This is significantly different from Mark's usage, suggesting that this passage is not a later creation by the early church. Witherington, *Christology*, 253.

65. In extrabiblical sources, it often referred to the payment offered to free slaves (BDAG, 605). Josephus talks about Eleazar the priest giving an expensive gold beam to the pillaging Crassus to protect the other temple artifacts. Josephus says, " . . . he gave this beam of gold as a ransom (λύτρον) for the whole (ἀντὶ πάντων)" (Josephus, *Ant.*, 14.107, trans. Whiston). For how the ransom saying would have been received in the first centuries based upon inscription evidence, see Collins, "Significance of Mark 10:45," 371–82. In some inscriptions devotees gave ransoms in order to be remitted of their known and unknown sins, which seems analogous to the current passage.

66. Gathercole, "Substitutionary Atonement," 162–64. Particularly applicable here is Exodus 21:30 where the law mandates that one pay a ransom in exchange for the loss of life.

67. The most persuasive essay on this is Watts, "Jesus' Death," 125–51. Witherington, though, makes a case for the influence of Isaiah 43 and God's giving of a "ransom" for his servant (*Christology*, 254).

68. Marcus argues that this alludes to Daniel's son of man in Dan 7:13–14. See Marcus, *Mark 8–16*, 749, 753. Even so, he does not think the influence of Daniel 7 displaces the influence of Isaiah.

previous verses.[69] In fact, both Jesus and Isaiah's servant benefit the "many."[70] Though I think an allusion to Isaiah's final servant song seems likely, the theological implications are present even if such an allusion is not. To put it briefly, the passage affirms that the death of Jesus is bound up with his larger purpose to bring salvation to Israel and ultimately the dawning of God's kingdom. His death is not at variance with his life and ministry but of one piece with it since it was for this that he "came." In addition, his death would be an exchange or a purchase that would secure the salvation of others.

Even though the ransom saying is important and confirms that Jesus' death coheres with his more encompassing mission of redeeming Israel, the passage is soteriologically ambiguous by itself. A ransom simply speaks of release, and this release can be accomplished in various ways. In fact, most atonement theories can speak of Jesus' death being a "ransom" in some way.[71] Without providing a thorough theological explanation for how Jesus' death will be salvific, the ransom saying continues a growing soteriological motif that reaches its fullest articulation in the Last Supper. In fact, Mark actually connects the ransom saying to the Last Supper sayings through his use of "many" (Mark 10:45). These are the same beneficiaries that are identified at the Last Supper when Jesus says, "This is my blood of the covenant, which is poured out for many" (Mark 14:24).[72] This intratextual link means that the two statements are inherently connected and the ransom saying points to the fuller theological articulation found at the Last Supper. In other words, Jesus is the ransom because he is the covenant-inaugurating sacrifice that atones for the sins of the many.

After the Last Supper, the rest of Mark continues to affirm and develop the saving significance of the cross. After the meal, Jesus and the disciples sing a hymn and go to the Mount of Olives (Mark 14:26). At this point, Jesus

---

69. Evans, *Mark 8:27—16:20*, 121.

70. Isaiah 53:11 speaks of the servant making "many righteous." In the ransom saying of Mark, the Son of Man's ransom is "for many." As a result, several scholars believe Mark's use of "many" alludes to Isaiah's servant. E.g. France, *Mark*, 419–21 and Evans, *Mark 8:27—16:20*, 122. However, this is contested in Dunn, *Jesus Remembered*, 812–15. Though I appreciate Dunn's caution, he completely overlooks the context of service that pervades the verses surrounding Mark 10:45, which make an allusion to Isaiah 53 more probable than he ascertains.

71. Witherington, for instance, avers the verse expresses a substitutionary view of the atonement (*Mark*, 290). Dowd and Malbon say it represents the Christus Victor theory of atonement ("Jesus' Death in Mark," 283–85). Hamerton-Kelly believes it speaks to the scapegoat mechanism in Girardian thought (*Gospel of the Sacred*, 71).

72. Chilton, *Feast of Meanings*, 118–19. The prepositions are different in each case, but this need not eliminate an intratextual connection. Mark 10:45 has "ἀντὶ πολλῶν" whereas Mark 14:25 has "ὑπὲρ πολλῶν."

tells his disciples "You will all become deserters; for it is written, 'I will strike the shepherd, and the sheep will be scattered'" (Mark 14:27). In the text, Jesus quotes from Zechariah 13:7, which he analogously applies to himself and his disciples. The quotation, however, alters the text of Zechariah in one particular way. In the MT and LXX texts of Zechariah 13:7, both attribute the striking to a "sword," not to a particular person. In Jesus' rendering, the subject of the sentence that performs the striking has been changed from the impersonal sword to the "I," who can be none other than God himself.[73] The alteration is theologically significant because it means the events that are about to transpire are not simply the vagaries of fate or the ire of Rome falling upon Jesus. Somewhere in the midst of all the various parties seeking to annihilate Jesus is the hand of God. Gibbs summarizes the theological significance well: "What Jesus now goes to experience is the hand of God, the Father's own hand, smiting him."[74] Though this might alarm some readers, the intentional alteration of Zechariah 13:7 requires such an association. Theologically speaking, it mandates that a theology of the cross desiring to follow the Gospels cannot remove God from the picture as if the cross were simply the result of human evil turning its venom upon Jesus as Girardian views of the atonement do. God, in one way or another, is involved in the process of striking the shepherd too and cannot be fully extracted from the situation.

The following pericope has Jesus and the disciples entering the Garden of Gethsemane to pray. In anguish, Jesus pleads, "Abba, Father, for you all things are possible; remove this cup from me; yet, not what I want, but what you want" (Mark 14:36). Several important things appear in this prayer. First, it is a reaffirmation that what is about to transpire in the crucifixion is a part of God's will. Second, Jesus calls what is about to happen to him the "cup." Intra-textually, this alludes back to the previous references to the Eucharistic cup (Mark 14:23) and the discourse with James and John regarding whether they were willing to drink the cup like Jesus would (Mark 10:38). Speaking of the "cup" might also denote God's judgment since this is what it symbolizes in several prophetic texts (Isa 51:17, 22; Jer 25:15–17; 49:12; 51:7; Ezek 23:31–33; Hab 2:16; Zech 12:2).[75] It is not entirely clear in the context of Mark whether this connotation is present, but the fact that the Passion predictions referred to Israel's exilic punishment makes it quite

---

73. Since there are no textual traditions that support this reading of the verse, the switch from the sword to the first person singular appears to originate either in Jesus or the early Christian community. See Menken, "Striking the Shepherd," 44–49 and Wright, "Jesus' Crucifixion," 137.

74. Gibbs, "Father's Wrath," 220.

75. Gibbs, "Father's Wrath," 221.

possible that being willing to drink the "cup" is another reference to Jesus bearing Israel's exilic punishment.

The atoning significance of Jesus' cross is carried deep into the very center of the Passion narrative. For Mark, Jesus' identity is inherently tied to the cross. Throughout the whole book, the human characters have failed to grasp the fullness of Jesus' identity. Even Peter's confession that Jesus is the Messiah in Caesarea, though accurate, is incomplete because Peter fails to understand how Jesus' messianic role involves suffering (Mark 8:27–33). However, characters on the periphery, like the demoniacs, have had an uncanny awareness of Jesus' identity that pierces through the obfuscation. For Mark, the most important breakthrough occurs in the ominous crucifixion scene. While Jesus is on the cross, darkness covers the region, and Jesus cries out "My God, my God, why have you forsaken me?" (Mark 15:34). The dying Galilean musters one last breath and expires. For many of the observers, this was the end of a charlatan's bid to be the Messiah. However, a centurion who "stood facing" Jesus on the cross sees just the opposite and proclaims: "Truly this man was God's Son" (Mark 15:39). Though a simple sentence, the sentence speaks volumes into the horrifying din of the crucifixion. Other human actors in the Gospel—even the disciples in certain ways—have been blinded and thus unable to "see," but the centurion "saw" Jesus' true identity.[76] The centurion's clairvoyance shatters the confusion over Jesus' identity that has plagued most of the characters in Mark's narrative. With the centurion's proclamation, Mark weds Jesus' identity to the crucifixion. Only when gazing at the cross, like the centurion, can one truly understand Jesus' identity and mission.[77] Moreover, we should not miss the fact that a centurion makes this proclamation. As a Gentile, he would have been viewed as one foreign to Israel's covenantal promises. However, his insight into Jesus' identity reveals that receiving the salvation Jesus offered is not limited to the Jewish people, but has taken on the universal thrust of Isaiah's hopes for restoration.[78] The Gentiles were identifying the presence of Israel's God active in Jesus of Nazareth, a sign of the restoration.

Yet, the scene with the centurion gazing at the cross advances another theologically significant point. When Jesus breathes his last upon the cross, Mark observes that "the curtain of the temple was torn in two, from top to bottom" (Mark 15:38). The statement jars the reader from the somber scene at Golgotha and transports her to an entirely different geographical location:

76. Gamel, "Salvation in a Sentence," 71–73. The "seeing" of the centurion contrasts with the blinding effects the parables were to induce: "They may indeed look, but not perceive, and may indeed listen, but not understand . . . " (Mark 4:12).

77. Carroll and Green, *Death of Jesus*, 29.

78. Gamel, "Salvation in a Sentence," 76.

the Jerusalem temple. Despite being a different location, the author sees the separate events constitutive of a single story that reaches its climax at this crucial moment. For Mark, the indictment against the temple that Jesus had pronounced with the action in the temple has come full circle. The temple's destruction has begun with the rending of the temple curtain.[79] More significantly, Mark wants his readers to realize the way to God is no longer through the temple and its cult, but now through the covenant-inaugurating death of Jesus Christ.[80] To be sure, the Last Supper sayings have prepared the reader for this point because they explain how Jesus' death on the cross "as a cultic sacrifice" can function as a replacement for the temple itself.[81] As one author put it so well: "Mark would have us know our Lord's entire ministry is a passion story, whereby he tears open the curtain of separation between God and man, and ensuring an everlasting *Yom Kippur*, that is, a Day of Atonement."[82] The sacrificial death of Jesus has made access to God available to all, even the Gentile centurion.

This much reveals that the theological implications of the Last Supper sayings are not alien pieces that Mark has assimilated from the tradition. The Last Supper sayings are fully integrated into his portrait of Jesus and the cross. Jesus, whose body was broken and whose blood was spilled out in the crucifixion, becomes the means by which human beings can be relationally connected with God. The rending of the veil establishes Jesus' death as the foundation upon which sinful humans can re-enter into a covenantal relationship with God. In his death, the hopes for Israel's restoration from exile were coming true. The covenant has been remade and the Gentiles were turning to God. It is thus entirely understandable why Jesus dies anticipating his next meal to be with his disciples in the kingdom. Israel's restoration was coming to pass and his death was an essential segue to this new state of affairs because it atoned for sin.

Conclusion

This analysis of Mark's Last Supper sayings has yielded several important insights. In the context of Mark, the Last Supper discourse casts Jesus' death in the light of the Passover festival. Though the Passover remembered YHWH's

79. France, *Mark*, 657.

80. If we take the temple action and the Last Supper as mutually explicatory events, then we can conclude that Jesus and his death replace the temple cult. See Wright, *Victory of God*, 558 and Antwi, "Atoning Sacrifice," 17–28.

81. Kilmartin, *Eucharist*, 55.

82. Scaer, "Mark's Sacramental Theology," 238.

past deliverance, the Last Supper anticipated a future rescue that was about to happen in and through Jesus, the eschatological arrival of the kingdom.[83] The words spoken over the bread and the wine explain the nature and means of this deliverance, indicating that Jesus' death would make atonement for the renewal of the covenant. This portrait, however, is not simply limited to the Last Supper discourse, for it finds corroboration in other places in Mark as well. The Passion predictions borrow the language of Israel's exilic punishment to indicate that Jesus' death would partake of Israel's judgment when he was "betrayed into human hands" (Mark 9:31) and handed "over to the Gentiles" (Mark 10:33). Such a picture is also given in the Garden of Gethsemane where Jesus seeks to do the Father's will and drink the "cup," which often referred to God's judgment. Finally, Mark's crucifixion scene, densely packed with the awareness of Jesus' identity flooding the centurion's consciousness and the temple veil rending in two demonstrates that Mark believed the death of Jesus made a new way of relating to God possible: the covenant was renewed.

---

83. The wedge that many seek to drive between Jesus' proclamation of the kingdom and his vicarious death for others is non-existent if we put Jesus in his context. Contra Gorringe, *God's Just Vengeance*, 81.

6

Matthew and Jesus' Death for the Forgiveness of Sin

As we transition from Mark to Matthew, the analysis of Mark will rarely be far from view given the strong likelihood that Matthew and Luke used Mark to write their Gospels. Matthew's dependence upon Mark is quite apparent in his narration of the Last Supper account because, with a few notable exceptions, Matthew's account of the Last Supper follows Mark rather precisely.[1] Since Matthew has assimilated many of the theological emphases that were present in Mark, the discussion on Matthew will not seek to repeat what has been said before in the chapter on Mark. It should be assumed that much of what is present in Mark's account is adopted by Matthew. In order to avoid the reduplication of material that does not significantly reveal Matthew's theological perspective, this section will primarily concentrate on the pieces that are unique to Matthew instead of including the material previously analyzed in Mark.

Matthew's Last Supper Sayings

A comparison between Mark and Matthew reveals that Matthew has introduced minor emendations to Mark's account of the Last Supper that reveal the theological points Matthew desires to make, though not all of Matthew's changes significantly alter the story. For example, though Matthew identifies the day of the Last Supper as the "first day of Unleavened Bread," he drops Mark's identification that this was "when the Passover lamb is sacrificed" (Mark 14:12; cf. Matt 26:17). This does not delete the Paschal setting because Matthew still has the disciples directly ask Jesus "Where do you want us to make preparations for you to eat the Passover?" (Matt 26:17). This alteration adds or subtracts nothing to the overall account of the Last Supper because the meal is ultimately still set within the context of the Passover.

---

1. A complete summary of the redactions can be found in Davies and Allison, *Matthew*, 3:456, 459–60, 465.

However, several of Matthew's redactions do have theological significance for his Last Supper account. When Matthew records Jesus' charge to the disciples to prepare the Passover, he adds a phrase absent in Mark. Jesus instructs the disciples preparing the Last Supper to inform their anonymous host that their teacher has announced: "My time is near (ὁ καιρός μου ἐγγύς ἐστιν)" (Matt 26:18). By adding this phrase, Matthew ties Jesus' message of the kingdom's imminent arrival with the events he is about to symbolize in the Last Supper. Throughout the Gospel, there have been many references to the coming "time (καιρός)," with many of the occurrences referring to the arrival of the kingdom.[2] In Matthew 8:29, the Gadarene demoniacs question Jesus: "Have you come here to torment us before the time (καιροῦ)?" In the exorcism of the demoniacs, the reference to the καιρός refers to the future restoration and judgment upon evil. In the parable of the weeds among the wheat, the kingdom of heaven is likened to the eschatological "harvest time (ἐν καιρῷ τοῦ θερισμοῦ)" (Matt 13:30). When the Pharisees and Sadducees fail to understand the eschatological significance of the recent events, Jesus faults them for failing to "interpret the signs of the times (τῶν καιρῶν)" (Matt 16:3), which again has eschatological overtones. In the parable of the wicked tenants, the owner sends servants to collect fruit when "the harvest time (ὁ καιρὸς τῶν καρπῶν) had come" (Matt 21:34) and the audience says the owner will lease it to others to "give him the produce at the harvest time (τοὺς καρποὺς ἐν τοῖς καιροῖς αὐτῶν)" (Matt 21:41). Throughout Matthew, καιρός often signifies the coming eschatological harvest and judgment. By inserting the comment that his καιρός was near, Matthew suggests that Jesus' death, which would be symbolized in the Last Supper, would precipitate the arrival of the kingdom.[3] Through the introduction of this phrase, Matthew has emphasized that Jesus' death will be the means by which the kingdom will arrive, even more so than Mark.

---

2. However, sometimes the word lacks a connotation of eschatological fulfillment (E.g. Matt 11:25; 12:1; 14:1; 24:45).

3. Senior, *The Passion of Jesus*, 59–61, 182. Jesus' main message was that "the kingdom of heaven has come near (ἤγγικεν γὰρ ἡ βασιλεία τῶν οὐρανῶν)" (Matt 3:2, 4:17; 10:7). In saying his καιρός was ἐγγύς, Jesus was connecting his death to the larger eschatological program of the kingdom that he had announced.

Comparison of Institutions Narratives in Mark and Matthew[4]

Mark 14:22–24	Matt 26:26–28
Bread Saying:	Bread Saying:
Καὶ ἐσθιόντων αὐτῶν λαβὼν ἄρτον εὐλογήσας ἔκλασεν καὶ ἔδωκεν αὐτοῖς καὶ εἶπεν· λάβετε, τοῦτό ἐστιν τό σῶμά μου.	ἐσθιόντων δὲ αὐτῶν λαβὼν ὁ Ἰησοῦς ἄρτον καὶ εὐλογήσας ἔκλασεν καὶ δοὺς τοῖς μαθηταῖς εἶπεν· λάβετε φάγετε, τοῦτό ἐστιν τό σῶμά μου.
Cup Saying:	Cup Saying:
καὶ λαβὼν ποτήριον εὐχαριστήσας ἔδωκεν αὐτοῖς, καὶ ἔπιον ἐξ αὐτοῦ πάντες. καὶ εἶπεν αὐτοῖς· τοῦτό ἐστιν τὸ αἷμά μου τῆς διαθήκης τὸ ἐκχυννόμενον ὑπὲρ πολλῶν.	καὶ λαβὼν ποτήριον καὶ εὐχαριστήσας ἔδωκεν αὐτοῖς λέγων· πίετε ἐξ αὐτοῦ πάντες. τοῦτο γάρ ἐστιν τὸ αἷμά μου τῆς διαθήκης τὸ περὶ πολλῶν ἐκχυννόμενον εἰς ἄφεσιν ἁμαρτιῶν.

When we come to the sayings over the bread and the cup, Matthew has made several changes, which can be seen in the chart above. Some of these are simply the introduction or alterations of conjunctions (insertions and transpositions of καὶ, γάρ, etc. or an alteration of καὶ to δὲ), which do not substantially change the sayings. In the bread saying, Matthew introduces more specificity than what one finds in Mark's account. He clarifies that Jesus is the one who is breaking the bread and identifies the disciples as the recipients of the bread rather than using the pronoun, αὐτοῖς. These kinds of changes do little to alter the force of Mark's rendering.

Probably the most significant alteration that Matthew makes to the bread saying is his introduction of the imperative φάγετε, which mirrors his later introduction of the imperative πίετε in the cup saying. In contrast, Mark leaves one to assume that they ate the bread and simply states "all of them drank" from the cup (Mark 14:23). Matthew's insertions of the imperatives, which were absent in Mark's account, likely reflect the framing of the passage for liturgical use wherein explicit commands would verbally instruct the people to partake of the Eucharistic elements.[5] If such a conclusion correctly explains why the imperatives were added, it does suggest that liturgical use would introduce minor changes to accommodate Eucharistic practice, but not enough to alter the meaning significantly.

---

4. In the chart, the words unique to each account have been underlined in order to show the changes Matthew introduced.

5. Davies and Allison, *Matthew*, 3:472.

Matthew's most significant additions come in the cup saying. Though Matthew follows Mark much of the way, he has introduced two significant changes in the cup saying. First, when Matthew records Jesus saying "this is my blood of the covenant, which is poured out for (περὶ) many" he changes Mark's ὑπὲρ to περὶ (Matt 26:28). The significance of this change is difficult to determine, but it has been argued that the change was intentionally adopted to bring the prepositional phrase into closer parallel with Isaiah's suffering servant.[6] In the discussion on Mark, we noted that Mark's "ὑπὲρ πολλῶν" was likely an allusion to Isaiah's suffering servant who made "many" righteous. If such is the case with Mark, it is also likely that Matthew's alteration of the prepositional phrase to "περὶ πολλῶν" was to make the connection with Isaiah's suffering servant even more apparent. This is the same preposition that the Septuagint used to identify those who benefited from the servant's death in Isaiah 53:4 LXX: "He suffers for (περὶ) us." If so, Matthew has brought the "for many" formula into greater conformity with Isaiah's suffering servant and makes such an allusion more probable, though the evidence is not conclusive.

The most substantial difference in Matthew's saying over the cup can be found in his addition at the end to the effect that the pouring out of Jesus' blood of the covenant would be "for the forgiveness of sins (εἰς ἄφεσιν ἁμαρτιῶν)." I argued earlier that Mark's saying over the cup alluded to the covenant sacrifice on Sinai in Exodus 24:8 and that this sacrifice was understood to effect atonement for sin, even if Mark does not say this explicitly. By adopting Mark's wording in the cup saying, Matthew likewise alludes to Exodus 24:8, but in contrast to Mark he makes the atoning significance of Jesus' death plainly visible by describing Jesus' "blood of the covenant" as that which is "for the forgiveness of sins" (Matt 26:28). In doing so, he adds further verification that the allusion to Moses' sacrifice on Sinai—which is present in both Mark and Matthew—possessed atoning significance.[7] Thus, even if Mark's allusion to the covenant sacrifice on Sinai fails to make the atoning function explicit, Matthew's account of the Last Supper certainly does. While I would suggest that Matthew's addition of this phrase indicates how we should read Mark's account, it is simply enough here to observe that Matthew makes it hard to deny the presence of atonement theology in the Gospels.

With the addition of the phrase "for the forgiveness of sins" to the words over the cup some have argued that Matthew has shifted the intertextual allusion away from Exodus 24:8 and Zechariah 9:11 and directed it

---

6. Kodell, *Eucharist*, 101 and Senior, *Gospel of Matthew*, 67–68.
7. Eubank, *Wages of Cross-Bearing*, 177.

toward the new covenant of Jeremiah 31:31–34.[8] This is indeed possible since Jeremiah's new covenant expected the forgiveness of Israel's sins. However, one is not forced to turn to Jeremiah's new covenant prophecy to explain Matthew's addition of the phrase "forgiveness of sins" to the Last Supper account. Observant scholars have noted that the same phrase is present in Mark 1:4 where John the Baptist is introduced "proclaiming a baptism of repentance for the forgiveness of sins (εἰς ἄφεσιν ἁμαρτιῶν)." However, Matthew's description of John's baptism has omitted this very phrase from the parallel account in his Gospel (Matt 3:1–6). According to Marshall, " . . . it looks as though Matthew has withheld the phrase in the story of John and kept it for use here."[9] If Marshall is right and Matthew has deliberately held the phrase "for the forgiveness of sins" in abeyance, then he has done so in order to make this the exclusive accomplishment of the cross. Consequently, Matthew's redactional relocation of this phrase removes a potential soteriological ambiguity for someone reading Mark in order to make sure the readers of Matthew understand the cross constitutes the moment when the forgiveness of sins was attained rather than baptism.[10] If Matthew has relocated the phrase "for the forgiveness of sins" from its original location in his Markan source and if the covenant sacrifice on Sinai did effect atonement as I have argued previously, all the pieces are in place for Matthew to affirm the atoning significance of Jesus' death as a covenant sacrifice without

---

8. For example, Clay Ham has argued that Matthew's addition of "forgiveness of sins" makes Jeremiah 31:31–34 the primary text being alluded to by the covenantal language of the Last Supper, though he does not rule out the influence of Exodus 24:8 and Zechariah 9:11. For support, he cites the fact that Jesus does not sprinkle blood on his disciples as Moses did in Exodus 24 nor does he renew the Mosaic covenant. Ham observes that Matthew has adopted the wording of Exodus 24:8, but has done so in a "typological" fashion in order to present a new idea. Ham is certainly right to see that Jesus has not blindly repeated an earlier ritual, but it is questionable whether this means the influence of Zechariah or Exodus is thereby lessened. If, as I argue above, Jewish and Christian exegesis of the Sinai covenant sacrifice saw it as atoning, then the addition of "forgiveness of sins" does not displace Exodus 24:8 but remains integral to it, even if it does introduce the influence of Jeremiah 31. See Ham, "Last Supper," 59–66. Cf. Marshall, *Last Supper*, 100.

9. Marshall, *Last Supper*, 100. Cf. Davies and Allison, *Matthew*, 3:474.

10. It was also Matthew's unique insertion of the phrase "forgiveness of sins" into the Last Supper sayings that led Heider to categorize Matthew's view of the atonement as "a vicarious sacrifice," which would pave the way for Anselm's theory of the atonement. Heider, "Atonement and the Gospels," 266. Others have argued that Matthew's relocation of the phrase is more indicative of his thoughts on baptism rather than his soteriology. See Luomanen, *Kingdom of Heaven*, 220–21. However, it seems more likely that the relocation is a reflection of both Matthew's soteriology and his theology of baptism rather than one to the exclusion of the other.

relying upon Jeremiah 31:31-34.[11] While Jeremiah 31:31-34 may still be in view, it would be misguided to suppress the importance of Exodus 24:8 and Zechariah 9:11 since the actual Greek wording, as in Mark's account, mirrors Exodus 24:8 and Matthew's emendations have heightened the eschatological hopes, resonating even more with Zechariah 9.

Integration with the Rest of the Gospel

Matthew's account of the Last Supper, though adapted from Mark's account, still coherently fits within the larger narrative of Matthew's Gospel, especially those parts that are uniquely Matthean. Matthew's Gospel—as more fully developed in the fourth chapter—begins with Jesus' genealogy that divided Israel's history into three epochs of fourteen generations (Matt 1:1-17). The last of these three eras spans from the Babylonian exile to the coming of the Messiah. With this opening to his Gospel, Matthew situates Jesus in the larger story of Israel's exile and restoration. As the Messiah, Jesus would bring Israel's exile to its end. By framing Jesus' life and ministry within the larger narrative of Israel's exile and restoration, Matthew likely presumes his reader will understand that the exile was punishment for Israel's faithlessness to the covenant. This is supported by some of the author's following comments. A few verses after the genealogy, the author introduces the significance of Jesus' name when an angel instructs Joseph to name Mary's son "Jesus, for he will save his people from their sins" (Matt 1:21b). Readers well-versed in Israel's story, would hardly miss the significance of this commentary. As the Messiah, Jesus was going to rescue his people, Israel, from their sins, which had resulted in their exilic punishment. In short, the promise of Jesus saving his people from their sins in Matthew 1:21 finds its fulfillment at the Last Supper where Matthew's redaction informs the reader that Jesus' "blood of the covenant . . . is poured out for the forgiveness of sins" (Matt 26:28). Thus, although Mark and Matthew share remarkable similarities in their versions of the Last Supper sayings Matthew, from his inaugural chapter onward, has uniquely set his narrative on a course that reaches its watershed moment at the Last Supper when all is explained.

Matthew's emphasis upon Jesus' name in the first chapter and the name's connection to Jesus' task of rescuing "his people from their sins," helps explain one of the other peculiar features of Matthew's Gospel. When Matthew is compared with Mark, Jesus' proper name is used far more frequently in the Passion accounts than the other Gospels, introducing it in

---

11. Luomanen, *Kingdom of Heaven*, 222-24.

places where Mark uses the third person pronoun.[12] If this is intentional on the part of Matthew, it is likely that he is purposefully recalling the name's meaning and identifying the cross as the event that saves God's people from their sin.

Like Mark, Matthew has a series of Passion predictions, which have prepared the reader for the comments delivered at the Last Supper and the events that follow it. Peter's confession of Jesus as the Messiah in Caesarea Philippi is followed by the first of these Passion predictions (Matt 16:21–23), which makes the cross and resurrection constitutive of Jesus' messianic mission. The second prediction follows Mark's emphasis of falling "into human hands," which again echoes Israel's punishment of exile (Matt 17:22). The final prediction likewise speaks of Jesus being handed "over to the Gentiles," another phrase echoing Israel's exile (Matt 20:18). Like Mark's account, this final prediction culminates with the ransom saying, which says ". . . the Son of Man came not to be served but to serve, and to give his life a ransom for many" (Matt 20:28). In discussing the ransom saying in the context of Mark, it was noted that financial analogies might better explain the term "ransom" than sacrificial imagery. The viability of financial metaphors seems more likely to be the case in Matthew because he uses the metaphor of sin as debt in both the Lord's prayer (Matt 6:12) and the parable of the unforgiving servant (Matt 6:23–35).[13] Given his predilection for understanding sin as debt elsewhere in his Gospel, Matthew's use of the ransom saying likely casts Jesus' death as a form of economic transaction.[14] To put it more precisely, as a ransom, Jesus' death would pay the sin debt of others.[15] Given his overt connection with Israel's exile in the opening chapter, one can reasonably

---

12. Carroll and Green, *Death of Jesus*, 50 and Senior, *The Passion Narrative*, 25n5. Senior suggests this is simply a result of Matthew's tendency to elucidate the characters and subjects that Mark leaves ambiguous. However, the clustering of "Jesus" in Matthew 26–27 is quite pronounced when compared with Mark: Matt 26:1, 4, 6, 17, 19, 26, 36, 49, 50, 51, 63, 71; 27:1, 11, 17, 20, 22, 27, 37, 55, 57. Several instances reveal a concerted effort to introduce the name "Jesus" even when Mark does not employ a third person pronoun: E.g. Matt 27:1, 11, 17, 20, 22, 37, 55.

13. There is some question whether the petition to "forgive us our debts, as we also have forgiven our debtors" (Matt 6:12) is to be taken metaphorically or literally. The most likely interpretation is the metaphorical one in light of Matt 6:14–15. See Nel, "Forgiveness of Debt," 87–106.

14. For a brilliant articulation of how Matthew's ransom saying connects with the notion of captivity and exile, see Eubank, *Wages of Cross-Bearing*, esp. 148–68. On the metaphor as sin as debt and its origin, see Anderson, *Sin* and Anderson, "Israel's Burden," 1–30.

15. As a result, scholars who force one to choose between Jesus' death being exemplary or atoning seem to be in err by positing and either/or situation. E.g. Luomanen, *Kingdom of Heaven*, 230.

argue that this sin debt payment would be taking on and sharing in Israel's very punishment.

Matthew, as noted in the fourth chapter, has also made a typological connection between Jesus and Moses throughout the book. This typological comparison continues into the Last Supper scene as well. There are little emendations in the account of the Last Supper, which appear to be intentional echoes of Moses' preparation of the Passover in Exodus. Davies and Allison suggest that the narrator's description of the disciples' preparation of the Passover ("the disciples did as Jesus had directed them, and they prepared the Passover meal") in Matthew 26:19 mirrors the Israelites' preparation of the Passover in Exodus 12:28.[16] This might not be convincing to all, but one is certainly on firmer ground to aver that Jesus' death as the inauguration of the covenant parallels and even surpasses the role of Moses who was the mediator of Israel's covenant with YHWH at Sinai.[17] Thus, the Last Supper, which draws on the trope of Jesus as the New Moses, adds another dimension to the manifold ways in which Jesus' ministry parallels Moses in the Gospel of Matthew.

After the Last Supper, Matthew shares many of the episodes following the Last Supper that appear in Mark. For example, Matthew has Jesus quoting from Zechariah 13:7 to predict that his followers will soon desert him (Matt 26:31–35). Matthew also includes Jesus praying in the garden, asking the Father if the cup could be bypassed. The heart and essence of this prayer, though not differing substantially from Mark's account, corresponds to the Lord's prayer given earlier in the Sermon on the Mount (Matt 6:9–13).[18] Thus, Jesus' prayer in the garden mirrors precisely the way he had taught his disciples to pray. Because the cup of suffering is the Father's will, he consents to drinking the cup just as he does in Mark.

When it comes to the crucifixion scene, Matthew also includes the rending of the temple curtain, but he adds several important elements. Immediately after the curtain is rent, the narrator comments, "The earth shook, and the rocks were split. The tombs also were opened, and many bodies of the saints who had fallen asleep were raised. After his resurrection they came out of the tombs and entered the holy city and appeared to many" (Matt 27:51b–53). The scene recalls Ezekiel's vision of the dry bones (Ezek 37:1–14) coming back to life, a point which is underscored by some of the

---

16. Davies and Allison, *Matthew*, 3:458.

17. Cooke, "Covenant Sacrifice," 33 and Davies and Allison, *Matthew*, 3:473.

18. Davies and Allison, *Matthew*, 3:497. The links include the similar address to the "Father," the desire for God's will to be done, and the desire to not enter into temptation.

lexical connections between the passages.[19] For example, Matthew speaks of the earth being moved, "ἐσείσθη" (Matt 27:51), and the LXX text of Ezekiel has a "σεισμὸς," an earthquake, occurring when Ezekiel was prophesying (Ezek 37:7). Additionally, Matthew mentions the opening of the tombs "μνημεῖα" (Matt 27:52–53) and the interpretation of Ezekiel's vision includes the promise that God would open up and bring Israel out of their tombs, "μνήματα" (Ezek 37:12). In Ezekiel's vision, the resurrection of the desiccated skeletons was a metaphor for God's future restoration of Israel. Here, the imagery has been profoundly altered. What was metaphorical (i.e. resurrection) has become a literal experience according to Matthew. The literal occurrence of resurrection for Jesus and other individuals affirms that Israel's restoration has begun in and through Jesus' death and resurrection.[20]

Conclusion

To conclude, the Gospel of Matthew has emphasized the forgiveness of sins and identified Jesus' death on the cross as the means by which Jesus would bring in the kingdom of God and Israel's restoration. Matthew, even more so than Mark, has explicitly established Jesus' death as an atonement for sin, which is most apparent in his addition of the phrase "for the forgiveness of sins" in the Last Supper sayings.[21] However, affirming that Matthew's emphasis falls on the forgiveness of sins does not mean this is the only dimension to salvation in Matthew.[22] As we saw in the fourth chapter, the arrival of the kingdom brought healing and restoration to the people to whom Jesus ministered. When Matthew identifies the cross as the moment which rips open the graves, he proclaims that the insidious force of death, one of the punishments for breaking the covenant, has met its match. The life-giving power of God is able to restore what death has destroyed. In addition, the arrival of the kingdom brings an ethical change to Jesus' followers. The way of salvation is not just emancipation from the threat of disease or death. As one writer put it, " . . . the way of salvation stressed by Matthew is *doing* the will of God."[23] This point is stressed most clearly in the Sermon on the Mount wherein Jesus does not abolish the law but instead heightens its expectations. In fact, the risen Christ's last words in the Gospel end by commanding his followers: "Go therefore and make disciples of all nations

19. Ibid., 3:633–35.
20. Senior, *Gospel of Matthew*, 166–67.
21. Gundry, "Salvation in Matthew," 411.
22. Gibbs, "Father's Wrath," 224–25.
23. Blair, "Jesus and Salvation," 307.

... teaching them to obey everything that I have commanded you" (Matt 28:19-20a). Continuing to live in the kingdom necessitates a different way of living life. Luomanen summarizes Matthew's holistic soteriology well: "Thus, on broad terms, Matthew's understanding of the content of salvation can be determined as the restoration of the wholeness of life under God's/Jesus' rule and in his presence."[24] For Matthew, Jesus' death is an eschatological event that ushers in this very wholeness, and we should make sure that this wholeness includes rather than excludes atonement for sin.

---

24. Luomanen, *Kingdom of Heaven*, 280. Despite this accurate assessment, Luomanen seems to downplay the atoning elements to Matthew's soteriology unnecessarily.

7

The Cross, Covenant, and Forgiveness in Luke

Luke's Last Supper Account

LUKE BEGINS HIS ACCOUNT of the Last Supper by identifying the day, like Mark and Matthew, as the day when "the Passover lamb had to be sacrificed" (Luke 22:7). Though Matthew and Mark fail to identify which disciples prepared the Last Supper, Luke has specified that the task fell to Peter and John (Luke 22:8). More frequently than the other Gospels, Luke reiterates multiple times that this is a Passover meal.[1] Moreover, Jesus begins the meal by saying, "I have eagerly desired to eat this Passover with you before I suffer; for I tell you, I will not eat it until it is fulfilled in the kingdom of God" (Luke 22:15-16). Not only does the statement affirm the paschal setting of the meal, it also explicitly combines Israel's past deliverance in the exodus with Jesus' proclamation that God's kingdom was about to dawn.[2] In other words, as they celebrated the Passover, they were on the cusp of God's restoration.

After this announcement, Jesus first takes a cup—not a loaf of bread, which is a marked departure from Matthew and Mark—and after blessing it says, "Take this and divide it among yourselves; for I tell you that from now on I will not drink of the fruit of the vine until the kingdom of God comes" (Luke 22:17-18). Luke's introduction of a cup before the bread has spawned debate over whether this reflects a different form of Eucharistic practice that celebrated the cup before the bread. Though possible, especially if one takes the shorter reading of the Last Supper as authentic, such arguments fail to take Luke very seriously. He has repeatedly informed the reader that this was a Passover meal. If later prescriptions for Passover provide a somewhat reliable picture of first century practice, their celebration of the Passover would have involved a series of cups, not simply one as in

---

1. By way of comparison, Mark has five mentions of the "Passover" (Mark 14:1, 12[2x], 13, 14), Matthew has four (Matt 26:2, 17, 18, 19), and Luke has six (Luke 22:1, 7, 8, 9, 11, 13).

2. Fitzmyer, *Gospel according to Luke*, 2:1390.

Eucharistic practice.³ Thus, when Luke speaks of a cup before the bread he is likely referring to one of the first cups that were drunk during the course of the Passover celebration, which should further support his depiction of the meal as a Passover celebration.⁴ Moreover, Luke's account has placed Jesus' expression of the kingdom's immanence in the first cup saying. Though Mark and Matthew place it at the end of the sayings over the bread and wine, Luke has placed it at the front, which only serves to emphasize the immanence of the kingdom even more so and to substantiate the point that the events symbolized by the meal, i.e. Jesus' death, will precipitate the arrival of the kingdom when "it is fulfilled" (Luke 22:16).

The very next step in the progression of the supper is the breaking of the bread. However, this is the point at which things become a bit more complicated simply because the supporting manuscripts have two vastly different readings of the account. The vast majority of manuscripts, including $\mathfrak{P}^{75}$, ℵ, A, B, and C, support the longer reading, which includes all of verses Luke 22:19–20:

> Then he took a loaf of bread, and when he had given thanks, he broke it and gave it to them, saying, "This is my body, which is given for you. Do this in remembrance of me." And he did the same with the cup after supper, saying, "This cup that is poured out for you is the new covenant in my blood."

However, in some manuscripts and translations, verses 19 and 20 are altered, transposed, or deleted entirely.⁵ The alternative option, the shorter reading, stops in the middle of Luke 22:19 and has abridged the word over the bread: "Then he took a loaf of bread, and when he had given thanks, he broke it and gave it to them, saying, 'This is my body.'" Thus, the two major variants of Luke 22:19–20 present vastly different portraits of what was said and therefore communicated at the Last Supper. Moreover, the adoption of the longer or shorter reading is theologically significant. If the shorter reading is deemed to be earlier and therefore more likely to reflect the original reading, Luke's Last Supper account lacks any reference to the inauguration

3. *m. Pesaḥ*, 10.2–7 (Neusner).

4. Ibid., 1397.

5. The Uncial D and some of the Italian translations (it[a, d, ff², i, l]) are missing the final part of Luke 22:19, "which is given for you. Do this in remembrance of me" and the entirety of 22:20, the cup saying. The it[b, e] translations also have the same abridged version of Luke 22:19 with no 22:20, yet Luke 22:19 has been transposed before Luke 22:17–18, which was most likely done in order to cohere with the traditional Eucharistic practice of sharing in the bread before the wine. The same thing occurs in syr[c] though the text has a fuller version of Luke 22:19. The version syr[s] has portions of Luke 22:20 interpolated throughout Luke 22:17–18, while syr[p] has dropped Luke 22:17–18 entirely. The text of these variants has been charted in Metzger, *Textual Commentary*, 149.

of the new covenant and removes the atoning implications that we observed in Mark and Matthew altogether. Furthermore, since Luke has only a few passages that suggest Jesus' death is an atonement for sin—one of which is the longer reading of Luke 22:19b–20—determining the viability of the longer reading is essential for understanding Luke's theology of the cross as a whole. Certainly, this question is also critical for ascertaining the nature of the Eucharistic pattern exhibited by Luke. If the shorter reading is authentic, then Luke betrays an inverted Eucharistic pattern where the wine was imbibed prior to the consumption of the bread. This particular investigation into Luke's understanding of Jesus' death proceeds with the assumption that the longer reading is earlier because it has more widespread textual support and, despite claims to the contrary, the theology of the longer reading seems required by the theological conclusions of the rest of the Gospel.[6]

Analysis of the Longer Reading of Luke's Last Supper Saying

Comparison of the Words of Institution in Mark and Luke[7]

Mark 14:22–24	Luke 22:19–20
Bread Saying:	Bread Saying:
Καὶ ἐσθιόντων αὐτῶν λαβὼν ἄρτον εὐλογήσας ἔκλασεν καὶ ἔδωκεν αὐτοῖς καὶ εἶπεν· λάβετε, τοῦτό ἐστιν τὸ σῶμά μου.	Καὶ λαβὼν ἄρτον εὐχαριστήσας ἔκλασεν καὶ ἔδωκεν αὐτοῖς λέγων· τοῦτό ἐστιν τὸ σῶμά μου τὸ ὑπὲρ ὑμῶν διδόμενον· τοῦτο ποιεῖτε εἰς τὴν ἐμὴν ἀνάμνησιν.
Cup Saying:	Cup Saying:
καὶ λαβὼν ποτήριον εὐχαριστήσας ἔδωκεν αὐτοῖς, καὶ ἔπιον ἐξ αὐτοῦ πάντες. καὶ εἶπεν αὐτοῖς· τοῦτό ἐστιν τὸ αἷμά μου τῆς διαθήκης τὸ ἐκχυννόμενον ὑπὲρ πολλῶν.	καὶ τὸ ποτήριον ὡσαύτως μετὰ τὸ δειπνῆσαι, λέγων· τοῦτο τὸ ποτήριον ἡ καινὴ διαθήκη ἐν τῷ αἵματί μου τὸ ὑπὲρ ὑμῶν ἐκχυννόμενον.

---

6. Textual support for the inclusion of Luke 22:19b–20 include: $\mathfrak{P}^{75}$, ℵ, A, B, C, L, T, W, Δ, Θ, Ψ, f[1], f[13], 157, 180, 205, 565, 579, 597, 700, 892, 1006, 1010, 1071, 1241, 1243, 1292, 1342, 1424, 1505 *Byz*, [E G H N] *Lect* along with several versions and Eusebian Canons (Basil) and Augustine. By comparison, the support for some form of omission is rather limited: D, it[a, d, ff, i, l, b, e], i, l, b, syr[c, s]. Furthermore, the main uncial support (D) has been noted for its liberal emendations. See Parker, *Codex Bezae*, 285–86 and Parker, "Codex Bezae," 43–50. Claims for the adoption of the shorter reading are often made on the basis of the internal evidence. See Ehrman, *Orthodox Corruption*, 233–37; Ehrman, "The Cup," 576–91; Parker, *Text of the Gospels*, 151–57; and Chadwick, "Shorter Text," 249–58.

7. The words in common are in plain script, while the words that are different have been underlined to highlight the differences in each account.

Assuming that the longer reading of Luke 22:19-20 is the earlier reading, what are the theological implications of the words given in Luke's account? After passing the first cup, the longer reading has the following: "Then he took a loaf of bread, and when he had given thanks, he broke it and gave it to them, saying, 'This is my body, which is given for you. Do this in remembrance of me'" (Luke 22:19). As in the other accounts, Jesus takes the paschal bread, which recalled Israel's redemption from Egypt.[8] The bread, however, no longer looks solely to Israel's past because the attention is now directed to the immediate future with Jesus' death looming on the horizon. To describe Jesus' prayer over the bread, Luke uses a different word for Jesus' blessing in his account, εὐχαριστήσας, which identifies this rite as a "Eucharist" (see chart above) from the beginning. Mark, though, uses the same word in the cup saying, so the term appears synonymous with Mark's εὐλογήσας and does not significantly alter the meaning, even though it likely situates this more explicitly in a liturgical context..

Although the accounts of Mark and Matthew have supplied little in the bread saying about the soteriological implications of Jesus' death, Luke has provided more. He specifically identifies his body as that which "is given (διδόμενον)." The word can be used in a generic way to refer to any kind of giving, but it can also refer to sacrificial giving.[9] In fact, when the verb occurs in conjunction with the preposition ὑπὲρ in the rest of the New Testament, the word most often refers to the sacrificial giving up of Jesus on behalf of his people.[10] This is the meaning that Fitzmyer suggests is utilized here, if not on the basis of the verb διδόμενον, then more certainly on the basis of the prepositional phrase "for you (ὑπὲρ ὑμῶν)" that identifies the beneficiaries of the gift.[11] By identifying his body as that which "is given for you," Jesus is indicating that he has chosen to forfeit his life sacrificially in order to benefit his disciples. While Luke's bread saying does not clarify how his death would benefit his disciples, it clearly confirms that it would. Luke also differs from Mark by adding the following command at the end of the bread saying: "Do (ποιεῖτε) this in remembrance of me." The present

---

8. *m. Pesaḥ.*, 10:5.

9. BDAG, 242. Particularly relevant here are 2 Cor 8:5; Matt 20:28; Mark 10:45; 1 Tim 2:6.

10. John 6:51; Gal 1:4; 1 Tim 2:6; Titus 2:14.

11. Fitzmyer, *Gospel according to Luke*, 2:1400-1401. ὑπὲρ with the genitive frequently signifies the beneficiaries of a particular action. BDAG, 1030. Wallace argues that ὑπὲρ frequently signifies substitution in many places in the New Testament. The substitutionary aspect seems implicit in this passage because, if an action is being performed for the benefit of someone else, one is doing it in their place. See Wallace, *Greek Grammar*, 383-89.

tense imperative (ποιεῖτε) likely bears the implication that this should be an ongoing practice for his disciples. As a result, Luke's bread saying seems much more intended for liturgical repetition.

Luke possibly alludes to a temporal interval between the bread saying and the cup saying since the next statement occurs "after supper," at which point Jesus takes a second cup and says, "This cup that is poured out for you is the new covenant in my blood" (Luke 22:20). In contrast to Mark, Luke places the attention on the cup rather than on the blood, but this should not be used to indicate that Luke has thereby suppressed the reference to blood. In referring to the cup, Luke surely intends to signify the contents of the cup, namely, the wine which Jesus equates with his blood. In the Old Testament, blood was equivalent to one's life, no doubt a realization that loss of blood quickly brought about one's demise (Lev 17:14). Thus, by equating the cup with Jesus' blood, Jesus is signifying his coming death. Like Mark and Matthew, Luke employs ἐκχυννόμενον to describe what will happen to the contents of the cup. As was noted earlier in the discussion on Mark, ἐκχυννόμενον, especially when used in conjunction with blood, was often used to describe the cultic act of sacrifice. The same association applies here as well, which means both the bread and the cup sayings in Luke use sacrificial language to describe Jesus' death. In addition, the cup saying also identifies the beneficiaries of this sacrifice using the same prepositional phrase "for you (ὑπὲρ ὑμῶν)" as he utilized in the bread saying. In light of this, it is clear that Luke's longer reading of the Last Supper emphasizes the sacrificial nature of Jesus' death, which is given in order to benefit his disciples. In fact, one can argue that Luke's institution narrative, which has used sacrificial language in both the bread and the cup saying, is more sacrificial than Mark's.

Thus far we have observed that both the bread and the cup saying affirm that Jesus' death would benefit his disciples, but what does Jesus' death accomplish for his disciples? The cup saying clearly specifies what is accomplished by Jesus death, for the cup is none other than "the new covenant in my blood" (Luke 22:20). Just like Matthew and Mark, Jesus' death will be the means by which the covenant with YHWH is inaugurated anew. However, Luke has one peculiar difference from Mark and Matthew in that he has identified this covenant as the "new covenant (ἡ καινὴ διαθήκη)." The addition of the adjective "new" changes the direction of the Old Testament allusion and brings the eschatological promises of Jeremiah 31 to the fore. The entire chapter of Jeremiah 31 anticipates God's restoration of Israel, of which the new covenant is one specific part of the larger vision of Israel's restoration. Since it is an essential part of Luke's understanding of the Last Supper, the passage can be quoted in full again here:

> The days are surely coming, says the Lord, when I will make a new covenant with the house of Israel and the house of Judah. It will not be like the covenant that I made with their ancestors when I took them by the hand to bring them out of the land of Egypt—a covenant that they broke, though I was their husband, says the Lord. But this is the covenant that I will make with the house of Israel after those days, says the Lord: I will put my law within them, and I will write it on their hearts; and I will be their God, and they shall be my people. No longer shall they teach one another, or say to each other, "Know the Lord," for they shall all know me, from the least of them to the greatest, says the Lord; for I will forgive their iniquity, and remember their sin no more (Jer 31:31–34).

We have already noted that Jesus' Last Supper had taken the Passover's orientation to Israel's past redemption in the exodus and redirected it toward what was about to be accomplished in the immediate future. This redirection from the past to the future is also present in the new covenant promise where YHWH promises that the new covenant "will not be like the covenant that I made with their ancestors when I took them by the hand to bring them out of the land of Egypt" (Jer 31:32). In a surprisingly similar way, Jesus' words of interpretation at the Last Supper do the same thing. Israel's salvation is no longer in the past but now at hand.

According to Jeremiah, the arrival of the new covenant would bring several things. First, God would put his "law within them." The exile had occurred because God's covenantal stipulations recorded in the law had been broken. The internalization of the law speaks to the transformation of God's covenant partner towards obedience. Thus, the new covenant would bring an ethical transformation of God's people, an internal transformation in which God would write the law "on their hearts." Second, YHWH says, "they shall all know me" (Jer 31:34), which implies that the knowledge of God will no longer be mediated by others. Finally, YHWH concludes with the reason why he could inaugurate a new covenant: " . . . I will forgive their iniquity, and remember their sin no more" (Jer 31:34). In the context of Israel's story, her sin and unfaithfulness had resulted in the exile and her punishment at the hands of foreign nations. The forgiveness of this sin would mean the end of the exile. In other words, Israel's restoration would commence when God forgave his people and inaugurated the new covenantal relationship with her. When Jesus says the cup is the "new covenant (ἡ καινὴ διαθήκη) in my blood," he is announcing to his listeners that this great eschatological hope, the forgiveness of sin and the repair of the covenant relationship, was coming true in his death. In other words, Jesus' death would be the event that ushered in the eschatological restoration of God's people. The age of Jeremiah's new covenant was dawning.

Even though Luke's account of the Last Supper has the clearest allusion to Jeremiah 31:31 of the Synoptics, this by no means excludes some of the other Old Testament texts like Exodus 24:8 and Zechariah 9:11. Jeremiah says nothing about the new covenant being sealed in blood, or as Jesus says, "in my blood (ἐν τῷ αἵματί μου)." The only other texts that combine the inauguration of the covenant with blood are Exodus 24:8 and Zechariah 9:11, which means these texts have not been displaced by moving Jeremiah 31:31 to the fore.[12] Their continued presence in Luke's version brings the atoning significance of Jesus' death into play too. In fact, by keeping all three passages (Jer 31:31–4; Exod 24:8; Zech 9:11) in view, one can conclude that the forgiveness of sins promised in the new covenant is made possible by Jesus' sacrificial death on the cross.[13]

The sequence of events after the distribution of the bread and the cup in Luke also differs from the other Synoptics. After passing the cup, Jesus announces that one of them will betray him, which instigates several disputes. The first concerns who would actually betray Jesus, but the second is a dispute regarding which of them was the greatest. Mark and Matthew record a similar dispute among the disciples regarding their importance. In both Matthew and Mark, Jesus authoritatively ends the dispute with the renowned ransom saying (Mark 10:45; Matt 20:28), which they both place earlier in their respective Gospels rather than at the Last Supper. In Luke, Jesus notoriously responds in a different way, without identifying his death as a ransom: "The kings of the Gentiles lord it over them; and those in authority over them are called benefactors. But not so with you; rather the greatest among you must become like the youngest, and the leader like one who serves. For who is greater, the one who is at the table or the one who serves?" (Luke 22:25–6). Instead of ending with the assertion that he would give his life as a ransom, Luke's version simply has Jesus saying, "But I am among you as one who serves" (Luke 22:27).

For many, this constitutes a Lukan redaction intentionally aimed at deleting any reference to atonement theology. However, there are several factors which do not warrant such a conclusion. First, its proximity to the Last Supper sayings clarifies for the reader that Jesus' service is his death

---

12. Nolland, *Luke 18:35–24:53*, 1054; Bornkamm, *Early Christian Experience*, 140; and Tan, *Zion Traditions*, 216. Tan affirms the twin allusion to Exodus and Jeremiah, but he fails to incorporate the Zechariah passage.

13. Thus, it is going too far to state flatly that "Luke avoids the particular Jewish belief of vicarious death" as asserted in Eben Scheffler, "The Meaning of Jesus' Death," 159.

as a covenant-inaugurating sacrifice.¹⁴ Mark and Matthew both situate the saying much earlier in their Gospels. With its location disconnected from the Last Supper, they had to make lexical connections to attach the ransom saying to the Last Supper, which they do by making sure both sayings have the same beneficiaries in view, namely, the "many." What Luke might lack in the absence of the word "ransom" or the prepositional phrase "for many" he has made up for by placing his discussion on service directly on the heels of the Last Supper account. The only kind of significant service in view is his death as a covenant-inaugurating sacrifice.¹⁵

Second, there are lexical connections that tie the saying about service immediately back to what just occurred at the Last Supper. In Jesus' rebuke of his disciples, he asks "For who is greater, the one who is at the table (ὁ ἀνακείμενος) or the one who serves? Is it not the one at the table (ὁ ἀνακείμενος)?" (Luke 22:27). This particular sentence is absent in Mark and Matthew's version of the ransom saying, yet its presence reveals Luke's emphasis. On the one hand, it constitutes an intra-textual allusion back to Jesus' teaching that the faithful servant will be served by his master at the banquet (Luke 12:35–38). On the other hand, Luke is referring to the events that have just been narrated regarding the Last Supper.¹⁶ At the Last Supper, Jesus served his disciples with a meal at a table, and this meal symbolized an ever greater service, namely, that he would give his life for their benefit. Luke's unique additions about being served at a table demand that we interpret his service in light of what just occurred at the Last Supper.

Third, many have observed that Luke's Passion narrative, including his Last Supper discourse, has followed a source other than Mark.¹⁷ This does

---

14. Cooke, "Covenant Sacrifice," 22; Scheffler, "Jesus' Death," 156; O'Toole, *The Unity of Luke's Theology*, 178; and Tannehill, "Theology of Luke-Acts," 200.

15. Following Poon, "Superabundant Table Fellowship," 228. Though Tannehill is aware Jesus' death constitutes his service for the disciples, he fails to find the soteriological implications. See Tannehill, "Theology of Luke-Acts," 202–3.

16. Luke 22:14 introduces the setting in a way that Mark does not: "When the hour came, he took his place at the table (ἀνέπεσεν), and the apostles with him." Though ἀναπίπτω need not imply the presence of a table, it was often used in the context of meals and therefore connoted the presence of a table or meal setting (BDAG, 70). The verb ἀνάκειμαι used in Luke 22:27 appears synonymous in the context. As a result, Luke's unique reference to serving at a table very likely builds upon the immediately preceding episode (i.e. the Last Supper), which occurred while they were reclining at the table.

17. Green, *Death of Jesus*, 46. For evidence, he shows that some of the words used in the passage are hapax legomena and depart from traditional Lukan style (e.g. φιλονεικία, ἐξουσιάζω, and εὐεργέτης). It is also hard to explain why Luke would reduce Mark's κατακυριεύω to the simpler κυριεύω. As a result, he concludes that Luke is using a source other than Mark. See also Marshall, *Last Supper*, 102 and Jeremias, *Eucharistic Words*, 98–99.

in fact seem to be the case since Luke has arranged events and sayings in the Last Supper account quite differently than Mark does, which is not true of Matthew's account that follows Mark quite closely. If Luke is relying upon a non-Markan source at this point, there is no need to see the absence of the word "ransom" in this saying as an intentional deletion of atonement theology. To put it bluntly, Jesus' service to his disciples is spelled out in the immediately preceding section where he interpreted his death as the inauguration of the new covenant.

At this point, it would be helpful to explain the significance of these observations. For the reasons noted above, the followers of Girard who rely upon Luke's version of the saying in order to suggest that we should not interpret Matthew and Mark's ransom saying sacrificially miss the point. Luke's saying on service derives its force from the Last Supper saying that immediately precedes it. Even if one believes Luke has intentionally deleted a theology of exchange from his form of the logion, it by no means allows one to delete such notions from Matthew and Mark as some of Girard's followers have done.[18] Furthermore, we cannot, as Bartlett does, use this logion as the hermeneutical key for understanding Luke's Last Supper sayings.[19] Quite frankly, the inverse occurs. Luke's Last Supper account defines the kind of service Jesus performs on behalf of his followers. It is the very service he has just discussed before them "at the table": he would give his life as a new covenant-inaugurating sacrifice, the very covenant that was to bring an end to Israel's sin.

Postlude

Luke's account of the Last Supper includes a few more conversations than what one finds in Mark and Matthew, most of which have some kind of connection with the passages already discussed. In fact, Jesus' statement about service is directly applicable to the disciples who will need to incarnate this form of leadership because Jesus turns and says to them, "You are those who have stood by me in my trials; and I confer (διατίθεμαι) on you, just as my Father has conferred (διέθετό) on me, a kingdom, so that you may eat and drink at my table in my kingdom, and you will sit on thrones judging the twelve tribes of Israel" (Luke 22:28–30).[20] Here is one of the most explicit

---

18. E.g., Williams, *Bible, Violence, and the Sacred*, 202.

19. Bartlett, *Cross Purposes*, 212.

20. Scott Hahn has argued that διατίθεμαι has the connotation of covenanting, instead of leaving a last will and testament. While this point is compelling, he has not persuaded me that the covenant in view during Luke's Last Supper sayings is predominantly the Davidic covenant. Hahn, *Kinship by Covenant*, 217–37.

assertions from Jesus that he stands in possession of the kingdom and serves as its king. In doing so, it is only to turn it over to his disciples who will receive this kingdom and judge the twelve tribes. Additionally, the statement affirms that Jesus' role in the kingdom—and hence Israel's restoration—is being passed on to his disciples who will function as Israel's judges. This saying following the Last Supper sayings again reminds the reader of the eschatological significance of what is about to transpire and affirms that the arrival of the kingdom is synonymous with the restoration of Israel.

A few other conversations occur before Luke ends the Last Supper discourse. Jesus first predicts that Peter will deny him three times despite Peter's avowal that he will be faithful to death. Then Jesus gives his disciples an enigmatic command to go and buy a sword (Luke 22:36). At this point, Jesus launches into a prediction formula: "For I tell you, this scripture must be fulfilled in me, 'And he was counted among the lawless (ἀνόμων)'; and indeed what is written about me is being fulfilled'" (Luke 22:37). This logion about buying swords has mystified many. Who exactly are the "lawless" ones? Some have argued it would be the disciples, hence the need to attain the swords, so they could be considered bandits.[21] Others have suggested that the "lawless" ones anticipate the coming crucifixion where Jesus is crucified alongside "criminals (κακοῦργοι)" (Luke 23:32). Without getting sidetracked by the particular identity of the lawless people, the more important part of this saying is the fact that Isaiah 53:12 is cited as the prophecy that "must be fulfilled in me" (Luke 22:37). In fact, this is the only citation of Isaiah 53 in the Synoptic Passion tradition. The necessity of this prophecy, which also describes the suffering and vindication of YHWH's servant, smoothly segues the reader into the betrayal, arrest, and crucifixion of the Messiah.[22] The events about to unfold mirror the experiences of the Isaianic servant who was also marred and maltreated by others, but ultimately was vindicated by God.

---

21. Minear, "Note on Luke 22:36," 128–34. Fitmyer, however, calls this view "strange." Fitzmyer, *Gospel according to Luke*, 2:1433.

22. Regardless of one's conclusion on Luke's use of the atoning dimension of Isaiah 53, Luke has cast Jesus in the role of Isaiah's suffering servant, which Joel Green has identified in the following: 1) the centurion's confession of Jesus as righteous in Luke 23:47; 2) The portrait of Jesus Luke develops on the Mount of Olives in Luke 22:39–46; 3) Luke alone has Jesus citing from Isa 52:13—53:12 in Luke 22:35–37; and 4) Luke uses Isaianic Servant language to explicate Jesus' identity (Luke 2:32; Acts 8:32–33). Green, "The Death of Jesus," 18–28. Cf. Larkin, "Use of the Old Testament," 325–35 and Marshall, *Luke*, 171–72. Marshall also argues that the use of παῖς in Acts 3:13, 26; 4:27, 30 identifies Jesus as the Isaianic servant, though this is not as compelling.

Integration with the Rest of Luke-Acts

Up to this point, I have argued that the longer version of the Luke's Last Supper tradition affirms that the new covenant era has dawned, being ushered in by Jesus' death, which is a covenant-inaugurating sacrifice. Though the notion of Christ's death as atonement is not the only theme present in the sayings, it certainly seems to be one of the dominant points of the text. However, if we are to conclude that Luke's Last Supper sayings also present Jesus' death as an atonement for sin, we can only do so by dissenting with the sentiment of much Lukan scholarship.[23] For example, consider Conzelmann's bold declaration that the author of Luke-Acts betrays "no trace of any Passion mysticism, nor is any direct soteriological significance drawn from Jesus' suffering or death. There is no suggestion of a connection with the forgiveness of sins."[24] Conzelmann's position is typical of many in the field. Even conservative scholars like Tannehill follow in his stead: "The death of Jesus is never interpreted as atonement for sins in the mission speeches of Acts, nor is the death of Jesus ever singled out as the basis for the release of sins or the salvation in Jesus' name which the missionaries are proclaiming."[25] For the most part, this view remains entrenched in Lukan scholarship with recent theologians still averring that Luke "originally contained not a single hit of atonement."[26] Thus, for many, Luke has either entirely expunged atonement theology from his account or repressed it.[27]

Some voices have cautioned against such an outright denial of Lukan atonement theology.[28] There have been a few attempts, with varying degrees of success, that have tried to find lingering evidence of an atonement theology in Luke-Acts. For example, Carpinelli has argued that Luke still retains

---

23. Regarding the recent state of Lukan research, see van Zyl, "Jesus' Death in Luke Acts," 533–57 and Reardon, "Recent Trajectories," 77–95.

24. Conzelmann, *Theology of St Luke*, 201. For similar conclusions, see Talbert, *Reading Luke*, 209, 212–13; Kümmel, "Current Theological Accusations," 134, 138; Tyson, *Death of Jesus*, 170; Haenchen, *Acts of the Apostles*, 92; Taylor, *The Passion Narrative*, 139; du Plessis, "The Saving Significance of Jesus," 523–40; Hultgren, *Christ and His Benefits*, 83–84; George, "La mort de Jésus," 186–217; and Bovon, *Luc le théologien*, 175–81.

25. Tannehill, *Gospel According to Luke*, 285.

26. Finlan, *Options on Atonement*, 38. Here he overlooks Acts 20:28 and predictably favors the shorter version of Luke's Last Supper saying.

27. Those seeing a suppression of atonement theology include: Käsemann, *Essays on New Testament Themes*, 92; Hengel, *The Atonement*, 34–35; Navone, *Themes of St. Luke*, 143; and Buckwalter, *Luke's Christology*, 74; cf. 254–57.

28. Marshall, *Last Supper*, 102.

a theology of expiation informed by the LXX.[29] For him, the decisive data lies in Luke's use of phrases like εἰς ἀνάμνησιν and εἰς μνημόσυνον, which reflect the expiatory rituals of almsgiving and other practices in ancient Judaism. In the context of Luke, Jesus' self-offering constitutes another cultic rite that memorializes God's atonement on behalf of his people. Thus, atonement theology can be unearthed in the underlying strata and assumptions in Luke, even though it might not find explicit articulation. Schroder and Fitzmyer take a different tack and emphasize Jesus' dialogue with the thief on the cross where the thief realizes that he is receiving his just deserts, whereas Jesus, the innocent one, can save repentant sinners.[30] Doble has argued that Luke does possess a *theologia crucis* without necessarily invoking atonement theology.[31] For him, Jesus is the δίκαιος who innocently suffers his fate and therefore receives vindication at the hand of God. Though interesting, these projects have hardly overturned the consensus view. At best they have undermined some of the confidence in the dominant view but have ultimately failed to supplant it. Probably the most supportive of Lukan atonement theology has been the recent work of David P. Moessner, but his voice has been a minority in the field.[32]

Some Lukan scholars are willing to grant the presence of atonement theology in the Last Supper and in Acts 20:28, which says that the church was "obtained with the blood of his Son," but still deny that this reflects Luke's own soteriology. For instance, Joel Green says that Luke has inserted this material (Luke 22:19–20 and Acts 20:28) into his narrative in a "mechanical" way to the effect that it is disconnected from his theological viewpoint.[33] According to him, both passages were adopted from Luke's sources and do not represent Luke's own thought. As a result, Green concludes that Luke has not "made this material more a part of his own thinking by integrating it into his style."[34] In other words, Luke 22:19–20 and Acts 20:28 are

---

29. Carpinelli, "My Memorial," 74–91.

30. Schroder, "Luke's Gospel," 337–46; Fitzmyer, *Luke the Theologian*, 210–22; and Fitzmyer, *Gospel according to Luke*, 1:22–23, 219–21.

31. Doble, *Paradox of Salvation*, 235. Unfortunately, his work ignores the Last Supper sayings and Acts 20:28, which jeopardizes the ability of his conclusions to speak definitively about all of Luke-Acts. A similar argument can be found in: Karris, "Jesus' Death," 65–74 and Karris, *Luke*, 101–4, 121.

32. Moessner, "Christ Must Suffer," 165–95.

33. Green, "God's Servant," 4. Regarding Acts 20:28, he says Luke "appears to be merely parroting ancient phraseology. He has not developed this motif. He has not 'owned' it." Cf., Ibid., 7 and Green and Baker, *Recovering the Scandal*, 70.

34. Green, "Message of Salvation," 24. In a more recent essay, he suggests Acts 20:28 and Luke 22:19–20 should caution interpreters from concluding that the notion of a substitutionary death is completely absent in Luke-Acts, though he does not think

free-floating bits of tradition that Luke has assimilated but not integrated into the manner in which his works present the soteriological effects of Jesus' death.[35]

Is this an accurate understanding of Luke-Acts? Does the longer reading of the Last Supper simply represent an instance where alien or partially digested concepts have been indiscriminately adopted because of Luke's allegiance to the traditions he inherited? In what follows, I will argue that the theology of the longer version of the Last Supper is not a free-floating relic of tradition, but a theological way of viewing Jesus' death that is woven into the larger narrative of Luke-Acts and is therefore integrated into his text.[36] In arguing this line of thought, I am not suggesting that Luke has developed a theology of atonement to the degree that Paul, Hebrews, or Mark does nor that Luke's soteriology is completely defined by a theology of atonement. Luke has certainly emphasized the exaltation/resurrection of Jesus as Israel's Davidic king more than Jesus' death as a means of atonement, and what follows is not meant to challenge that he emphasizes the resurrection more than Christ's death. With this caveat in place, I contend that scholars ignore considerable evidence when they avouch that Luke has no theology of atonement or that the two places where it appears are simply portions that have been "mechanically" adopted by Luke.

To begin, Luke speaks of Jesus either forgiving or offering the "forgiveness of sins" more than any other New Testament author, which is surprising given that atonement theology seems more securely rooted in Matthew and Mark.[37] Assertions like Green's can only be made if we ignore the obvious, though latent, connection between the inauguration of the new covenant at the Last Supper and YHWH's promise in the new covenant prophecy to forgive Israel's "iniquity and remember their sin no more" (Jer 31:34). By

---

these texts are indicative of all of Luke's soteriology. Nevertheless, they do preclude one from discrediting any presence of substitution. Green, "Significance of Jesus' Death," 71–85.

35. Zehnle, "Salvific Character of Jesus' Death," 439–40. Green writes, "In summary, Luke was certainly aware of the interpretation of Jesus' death as the basis for human salvation, but he did not choose to develop this notion as a critical or significant element either of his understanding of the crucifixion of Jesus or of his soteriology." Green, "Message of Salvation," 24.

36. Some have contended this is present in Luke. See Steyn "Soteriological Perspectives," 96.

37. Matthew: 9:2, 5–6; 12:31; 18:21; 26:28. Mark: 1:4; 2:5–10; 3:28–29. Johannine Literature: John 20:23; 1 John 1:9; 2:12. Paul: Col. 1:14. General Epistles: Heb 9:22; Jas 5:15. By comparison Luke-Acts contains a far more extensive affirmation that Jesus provides the forgiveness of sins: Luke 1:77; 3:3; 5:20–24; 7:47–49; 24:47; Acts 2:38; 5:31; 10:43; 13:38; 26:18.

positing Jesus' death as the inauguration of the new covenant—elements that he has likely taken from tradition but still employed in his own theological portrait—Luke emphasizes the new covenant blessings of forgiveness to those who repent and believe throughout his narrative. In fact, one can put it more forcefully: the characters in Luke-Acts are only able to speak of God's offer of forgiveness on the basis of the new covenant's inauguration, which the Last Supper identifies with Jesus' sacrificial death.

Jesus' Meals with Sinners

The theology of the Last Supper explains some of the unanswered questions that have lingered throughout the Gospel. As a meal, the Last Supper stands at the zenith of a series of meal scenes in Luke that have slowly been building towards the theological explanation provided in the Last Supper. In fact, Luke has recorded Jesus' practice of eating at table more than any other Synoptic, and scholars have long noted that the meals Jesus had were tactile experiences of the kingdom's arrival.[38] As one author put it, eating a meal with Jesus "was both the offer in the present of the possibility of a new kind of relationship with God and with one's neighbor, and an anticipation of the fellowship to be expected in the future in the consummated kingdom of God."[39] Thus, when Jesus shared a meal he was symbolically enacting the forgiveness and inclusion offered in the kingdom.

It is noteworthy that Jesus' dinner guests were often the unsavory sort, earning Jesus the reputation of being "a glutton and a drunkard, a friend of tax collectors and sinners!" (Luke 7:34). To illustrate why Jesus received such criticism, Luke follows the charge with a story where Jesus dines at a Pharisee's house. During the meal, a woman bearing the scornful opprobrium of "a sinner" came into the house and broke an alabaster jar of ointment over his feet (Luke 7:37). Jesus' host is repulsed by the presence of such a notorious sinner whom Jesus permits to touch him. Despite offending his host, Jesus uses this as an instance to make a theological point. He tells the story about a lender canceling the debts for two people who owed vastly different amounts to show that the one who was forgiven the greater debt would love more (Luke 7:41–43). At the end of the episode, Jesus turns to the woman and says, "Your sins are forgiven" (Luke 7:48). The pronouncement of forgiveness perplexes those at the table and they ask, "Who is this who even forgives sins?" (Luke 7:49). The question, of course, is meant to

---

38. It is quite likely that Jesus' practice of eating meals was directly relevant to the social issues of Luke's day. See Smit, *Fellowship and Food*, 199.

39. Crockett, *Eucharist*, 6.

raise the curiosity of the reader. Who does Jesus think he is anyway? Luke never answers the question in this episode, but he leaves the reader mulling over the question. What is left unanswered in this episode finds its explanation in a later meal, the Last Supper, where Jesus' death inaugurates the new covenant, which brings forgiveness to Israel. Because Jesus is the one whose death inaugurates the new covenant and ushers in the fullness of the kingdom, Jesus has the authority to forgive sins.

Post-Resurrection Meal in Emmaus

Not only do the earlier meal scenes with notorious sinners anticipate the theology of the Last Supper, but the post-resurrection meals also look back to the Last Supper. The first of these meal episodes begins when the risen, but unrecognized Lord happens upon two disciples traveling toward Emmaus deliberating over the Passion events. As Jesus joins the pair, the narrator explains that "their eyes were kept from recognizing him" (Luke 24:16). When Jesus appears ignorant regarding the crucifixion and resurrection reports, the two quickly inform him about the crucifixion, which not only exterminated Jesus' life but also their hopes "that he was the one to redeem (ὁ μέλλων λυτροῦσθαι) Israel" (Luke 24:21).[40]

The account is thick with irony. The disciples who believe the crucifixion has extinguished the hope that Jesus could redeem Israel no longer recognize his physical appearance. In fact, the disciples verbally reveal their incomprehension of Jesus' identity because they describe him as just "a prophet mighty in deed and word" (Luke 24:19), but nothing more. To compound the irony, the disciples believe that Jesus is the one who is ignorant of the recent happenings in Jerusalem, but in reality they are ignorant. They fail to see what God was doing in and through the death and resurrection of Jesus Christ.[41] Thus, their physical inability to recognize Jesus mirrors their spiritual myopia.

In response to their confusion, the risen Jesus does not dismiss their hopes as unfounded but instead affirms them through a different means. To put it in the words of the disciples, the risen Lord does not deny that he is the one to "redeem Israel," but redefines how this would occur, namely, through death and resurrection. In fact, the risen Christ seems incredulous with the disciples on the road to Emmaus for failing to recognize this and

40. I disagree here with those who believe λυτρόω simply speaks of liberation because they fail to see that Luke continues to connect this to the necessity of death and resurrection and ultimately to the forgiveness of sins. E.g. Zehnle "Lucan Soteriology," 439.

41. Weatherly, "Eating and Drinking," 21.

responds to their quandary by saying: "Oh how foolish you are, and how slow of heart to believe all that the prophets have declared! Was it not necessary that the Messiah should suffer these things and then enter into his glory?" (Luke 24:25–26). Jesus' response does two things. First, it establishes Jesus as more than a prophet, which is all that the disciples had been able to say about him. Jesus is the Messiah, the one to whom the prophets pointed. Second, it presumes that the Old Testament prophecies necessitated the suffering of the Messiah. Therefore, his death was not the annihilation of their hopes for redemption, but following the course that the prophets predicted. Despite receiving a thorough lesson on biblical prophecy, the disciples still do not recognize Jesus, even though the Scriptural precedent for his death and resurrection was traced through the Old Testament, "beginning with Moses and all the prophets" (Luke 24:27). They implore the unrecognized Jesus to stay for the night, and he consents after demurring for a time.

The next scene is essential for seeing how this episode connects to the Last Supper. Seated at the table Jesus "took bread, blessed and broke it, and gave it to them" (Luke 24:30). The setting and the actions of Jesus at the meal intentionally reduplicate Jesus' actions at the Last Supper and cast this post-resurrection meal as a Eucharistic meal, even if the wine is absent.[42] It is only at this point, at the breaking of the bread, when "their eyes were opened, and they recognized him; and he vanished from their sight" (Luke 24:31). Their former inability to see and understand Jesus vanishes upon the breaking and blessing of the bread, both Eucharistic actions.

What occurs at the meal in Emmaus is something akin to Mark's centurion gazing at Jesus on the cross. The reader will recall that, for Mark, it is only by gazing upon the cross that the human centurion understands

---

42. Compare Luke 22:19: "λαβὼν ἄρτον εὐχαριστήσας ἔκλασεν καὶ ἔδωκεν αὐτοῖς" with Luke 24:30: "λαβὼν τὸν ἄρτον εὐλόγησεν καὶ κλάσας ἐπεδίδου αὐτοῖς." Several scholars concur that an intratextual allusion to the Last Supper is present. See LaVerdiere, *Dining in the Kingdom*, 170; O'Toole, *Luke's Theology*, 46–47, 202–3, 254–55; and Dupont, "Meal at Emmaus," 116–19. Dupont bases his conviction upon the fact that the "breaking of bread (τῇ κλάσει τοῦ ἄρτου)" in Acts 2:42 most certainly has the Eucharist in view. Thus, it is likely present here as well. Not all, however, are convinced that a Eucharistic meal is implied in the Emmaus account. E.g. Nolland, *Luke 18:35–24:53*, 1208; Plummer, *Gospel according to S. Luke*, 556; and Morris, *Gospel according to St. Luke*, 340. Against the argument that the Emmaus disciples were not present at the Last Supper, one can respond by saying this is a literary work and the reader has been privy to the Last Supper events even if these two disciples were not. Some have noted it could allude to the feeding miracle of Luke 9. However, the verbal parallel with Luke 9:16 is too inexact ("λαβὼν δὲ τοὺς πέντε ἄρτους καὶ τοὺς δύο ἰχθύας ἀναβλέψας εἰς τὸν οὐρανὸν εὐλόγησεν αὐτοὺς καὶ κατέκλασεν καὶ ἐδίδου τοῖς μαθηταῖς") for this to be the primary allusion. In my view, the close verbal parallels indicate the Emmaus account should be read Eucharistically.

Jesus' identity as God's Son. The same phenomenon is occurring here, only the event that provides the insight into Jesus' identity and mission is not the crucifixion but the Eucharist, which supplies the soteriological significance of the crucifixion.[43] The disciples of Emmaus who cannot believe a redeeming Messiah could suffer such an ignominious death realize in the Eucharistic act of breaking bread that the crucified one was and still is the Messiah.[44] By locating the moment of recognition at the point of breaking bread and not with Jesus' recitation of Scripture, Luke reveals that it is not simply Scriptural precedent that necessitates Jesus' death but the theological rationale provided at the Last Supper.[45] The Scriptural antecedents were only "a preparation" for the understanding that was about to dawn, but not an efficient cause of it.[46] As a result, the Eucharistic breaking of bread, which looks back to the Last Supper before the crucifixion provides the theological explanation for how Jesus can be a redeeming Messiah in spite of his death.[47] The upshot of all of this is that the Emmaus episode has led the reader right back to scene of the Last Supper where Jesus broke bread and dispersed the wine, saying that these elements were symbolic of his coming death on behalf of his followers, which would inaugurate the new covenant. Thus, if we are going to understand Luke's point in the Emmaus episode correctly, Jesus is not the redeeming Messiah in spite of his death but *by means* of his death.

The Emmaus episode also warrants a reassessment of the claim that Luke's theology has deleted Mark's notion of "ransom theology" from his account. For many, Luke's failure to restate Mark's saying to the effect that Jesus will give his life as a λύτρον (ransom) mandates a significant departure from Markan atonement theology. However, the issue should not be decided simply on the basis of this one saying. Though Luke never uses the noun λύτρον, he does use other cognates of word throughout his Gospel to describe what God would do in and through Jesus. The opening lines of Zechariah's *Benedictus* declares: "Blessed be the Lord God of Israel, for he has looked favorably on his people and redeemed (ἐποίησεν λύτρωσιν)

---

43. The point of the episode, unlike the one that follows it, is not to provide apologetic evidence for the resurrection. Dupont, "Meal at Emmaus," 109–10. Instead, the account is making the theological point that Jesus, not simply in spite of, but by means of death and resurrection, has fulfilled Israel's hopes for redemption.

44. Thus, the conclusion that Carroll and Green take on this passage is still a halfway house towards penetrating into what Luke is actually communicating in this episode. They write that Luke "goes on to show only that the cross was not a contradiction of such longings, not that the cross was directly instrumental in instigating God's redemption" (Carroll and Green, *Death of Jesus*, 267–68).

45. Contra Caird, *Gospel of St Luke*, 258–59.

46. Dupont, "Meal at Emmaus," 120.

47. Ibid., 120–21.

them" (Luke 1:68). Likewise, Anna the prophetess who greets the newborn Jesus in the temple was delighted to see the infant Jesus for she was "looking for the redemption (λύτρωσιν) of Jerusalem" (Luke 2:38). For Luke, Jesus inaugurates the redemption of God's people and he opens his Gospel by affirming that such hopes will be met in Jesus.

To be sure, λύτρωσις has a broad semantic range. One the one hand, it can simply speak of redemption as liberation from some kind of bondage without any kind of exchange being in view. On the other hand, it can describe the act of liberating someone or something by means of an exchange or purchase.[48] It is difficult to know how Luke uses the word, but it is certainly possible that its use in Zechariah's blessing implies an exchange since the redemption that God is bringing through Jesus will result in the "forgiveness of sins" (Luke 1:77).[49] The only other use of λύτρωσις in the New Testament does in fact employ this meaning.[50] In the LXX, the word is most frequently used to capture the notion of an exchange where something is given in order to purchase something else.[51] If Luke was influenced by the LXX, then his usage of λύτρωσις likely implies that God's liberation of

---

48. BDAG, 606.

49. In this portion of the Benedictus, Zechariah is speaking directly about John the Baptist and says "you will go before the Lord to prepare his ways, to give knowledge of salvation to his people by the forgiveness of their sins" (Luke 1:76b–77). John himself would soon be "proclaiming a baptism of repentance for the forgiveness of sins" (Luke 3:3). Though it could be that the Benedictus' allusion to the forgiveness of sins points simply to his future ministry of baptism, the Benedictus suggests that John will not be accomplishing this in his ministry, but will be witnessing to something that God will do in bringing salvation to his people. As such, it has in view what will be developed later in the Gospel as well—which finds its fullest articulation in the Last Supper—and not just John's baptism.

50. "[Jesus] entered once for all into the Holy Place, not with the blood of goats and calves, but with his own blood, thus obtaining eternal redemption (λύτρωσιν)" (Heb 9:12).

51. The word referred to purchasing a good many things like buying back property that had been sold to pay debts (Lev 25:29, 48) or the necessary payment required to buy back from YHWH the firstborn of any womb (Lev 18:16–17). Caleb's daughter who is allotted land in the arid southern portion of the land asks for a λύτρωσιν "of water" (Judges 1:15). Psalm 49:8 (48:9 LXX) speaks about the human inability to give a "ransom," a λυτρώσεως, for one's life to pay for their iniquities. Psalm 130 again invokes the purchasing connotation: "O Israel, hope in the Lord! For with the Lord there is steadfast love, and with him is great power to redeem (λύτρωσιν). It is he who will redeem (λυτρώσεται) Israel from all its iniquities" (Ps 130:7–8; 129:7–8 LXX). Only two instances in the Old Testament fail to invoke the connotation of purchasing or paying something as a means of liberating it. Psalm 111:9 (110:9 LXX) speaks of God sending "redemption (λύτρωσιν) to his people," a usage which does not necessarily have the notion of an exchange or purchase in view. The final occurrence is Isaiah 63:4 where YHWH declares "For the day of vengeance was in my heart, and the year for my redeeming work (λυτρώσεως) had come," which refers to YHWH's war against Israel's enemies.

his people will occur on the basis of an exchange or purchase, which he develops most explicitly in the Last Supper scene.

For much of the Gospel, the language of redemption fades into the background. However, it emerges again at the very end of the Gospel on the road to Emmaus, but this time Luke uses the verb form.[52] The two despondent disciples tell the risen Christ "we had hoped that he was the one to redeem (λυτροῦσθαι) Israel" (Luke 24:21). In fact, Luke had given such hopes to his readers in Zechariah's *Benedictus*, so the disciples on the road to Emmaus articulate the very questions facing Luke's readers: Can Jesus still be Israel's redeeming Messiah if he dies on the cross? Luke's risen Jesus traces the hope for Israel's redemption right through the cross, indicating it was "necessary that the Messiah should suffer these things and then enter into his glory" (Luke 24:26), which affirms rather than denies the necessity of Israel's redemption. To put it simply, the risen Lord indicates the suffering and resurrection of the Messiah are essential to accomplish the redemption of Israel, and this realization only dawns at the moment of breaking bread.[53]

---

52. The verb form is only used two more times in the New Testament, and each time it implies a purchase or exchange. For example, Titus 2:14 says: "He it is who gave himself for us that he might redeem (λυτρώσηται) us from all iniquity and purify for himself a people of his own who are zealous for good deeds." In a similar manner, 1 Peter 1:18–19 says: "You know that you were ransomed (ἐλυτρώθητε) from the futile ways inherited from your ancestors, not with perishable things like silver or gold, but with the precious blood of Christ, like that of a lamb without defect or blemish."

Its use in the Pentateuch often involves the exchange of a payment in order to free something else. Exod 13:13, 15; 34:20; Lev 19:20; 25:25, 30, 33, 48–49, 54; 27:13, 15, 19, 20, 27, 28–29, 31, 33; Num 18:15, 17. Other texts outside of the Pentateuch also carry the explicit connotation of an exchange: Ps 49:7 (48:8 LXX); 49:15 (48:16 LXX); Isa 52:3.

In several instances, the action of redeeming is set in parallelism with or infers the means by which sins are forgiven: Ps 103:4 (102:4 LXX); 130:8 (129:8 LXX); Isa 44:22–24; Dan 4:27. In Daniel 4:27 LXX, the translator assumes that the giving of alms will be a means of redeeming the king from his sins.

At other points, the explicit notion of exchange is absent, and the action of "redeeming" is more equivalent to rescuing someone from calamity. From slavery in Egypt: Exod 6:6; 15:13; Deut 7:8; 9:26; 13:5 (LXX 13:6); 15:15; 21:8; 24:18; 2 Sam 7:23; 1 Chron 17:21; Neh 1:10; Ps 74:2 (73:2 LXX); 78:42 (77:42 LXX); 106:10 (105:10 LXX); Mic 6:4. Of David's rescue from adversity: 2 Sam 4:9; 1 Kgs 1:19; Ps 7:2 (7:3 LXX); 31:5 (30:6 LXX); 32:7 (31:7 LXX); 34:22 (33:23 LXX); 55:18 (54:19 LXX); 59:1 (58:2 LXX); 69:18 (68:19 LXX); 144:10 (143:10 LXX). Of the political rescue of Israel under oppression: Esth 4:17 LXX; Ps 25:22 (24:22 LXX); 26:11 (25:11 LXX); 44:26 (43:27 LXX); 77:15 (76:16 LXX); Hos 7:13; Mic 4:10; Zeph 3:15; Zech 10:8; Isa 41:14; 51:11; 62:12; 63:9; Jer 15:21; 31:11 (38:11 LXX). Protection from general adversity: Ps 71:23 (70:23 LXX) 72:14 (71:14 LXX); 107:2 (106:2 LXX); 119:134 (118:134 LXX); 119:154 (118:154 LXX); 136:24 (135:24 LXX); Prov 23:11; Isa 35:9; 43:1, 14; Lam 3:58; 5:8; Dan 3:88 (LXX); 6:28 (LXX). Redemption from death: Hos 13:14.

53. In light of this, Carpinelli misses the point when he believes that redemption

If the Emmaus episode does invite the reader to return to the Last Supper scene as I have contended, then the Last Supper scene more fully explains how Jesus redeems Israel: his death would be the purchase or moment of exchange ushering in the new covenant era. If this accurately articulates Luke's use of redemption in the Emmaus account, then certain scholars err when they confidently conclude that Luke, simply by choosing not to use λύτρον in one place where Mark did, thus sanitized his account of ransom language or atonement theology.

Post-Resurrection Meal in Jerusalem

Luke's account of the resurrected Lord continues with one more scene in the Gospel. The end of the Emmaus account transitions seamlessly into the next meal scene wherein the Emmaus disciples return to Jerusalem to inform the eleven disciples. When they report their encounter of the risen Lord, they announce that "he had been made known to them in the breaking of the bread (ἐν τῇ κλάσει τοῦ ἄρτου)" (Luke 24:35). Such an introductory statement serves to keep the Emmaus account in view and therefore connects the next meal in Jerusalem with what happened before at Emmaus. Furthermore, it reiterates the former point made to the effect that it is the Eucharistic act of breaking bread—with its rearward focus on the content of the Last Supper sayings—that allows one to penetrate into the mysterious nature of this Messiah.[54]

While the Emmaus disciples are recounting their prior experience of the risen Lord, Jesus appears again to those who were gathered. This time, instead of breaking bread, Jesus has a fish (Luke 24:42–43).[55] At the end of this encounter with the resurrected Lord, Jesus again "opened their minds to understand the scriptures" (Luke 24:45) and affirms that the death and resurrection of the Messiah follow the Scriptural expectations: "Thus it is written that the Messiah is to suffer and to rise from the dead on the third day, and that repentance and forgiveness of sins (εἰς ἄφεσιν ἁμαρτιῶν) is

and expiation are entirely separate domains since Luke often weds them together. Carpinelli, "My Memorial," 80–82, 88.

54. Some, unfortunately, only see the connection with the feeding miracles and not the Eucharistic connection. E.g. Parker, *Living Text*, 154 and Poon, "Superabundant Table," 229–30.

55. Together these post-resurrection meals in which Jesus eats both bread in the first and fish in the second recall Jesus' earlier feeding miracle where he miraculously multiples food for his listeners (Luke 9:10–17). Moloney, *Body Broken*, 109–10. In addition, this second appearance wherein Jesus dines on a fish demonstrates the physicality of his resurrection because "a ghost does not have flesh and bones as you see that I have" (Luke 24:39).

to be proclaimed (κηρυχθῆναι) in his name to all nations, beginning from Jerusalem" (Luke 24:46-47). Though short, this quotation does two important things. First, it introduces the notion that forgiveness of sins is bound up with the Messiah's suffering and resurrection.[56] Second, it imparts to Jesus' disciples the same role of proclamation that he had assumed in the synagogue in Nazareth at the beginning of the Gospel and expands it to include the Gentiles.[57] In Luke 4, Jesus read from Isaiah 61 to appropriate the Isaianic prophecies "He has sent me to proclaim (κηρύξαι) release (ἄφεσιν) to the captives" and "to let the oppressed go free (ἀφέσει)" (Luke 4:18) to himself. Jesus' final appearance to the disciples imparts this role of proclamation to his followers and clarifies the nature of the ἄφεσις Jesus brings, namely, the forgiveness of sins. In essence, Jesus has bequeathed his ministry of the kingdom and the proclamation of the forgiveness of sins to his disciples.

At this point, if we take a step back and ask ourselves what passage has laid the theological groundwork for Jesus to pass his role of preaching about the kingdom and the forgiveness of sins on to his disciples, are we not directed back to the Last Supper? It was there that Luke's unique version of the Last Supper discourse has Jesus saying, "I confer on you, just as my Father has conferred on me, a kingdom" (Luke 22:29). Jesus had given his disciples authority in the kingdom at the Last Supper, and this final meal scene further elaborates by explicitly endowing them with the responsibility of proclaiming the presence of the kingdom. In addition, the connection of Jesus' death to the forgiveness of sins is theologically connected to the longer version of the Last Supper sayings which characterizes Jesus' death as the event inaugurating the new covenant, the same covenant that would bring the forgiveness of sin. Let us also not forget that the literary transition from Emmaus to Jerusalem hinged upon the realization that Jesus "had been made known to them in the breaking of the bread" (Luke 24:34), which connected this final meal scene to the Emmaus account and ultimately the Last Supper. This final meal scene, anticipating the apostolic ministry that commences in Acts, reveals that the disciples' proclamation of the forgiveness of sins is contingent upon the theological rationale that was explicated at the Last Supper, namely, the inauguration of the new covenant promises through the suffering Messiah.

---

56. Morris, *Luke*, 343.
57. Caird, *Gospel of St Luke*, 261.

New Covenant in Acts

Given this theological grounding for the new covenant in the book of Luke, we should be unsurprised that it would appear in Luke's second volume, Acts. That is precisely what we do find, though this time it comes on the lips of the character Paul. Acts 13 contains one of the most developed summaries of Paul's preaching in Acts and therefore informs the reader of the kinds of sermons that Paul often preached. At the end of this sermon, Paul says "Let it be known to you therefore, my brothers, that through this man forgiveness of sins is proclaimed to you; by this Jesus everyone who believes is set free from those sins from which you could not be freed by the law of Moses" (Acts 13:38–39).[58] Essentially, Paul is fulfilling the very commission that Jesus imparted to his disciples at the end of Luke since he is proclaiming the forgiveness of sins in the name of Jesus (Luke 24:46–47). However, there is one very important addition made in this passage. Paul contrasts the old covenant ("the law") mediated by Moses with the forgiveness of sins now offered through Jesus. Though there is no explicit affirmation in the passage that the new covenant has been inaugurated, it is hard to imagine that anyone remotely familiar with Jeremiah's promise of a new covenant would miss the theological assumption latent here: Jesus constitutes the turning point in the eras.[59] Israel's former exile, which was punishment for breaking the Mosaic law, has ended. Through Jesus the forgiveness of sins, the promised state of affairs in the new covenant, has been made available.

This should be nothing new to the reader of Luke-Acts, for this is precisely what Luke laid out in the Last Supper sayings where Jesus' death was described as the inaugurating sacrifice of the new covenant. In addition, it confirms that Jesus' commission to the disciples in Luke 24:47 to proclaim "the forgiveness of sins" finds its ideological basis in the Last Supper's affirmation that Jesus' death inaugurates Jeremiah's new covenant. In other words, Luke's utilization of "the forgiveness of sins" cannot be divorced from the inauguration of the new covenant, which finds its clearest expression in the longer reading of Luke 22:19–20. It was there that Jesus connected the new covenant's inauguration to his death, a point which was reiterated in the Emmaus account. Thus, rather than separating Jesus' death, the new covenant, and the forgiveness of sins into separate realities, Luke makes

---

58. Most commentary on these verses has been distracted by the question of whether the passage accurately reflects Paul's teaching and have not directed enough attention to how Luke frames his narrative of salvation history in both volumes. E.g. Lüdeman, *Acts of the Apostles*, 172–73 and Barrett, *Acts of the Apostles*, 1:649–52.

59. Thus, those who suggest the "new covenant" ideology is foreign to Luke overlook what seems quite apparent in texts like the above. E.g., Ehrman, "The Cup," 578–79.

them constitutive of the redemption that God is working on his people's behalf.

While this is a small sampling of Luke-Acts, it nevertheless tells a different story than the one most scholars have been telling about Luke-Acts. Luke's longer version of the Last Supper is not free-floating flotsam he has assimilated from tradition. To the contrary, Luke has intertwined the theological implications of the Last Supper into his larger story of God's salvation of his people. Luke 24 and Acts 13 reveal that there are ideological connections between the Last Supper and the rest of Luke-Acts. Only the longer reading of Luke's account of the Last Supper explains why the Messiah's death would serve Israel's redemption. Moreover, only the longer reading speaks to the inauguration of the new covenant, a theological presupposition that gives rise to Luke's frequent references to forgiveness and the belief that the era of Israel's culpability under Moses' covenant had ended with Jesus (Acts 13). All of this indicates that the longer reading is likely authentic because it is deeply connected to the rest of Luke-Acts and that it functions as the theological crescendo capable of integrating several different aspects of Luke's narratives into a coherent hole.

Conclusion

The analysis of Luke's Last Supper account as it comes to us in the longer reading demonstrates that atonement theology is not an aberration of Lukan theology but is rather bound up in Luke's larger understanding of how God's salvation has occurred through Jesus Christ. Based upon the various intra-textual connections present in Luke-Acts, we cannot dismiss this theology as if it were simply borrowed from prior sources or somehow suppressed in his work. From all appearances, it seems intentionally woven into the larger narrative. Now this is not to suggest that Luke has simply reiterated the soteriology that one finds in Mark and Matthew. Scholars have long noted that Luke has different emphases than the other Gospels and focuses more on the resurrection and vindication than Jesus' death.[60] To be sure, Luke's soteriology is much broader than atonement.[61] The point that I wish to underscore is that the analysis here requires us to include rather than exclude a theology of atonement if we are to represent Luke's soteriology accurately.

---

60. Though I agree with Zehnle that the resurrection plays a vital role in Luke's soteriology, I do not think Luke's soteriology is completely located in the resurrection to the exclusion of Jesus' death. So Zehnle, "Jesus' Death," 431. The necessity that Luke connects to both the cross and the resurrection means that one cannot locate God's saving activity only in the resurrection. See Carroll and Green, *Death of Jesus*, 67.

61. See Steyn, "Luke's Gospel," esp. 77, 90, and 94–96.

Having come to the end of the analysis of the Last Supper sayings in the Synoptics to which we have devoted the last three chapters, we have seen a great deal of commonality among them regarding the significance of Jesus' death. Mark and Matthew have both cast Jesus' death as a covenant sacrifice, and Matthew has made it clear that this was for the "forgiveness of sins," something which seems implicit in Mark's account. Luke reiterates essentially the same thing when he specifies that Jesus is the sacrifice of the new covenant, and the force of this is not lost on him with his frequent mention of the forgiveness of sin. For all three Gospels, Jesus' death is one of the primary means by which the forgiveness of sin and hence Israel's restoration comes to pass.

Furthermore, this understanding of the Synoptic portrait of the cross fits coherently within the larger narrative structure that was developed in chapters three and four. In them, I argued that the Synoptics insert their narratives about Jesus into the larger story of Israel's exile and hoped-for restoration, which is a story about a broken covenant (i.e. sin) and the prophetic hopes that a Spirit-endowed descendent of David would one day bring restoration to his people. As we noted, the Synoptics successfully connected Jesus to the hopes for restoration that appear in the prophetic corpus and the Second Temple Jewish literature, which allows them to herald Jesus as a saving figure because he inaugurates Israel's restoration. If the Synoptics see Jesus' ministry within the larger story of Israel awaiting restoration, it only seems logical that they would also see his tragic death on the cross as an important element in this story. Such is precisely what one finds. All three of the Synoptics indicate that Jesus' death was the means by which God renewed his covenant, which is affirmed in the Last Supper sayings.

While this is an important observation and once again shows how Jesus fulfills the hope for a renewed covenant relationship, I believe we are now in a position to say a bit more about why Jesus' death can bring forgiveness and renew the covenant. As we observed in the prior three chapters, the language the Synoptics used to frame Jesus' death in the prediction sayings (where he would be given "into human hands" and "over to the Gentiles") mirrors the language of Israel's exile in the Septuagint. This insight combined with the analysis of the Last Supper sayings allows us to say that Jesus' death acquires forgiveness and renews the covenant because he enters into solidarity with and bears Israel's exilic punishment. The end of Deuteronomy had given Israel two options: "See, I have set before you today life and prosperity, death and adversity" (Deut 30:15). Death was the punishment for breaking the covenant. It is precisely this punishment that Jesus suffers under the hands of the Romans, the dominating empire. Therefore, his death can be understood as bearing the covenant curses to emancipate the covenant people from their sin. I believe that this is precisely the kind of logic operative in the Last Supper sayings when they use sacrificial language to describe Jesus' death, not just to say that Jesus relinquished his right to life, but to avow that in doing so he was making forgiveness possible.

Now this is not to say that death has the final word in the Gospels. In fact, it is quite the opposite. Resurrected life dominates the landscape. Here again, against the backdrop of Israel's hopes for restoration, the resurrection of Christ finds its place. In Ezekiel's vision of dry bones (Ezek 37:1–14), resurrection functioned as a metaphor of Israel's coming restoration and her return to the land. Resurrection would be the moment when the nation itself was restored. For the Gospels, what had once been a metaphor or a symbol of Israel's restoration had now become the literal experience of Israel's Messiah. If the divine Spirit had breathed new life into Israel's Messiah then the restoration of Israel had truly begun, and this restoration was now to be found in a singular person, Jesus of Nazareth. The metaphor had morphed into history and now the restoration of the nation was focalized on a particular individual who suffered on behalf of his people and thereby re-covenanted his people to their God.

Having reached these conclusions about the Last Supper sayings, which seem all the more credible set against the hermeneutical backdrop that we sketched in chapters three and four, we can return to the question with which this volume began, the biblical viability of Girard's soteriology. To what degree do the conclusions and interpretations drawn here affect the approach to salvation offered by Girard? The following chapter will address these concerns more closely.

8

Assessing the Biblical and Theological Foundations of Girard's Soteriology

Evaluating Girardian Soteriology

AFTER INVESTIGATING THE LAST Supper sayings' contributions to the soteriological implications of Jesus' death in the Synoptic Gospels along with other passages dealing with the cross, it is time to return to Girard's soteriology. In light of the exegetical analysis of the preceding chapters, it has become apparent that, despite Girard's claim that the Gospels unequivocally support his thesis, the Synoptic Gospels actually challenge the current formulations of Girard's soteriology and thereby preclude his ability to claim the entirety of the Gospels for support. This particular section summarizes several ways in which Girard's soteriology differs from the hermeneutical and exegetical conclusions made in the preceding chapters.

Girard's Hermeneutics

In the third and fourth chapters, we observed that Girard's hermeneutical approach to the Gospels proceeded upon several questionable assumptions. First, instead of deriving the "state of deprivation" or the human need for salvation from the story the Gospels are telling, Girard borrows one from his theory of humanity's origins. For Girard, human culture is founded upon the innocent victim who was unjustifiably executed in the original murder. In an effort to justify itself and remove its culpability, humanity has convinced itself that all such victims are worthy of their punishment. According to Girard, this ideology governs mythological texts, and only the Gospels succeed in revealing the truth that such victims are innocent. Nevertheless, aside from a few oblique possibilities and some structural similarities, it is not clear that the Gospels presume the scapegoat mechanism as the "state of deprivation" that needs to be remedied for human salvation.

In fact, the Gospels presuppose a different "state of deprivation." As the third and fourth chapters argued, the Synoptic Gospels situate Jesus within the larger story of Israel and her restoration from exile, a story that began in the Old Testament and finds its culmination in the New Testament. Furthermore, the Gospels' manifold and explicit dependence upon the prophetic texts—something which cannot be said of mythological texts—and their frequent allusions to the Jewish hopes for restoration indicate that the Synoptic writers believe the problem Jesus addresses is Israel's lack of complete restoration from its exilic punishment, which was to bring blessing to the world. When the Synoptics herald Jesus as savior, they do so within the purview of this particular story and this particular "state of deprivation," which does not appear in Girard's soteriology.

Second, since Girard's understanding of humanity's need—as derived from his structural analysis of mythological and persecutory texts—determines how Christ functions as a savior, an external body of literature becomes the hermeneutical key for unlocking the New Testament's claim that Jesus is the savior of humankind. At the core of Girard's soteriology lies the assumption that the biblical texts are intertextually related to mythological texts.[1] For him, a polemical exchange with mythology reverberates throughout the biblical narrative, which is especially true of the Passion account. Though the comparison between the Bible and mythology is a necessary and worthwhile endeavor in its own right, presupposing such a dialectical interchange unfortunately makes this polemical intertextuality the governing force of the meaning of the biblical text. In fact, it reduces the biblical narrative and the interpretation of the Passion to the subversion of mythology, which fails to acknowledge the many other things the biblical texts are trying to communicate.

When he does defend his hermeneutic, Girard contends that, in conjunction with Christian tradition, he reads the Gospels from Christ backwards, thereby privileging the New Testament over the Old Testament.[2] He thus claims that Christ functions as the hermeneutical key to the entire Bible. This is true regarding the relationship he presupposes between the two parts of the canon, but it certainly does not describe the entirety of Girard's hermeneutical approach to the biblical canon. In Girard's exegesis, his narrative of human origins and his interpretation of mythology govern and set the framework for his interpretation of the Gospels. To put it bluntly, Girard does not start with Christ as a saving figure and then work back-

---

1. He does qualify this claim, noting that not all biblical narratives are anti-myths. Nevertheless, he does admit that his exegesis presupposes a great degree of intertextuality vis-à-vis mythical texts. See Girard, *Evolution and Conversion*, 200–204.

2. Girard, *Things Hidden*, 274–75.

wards into the Old Testament.[3] Rather, Girard begins with his meta-theory of humanity in subjection to the scapegoat mechanism. This construct becomes the governing lens of the Bible more generally, but also dictates how Christ can be a savior more specifically.

For proof that this is the case, one only needs to trace the historical publication of Girard's major works. The first of his major works, *Deceit, Desire, and the Novel* (1961), developed his notion of mimetic desire, and the concept of mimetic desire is most often the first essential piece to understanding Girard's soteriology.[4] The second major work, *Violence and the Sacred* (1972), drew from ethnology to explain that human culture was founded on the innocent murder, the cataclysmic effect of mimetic desire, and that natural human religion was nothing other than the deification of scapegoats.[5] Only after these ideological precursors were in place did Girard go on to explain how the Gospels reveal the truth of the scapegoat in *Things Hidden since the Foundation of the World* (1978).[6] Despite what some of his followers like Alison contend, Girard's soteriology begins with his narrative of human origins and the scapegoat mechanism as developed through ethnology and his reading of mythology. Since Girard never reads the Bible apart from mythological texts and since the nature of humanity's problem is quintessentially enshrined in these texts, Girard's interpretation of the Gospels cannot exist without its polemical relationship with mythology and its obfuscation of the scapegoat mechanism. Though one might be able to say that the cross is the hermeneutical key for interpreting mythology, the relationship is not unilateral for Girard and those who follow him. In fact, because the Gospels and mythological texts exist in a dialectical exchange for Girard, one could say mythology is as much a hermeneutical key for the Passion as the Passion is for mythology. The two are mutually explicatory.

The problem with this approach is that it imposes a polemical interchange between the Bible and mythology in places where biblical scholars have rarely drawn the battle lines and where one is hard pressed to find it. Certainly the Bible has places where it contravenes the metaphysical commitments of mythological texts and idolatrous practices, but Girard has placed the battle lines in the center of the Passion account. Consequently,

---

3. I am not suggesting that this is what one must do in order to make Christ the center of salvation history. Even the approach I have taken here assumes that we need an understanding of the human problem before we can talk about how Jesus is a solution in that regard. The issue is the place from whence one derives this understanding of the human problem.

4. The original French version was published as Girard, *Mensonge romantique*.

5. The original French version was Girard, *La violence*.

6. The French original was Girard, *Des choses chachées*.

this makes Girard's soteriology contingent upon the belief that the Passion accounts intentionally undermine mythology or at least his understanding of it. Furthermore, it allows a group of texts, which are likely not in the Gospel writers' purview to the degree and in the manner that he presupposes, to set the agenda for how Jesus functions as a Savior.

Girard's presupposition of a polemical relationship between the biblical texts and mythology leads to another problem, namely, Girard offers some unconvincing interpretations of select biblical passages in order to ground his soteriology more firmly in the biblical texts. For example, in earlier chapters we noted that Isaiah 40:3–4 anticipates God's work of restoring Israel from exile when the author writes that a " . . . voice cries out: 'In the wilderness prepare the way of the Lord, make straight in the desert a highway for our God. Every valley shall be lifted up and every mountain and hill be made low; the uneven ground shall become level, and the rough places a plain." As previously noted, most Old Testament scholars have interpreted the imagery of making a "way" and a "highway" in the wilderness as a reference to the new exodus, when God would lead his people back from the exile. Even ancient readers of Isaiah 40 interpreted it as heralding a return from exile, so this is not simply a matter of modern interpreters taking the text in a new direction.[7] In addition, the Synoptic Gospels draw upon this expectation of God's intervention on Israel's behalf, to situate the ministries of Jesus and John the Baptist, establishing their work as the culmination of Israel's hopes for restoration from exile. The consensus of modern biblical scholarship has taken Isaiah 40 and its adoption by the Gospel writers as an anticipation of God's restoration of his people when he was to lead them back from exile.

Despite the explanatory value of this interpretation of Isaiah 40, especially within its historical context, Girard believes the common scholarly interpretation misses the point because, underneath it all, he believes the passage must be talking about a mimetic crisis. When Isaiah writes that "Every valley shall be lifted up, and every mountain and hill be made low; the uneven ground shall become level, and the rough places a plain," Girard avers this can only be fully understood as a reference to the initial stages of the mimetic crises where the community embarks on a war against everyone.[8] Regarding these verses from Isaiah he writes, " . . . I think it is necessary to see there an image of those mimetic crises whose essential feature is the loss of differences, the transformation of individuals into *doubles* whose

---

7. Bar 5:5–7; *Pss. Sol.* 11:4.

8. Girard, *Evolution and Conversion*, 209; Girard, *I See Satan*, 29–31; and Girard, *Things Hidden*, 199. See also Hamerton-Kelly, *Gospel of the Sacred*, 61.

perpetual conflict destroys culture."[9] In other words, the flattening of the mountains and valleys does not depict a future rebuilding of a highway to allow the exiles to return to their homeland but is rather a symbolic picture of the erasure of difference among a community at conflict.[10]

Such an interpretation, though creative, strains credulity for the immediate literary and even presumed historical context speaks of the end of exile and Israel's ensuing restoration. What in the context actually indicates this is the beginning phase of a mimetic crisis other than Girard's presupposition that the Bible is engaged in diffusing the scapegoat mechanism? The geographical imagery is much more easily connected with the processes of building a road for the returning exiles than with a mimetic conflict, though Girard is certainly on firmer footing when he identifies the suffering servant's death in Isaiah's final servant song as the culmination of a mimetic crisis.[11] Nevertheless, for Girard to suppose that the opening verses of Isaiah 40 must have a mimetic crisis in view cannot be supported, even if the final servant song culminates in one.

Girard is also aware that Isaiah 40:3–5 establishes the trajectory of the Gospels and Jesus' role as a Savior, and this might explain Girard's efforts to inscribe mimetic rivalry into the text of Isaiah 40. According to him, when the Gospels utilize Isaiah 40:3–5 to situate Jesus' ministry, they imply that Jesus will inaugurate another "mimetic cycle" like Isaiah's suffering servant.[12] Unfortunately, Girard misses a vital opportunity to understand Israel's hopes for restoration in Isaiah and how those hopes become the leitmotif for the Gospels themselves. Instead of grasping this insight, Girard's controlling narrative of mimetic rivalry has conscripted Isaiah 40 to support his presupposition that the Bible unveils the mimetic contagion. As a result, he has likely disinterred a mimetic conflict where none actually existed in the biblical text.

A similar effect can be seen in Girard's interpretation of the parable of the wicked tenants (Matt 21:33–44; Mark 12:1–12; Luke 20:9–19). Girard's reading of the parable is placed within his larger word study of σκάνδαλον in the New Testament. Though σκάνδαλον and its cognates are absent from the Lukan version of the parable, the allusion to someone stumbling over a

---

9. Girard, *I See Satan*, 29.

10. Girard is aware that Old Testament scholars differ with his interpretation and responds in the following way: "The text speaks of flattening—that is clear—but it does not speak about it flatly. It presents flattening as a subject so grand and impressive that to limit its scope to the construction of a great highway, even for the greatest of monarchs, seems to me too narrow a view of it" (Ibid.).

11. Ibid., 29–30.

12. Ibid., 30.

stone (Luke 20:18) allows him to link it with his larger discussion. Believing that many misunderstand this theme, he states that the σκάνδαλον or the stone of stumbling can be equated with the mimetic conflict. For Girard, the use of σκάνδαλον in the Bible refers to the model of one's mimetic desire who simultaneously functions as the "obstacle" prohibiting one's acquisition of a particular desire, hence the stumbling effect.[13] This very obstacle, the one that becomes the victim, is eventually deified if the entire process runs unhindered.[14] Thus, Luke's reference to the stone of stumbling takes up this very theme according to Girard. He finds further confirmation of his conclusion in the violent murder of the son at the hands of the wicked tenants, thus making the entire parable one "that reveals the founding murder."[15] According to Girard, the quotation of Psalm 118 at the end of the parable confirms that the passage has the foundational murder in view:

> The quintessential scandal is the fact that the founding victim has finally been revealed as such and that Christ has a role to play in this revelation. That is what the psalm quoted by Christ is telling us. The entire edifice of culture rests on the cornerstone that is the stone the builders rejected. Christ is that stone in visible form. That is why there can be no victim who is not Christ, and no one can come to the aid of a victim without coming to the aid of Christ. Mankind's failure of intelligence and belief depends upon an inability to recognize the role played by the founding victim at the most basic level of anthropology.[16]

Thus, for Girard, since the parable contains an unjust lynching and a reference to the stumbling typical of the mimetic crisis, it must speak of humankind's inability to recognize its murderous nature. For him, the passage supports the contention that the Gospels reveal the nature of humanity to us by exposing the scapegoat mechanism.

Schwager's exegesis of the same parable is a bit more cautious. He still follows Girard in emphasizing the passage's emphasis upon rivalry with God, but he locates the emphasis in a different place.[17] Rather than seeing the reference to stumbling as suggestive of the mimetic conflict, Schwager focuses on the theme of rejection and vindication, making this pattern paradigmatic for the Gospel. For Schwager though, the citation of Psalm 118 serves to demonstrate that the "collective blindness" of the Jerusalem

13. Girard, *Things Hidden*, 416.
14. Ibid., 421.
15. Ibid., 428.
16. Ibid., 429.
17. Schwager, "Christ's Death," 114–15.

leadership will advance "the process of revelation."[18] In other words, the rejection by the Jerusalem leadership will be the means by which God reveals humanity's bent towards violence.

Though Girard and Schwager offer intriguing observations about this passage, both of them offer incomplete interpretations in comparison with what has been advanced in former chapters. Their exegesis of the passage is unconvincing for several reasons. First, the vineyard's symbolization of Israel is ignored and there is no correlation between the servants being sent with God's former emissaries, the prophets, though this part is present in Schwager.[19] Second, equating the stone of stumbling in Luke and Matthew with the mimetic conflict, as Girard does, overextends the imagery. Though Girard is aware of the Old Testament passages that are likely being alluded to here, he fails to see the connection the passage makes between the "stone" and the temple itself, which we identified in previous chapters. For Girard, the stumbling stone can serve no other purpose than as an allusion to the mimetic crisis. Third, both fail to see the passage's connection with the temple and the implications that Jesus' community will now function as some kind of new, spiritualized temple. Though I can agree with both that the passage is about the rejection of the son, the text has wider implications that become visible only when read against the background of Israel's hopes for restoration, one of which was the reconstruction of the temple of YHWH.

Girard's interpretation of this parable reveals that one's presupposed soteriological narrative determines how one interprets select passages. When Girard's anthropological narrative is presumed to be the operative "story behind the story," subtle allusions to elements of the mimetic crisis can be found in something as ambiguous as a stumbling stone. While I do not deny that the parable expects the future rejection of the son (i.e. Jesus), I suggest that when the passage is read in light of the story of Israel awaiting restoration, Jesus' comments reveal that his followers will function as a fulfillment of Israel's hopes for a new eschatological temple. In addition, when the passages of the Gospels are read in light of the larger story of Israel, the interpretations appear much more credible and historically rooted in the Jewish world of the first century.

The same can be said for Girard's articulation of Jesus' proclamation of the Kingdom. Instead of seeing the Kingdom from the vantage point of the Jewish hopes for restoration, Girard forces the proclamation of the Kingdom into, what appears to be, a foreign mold. For Girard, the Kingdom of God is the antithesis of the Kingdom of Satan, and, with his demythologized

---

18. Schwager, *Scapegoats*, 141.
19. Ibid., 140–41.

notion of the demonic realm, the Kingdom of Satan is the self-perpetuating system of violence founded upon "the unanimous and spontaneous murder of a scapegoat."[20] Jesus' proclamation of the Kingdom is therefore the announcement regarding the attenuation of the scapegoat mechanism's power because the exposure of its principles will render it ineffective.[21] Girard's most complete definition of the Kingdom puts it thusly: "The Kingdom of God means the complete and definitive elimination of every form of vengeance and every form of reprisal in relations between men."[22] Ultimately, this is "the Kingdom of love" which is the converse of violence and murder that typifies the Kingdom of Satan.[23] To refuse to enter the kingdom " . . . means refusing the knowledge that Jesus bears—refusing the knowledge of violence and all its works."[24] Thus, the proclamation of the Kingdom is an invitation to a nonviolent lifestyle.[25]

Now, Girard is not wrong to suggest that entering the Kingdom of God would constitute the way of love or that it would call us to relinquish our desires to seek vengeance. The Sermon on the Mount does as much. Nevertheless, Girard errs when he reduces the pluripotent symbol of the kingdom into being solely the privation of violence and presence of love. The Kingdom is certainly this, but it is much more in the Gospels. The arrival of the Kingdom, as noted in the third and fourth chapters, takes up Israel's story of God as King. As such it would have spoken not simply of an invitation away from violence but also of a recognition that God was about to make good on his hopes for restoration. The coming of the Kingdom was about more than humans acting differently. It was about God renewing his covenantal relationship with his people and re-gathering them to himself.[26] Nevertheless, by adopting a view of the Kingdom that simply juxtaposes itself to the scapegoat mechanism, Girard's notion of the Kingdom unfortunately lacks these dimensions that seem to be bound up with the connotation of the Kingdom in the first century and in the Gospels.

---

20. Girard, *Scapegoat*, 187.
21. Ibid., 189–90.
22. Girard, *Things Hidden*, 197.
23. Ibid.
24. Ibid., 208.
25. One can also wonder whether Girard's assertion that Jesus' self-identification as "Son of man" is rooted in Ezekiel not Daniel is an intentional effort to remove Jesus from the potentially violent associations the kingdom of God has in Daniel. Ibid., 207.
26. Girard is right that the Kingdom arrives at a particular point in history, to a Jewish people who had been "prepared . . . by the Old Testament to throw themselves into the great adventure of the Kingdom" (ibid., 201, original emphasis not included). The question is precisely in what this preparation consists.

Investigating Girard's exegesis of these selected passages and themes reveals that the larger narrative one presupposes when reading the Gospels governs how particular passages and symbols are interpreted. As observed in the aforementioned examples, Girard's decision to read the Gospels vis-à-vis mythological texts has led him to overlook the ways in which the Gospels retell the story of Israel, not as an exodus from mythological delusion to revelation, but from exile to restoration. In a few of these instances, particularly with the interpretation of Isaiah 40, it has resulted in an unfortunate distortion of the text to the point that Girard introduces mimetic crises in places where they are not apparent. Thus, hermeneutical presuppositions are not inconsequential. They run the risk of imposing alien meaning as much as they offer the potential of unveiling the text's meaning.

Girard's Theology

In addition to issues surrounding hermeneutics, the previous chapters also identified how the Synoptics see the death of Jesus effecting salvation. On several occasions we have seen that the Gospels challenge and undermine the validity of some assertions essential for Girard's soteriology. In what follows, I identify three areas where the exegesis of the former chapters challenges core tenets of Girard's soteriology.

Sacrificial Language

To begin, the analysis of the Last Supper sayings has shown that sacrificial language is more constitutive of the Gospels than Girard allowed, at least in his earlier formulations. In *Things Hidden since the Foundation of the World*, Girard claimed, "The rare examples of sacrificial language can be taken as metaphorical in view of the absence of any specific theory of sacrifice comparable to that of the Epistle to the Hebrews or the range of theories that develop later."[27] The previous analysis of the Last Supper sayings has called this assertion into question. We have seen that the Last Supper sayings do frame the importance of Jesus' death with sacrificial language and that when they do so, especially in the case of Matthew, they appear to be operating with the atoning logic present in Hebrews. Thus, the initial distance that Girard placed between the Gospels and Hebrews does not truly exist.

At this point, my assessment differs from William Newell's analysis of Girard, who also argued that Christian theology was more sacrificial than Girard allowed. However, to support his disagreement, he leaned exclusively

27. Ibid., 243.

on the book of Hebrews: "The hole we perceive in Girard's hypothesis is that rendering Jesus' death non-sacrificial does not jibe with the rest of the New Testament, especially Hebrews 10, and with tradition."[28] Though Newell disagrees with Girard's perspective on Christianity, he still believes that the Gospels are different from the book of Hebrews, writing: " . . . the Gospels do not define the death as a sacrifice, they offer us a phenomenology of it."[29] In another place, he writes, "Nowhere in the gospels will one find a theory of sacrifice as one finds in the Epistle to the Hebrews."[30] On this point, Newell's analysis falls short. As we have seen, the Last Supper sayings do not simply offer a "phenomenology" of sacrifice but define Jesus' death as a covenant sacrifice by using language allusive of Exodus 24:8. Moreover, as we have argued, the Targums portrayed the covenant sacrifice as atoning, which is the same way it was understood in Hebrews. When Matthew adds the phrase, "for the forgiveness of sins," to his allusion to the covenant sacrifice, we are in the theological orbit of the Targums and Hebrews. Thus, the alleged difference that Girard and Newell identify between the Gospels and Hebrews actually vanishes upon closer inspection of the Last Supper sayings.[31]

Though Girard initially opposed the language of "sacrifice" as a means of categorizing Jesus' death in *Things Hidden since the Foundation of the World*, he has since made a significant adjustment by conceding that Jesus' death can be called a "sacrifice," even though he has carefully qualified what he means by adopting such language.[32] His adoption of sacrificial language turns upon "a distinction between sacrifice as murder and sacrifice as renunciation," with the latter being the only permissible manner of applying the term to Christ's death.[33] Girard further defines the appropriate use of "sacrifice" as "a movement toward freedom from mimesis as potentially rivalrous acquisition and rivalry."[34] It is this definition that he has continued to uphold in *Evolution and Conversion* where he says there is a difference between "sacrifice as murder" and "sacrifice as the readiness to die in order

---

28. Newell, *Desire in René Girard*, 159; see also 163, 181, 220.

29. Ibid., 159.

30. Ibid., 181.

31. Newell does cite the Last Supper sayings in parentheses at one point but fails to elucidate their significance and reiterates the centrality of Hebrews in the sacrificial theology of the New Testament. Ibid., 173–74, 189, 194.

32. One of the earliest statements in this regard is Girard's essay, "Mimetische Theorie und Theologie," 15–29. The acceptance of the term "sacrifice" is most apparent in *Evolution and Conversion*, esp. 215.

33. Girard, *Girard Reader*, 272.

34. Ibid.

not to participate in sacrifice as murder."³⁵ In this same work, he further augments the distinguishing features of the acceptable form of sacrifice by saying that there is a "difference between the archaic sacrifice, which turns against a third victim the violence of those who are fighting, and the Christian sacrifice which is the renunciation of all egoistic claiming, even to life if needed, in order not to kill."³⁶ In fact, he claims there is actually "no non-sacrificial space," but only a transition from one form of sacrifice to the other.³⁷

Nevertheless, even though Girard has become more amenable to applying sacrificial language to Christ's death, he still opposes the kind of thought that would connect sacrifice with atonement because atonement would involve turning some form of violence "against a third victim" who would bear punishment or expiate sins on behalf of another. Thus, regarding the ability to describe Christ's death as a sacrifice of atonement, it is likely that his earlier assertion would still obtain: "The rare examples of sacrificial language [in the Gospels] can be taken as metaphorical in view of the absence of any specific theory of sacrifice comparable to that of the Epistle to the Hebrews or the range of theories that develop later."³⁸

The former analysis of the Last Supper sayings suggests there is more to the sacrificial language employed to describe Christ's death than just a refusal to capitulate to the human penchant for murder or mimetic rivalry. Certainly Girard is right that Jesus freely renounced his claim to life, but he is wrong to say it was nothing more in the Gospels. As explained in the fifth and sixth chapters, the language of Matthew and Mark's Last Supper discourses invokes the wording of the covenant sacrifice on Sinai (Exod 24:8) to signify the soteriological value of Jesus' death. Matthew has especially made Jesus' death the means by which forgiveness is acquired and this same affirmation can be deduced from Luke's Gospel as well. Moreover, when the Last Supper is read alongside of other passages like the ransom saying and the predictions of Jesus' death which use language reminiscent of Israel's exilic punishment to depict Jesus' death, one can see that the sacrificial language means more than the relinquishment of Jesus' life. Instead, the sacrifice involves Jesus entering into and experiencing Israel's exilic punishment in order to bring restoration.

---

35. Girard, *Evolution and Conversion*, 215.
36. Ibid.
37. Ibid., 216.

38. Girard, *Things Hidden*, 243. Although, one should note his view on the book of Hebrews did change.

Not only does the exegesis of the Last Supper and supporting passages challenge Girard, those who have adopted his interpretation of the Gospels are also called into question.[39] For example, one can agree with theologians like Hamerton-Kelly who see the Last Supper as a reversal of traditional sacrifice where "instead of the worshiper giving to the god, the god is giving to the worshiper."[40] Certainly, the covenant sacrifice of Jesus results from the divine initiative, but Hamerton-Kelly fails to see that Jesus as the covenant sacrifice provides atonement for his followers in the process. In the same vein, our analysis has shown that Bruce Chilton errs when he writes that the "'blood' and 'body'" of the Last Supper do not need to be "identified with Jesus' death."[41] Chilton's assertion that the Last Supper represents the moment at which Jesus made sharing meals together a replacement of the temple cult is not only quite speculative, it cannot be supported by the evidence in the Last Supper sayings themselves. As we have seen, the allusions present in the passages depict Jesus as the covenant sacrifice. Jesus is not substituting a meal for the temple cult; he is substituting himself and this is found most poignantly in the rending of the temple veil. Moreover, our analysis of Luke's account of the Emmaus road encounter has demonstrated that the Last Supper sayings provide the essential insight for understanding Jesus as a dying-yet-still-redeeming Messiah. We cannot fully understand the importance of the Last Supper unless we see it as a meal that establishes Jesus as the covenant sacrifice that inaugurates Israel's restoration.

Moreover, one cannot play the Synoptics against one another, as some of Girard's followers have done. Some treat Luke as the authoritative interpreter of the Synoptic tradition whose omission of the ransom saying should purportedly dictate how one interprets both Luke's Last Supper discourse and the soteriology of Mark and Matthew who do include the ransom saying.[42] As we have already noted, it is unwise to put too much weight on Luke's absence of the ransom saying, for he appears to be following a different source. Moreover, when he does insert his version of the saying after the Last Supper, his specific variation of the saying actually points the reader back to the Last Supper to understand the kind of service that Jesus would do for his people. Thus, the service is interpreted in light of the Last

---

39. Contrary to Schwager, the interpretation of the "kingdom of God" as a revelation of God's benevolent nature does not need to be juxtaposed to a notion of Christ's death as atonement. See Schwager, "Christ's Death," 111.

40. Hamerton-Kelly, *Gospel of the Sacred*, 44.

41. Chilton, *Feast of Meanings*, 68. He is followed by Heim, *Saved from Sacrifice*, 232.

42. E.g., Williams, *Bible, Violence, and the Sacred*, 202 and Bartlett, *Cross Purposes*, 212.

Supper saying and not vice versa. Finally, to use Luke to suppress any kind of atonement theology in Mark or Matthew is to overlook the fact that Mark and Matthew are independent works in their own right. While Luke needs to be granted freedom in presenting his own portrait of Jesus, one should not use Luke to fetter the theological voices of Mark and Matthew.

Finally, one cannot dismiss the theological implications of the Last Supper sayings by assuming that the New Testament uses "sacrificial language" simply to subvert it.[43] Contrary to some of Girard's followers, it is not simply a necessary bridge to carry people from a deficient understanding of human culture to a revelation of its vicious origins. The analysis of the previous chapters has confirmed this. To summarize, the Gospels depict Jesus' death as a sacrifice in order to explain that his death will benefit his followers by atoning for sin and ushering in the age of restoration. If the sacrificial language were only utilized to subvert the sacrificial logic, it is entirely incumbent upon those who make this assertion to provide criteria to prove this is the case since sacrificial logic was commonplace in the first century.[44] Thus, if the Gospel writers were to use sacrificial language to subvert such ideology, they would have to make themselves overtly clear to avoid any confusion on the part of the reader. If the Gospels are read as literary products from their place and time, there is nothing in the Gospels constituting an intentional effort to undermine sacrificial theology in a way that would have been apparent to a first century reader. All indicators suggest they were working with and presupposing such logic.

The Cross and Causality

Girard and his followers have also contended that the cross is solely the product of human violence, which means that God cannot be credited or associated with the violence at the cross. After all, if the cross were simply the result of a mimetic crisis, then humans would be the only culpable party. Girard affirms on multiple occasions that the Gospels portray God the Father apart from violence and therefore innocent of the cross's violence. For example, on one occasion he writes: "If we keep to the passages that relate specifically to the Father of Jesus, we can easily see they contain nothing which would justify attributing the least amount of violence to the deity."[45]

---

43. For some, "sacrificial language" is a necessary linguistic accommodation to move people beyond it. E.g. Heim, *Saved from Sacrifice*, 13 and Williams, *Bible, Violence, and the Sacred*, 223–24.

44. For example, the martyr stories of 2 and 4 Maccabees ascribe atoning value to the unjust deaths of the Jewish martyrs.

45. Girard, *Things Hidden*, 182; cf. 189.

According to Girard, any notion that God participated in the crucifixion of the Son "appears contrary to both the spirit and the letter of the Gospels."[46] If there is any way in which God contributes to Jesus' death it is simply this: "There is no other cause for his death than the love of one's neighbour lived to the very end, with an infinitely intelligent grasp of the constraints it imposes."[47] In one of his most direct statements on the causality of the cross, he writes: "Neither the son nor the Father should be questioned about the cause of this event, but all mankind, and mankind alone."[48] Thus, Girard explicitly dismisses any role that the Father or the Son might play in the crucifixion other than the choice to love. In short, it seems that Girard wants to posit God with willing a particular end, namely, the dissolution of the scapegoat mechanism, without willing or causing the means to that particular end, the cross. Certainly these assertions are in keeping with Girard's desire to see God freed from violence, but it deserves to be asked whether this accurately reflects the Gospels like he avouches.

The previous chapter has given several reasons to question Girard's ability to claim the Gospels as support in this regard. Jesus' prayer in the Garden of Gethsemane indicates that the ensuing events are the Father's "will" (Matt 26:39; Mark 14:36; Luke 22:42), and Jesus consents to the Father's will by accepting the path of the cross. Moreover, if the "cup," which Jesus must drink is symbolic of God's judgment, then the Father's will is not simply the salvation of humanity but accomplishing this salvation via the cross as an atoning act. Though good-intentioned theologians aver God is never associated with the violence of the cross, the Gospels suggest a more complicated picture, especially in Gethsemane.

Probably the most formidable example in this regard is the intentional change that was introduced into the citation of Zechariah 13:7 where Jesus says, "I will strike the shepherd, and the sheep will be scattered" (Matt 26:31; Mark 14:27). As noted earlier, the LXX and MT both have an impersonal sword striking the shepherd, but the Gospels' citation has significantly altered the subject of the sentence to make God the actor and hence grant him a role in the cross, even its violent aspects. Although this passage does not delete the culpability of those crucifying Jesus, it does obviate theologians' ability to say that the Gospels never portray God involved—however one might understand this particular involvement—in the violence of the cross. It is perhaps ironic that in a book whose title alludes to the kind of language

---

46. Girard, *I See Satan*, 21; cf. Girard, *Things Hidden*, 214. In the latter text, Girard contrasts his position with the "usual writings on the subject" wherein "the death of Jesus derives . . . from God and not from men . . . ."

47. Girard, *Things Hidden*, 211.

48. Ibid., 213.

present in this very verse, *Stricken by God?*, not a single one of Girard's followers addresses this particular verse, though there are multiple claims throughout that divine "violence" is absent from the New Testament.[49]

In addition, the former analyses suggest that the "necessity" the Gospels find in the cross differs from how Girardian soteriology typically explains it. Following Girard, Alison contends that when the New Testament defines the cross as "necessary"—which is phraseology peculiar to the Lukan presentation of the cross—the "Gospels do not attempt to attribute this 'necessity' to anything in God . . . ."[50] For him, the violence of the cross is entirely "anthropological" in its origin. Because human culture is captivated by the scapegoat mechanism, the crucifixion must necessarily result. According to Alison, the only "theological reason" behind the cross is that it occurs simply "so that the Scriptures be fulfilled . . . ."[51] This fulfillment of Scripture, however, does not mean "that there is some divine plan to kill Jesus" because it is simply speaking about the human penchant for death, especially of those who challenge cultural order.[52] Schwager too, explained the "necessity" of the cross as a result of humanity's hatred for the divine, which could only be broken by the divine forgiveness offered at the cross.[53] For both, the necessity of the cross lies within humanity rather than within God.

However, trying to limit the "necessity" of the cross to human nature—at least as it is understood in Girardian soteriology—and Old Testament prophecies still does not fully reflect the presentation in the Synoptics, especially when the Emmaus episode is taken into account. On the road to Emmaus the unrecognized Jesus asks the perplexed disciples, "Was it not necessary that the Messiah should suffer these things and then enter into his glory?" (Luke 24:26). The risen Jesus' recounting of the Old Testament prophecies fails to bring awareness of Jesus' identity, which indicates that the theological necessity for the crucifixion is more than simply fulfilling Scripture, contrary to Alison's proposal, though this is certainly a part of it. It is not until Jesus participates in the Eucharistic act of breaking bread that the disciples understand why it was "necessary" for the Messiah to die in

---

49. Jersak and Hardin, eds., *Stricken by God*. Regarding "violence" being absent from the divine in the New Testament, see Northey, "The Cross," 366. The title of the book is reminiscent of Isaiah 53:4 that says the servant was "struck down" by God, but failing to engage Zechariah 13:7 in the context of the Gospels is necessary to prove the point.

50. Alison, *Being Wrong*, 171; cf. Heim, *Saved from Sacrifice*, 114.

51. Alison, *Being Wrong*, 171.

52. Ibid.

53. Schwager, *Scapegoats*, 190–200.

order to redeem Israel. For the reader of Luke, the Emmaus episode's emphasis on the Eucharistic act of breaking bread is a direct allusion to the Last Supper, which reminds one that Jesus' death is the sacrifice that inaugurates the new covenant. Therefore, the theological dimension behind the necessity of the cross cannot be limited solely to fulfilling prophecy, even for the Gospel of Luke. The texts suggest that, more than just fulfilling prophecy, the theological necessity behind the cross requires Jesus' death as the means by which God will redeem his people from sin, which is precisely what the Last Supper sayings reveal.

Other followers of Girard attempt to distance God from the violence of the cross by arguing that only Jesus' opponents believe his death will be redemptive. For example, Heim writes: "The Gospels make clear that it is Jesus' antagonists who view his death as a redemptive sacrifice, one life given for many."[54] Hardin, who follows Heim on this point, blames advocates of the penal substitution theory for inverting "the meaning of the death of Jesus" and making the sacrificial death a part of God's will.[55] For most Girardian thinkers, the belief in a redemptive death is the ideology of the crowds, not that of Jesus himself. To return to Heim again, he contends that adopting a view of Jesus' death as redemptive means that one is "entering the passion story on the side of Jesus' murderers."[56] However, the Last Supper sayings, especially as they have been understood in the previous chapters, certainly dispute such an assertion. The Last Supper sayings are not uttered by those plotting Jesus' death. Rather, Jesus speaks them. If one is to follow good hermeneutical practice and privilege Jesus' words over those of the crowds, then one cannot dismiss them as irrelevant. As we have seen in the previous chapter, the Synoptic Jesus articulates a view that his death is a covenant sacrifice that will instantiate the kingdom and the covenant. Adopting such a viewpoint is not assuming the ideology of the crowds, but that of the Gospels' central character, Jesus.

Thus, the Gospels deliver a more complicated picture of the Father's relationship to the cross than what Girard and his followers have allowed. In the Gospels, the cross is not solely the will of humanity, for the cross is the Father's will too. One can certainly understand the desire to create a pristine view of the Father cleansed of all involvement with violence, even the violence of the cross. However, the Gospels cannot be counted on for support in this regard. To put it simply, the Gospels put forth a more complicated view of the Father's relationship to the crucifixion of Jesus where the Father

---

54. Heim, *Saved from Sacrifice*, 125.
55. Hardin, "Nonviolent Atonement," 249.
56. Heim, *Saved from Sacrifice*, 126.

wills the cross and can in some fashion be said to "strike the shepherd," though this never eclipses humanity's participation or responsibility for the evil in the cross.

The Effects of the Cross

Within Girardian soteriology, the cross has a direct impact upon humankind, but it is rarely articulated in a way that suggests there is any impact on God's relationship to humans. According to Girard, the cross solely resolves the problem of humanity's misunderstanding concerning the culpability of its victims. Other followers of Girard, like Schwager and Alison, have expanded upon this to include the notion that the cross and resurrection reveal God's goodness to humankind as well. Nevertheless, even with the introduction of the more positive dimension of the cross's significance, the main object affected by the death and resurrection remains humanity's understanding. For most Girardians, the death and resurrection have no effect on humanity's relationship with the divine, unless it finally clears away the misconceptions about God that have kept humans from pursuing such a relationship. Regardless, if the cross changes anything in the divine-human relationship, it is located on the human side of the relationship.

Nevertheless, there are some exceptions in this regard, and Heim has the most robust articulation regarding how the cross, as understood within a Girardian framework, could be construed to speak of a reconciliation between God and humanity. He writes:

> I unequivocally advocate a reversal of polarity in our common theology of the cross. We are not reconciled with God and each other by a sacrifice of innocent suffering offered to God. We are reconciled with God because God at the cost of suffering rescued us from bondage to a practice of violent sacrifice that otherwise would keep us estranged, making us enemies of the God who stands with our victims.[57]

This is a helpful way of articulating how a Girardian understanding of the cross can still speak of reconciliation with God, and it allows Heim to fill a lacuna that is missing in other Girardian thinkers.

For as helpful as such a contribution is, though, it seems to collapse all of the various sins into that of victimizing others. In fact, Heim seems to do just this a few pages later: " . . . many if not all of our individual sins are tributary to sacrifice in that they sow the conflicts that flower in social

57. Ibid., 320.

crisis and lead to redemptive violence."[58] Can the biblical view of sin be entirely summarized under the umbrella of victimization? This is where the covenantal backdrop of the Last Supper sayings becomes relevant. The Ten Commandments, the heart of the covenantal expectations, begin with expectations of faithfulness to YHWH. Even though the final commandments regulate one's relationship with other human beings, the first four deliver expectations for humanity's relationship with the divine. To equate the commandments requiring exclusive loyalty to YHWH with an injunction to protect the victim constitutes a simplistic reduction in what those commands expect from YHWH's covenant partner. Thus, one seems hard pressed to summarize human sin under the sole category of victimization since the biblical view of sin is more expansive and includes prohibitions against worshipping other gods, against making images, and against the misuse of the divine name. If human sin includes more than victimization of other humans, then there will need to be an explanation for how humans can be reconciled to God besides the cessation of victimizing activities.

To return to the question of whether the cross and resurrection change anything in God's relationship with humankind, the Last Supper sayings beg for a more encompassing understanding once again. As we have seen, the recurring history of Israel was one of covenant disintegration and subsequent renewal. Israel's covenantal relationship with YHWH involved both a vertical dimension with God and a horizontal dimension with others under the covenant, and one cannot collapse one into the other but must allow both dimensions to exist simultaneously.[59]

All of the most substantiated versions of the sayings over the bread and cup that have come down to us in the New Testament cast Jesus' death within the context of Israel's covenantal relationship with YHWH. Regardless of whether one follows Mark and Matthew seeing the "blood of the covenant" as earlier or adopts Luke's "new covenant" as a better representation of the original, all four thrust the notion of the covenant to the fore. As a result, we cannot simply see the cross and resurrection as solely altering a change within humanity or humanity's understanding of God. The covenantal relationship involved two parties that were formerly estranged who can now enter back into a relationship once again. Moreover, if the Old Testament does provide a theological background, one can find several examples of YHWH willingly choosing to divorce his faithless spouse. If the covenantal relationship were to be resumed, one cannot say the change would solely be on the human side. Its resumption would imply that YHWH, who had willingly

---

58. Ibid., 321–22.
59. Levenson, *Sinai and Zion*, 53.

severed the relationship earlier, has again volitionally entered back into the relationship. Therefore, on the basis of the Last Supper sayings we can conclude that the cross and resurrection, at a minimum, signify a change in God's treatment of his covenant partner and constitute the effectual cause of that change, though this would not constitute a change in God's own nature.

Evaluating the Consistency of Girardian Thought

Those adhering to a Girardian understanding of the atonement will likely object to the exegesis of the Gospels taken thus far since it would supposedly re-inscribe God in violence, the very thing from which the cross purportedly saves us in a Girardian account. Now I have no intention of portraying God as a diabolic deity who delights in death, but merely wish to point out that, despite the contributions that Girard has made to Christian theology, his ability to claim the New Testament Gospels for support is flawed. Moreover, before the reader rushes to condemn the exegesis of the Gospels that has been established heretofore, I would invite the reader to a closer inspection of Girard's thought on its own terms and agendas. In this next portion, I contend that when Girard's theology is analyzed closely, it becomes apparent that Girard's thought is unable to free itself entirely from divine violence in significant ways.[60]

Human Origins

Of the various theological imbroglios that result from Girard's theory, the first concerns Girard's account of original sin, which jeopardizes an ability to affirm that God created human beings in goodness. The problem originates when Girard maps his theory of human nature onto the Darwinian evolution of human beings.[61] For Girard, animals utilize imitation just like humans, so humans share imitative behaviors with their ancestors. The main difference between animals and humans, though, is that animals lack "acquisitive behaviors"[62] and have some kind of instinctual resistance toward killing the less dominant members of the species, even if such a

---

60. Many, however, proclaim that Girard has achieved this goal. For example, Shults positively affirms that Girard "... provides a way of relating culture to the cross without a divine sanctioning of violence." Shults, *Christology and Science*, 93.

61. For attempts to defend Girard on this point, see Palaver, *Mimetic Theory*, 223–26 and Kirwan, *Philosophy and Theology*, 141.

62. Girard, *Things Hidden*, 91 (emphasis has been removed).

member were a former competitor.[63] While the animals of lower status will imitate the dominant animals for the sake of their corporate protection, imitation among animals precludes excessive rivalry and hence destructive social conflict. However, as this power of imitation increases among human ancestors, so does its power to induce acquisitive rivalry.

Girard's account of human origins becomes theologically problematic when he makes the appearance of human beings in the evolutionary process simultaneous with the point when acquisitive rivalry increases to where it must find its resolution in the scapegoat mechanism. Girard writes, "Beyond a certain threshold of mimetic power, animal societies become impossible. This threshold corresponds to the appearance of the victimage mechanism and would thus be the threshold of hominization."[64] As a result, Girard makes the emergence of humans coterminous with the occurrence of the scapegoat mechanism.[65] He affirms this again a few pages later: "Between what can be strictly termed animal nature on the one hand and developing humanity on the other there is a true rupture, which is collective murder, and it alone is capable of providing for kinds of organization, no matter how embryonic, based on prohibition and ritual."[66] In other words, only the scapegoat mechanism provides the decisive fissure, separating humans from the rest of the animal kingdom. Girard has even reiterated this point of view in a more recent interview with Phil Rose, where he affirms that the "mechanism of hominization" is none other than "the victimage mechanism."[67] Translating this into theologically relevant paradigms highlights the core of the conflict. In short, human beings are essentially "created"—i.e. differentiate themselves from animal societies—by the Fall, namely, the scapegoat mechanism.

By making the actuation of the scapegoat mechanism the point of humanity's emergence, Girard imperils the prospect of affirming that God created humanity in goodness.[68] In Girard's account, there is no primordial state of human goodness or innocence that is later disturbed by the scapegoat mechanism.[69] In fact, when Phil Rose directly queried him

63. Girard, *Violence and the Sacred*, 145.

64. Girard, *Things Hidden*, 95.

65. Alison concurs: "The emergent difference that we later call a victim is at the root of our hominization." Alison, "Conversion's Adventure," 27.

66. Girard, *Things Hidden*, 97.

67. Phil Rose, "Conversation with René Girard," 29.

68. For similar conclusions, see Adams, "Loving Mimesis," 279 and Rose, *Broken Middle*, 147.

69. Part of the problem is that Girard makes the scapegoat mechanism a ubiquitous feature of human societies. Even Hobbes did not think the war of all against all totalized human societies to such a degree. Hobbes, *Leviathan*, 92–98.

about this problematic issue in a recent interview, Girard sidestepped the issue by redirecting the focus onto a different theological question.[70] Either Girard failed to grasp the importance of Phil Rose's question regarding the absence of original goodness or he did understand the question and redirected it because he lacks a convincing explanation for how his understanding of human origins coheres with a belief that God created humanity in goodness. Failure to affirm such a tenet ushers in a number of questions related to theodicy.

Girard has suffered criticism on this point, and some have categorized his theory as some version of Gnosticism with its view of a diabolic creator deity. In response, Depoortere and Kerr have both attempted to repudiate the charges by arguing that, though violence might have a "historical" priority in Girard's account of human origins, it is not an "ontological priority."[71] They contend that, even though hominization proceeds by the violence of the scapegoat mechanism, God's end goal, as revealed in the cross and resurrection, is the kingdom of peace. Thus, even if God originally used the scapegoat mechanism as a means for human evolution, it is certainly not his teleological desire for humanity.

Depoortere and Kerr successfully demonstrate that Girard's system does not construct an ontological dualism where good and evil are on equal playing fields, and their arguments persuasively refute Girard's association with Gnosticism on this issue. Nevertheless, a serious problem still remains, and this is the problem from which Depoortere and Kerr cannot emancipate Girard. Even if God's teleological goal for humanity constitutes inhabiting the peaceful kingdom modeled after Christ's nonviolent behavior, Girard's account of human origins says that God has, at a minimum, permitted and perhaps even chosen the violence of the scapegoat mechanism as the means by which humans would evolve and come into being. This contrasts with the traditional Augustinian framework and the account of Genesis, where humans are first created in a state of innocence, and God permits humans to choose evil out of respect for human freedom. In contrast, for Girard, there is no pre-lapsarian state of human innocence. In order to create the peaceful kingdom on earth, God has allowed the evil of the scapegoat mechanism

70. Rose, "Conversation with René Girard," 24–26. When Rose asks about the goodness of creation, Girard responds as if Rose were asking about how one should understand the expulsion of Adam and Eve from the Garden, which is not answering the question that was put forth. Instead Girard turns to John 1:11 ("He came to what was his own, and his own people did not accept him.") to argue that humans first expel God rather than God expelling humans as the Garden of Eden depicts, which was not the central point of the question.

71. Depoortere, *Christ in Postmodern Philosophy*, 88 and Kerr, "Rescuing Girard's Argument?" 392–95.

to be the means of bringing humanity into being. Thus, humanity is created as already fallen because the Fall is the very mechanism of humanity's emergence.

This way of framing human origins compromises one's ability to claim that God is free of violence because violence is not a secondary development for humanity but its original state. If humans were always in a fallen state, one can legitimately wonder if the creator is not partially to blame for the current state of affairs. Moreover, instead of evil being the parasitic privation of goodness, as an Augustinian account would have, evil possesses the creative potency to generate new ways of being. Instead of delivering a portrait of the divine free of violence, Girard has constructed a view of human origins that compromises his assertions that God cannot be assimilated with "violence" in all of its forms. If God foresees that the scapegoat mechanism will be essential for the emergence of humanity and still elects this way of bringing humanity into being, then God seems morally compromised by utilizing the violence perpetrated against an innocent victim in order to bring rational creatures out of the animal kingdom only to "create" them as members in the kingdom of Satan. In fact, God appears to be a cosmic utilitarian willing to allow or employ evil in order to produce a greater good, namely, human creatures capable of higher rational and symbolic ordering.

Violence as the Means of Salvation

The second issue for Girardian soteriology arises from the very fact that, biblical texts aside, the violence of Jesus' cross must remain an essential element, for only the cross can diffuse the knowledge of the innocent victim necessary for humanity's salvation. In a Girardian account of the cross, humans are faulted for the violence, which seems to remove God from culpability, at least initially. However, when Girardian soteriology is pressed to articulate God's will for humanity's salvation, one is forced to reckon with the fact that God might, in fact, will violence against the son. To put it another way, if God truly desires a different cultural order than the one that has governed humanity from its infancy as the Girardian perspective suggests, then the cross must be willingly permitted in order to procure the saving revelation. Girard appears to affirm something along these very lines when he writes: "Jesus willingly and knowingly accepts to undergo the fate of the scapegoat to achieve the full revelation of scapegoating as the genesis of all false gods."[72] In this section, he maintains that Jesus chooses to embrace the violence on the cross in order to bring salvation to others.

---

72. Girard, "Violence Renounced," 319 (original emphasis removed).

On the same page, he writes: "God willingly becomes the scapegoat of his own people not for the purpose of evacuating internal violence through the old mythical misunderstanding but for the opposite reason, for clearing up once and for all such misunderstandings and raising humankind above the culture of scapegoating."[73] Thus, Girard describes the cross as something that is "willingly" chosen in order to deliver the saving revelation.

This is precisely where the problem arises. If the violent suffering of an innocent victim (i.e. Jesus) is the only means by which the "ontological priority" of the kingdom can be attained and the scapegoat mechanism can be deconstructed, God becomes complicit in the violence of the cross to the degree that he wills to accomplish human salvation through this very means. By implication then, God's desire and will for human salvation via the cross means that God has to allow and even desire the scapegoat mechanism to run its course with Jesus if he is going to accomplish the greater good of humanity's salvation. However, if scapegoating is the very problem with humanity and the very essence of its sin, basically that it is willing to sacrifice innocent victims, why is God justified in willing and embracing violence for the Son? It would appear Girard's approach to soteriology finds itself thrust upon the horns of the dilemma in the very event that it has tried to interpret as the paramount revelation of violence.

Finlan also put his finger on this very weakness within Girardian thought, declaring: "For Girardian theory to work, God needs to reject *all* scapegoating. Using it once is once too often."[74] Though Finlan finds this a point of contradiction within Girardian soteriology, he does try to rescue Girardian soteriology by differentiating between "a God-caused death and a God-anticipated death."[75] Though a "God-caused death" is hopelessly irredeemable in his perspective, a "God-anticipated death" remains a more viable option in his view. However, distinguishing between these two options in Girardian thought is a bit complicated if not impossible. In the Girardian theory, God certainly anticipates the violence of the cross because of humanity's past behavior.[76] However, just because God anticipates such a death does not necessarily remove his complicity. In the Girardian account of salvation, God must still remain a factor to the degree that he chooses to participate in the rescue of humanity in this way. Cognizant that the cross is essential for humanity's salvation and that the incarnation will lead to Jesus' victimization (so Schwager), he still chooses to go through with the events

---

73. Ibid., 319.
74. Finlan, *Options on Atonement*, 106.
75. Ibid.
76. Girard, *Things Hidden*, 213.

that will knowingly precipitate the cross. Heim, who is more honest than most of Girard's followers on this point, concedes that at the cross, "Jesus has become ... an accomplice of Satan in something that is unqualifiedly evil. Even though ultimately this may be seen as a deep wisdom that ensnares and defeats Satan, it requires that God is not only willing to suffer in body and spirit, but also willing to suffer the moral ambiguity reflected in this exchange...."[77] Heim, I believe, is right to put it in these terms. God becomes an "accomplice" in the violence of the cross. God permits one to be victimized to accomplish the greater good.

Marlin Miller has been more perceptive than some other followers of Girard in this regard and attempted to circumnavigate the predicament by distinguishing God's willful choosing of the cross from "God's allowing people to respond by opposing and killing Jesus."[78] As he continues, Miller casts the choice to God as if it were a decision between either "obedience unto death" or "killing enemies with supernatural power."[79] However, this is a disingenuous way of arranging the options because the real choice put to a Girardian point of view is whether God wills to save humans through the kind of violence necessary to expose the scapegoat mechanism or whether God will refuse to play a role in this matter and let humans languish in their violence. One can appreciate what Miller is trying to do yet still find the attempt unsuccessful because God still chooses the route of the cross in order to save humanity, which will knowingly require the victimization of one more innocent victim.

Not surprisingly, several of Girard's commentators overlook this fact. For example, Anthony Kelly who ascribes to Girard's view of the cross asserts: "The victimization of some can never be the precondition of a full life for others."[80] Unfortunately, he fails to note that Girard's system still requires *one* to suffer for the benefit of others. Similarly, Ted Grimsrud overlooks the contradiction in Girardian thought: "Girardians associate sacrifice with sacred violence. Sacrificial theology does not help us overcome the problem of violence. Rather, such theology pictures ultimate reality (the heart of God itself) as requiring violence—the death of innocent victims. Thus ultimately sacrifice does not provide the means to genuine salvation and *shalom* but only feeds the spiral of violence."[81] Though the Girardian viewpoint no longer has the divine demanding sacrifices, in Girardian soteriology the

77. Heim, *Saved from Sacrifice*, 152–53n12.
78. Miller, "Girardian Perspectives," 39.
79. Ibid.
80. Kelly, "Beyond Locked Doors," 83.
81. Grimsrud, "Scapegoating No More," 51.

sacrifice of one innocent victim does remain "the means to genuine salvation" since the Son must endure unjustified violence for the rest of humanity. Thus, attaining the kingdom of God, even in Girardian soteriology, requires the sacrifice of at least one innocent person, the Son.

Though Girard has statements that acknowledge God's willful choosing of the cross, as noted above, he has other statements that explicitly deny any such complicity with the violence of the cross. For example, he writes: "If the fulfilment, on earth, passes inevitably through the death of Jesus, this is not because the Father demands this death, for strange sacrificial motives. Neither the son nor the Father should be questioned about the cause of this event, but all mankind, and mankind alone."[82] Because the human problem is such that it requires violence in order to bring salvation, Girard tries to remove God from being responsible for the violence of the cross in any way.

In *Things Hidden since the Foundation of the World*, Girard turns to Solomon's judgment between two women vying for possession of the same child to make the case that God can adopt the way of the cross without choosing the evil of violence by reading the narrative as a parable. While the quarrel and the competing claims of the mothers coincide perfectly with Girard's description of a mimetic crisis, he uses the narrative to expose a difference between the illegitimate form of sacrifice and the mother's self-offering. When Solomon threatens to divide the child in two, the real mother relinquishes all claims to the child. As a result, she risks not only her future with the child, but also risks being thought a schemer and a liar. In light of this, one can say the mother truly does give up something of herself, but Girard was reluctant, at this point in his career anyway, to label this a sacrifice. To avoid associating such an act with sacrifice, he introduces a primary distinction. For him, death is constitutive of sacrificial language, but the mother is not truly pursuing death as such. Although she has jeopardized her own life and reputation, she does it *"in order to save life,"* namely, the life of her child.[83] Girard indicates that this mother is "the most perfect *figura Chrsti* that can be imagined."[84] For Girard, Solomon is analogous to the Father. Neither wants the death or sacrifice of the son. Jesus, comparable to the good mother, must likewise renounce his claim to life. Thus far, the comparison between the two accounts holds. However, there is a striking difference in these parallels that Girard fails to mention. In the judgment of Solomon, violence is only ever threatened. The mere threat efficaciously brings the truth to light. However, in the case of Jesus, the truth can only

82. Girard, *Things Hidden*, 213.
83. Ibid., 241 (emphasis is his).
84. Ibid.

be revealed through actual violence, and this is something that the Son and Father know beforehand, a point which Girard seems to acknowledge on occasion.[85] Surely, the cross is not the ultimate end intended from a Girardian point of view, but this does nothing to eliminate the fact that the cross is knowingly chosen as the means to redemption, even if these conditions were necessitated by humanity's fallen state. In the end, neither Girard nor any of his defenders successfully diffuse the charge that God must, to some degree, still choose the violence of the cross.

As a result, the attempts to make humanity solely responsibility for the cross's violence are unsuccessful even in a Girardian account. In the case of Girard, one finds the statements removing God from culpability in conflict with those that posit his willing choice in the matter. Girard cannot have it both ways. Furthermore, even if human sin demands that salvation must occur through the lynching of an innocent victim, the Father and Son still consent to this very manner of procuring salvation. Even though humanity is the initial "cause" which establishes the route by which salvation must occur in Girardian soteriology, it is still God who agrees to gain salvation in just this way. Whether this choice is described as a passive allowance or an active choice seems to make little difference, for God must elect the violence of the cross in some way for us to be able to speak of the event theologically. Only if the cross were truly an unintended accident, then one could successfully remove God from complicity in its violence. Consequently, it would at the same time preclude any theological reflection about what God was accomplishing in and through Jesus' death. However, Girardian soteriology does not believe that the cross is an accident, but the deliberate means by which God saved humankind. As a result, it must accept God's complicity in the event if it is to continue making theological claims about it.

Since God is willing to enact the events that will knowingly lead to the Son's victimization in order to attain salvation, one cannot say with Girard that God "never acts by means of violence, is never responsible for any violence, and remains radically opposed to violence."[86] Instead, God appears utilitarian, willing to use violence on at least one occasion against the Son

---

85. Girard writes in *I See Satan Fall like Lightning* that the only reason God allowed the temporary enslavement to the victim mechanism was "because God knew beforehand that at the right time Christ would overcome his adversary by dying on the Cross. God in his wisdom had foreseen since the beginning that the victim mechanism would be reversed like a glove, exposed, placed in the open, stripped naked, and dismantled in the Gospel Passion texts, and he knew that neither Satan nor the powers could prevent this revelation" (151). Though God is not gambling with the outcome, he foresees the exact steps necessary to undo the scapegoat mechanism and still chooses to walk down the morally ambiguous path.

86. Girard, *Things Hidden*, 214.

in order to bring about a world without violence. The violence of the cross becomes a means to the peaceful end, but this requires God to be complicit in the very thing he is trying to exorcise. This, unfortunately, jeopardizes God's goodness in a Girardian account. If earlier versions of Christus Victor theory were deemed inadequate because God compromised his character by deceiving the devil in order to gain human salvation, the same might be the fault of Girardian soteriology. God must compromise his nonviolent character in order to attain the saving knowledge for humanity.

Conclusion

In the final analysis, Girard's soteriology faces challenges from two fronts: biblical exegesis and internal consistency. Among the issues arising in biblical exegesis, we have seen that Girard's interpretation of the biblical texts is dependent on the assumption that the biblical texts are involved in a polemical exchange with mythology. As we have observed, this presupposition ultimately misconstrues several significant passages because they are read from the vantage point of Girard's narrative of human origins and the scapegoat mechanism. More significantly, Girard's hermeneutical approach has positioned the Gospels in the wrong conversation, i.e. the emancipation of humanity from a cultural of scapegoating. As demonstrated in earlier chapters, the Gospels continue the story of Israel's exile and restoration and situate Jesus as the redeemer in that story. Based upon this, one can contend that a more holistic understanding of the Gospels must proceed with this story in view.

Girard's hermeneutical approach also translates into theological assertions that stand in contrast to the Gospels, at least the conclusions reached herein. The Last Supper sayings cast Jesus' death as a sacrifice, not simply as a way of designating it as a renunciation of his life but to explain how his death would benefit his followers. In the case of Matthew, Jesus' death was "for the forgiveness of sins," which infuses Jesus' death with atoning value. Moreover, the Gospels' picture of the Father's relationship with the cross's violence is not nearly as removed as some might like. The Gospels paint a much more complicated portrait where the shepherd is stricken and the cross is necessary for the redemption of God's people. Thus, the Gospels give us a much more complicated view of the Father's relationship to the cross and its violence than what Girard would allow. Additionally, the cross does not simply change humanity but also can be said to change the conditions that allow God's covenantal relationship with humans to be resumed. Thus, the cross does not simply remove the relational barriers solely on the human side. If the covenantal relationship is restored like the Last Supper sayings indicate, then it seems that the conditions for reconciliation, some of which might be demands from the divine side, have been met. For these reasons, several of Girard's significant theological assertions fail to be compelling on biblical grounds.

Not only do the Gospels challenge Girard's theological formulations, but Girard faces the problem of internal inconsistencies within his own work. A close analysis of Girard's writings reveals that he has not fully succeeded in removing violence from God either. In the evolutionary emergence of humans and at the cross, God appears willing to use violence to accomplish a greater good that could not otherwise occur. Even though the good accomplished proportionally outweighs the evil allowed, Girard complicates his portrait of God in these two instances. In light of these observations, it does not appear that Girard's soteriology has attained the moral high ground of a God completely free from violence nor has he delivered a soteriology that would ask humans to renounce all forms of violence.[87] Because God did become complicit with violence to accomplish a greater good, one can legitimately wonder whether Girard's thought has the theological consistency to denounce other soteriologies as violent or sacrificial and therefore deficient on these grounds.

Now this is not to say that Girardian soteriology more broadly speaking could not be emended to be more internally consistent, though it is doubtful whether it could surmount all of the above issues entirely. One could imagine a revision to Girard's theory of human origins that might locate human emergence in a state of innocence rather than having the scapegoat mechanism be the point of demarcation between humans and animals. However, the one criticism that appears incapable of circumnavigation would be the fact that God, if he desires to save humanity, must somehow remain complicit in the violence at the cross from a Girardian point of view. If this cannot be overcome, Girardian thought—both in its original formulation by Girard and in its development by his followers—suffers from an internal inconsistency where God is willing to become an accomplice with "evil" in the form of scapegoating to effect a greater good, namely, the emancipation of humanity from its violence. In fact, God does not appear all that different from archaic societies because he too believes that the sacrifice of the innocent victim, i.e. the Son, will bring peace on earth. The only difference is that God was right whereas humans have

---

87. Girard even allows for a violent response to terrorism. See Rose, "Conversation," 34. See also Williams, *Bible, Violence, and the Sacred*, 244–45.

always been wrong because the scapegoat mechanism could only deliver the simulacra of peace.

9

Girard, Renewing the Covenant, and Ways Forward

IF THE ARGUMENTS AND the observations of the previous chapter obtain, what options are left for Girardian soteriology? There should, of course, be a concerted effort to frame a more internally consistent theology regarding God's relationship to violence. It is likely that Girardian theorists can produce a more amenable account of human origins that affirms God's creation of humans apart from violence. Whether Girardian soteriology can fully avoid God's complicity in violence at the cross without degenerating into semantic word-plays should at least be explored, though it may not prove successful in the end. However, the more troubling issue for Girardian soteriology that requires more wholesale revision is the biblical counter-evidence that has been explored in the previous chapters. For as much as modern interpreters might want the Gospels to emancipate God from any involvement with violence or provide a non-sacrificial interpretation of the cross, one is forced to reckon with quite the opposite, for God is the one striking the shepherd and Jesus' death is depicted as a new covenant sacrifice that acquires the forgiveness of sins. As a result, Girardian soteriology has, from what I can foresee at this moment, several alternatives if the evidence of the preceding chapters should prove persuasive.

Future Courses for Girardian Soteriology

Abandoning the Global Claim: "a Canon within the Canon"

The first option is to retreat from Girard's global affirmation that the Gospels entirely affirm his soteriology.[1] Consider, for example, his assertion to the following effect: "There is nothing in the Gospels to suggest that the death of Jesus is a sacrifice, whatever definition (expiation, substitution, etc.) we may

---

1. Girard, *Things Hidden*, 243.

give for that sacrifice."² Though one might be able to fault the evangelists with introducing the language and logic of atonement at a later date, Girard closes the door on this facile way around the problem by averring that the Gospel writers faithfully transmitted the saving revelation.³ Thus, because Girard's soteriological affirmations are grounded upon his assertions that the Gospels speak unequivocally about Jesus accomplishing salvation and that they are accurate conduits of the saving revelation, any evidence to the contrary imperils his soteriological claims.⁴

Unfortunately, the prospects of Girard's soteriology are jeopardized by the fact that the Gospels do have passages that see Jesus as a sacrifice who will provide atonement for God's people and renew his covenant with them, and these elements are located precisely in the passages that Girard ignores. Even though several of his followers have tried to offer interpretations of these passages consistent with Girardian soteriology, they have not proven persuasive, especially when we read the Gospels as documents situated within the larger story of Israel's exile and restoration.

Nevertheless, despite such counter-evidence, one need not surrender Girardian soteriology altogether. One could put forth a less comprehensive thesis about the Gospels and contend that a selection or a portion of the Gospel texts deconstructs the scapegoat mechanism, even if other passages rehabilitate it. Thus, instead of trying to bend the problematic texts into conformity with Girardian soteriology, one could simply concede that certain passages do portray the cross as a result of divine intentionality. Perhaps the counter-evidence could be dismissed as later human projections into the Gospel accounts that have failed to make sense of the saving revelation. Regardless of how it gets fleshed out, this particular alternative would simply retreat from Girard's global claim regarding the Gospels and concede that there are passages that counter Girard's soteriology.

In fact, Girard's interpretation of the Old Testament provides the resources for such a way forward.⁵ For instance, Girard's exegesis of the book of Job conceded the presence of conflicting evidence. Even though Job utters statements that credit God with the calamities of his life (e.g. Job 19:2–7; 30:9–15), Girard says that these are instances when Job has succumbed to the myth of the persecutors.⁶ As a result, he contends, "In most

---

2. Ibid., 181.
3. Girard, *Evolution and Conversion*, 216 and Girard, *Scapegoat*, 163.
4. Girard, *Things Hidden*, 185–90.
5. For instance, when Isaiah's Fourth Servant Song implicates YHWH in the death of the Servant, he believes this is the result of "a later interpretation that falsifies the text." Girard, *Things Hidden*, 227.
6. Girard, *Job*, 125–29.

of the Dialogues, the God of Job is not the Yahweh of the Bible."[7] In contrast to the views of Job's friends and Job's own capitulations to the mythological viewpoint, Girard identifies two passages as the main revelation of the book that rise above the mire of the mythological viewpoint: Job 16:12–21 and 19:25–27.[8] Both of these texts constitute the "audacious revolt of the scapegoat" that refuses to crumble to the view of the crowd and instead clings to the belief that "God lends an ear to the victim."[9] Instead of allowing the various theological viewpoints expressed in Job to stand in unresolved tension or trying to synthesize them together into a coherent portrait, Girard sees the theology and discourses condemning Job as an attempt to suppress the true revelation that Job, the scapegoat, is innocent of the wrongs being foisted upon him.[10] The book of Job is thus a conflicted text that simultaneously includes both the revelation of the innocent victim and the mythological condemnation of the crowds, but Girard privileges only a very minute portion of the book as revelation. From a Girardian point of view, it is not too far of a leap to say that the Gospels are similar in that they also contain both revelation and the condemnation of the scapegoat.

Girard openly admits that the anti-mythological bent of Job is a minor theme that is on the verge of extinction in the book. However, in order to privilege these two passages to discredit the more numerous passages condemning Job, Girard appeals to another group of texts, the Gospels:

> For the Dialogues to be interpreted as they should, as I have already mentioned, we must choose the side of the victim against the persecutors, identify with him, and accept what he says as truth.... As it has come down to us, the Book of Job does not insist enough on our hearing the complaint of Job: many things divert us from the crucial texts, deforming and neutralizing them with our secret complicity. We need, therefore, another text, something else, or rather someone else to come to our aid: the text of the Passion, Christ, is the one to help us understand Job, because Christ completes what Job only half achieves, and that is paradoxically what in the context of the world is his own disaster, the Passion that will soon be inscribed in the text of the Gospels.[11]

---

7. Ibid., 132.
8. Ibid., 138–40.
9. Ibid., 138.
10. Ibid., 143.
11. Ibid., 163.

Thus, in his approach to Job, which is paradigmatic of his approach to much of the Old Testament, the Gospels become the text that verifies the true import of Job.

Girard's exegesis of Job reveals the inherent problem of this particular option and perhaps illumines why Girard felt compelled to contend the Gospels are in full support of his position. In his exegesis of Job, Girard is able to lean upon the Gospels as the hermeneutical key which identifies the transcendent viewpoint in the conflicted text. In essence, the Gospels function as the Archimedean point by which Girard is able to clear away the mythological viewpoint. With the Gospels—presumably unadulterated by any kind of "sacrificial theology"—in hand, Girard can dismiss the passages that justify Job's condemnation. If, however, the Gospels no longer remain the ciphers which decode all other texts but are themselves conflicted texts, then not only do his conclusions of Job crumble, but humanity is left without access to an immaculate, transcendent viewpoint that can speak unequivocally for God. Moreover, if the Gospels are conflicted texts that re-inscribe God in violence and situate Jesus' death as a sacrifice that accomplished the forgiveness of sin, Girard provides no other texts to which one might appeal to verify that the sacrificial viewpoint is wholly in error. Furthermore, if the biblical tradition can no longer serve as the sure ground upon which to assess the world, admitting that the Gospels are conflicted texts threatens to destabilize Girard's wider anthropological assumptions since the exposure of mythology and humanity's penchant for justifying its victims only comes through the Gospel texts.[12] The only remaining group of texts that might serve in such a fashion is Girard's own oeuvre.

In one of the debates regarding Girardian thought, Schwager retreated to this very conclusion. In the conversation, Schwager was asked to identify the master text from which he could discern the workings of the scapegoat mechanism. Schwager admitted that one can only categorize a story like the Joseph cycle in Genesis as "plus révélatrice" on the basis of what appears to be an arbitrary criterion.[13] One of the interlocutors pressed Schwager for a criterion upon which to judge the more revelatory texts since one can find ample support for divine violence in the Bible. Though Schwager responded by pointing toward the Gospels, he was forced to qualify his criterion further as "la théorie de Girard" rather than making his criterion the Gospels alone.[14] Thus, the Gospels, as a whole, do not

12. This potential weakness was noted by Jean-Michel Oughourlian in the dialogue contained in Girard, *Things Hidden*, 185.

13. Dumouchel, *Violence et vérité*, 87. The English translation is available in Goodhart, *Prophetic Law*, 29.

14. Dumouchel, *Violence*, 88 and Goodhart, *Prophetic Law*, 30.

form the criterion for identifying revelation in the Bible, but rather Girard's interpretation of the Gospels do.[15]

Schwager's concession on this point corroborates the problematic nature of adopting this solution to the counter-evidence. Conceding that only a portion of the Gospels contain the saving revelation subjects Girardian thought to the old saw of being nothing more than another "canon within the canon." Klug aptly summarizes the deficiencies of such an approach: "The simple fact is that the Bible itself supports no formula whatever, whereby the Word of God and Scripture are to be sifted like flour from grit."[16] Continuing on, he writes, "Holy Scripture does not allow itself to be split down the middle arbitrarily into that which is human and that which [is] divine."[17] This, however, would be precisely what this particular revision to Girardian soteriology would need to do, and this is not merely giving one set of passages a more significant role in one's theology.[18] It would require distinguishing strands in the Gospels that represent the "divine" viewpoint from those that represent the "human" viewpoint. Statements that fall from the lips of Jesus (the Last Supper sayings, the Ransom logion, etc.) would need to reflect later accretions to the tradition, and one might even marshal historical Jesus research for support. If Girardian thought is to be revised along these lines, it would require a decision to ignore or delete the passages in contradiction with Girardian soteriology, and this would always be susceptible to the charge of being a capricious, arbitrary, and ideologically self-serving choice. Furthermore, the nagging problem of God's complicity in violence at the cross would remain a perpetual concern because the violence of the cross would still remain necessary for the diffusion of the saving revelation. For these reasons, other options are more preferable, though some no doubt have taken and will take this first option.[19]

Assimilation 1: One Theory among the Many

If one wished to align Girardian theory in more accord with the biblical texts, especially as they have been interpreted in the prior chapters, and

---

15. Schwager's concession places Girardian soteriology in the crosshairs of Dunnill's criticism: "The effect is in fact to imprison Christology within his bold but inadequate theory, because salvation would then come to lie, not in the cross and resurrection, but in apprehending the Girardian understanding of violence." Dunnill, *Sacrifice and the Body*, 159.

16. See Klug, "End of the Historical-Critical Method," 290.

17. Ibid.

18. Contra Rogness, "Canon," 436, 438.

19. E.g. Baker, *Executing God*, 18, 90.

not simply reject the counter-evidence, a more radical reconfiguration of Girardian theory would be necessary. As a beginning first step, Girardian soteriology would have to be unseated from its claim to be the quintessential explanation of the cross. This is necessary because, in its current form, Girardian soteriology has made itself incommensurable with any atoning understanding of the cross.[20] In effect, Girardian theory paradoxically—even contradictorily so—ends up scapegoating "sacrificial Christianity" as part of the problem within humanity that must be overcome.[21] As we have seen, these are precisely the elements that remain stubbornly embedded in the Gospel narratives. If one is going to redraw Girardian soteriology along biblical lines and delete its scapegoating of other atonement theologies, then it will have to be reformulated so it can coexist alongside of other theories or soteriologies that might include penal elements.

There are two ways in which this process might proceed after this point, both of which require some form of assimilation with other theories of the atonement. In the first way, all of the atonement theories—from Christus Victor up through Girard's scapegoat theory—could be relativized in a way that acknowledges their particular insights without affording any one theory the power of fully explaining the cross. Thus, none of the views would be able to explain the atonement *in toto*. Joel Green's "Kaleidoscopic View" of the atonement closely approximates this view.[22] Though the atonement metaphors in Green's account derive from the biblical metaphors, he demands that we cease trying to privilege one metaphor over another. Instead, the metaphors all contain insights that must be retained, though some may be granted more precedence during eras where they prove more relevant. Nevertheless, the failure of any one theory or metaphor to exhaust the inner workings of the atonement betrays the transcendent mystery inherent in the atonement. Thus, each theory or metaphor would be essential to understanding God's salvation of humankind but could never satisfactorily explain its totality.

In such a paradigm, Girardian soteriology could uniquely contribute the insight that the cross is a revelation of humanity's injustice and that humankind is willing to conscript notions of law, justice, and the power of the state in order to muffle the voice of innocent victims for the sake of peace. As such, it would serve as an enduring reminder of humanity's pernicious

---

20. Girard, *Things Hidden*, 180–81. See also Dizdar, "Finding the Way," 46.

21. Dunnill, *Sacrifice and the Body*, 160. In an interview with Richard Golsan, Girard concedes that assuming a particular theological position and disagreeing with another constitutes scapegoating, though being a minor form of it. See Golsan, *Girard and Myth*, 135.

22. Green, "Kaleidoscopic View," 157–85.

tendency to justify its sinful behavior. At the same time, Girardian soteriology, though offering a valid criticism of human law and its connection with the divine law, could not fully deliver a wholesale rejection of a soteriological view in which God would enforce boundaries or punish sin. In short, Girardian soteriology would no longer be able to expel certain theories of the atonement like satisfaction or penal substitution theories but would have to concede that these theories do in fact offer some insight into the mystery of the atonement. Whether the plethora of views that have been offered throughout church history can find some logical unity in the aggregate or whether they can coherently exist alongside of each other are questions worth exploring. The detriment of this particular approach resides in its tenuous unification of diverse—sometimes even conflicting—viewpoints and the admission that, if there is a logic driving God's salvation of humankind, it is not fully intelligible to us.[23]

Assimilation 2: Supporting a Governing Theory

The second manner of assimilating Girardian soteriology would be to place it into an interpretive framework where another governing theory provided the logical soteriological structure. In this option, Girardian theory would play a subservient role, further explaining another theory, though making valid contributions on its own. One could, for instance, make Christus Victor the controlling theory and incorporate Jesus' ability to resist caving to the mimetic contagion as one of ways in which God conquers evil. If such an approach is to be informed by the biblical exegesis of the former chapters, it will have to retain a penal or satisfaction element in some fashion. Perhaps N. T. Wright's soteriology would be amenable to this, for he elevates Christus Victor as the dominant atonement theory, making it the gravitational center around which all of the other theories revolve.[24] Underneath this particular umbrella, Wright includes a penal element of the cross.[25] In addition, Wright also sees a dimension of God's victory over evil including the exposure of the political authorities.[26] Though Wright's account is largely informed by his historical reconstruction of the events and political wrangling that led to the crucifixion, one could just as soon borrow insights from Girard's anthropology and soteriology in order to elucidate more

---

23. In fact, Green's "kaleidoscopic view" was criticized on the grounds that it appears to presuppose no internal logic. See Boyd, "Christus Victor Response," 187.
24. Wright, *Justice of God*, 95.
25. Ibid.
26. Ibid., 79–80.

thoroughly the psychological forces that put Jesus on the cross. Of course, Girard's mimetic theory and its corresponding explanation of the cross would not be adopted wholesale, but they could be utilized to construct a more robust account of the crucifixion and the battle that was waged with the powers.

A Future Course for Soteriology

Of the options presented above, I would offer the final one as the most congruent with the exegetical conclusions of the former chapters. Moreover, the centrality of the covenantal motif present in the Last Supper sayings and the larger biblical canon suggest that a theory of atonement that privileges the story of God in covenant with his people might be better suited to serve as the governing motif into which various atonement theories could be assimilated. Regrettably, theologians have rarely turned to the covenantal motif in order to ground and frame their understanding of the atonement.[27] The recent publication of Michael Gorman's *The Death of the Messiah and the Birth of the New Covenant: A (Not So) New Model of the Atonement* might serve to encourage others to recast the atonement in this regard.[28] Nevertheless, it is an often overlooked area that is pregnant with promise not only because of its biblical roots but also because it can gather various atonement theories and the different dimensions of salvation under its wings.

The potential of the covenantal approach to assimilate aspects of the various atonement theories is significant. For example, it can incorporate the very penal elements that have been identified in the Last Supper sayings. Jesus' death identifies with Israel specifically and humanity more generally in that he takes on the punishment for breaking the covenantal expectations. However, the atonement and salvation would by no means be limited to a legal transaction or the assumption of a punishment. The new covenant promises reveal that God's intended salvation was not simply removing the punishment the erring covenant partner deserved but included the moral transformation of his people so they would keep his covenant in the future. In order to resume and fortify the covenant relationship, their guilt for breaking the covenant had to be removed and the partner's character had

---

27. Theologians who have used the covenantal motif to construct their soteriology include the following thinkers: Torrance, *Atonement*; Shelton, *Cross and Covenant*; Vanhoozer, "Atonement in Postmodernity," 367–407; Vanhoozer, *The Drama of Doctrine*; and Balthasar, *The Old Covenant*, esp. 388–416; and Balthasar, *The New Covenant*, esp. 33–40.

28. Gorman, *Birth of the New Covenant*. This work is an expansion of a former essay: Gorman, "Effecting the New Covenant," 26–59.

to be molded in order to be the faithful partner that God desired. Thus, the divide between justification and sanctification that has dogged much Protestant theology could be unified around God's desire to renew the covenant with his wayward people and recreate them into his intended covenant partners.[29]

Within this framework, Girardian anthropology could play an informative role about the nature of human beings. In Girardian thought, the cross is a revelation of human sin, and this very insight would be reframed but still utilized in a reconstructed atonement theology drawn upon covenantal lines. The Gospel writers do not simply describe the cross as Jesus' adoption of Israel's exilic punishment. They also reveal that the cross was the result of religious and political leaders trying to protect their power. What is most striking in the accounts of the Passion is that the religious leaders appealed to the covenantal expectations, the Mosaic law, in order to justify their collusion in Jesus' death (Mark 14:64). These religious trials reveal that humans possess the sinister ability of justifying their violence and sin through appealing to the covenant itself. When one's adherence to the covenant departs from its *telos* of love, the covenantal expectations can become a means of victimization and oppression. The wrangling and petty posturing for power that ultimately hangs Jesus on the cross is not the intended outcome of the covenant. In fact, one can say just the opposite: the crucified Jesus who faithfully fulfilled the *telos* of the covenant to the end remains the example *par excellence* of covenant faithfulness. Instead of following the morally scrupulous religious leaders who are willing to dispense with an opponent on religious grounds, incorporating Girard's insights would point to the fact that Jesus' demonstration of love and forgiveness reveals the true ethos of the covenant.

By the same token, incorporating the insights of Girardian soteriology would also question our ability to map divine justice onto the canons of human justice in all instances. As a result of incorporating Girardian soteriology, one would be forced to part ways with those who, like Calvin, do equate human justice with divine justice, especially in the Passion narratives. In Calvin's exposition of the atonement, he makes it essential that Christ dies as a criminal condemned in a human court of law.[30] Only by being condemned in a human court of law can Jesus also receive the divine punishment for sin. Calvin even goes so far as to claim: "Had he been cut off by assassins, or slain in a seditious tumult, there could have been no kind of satisfaction in such a death."[31] Because Calvin directly interweaves

---

29. See Meilaender, *Freedom of a Christian*, 49–53.
30. Calvin, *Institutes*, 2.16.5.
31. Ibid.

justice on the human plane with divine, he is unable to separate the two at the cross sufficiently and makes the human courts' condemnation of Jesus the organ of divine justice.[32] In so doing, Calvin forfeits any ability to find in the condemnation of Jesus an exposure or revelation of human depravity, much less a critique of the political authorities that put Jesus on the cross..

At this juncture, it might seem that one is forced to embrace either Girard or Calvin wholesale. It could appear that, if one affirms a penal aspect to the cross, one is forced to walk the entire way with Calvin and see Pilate's condemnation of Jesus as a mechanism of the divine court of justice. On the other hand, it might appear that, if one wishes to see the cross as a revelation of human sinfulness and injustice, one must jettison any assumption of divine punishment in the cross and follow Girard.

However, we are not forced to choose between the two. In fact, adopting the covenantal motif as the governing framework for the atonement provides a way of assimilating both. In Miroslav Volf's masterful work, *Exclusion and Embrace*, he explains that an essential component of renewing ruptured relationships—ones that have been broken because one of the parties has broken their covenanted agreements—with other people requires a willingness to suffer injustice. In order to re-establish a broken relationship, Volf believes that "injustice" must accompany any such overture for continued relationship. An innocent party undoubtedly must give more than the requirements of retributive justice would dictate and suffer a loss of some kind:

> If such suffering of the innocent party strikes us as unjust, in an important sense it *is* unjust. Yet the 'injustice' is precisely what it takes to renew the covenant. One of the biggest obstacles to repairing broken covenants is that they invariably entail deep disagreements over what constitutes a breach and who is responsible for it.... In a world of clashing perspectives and strenuous self-justifications, of crumbly commitments and strong animosities, covenants are kept and renewed because those who, from their perspective, have not broken the covenant are willing to do the hard work of repairing it.[33]

Though Volf's comments describe the reconstitution of human relationships, the same thing could be said about God's resumption of the covenant with his people. From God's perspective, there was no reason for him to renew the relationship. Measured by the standards of retributive justice and the conditions established by the covenant, God had no reason to endure

---

32. See the helpful analysis in Vidu, *Atonement*, 118–32.
33. Volf, *Exclusion and Embrace*, 155(emphasis is his).

the cross. In fact, retributive justice would have directed the punishment at the other party in the covenant, human beings. However, God was willing to endure the injustice of the cross in order to maintain the covenantal relationship. What God in Jesus suffers at the cross is nothing less than a gross infraction of the covenant even though his death was erroneously justified on those same grounds. Thus, on the one hand, we can stand with Girard and call the cross an unjust annihilation of a covenant partner that was propped up by the distorted interpretations of the covenant.

On the other hand, we can stand with the Gospel writers and other theories of atonement that have found in the cross a penal or satisfaction element. Volf's comments again provide a point of entry for the discussion. He describes the story of the cross in relationship to the covenant in the following way: "For the narrative of the cross is not a 'self-contradictory' story of a God who 'died' because God broke the covenant, but a truly incredible story of God doing what God should neither have been able nor willing to do—a story of God who 'died' because God's all too human *covenant partner* broke the covenant."[34] Volf's final line can be taken in two ways, and he unfortunately leaves its meaning rather ambiguous. In the first way, which would simply be affirming Girard, the execution of Jesus is a breach of the covenant. When the religious leaders turned against Jesus and pandered for his death, they broke the covenantal expectations. In the second way, Jesus' death occurred as a punishment for Israel's sin. Though Volf does not indicate which of the two he means, I think both meanings can be held simultaneously.

The former chapters of the present work illumine the way at this point. As we have seen, the consequences for breaking the covenant included God's abandonment of his people to exile under foreign powers and death itself. The Gospels assume Israel's state of exile and her hopes for restoration as the governing script in which Jesus lives and announces God's imminent restoration. In light of this, it is not hard to understand why the Gospel writers depict Jesus' death in the language of Israel's exile. Jesus is handed "over to the Gentiles" (Mark 10:33), just like Israel was. Nor is it difficult to understand why if Jesus, as the innocent representative of his people, would unjustly suffer at the hands of the Romans, the Gospel writers would think that he would thereby inaugurate a new covenant between God and his people. By being faithful to the covenant to the point of death *and* suffering the punishment for his people's previous breaches of the covenant, Jesus would renew that same relationship through suffering the injustice of the cross. Precisely by voluntarily entering into Israel's exile, into the human

---

34. Ibid (emphasis is his).

condition where violence and death are the natural consequence for human sin, God revealed he still wants to be in relationship with Israel in particular and humanity in general. Therefore, by allowing a covenantal framework to govern the atonement, we can affirm with Girard that the cross is an act of injustice and a revelation of Israel's failure to keep the covenant. On the other hand, we can also understand and affirm the Gospels' description of the cross as a punishment.[35] Posturing the renewal of the covenant as the encompassing motif for soteriology holds a number of fascinating potentials like the integration noted above, and theologians would be well served should they employ it more frequently.

Conclusion

Our journey has thus come to an end. After beginning with a summary of Girard's theory and his reading of salvation history, we then observed the manner in which several key thinkers have adopted and adapted Girard with special attention to the passages that would become the focus of the exegetical portions of the study. From there we traveled through the Old Testament and paid particular attention to Israel's covenant with YHWH, their experience of exile from the land, and the promises of restoration. In addition, we noted that hopes for restoration endured in Second Temple Judaism long past the physical return under Cyrus and that these hopes informed the Synoptic writers and their presentation of Jesus as a savior. In making these observations, though, we were already beginning to frame the soteriological need differently than Girard. As we observed, there is good reason to conclude that the Gospels are written within the larger story of Israel waiting for restoration rather than the story of humanity enslaved to sacrificial and mythical thought. When our attention turned to those passages dealing with the cross, particularly the Last Supper sayings, we found several instances where Jesus' death was cast in sacrificial language or it was presumed that Jesus' death was participating in Israel's exilic punishment. Unfortunately, these discoveries are detrimental to Girardian soteriology and require modification should the Gospels continue to be claimed for support. Nevertheless, despite the presence of passages that challenge Girardian soteriology, there are ways it could be amended in order to account for the problematic issues we have seen thus far.

---

35. Vidu wants to do something similar, but his appeal to divine simplicity only serves to make human actions incommensurable with divine actions. He does not adequately explain how the cross is both an injustice and a divine punishment. Vidu, *Atonement*, 271.

While future efforts could be devoted to modifying Girardian soteriology in light of the exegesis in this study, our inquiry has opened up another vista that holds potential for casting soteriology in light of the biblical narrative: God in covenant with humankind. Exactly what it would look like to develop a soteriology rooted in the covenantal motif has neither been fully nor satisfactorily traced out, in my opinion.[36] Though biblical exegetes have long noted the preponderance of the covenant motif, theologians have only rarely adopted it as the governing framework for their soteriology. The fields are ripe for harvest and future soteriological work might benefit us all with efforts devoted to mining the theological ore of the covenantal motif in Scripture. If the theology of atonement is to move beyond being a theological abstraction from Jesus' story and is to be read as the story of God in relationship with human beings, then the covenant motif might prove conducive for the task.

---

36. For example, Gorman, though correct that the New Testament writers emphasize the effects over the mechanics of the atonement, seems to underplay their existence in certain portions of Scripture. Gorman, *Birth of the New Covenant*, 210.

Bibliography

Abegg, Martin G. "The Concept of the Qumran Sectarians." In *The Concept of the Covenant in the Second Temple Period*, edited by S. E. Porter and J. C. R. de Roo, 81–97. Leiden: Brill, 2003.

Abelard, Peter. *Commentary on the Epistle to the Romans*. Translated by Steven R. Cartwright. Washington, D.C.: Catholic University of America Press, 2011.

Adams, Rebecca. "Loving Mimesis and Girard's 'Scapegoat of the Text.'" In *Violence Renounced*, edited by Willard M. Swartley, 277–307. Telford, PA: Cascadia, 2000.

Adams, Rebecca and René Girard. "Violence, Difference, Sacrifice: A Conversation with René Girard." *Religion & Literature* 25, no. 2 (1993) 11–33.

Alberg, Jeremiah. "Grace Can Be Violent: Flannery O'Conner's Novelistic Truth." In *Girard's Mimetic Theory across the Disciplines*, edited by Scott Cowdell et al, 150–68. New York: Continuum, 2012.

Alison, James. *The Joy of Being Wrong: Original Sin Through Easter Eyes*. New York: Crossroad, 1998.

———. *Knowing Jesus*. Springfield, Ill: Templegate, 1994.

———. "'Like Being Dragged through a Bush Backwards': Hints of the Shape of Conversion's Adventure." In *Girard's Mimetic Theory across the Disciplines*, edited by Scott Cowdell et al, 19–33. New York: Continuum, 2012.

———. *Living in the End Times: The Last Things Re-imaged*. London: SPCK, 1997.

———. *On Being Liked*. New York: Crossroad, 2003.

———. *Raising Abel: The Recovery of Eschatological Imagination*. New York: Crossroad, 1996.

Allison, Dale C., Jr. *Constructing Jesus: Memory, Imagination, and History*. Grand Rapids: Baker Academic, 2010.

———. *The New Moses: A Matthean Typology*. Minneapolis: Fortress, 1993.

Anderson, Bernhard W. *From Creation to New Creation: Old Testament Perspectives*. Minneapolis: Fortress, 1994.

Anderson, Gary A. "From Israel's Burden to Israel's Debt: Towards a Theology of Sin in Biblical and Early Second Temple Sources." In *Reworking the Bible*, edited by Devorah Dimant et al, 1–30. Leiden: Brill, 2005.

———. *Sin: A History*. New Haven: Yale University Press, 2009.

Antwi, Daniel J. "Did Jesus Consider His Death to be an Atoning Sacrifice?" *Int* 45 (1991) 17–28.

Astell, Ann W., and Sandor Goodhart, eds. *Sacrifice, Scripture, and Substitution: Readings in Ancient Judaism and Christianity*. Notre Dame: University of Notre Dame Press, 2011.

Attridge, Harold W. *The Epistle to the Hebrews: A Commentary on the Epistle to the Hebrews.* Edited by Helmut Koester. Philadelphia: Fortress, 1989.

———. "Historiography." In *Jewish Writings of the Second Temple Period*, edited by Michael E. Stone, 157–84. Assen: Van Gorcum, 1984.

Backhaus, Knut. "Hat Jesus von Gottesbund gesprochen?" *Theologie und Glaube* 86 (1996) 343–56.

Bahr, Gordon J. "Seder of Passover and the Eucharistic Words." *NovT* 12 (1970) 181–202.

Bailey, Kenneth E. *Jesus through Middle Eastern Eyes: Cultural Studies in the Gospels.* Downers Grove, IL: IVP Academic, 2008.

Bailie, Gil. "Sacrificial Violence in Homer's *Iliad*." In *Curing Violence*, edited by Mark I. Wallace, 45–70. Sonoma, CA: Polebridge, 1994.

———. *Violence Unveiled: Humanity at the Crossroads.* New York: Crossroad, 1995.

Baker, Sharon L. *Executing God: Rethinking Everything You've Been Taught about Salvation and the Cross.* Louisville: Westminster John Knox, 2013.

Baltzer, Klaus. *Deutero-Isaiah: A Commentary on Isaiah 40–55.* Edited by Peter Machinist. Translated by Margaret Kohl. Minneapolis: Fortress, 2001.

———. *The Covenant Formulary: In Old Testament, Jewish, and Early Christian Writings.* Translated by David E. Green. Philadelphia: Fortress, 1971.

Barrett, C. K. *The Acts of the Apostles: A Shorter Commentary.* London: T & T Clark, 2002.

———. *A Critical and Exegetical Commentary on the Acts of the Apostles.* 2 vols. Edinburgh: T & T Clark, 1994.

Bartlett, Anthony. *Cross Purposes: The Violent Grammar of Christian Atonement.* Valley Forge, PA: Trinity, 2001.

Barton, George A. "The Date of the Epistle to the Hebrews." *JBL* 57 (1938) 195–207.

Bauckham, Richard. "The Restoration of Israel in Luke-Acts." In *Restoration: Old Testament, Jewish, and Christian Perspectives*, edited by James M. Scott, 435–87. Leiden: Brill, 2001.

———. "Son of Man: 'A Man in My Position' or 'Someone.'" *JSNT* 23 (1985) 23–33.

Bauer, Walter. *A Greek-English Lexicon of the New Testament and Other Early Christian Literature*, edited by Frederick W. Danker. 3d ed. Chicago: University of Chicago Press, 2000.

Beale, G. K. *We Become What We Worship: A Biblical Theology of Idolatry.* Downers Grove, IL: IVP Academic, 2008.

Beale, G. K., and D. A. Carson, eds. *Commentary on the New Testament Use of the Old Testament.* Grand Rapids: Baker Academic, 2007.

Beaton, Richard. "Isaiah in Matthew's Gospel." In *Isaiah in the New Testament*, ed. Steve Moyise and Maarten J. J. Menken, 63–78. London: T & T Clark, 2005.

Beck, Norman A. "Last Supper as an Efficacious Symbolic Act." *JBL* 89 (1970) 192–98.

Beilby, James, and Paul R. Eddy, eds. *The Nature of the Atonement: Four Views.* Downers Grove, IL: IVP Academic, 2006.

Bellinger, William H. Jr., and William R. Farmer, eds. *Jesus and the Suffering Servant: Isaiah 53 and Christian Origins.* Harrisburg, PA: Trinity, 1998.

Benoit, P. "The Accounts of the Institution and What They Imply." In *The Eucharist in the New Testament*, translated by E. M. Stewart, 71–101. Baltimore: Helicon, 1964.

Bird, Michael F. *Are You the One Who is to Come? The Historical Jesus and the Messianic Question.* Grand Rapids: Baker Academic, 2009.

Bird, Phyllis A. "'Male and Female He Created Them': Genesis 1:27b in the Context of the Priestly Account of Creation." In *'I Studied Inscriptions from before the Flood': Ancient Near Eastern, Literary, and Linguistic Approaches to Genesis 1–11*, edited by Richard S. Hess and David Toshio Tsumura, 329–61. Winona Lake, IN: Eisenbrauns, 1994.

Billings, Bradly S. "The Disputed Words in the Lukan Institution Narrative (Luke 22:19b-20) A Sociological Answer to a Textual Problem." *JBL* 125 (2006) 507–26.

———. *Do This in Remembrance of Me: The Disputed Words in the Lukan Institution Narrative (Luke 22.19b-20): An Historico-Exegetical, Theological and Sociological Analysis*. London: T & T Clark, 2006.

Blair, Edward P. "Jesus and Salvation in the Gospel of Matthew." *McCormick Quarterly* 20 (1967) 301–8.

Blocher, Henri. "Old Covenant, New Covenant." In *Always Reforming: Explorations in Systematic Theology*, edited by A. T. B. McGowan, 140–70. Downers Grove, IL: IVP Academic, 2006.

Blomberg, Craig L. "Matthew." In *Commentary on the New Testament Use of the Old Testament*, edited by G. K. Beale and D. A. Carson, 1-109. Grand Rapids: Baker Academic, 2007.

Bockmuehl, Markus. *This Jesus: Martyr, Lord, Messiah*. Edinburgh: T & T Clark, 1994.

Boda, Mark J. *A Severe Mercy: Sin and Its Remedy in the Old Testament*. Winona Lake, IN: Eisenbrauns, 2009.

Boersma, Hans. *Violence, Hospitality, and the Cross: Reappropriating the Atonement Tradition*. Grand Rapids: Baker Academic, 2004.

———. "Violence, the Cross, and Divine Intentionality: A Modified Reformed View." In *Atonement and Violence*, edited by John Sanders, 47–69. Nashville: Abingdon, 2006.

Bokser, Baruch M. "Was the Last Supper a Passover Seder?" *Bible Review* 3, no. 2 (1987) 24–33.

Bolt, Peter G. *The Cross from a Distance: Atonement in Mark's Gospel*. Downers Grove, IL: InterVarsity, 2004.

Bornkamm, Günther. *Early Christian Experience*. London: SCM, 1969.

Bottum, J. "Girard among the Girardians." *First Things* 62 (March 1996) 42–45.

Bovon, François. *Luc le theologian: Vingt-cinq ans de recherché (1950–1975)*. Neuchâtel: Delachaux & Niestlé, 1978.

Breytenbach, Cilliers. "Das MarkusEvangelium, Psalm 110,1 und 118,22f: Folgetext und Prätext." In *The Scriptures in the Gospels*, edited by C.M. Tuckett, 197–222. Leuven: Leuven University Press, 1997.

Brock, Rita Nakashima. "And a Little Child Will Lead Us: Christology and Child Abuse." In *Christianity, Patriarchy, and Abuse*, edited by Joanne Carlson Brown and Carole R. Bohn, 42–61. New York: Pilgrim, 1989.

Brown, Joanne Carlson. "Divine Child Abuse?" *Daughters of Sarah* 18, no. 3 (1992) 24–28.

Brown, Joanne Carlson, and Rebecca Parker. "For God so Loved the World?" In *Christianity, Patriarchy, and Abuse: A Feminist Critique*, edited by Joanne Carlson Brown and Carole R. Bohn, 1–30. New York: Pilgrim, 1989.

Brown, Raymond E. *The Death of the Messiah: From Gethsemane to the Grave, a Commentary on the Passion Narratives in the Four Gospels*. 2 vols. New York: Doubleday, 1994.

―――. *An Introduction to the New Testament*. New York: Doubleday, 1997.
Brown, Schuyler. "The Mission to Israel in Matthew's Central Section (Mt 9 34–11 1)." *ZNW* 69 (1978) 73–90.
Brownlee, William H. *Ezekiel 1–19*. Waco: Word, 1986.
Broyles, C. C. "Gospel (Good News)." In *Dictionary of Jesus and the Gospels*, edited by Joel B. Green et al., 282–86. Downers Grove, IL: InterVarsity, 1992.
Brueggeman, Walter. *Theology of the Old Testament: Testimony, Dispute, and Advocacy*. Minneapolis: Fortress, 1997.
Bryan, Steven M. *Jesus and Israel's Traditions of Judgment and Restoration*. Cambridge: Cambridge University Press, 2002.
Buckwalter, H. Douglas. *The Character and Purpose of Luke's Christology*. Cambridge: Cambridge University Press, 1996.
Burkill, Alec T. "The Last Supper." *Numen* 3 (1956) 161–77.
Caird, G. B. *The Gospel of St Luke*. London: Adam & Charles Black, 1963, 1968.
Calvin, John. *Institutes of the Christian Religion*. Edited by John T. McNeill. Translated by Ford Lewis Battles. 2 vols. Louisville: Westminster John Knox, 1960, 2006.
Carpinelli, Francis G. "'Do This as My Memorial' (Luke 22:19): Lucan Soteriology of Atonement." *CBQ* 61 (1999) 74–91.
Carroll, John T., and Joel B. Green. *The Death of Jesus in Early Christianity*. Peabody, MA: Hendrickson, 1995
Casey, Maurice. *Aramaic Sources of Mark's Gospel*. Cambridge: Cambridge University Press, 1999.
―――. *Son of Man: The Interpretation and Influence of Daniel 7*. London: SPCK, 1979.
―――. "Where Wright is Wrong: A Critical Review of N. T. Wright's *Jesus and the Victory of God*." *JSNT* 69 (1998) 95–103.
Chadwick, Henry. "The Shorter Text of Luke 22:15–20." *HTR* 50 (1957) 249–58.
Childs, Brevard S. *Isaiah*. Louisville: Westminster John Knox, 2001.
―――. *The Book of Exodus: A Critical, Theological Commentary*. Philadelphia: Fortress, 1974.
Chilton, Bruce D. *Abraham's Curse: Child Sacrifice in the Legacies of the West*. New York: Doubleday, 2008.
―――. "The Eucharist and the Mimesis of Sacrifice." In *Sacrifice, Scripture, and Substitution*, edited by Ann W. Astell and Sandor Goodhart, 140–54. Notre Dame, IN.: University of Notre Dame Press, 2011.
―――. *A Feast of Meanings: Eucharistic Theologies from Jesus through Johannine Circles*. Leiden: Brill, 1994.
―――. "Jesus' Dispute in the Temple and the Origin of the Eucharist." *Dialogue* 29, no. 4 (1996) 17–28.
―――. *The Temple of Jesus: His Sacrificial Program within a Cultural History of Sacrifice*. University Park, PA: Pennsylvania State University Press, 1992.
Churgin, Pinkhos. *Targum Jonathan to the Prophets*. New Haven: Yale University Press, 1907.
Cohen, Shaye J. D. *From the Maccabees to the Mishnah*. 2d ed. Louisville: Westminster John Knox, 2006.
Cohn, Robert G. "Desire: Direct and Imitative." *Philosophy Today* 33 (1989) 318–29.
Collins, Adela Yarbro. *Mark: A Commentary*. Edited by Harold W. Attridge. Minneapolis: Fortress, 2007.
―――. "Mark's Interpretation of the Death of Jesus." *JBL* 128 (2009) 545–54.

———. "The Influence of Daniel on the New Testament." In John J. Collins, *Daniel: A Commentary on the Book of Daniel*, edited by Frank Moore Cross, 90–123. Minneapolis: Fortress, 1993.
Collins, John J. "Testaments." In *Jewish Writings of the Second Temple Period*, edited by Michael E. Stone, 325–55. Assen: Van Gorcum, 1984.
———. *The Scepter and the Star: Messianism in Light of the Dead Sea Scrolls*. 2nd ed. Grand Rapids: Eerdmans, 2010.
Collins, John J. and Adela Yarbro Collins. "The Significance of Mark 10:45 among Gentile Christians." *HTR* 90 (1997) 371–82.
Combrink, H. J. Bernard. "Salvation in Mark." In *Salvation in the New Testament: Perspectives on Soteriology*, edited by Jan G. van der Watt, 33–65. Leiden: Brill, 2005.
Conzelmann, Hans. *The Theology of St Luke*. Translated by Geoffrey Buswell. New York: Harper & Row, 1961.
Cooke, Bernard J. "Synoptic Presentation of the Eucharist as Covenant Sacrifice." *TS* 21 (1960) 1–44.
Cowdell, Scott. "Hard Evidence for Girardian Mimetic Theory? Intersubjectivity and Mirror Neurons." In *Girard's Mimetic Theory across the Disciplines*, edited by Scott Cowdell et al., 219–26. New York: Continuum, 2012.
———. *René Girard and Secular Modernity*. Notre Dame, IN: University of Notre Dame Press, 2013.
Crockett, William R. *Eucharist: Symbol of Transformation*. New York: Pueblo, 1989.
Crossan, John Dominic. *The Historical Jesus: The Life of a Mediterranean Jewish Peasant*. San Francisco: HarperSanFrancisco, 1991.
Daly, Robert J. "Eucharistic Origins: From the New Testament to the Liturgies of the Golden Age." *TS* 66 (2005) 3–22.
———. "Phenomenology of Redemption? Or Theory of Sanctification." *TS* 74 (2013) 347–71.
———. *Sacrifice Unveiled: The True Meaning of Christian Sacrifice*. London: T&T Clark, 2009.
Daniels, T. Scott. "Passing the Peace: Worship that Shapes Nonsubstitutionary Convictions." In *Atonement and Violence: A Theological Conversation*, edited by John Sanders, 125–48. Nashville: Abingdon, 2006.
Darr, John A. "Mimetic Desire, the Gospels, and Early Christianity: A Response to René Girard." *Biblical Interpretation* 1 (1993) 357–67.
Davies, W. D. and Dale C. Allison, Jr. *A Critical and Exegetical Commentary on the Gospel According to Matthew*. 3 vols. London: T & T Clark, 2004.
Delorme, J. "The Last Supper and the Pasch in the New Testament." In *The Eucharist in the New Testament*, translated by E. M. Stewart, 21–67. Baltimore: Helicon, 1964.
Dennis, John. A. *Jesus' Death and the Gathering of True Israel: The Johannine Appropriation of Restoration Theology in Light of John 11:47–52*. Tübingen: Mohr Siebeck, 2006.
Depoortere, Frederick. *Christ in Postmodern Philosophy: Gianni Vattimo, René Girard, and Slavoj Žižek*. London: T & T Clark, 2008.
Dizdar, Draško. "Finding the Way: How to Study Scripture with the Help of Scripture and the Desert Fathers." In *Girard's Mimetic Theory across the Disciplines*, edited by Scott Cowdell et al., New York: Continuum, 2012.

Doble, Peter. *The Paradox of Salvation: Luke's Theology of the Cross*. Cambridge: Cambridge University Press, 1996.
Dodd, C. H. *The Parables of the Kingdom*. Digswell Place, Welwyn: James Nisbet, 1935, 1958.
Domenach, Jean-Marie. "Voyage to the End of the Sciences of Man." Translated by Mark R. Anspach. In *Violence and Truth: On the Work of René Girard*, edited by Paul Dumouchel, 152–9. Stanford: Stanford University Press, 1988.
Dowd, Sharyn E. and Elizabeth S. Malbon. "The Significance of Jesus' Death in Mark: Narrative Context and Authorial Audience." *JBL* 125 (2006) 271–97.
Duhm, Bernhard. *Das Buch Jesaja*. Göttingen: Vandenhoeck & Ruprecht, 1892.
———. *Violence et vérité: autour de René Girard*. Paris: B. Grasset, 1985.
Dunn, James D. G. *Christology in the Making: A New Testament Inquiry into the Origins of the Doctrine of the Incarnation*. Philadelphia: Westminster, 1980.
———. "Jesus and the Kingdom: How Would His Message Have Been Heard?" In *Neotestamentica et Philonica: Studies in Honor of Peder Borgen*, edited by Peder Borgen et al, 3–36. Leiden: Brill, 2003.
———. *Jesus Remembered*. Grand Rapids: Eerdmans, 2003.
———. "Review of *Jesus and the Victory of God*." *JTS* 49 (1998) 727–34.
———. "The Danielic Son of Man in the New Testament." In *The Book of Daniel: Composition and Reception, Volume Two*, edited by John J. Collins and Peter W. Flint, 528–49. Leiden: Brill, 2001.
Dunnill, John. *Covenant and Sacrifice in the Letter to the Hebrews*. Cambridge: Cambridge University Press, 1992.
———. "Methodological Rivalries: Theology and Social Science in Girardian Interpretations of the New Testament." *JSNT* 62 (1996) 105–119.
———. *Sacrifice and the Body: Biblical Anthropology and Christian Self-Understanding*. Farnham, Surrey: Ashgate: 2013.
du Plessis, I. J. "The Saving Significance of Jesus and His Death on the Cross in Luke's Gospel—Focussing on Luke 22:19b–20." *Neot* 28 (1994) 523–40.
Dupont, Jacques. "The Meal at Emmaus." In *The Eucharist in the New Testament*, translated by E. M. Stewart, 105–21. Baltimore: Helicon, 1964.
Eagle, David E. "Anthony Bartlett's Concept of Abyssal Compassion and the Possibility of a Truly Nonviolent Atonement." *Conrad Grebel Review* 24 (2006) 66–81.
Eberhart, Christian A. *The Sacrifice of Jesus: Understanding Atonement Biblically*. Minneapolis: Fortress, 2011.
Eckhardt, Benedikt. "Reclaiming Tradition: The Book of Judith and Hasmonean Politics." *Journal for the Study of the Psedepigrapha* 18 (2009) 243–63.
Eddy, Paul R. and James Beilby. "The Atonement: An Introduction." In *The Nature of the Atonement: Four Views*, edited by James Beilby and Paul R. Eddy. Downers Grove, IL: InterVarsity, 2006.
Edwards, James R. *The Gospel According to Mark*. Grand Rapids: Eerdmans, 2002.
Ehrman, Bart D. "The Cup, the Bread, and the Salvific Effect of Jesus' Death in Luke-Acts." *SBLSP* 30 (1991) 576–91.
———. *The Orthodox Corruption of Scripture: The Effect of Early Christological Controversies on the Text of the New Testament*. Rev. ed. New York: Oxford University Press, 2011.
Eichrodt, Walther. *Theology of the Old Testament*. Translated by J. A. Baker. 2 vols. Philadelphia: Westminster, 1961.

Ellingworth, Paul. *The Epistle to the Hebrews: A Commentary on the Greek Text*. Grand Rapids: Eerdmans, 1993.
Epp, Eldon J. "Disputed Words of the Eucharistic Institution (Luke 22, 19b–20): The Long and the Short of the Matter." *Bib* 90 (2009) 407–16.
Eppstein, Victor. "The Historicity of the Gospel Account of the Cleansing of the Temple." *ZNW* 55 (1964) 42–58.
Eubank, Nathan. *Wages of Cross-Bearing and Debt of Sin: The Economy of Heaven in Matthew's Gospel*. Berlin: Walter de Gruyter, 2013.
Eusebius, *Eusebius' Ecclesiastical History: Complete and Unabridged*. Translated by C. F. Cruse. Rev. ed. Peabody, MA: Hendrickson, 1996, 2006.
Evans, Craig A. "Aspects of Exile and Restoration in the Proclamation of Jesus and the Gospels." In *Exile*, edited by James M. Scott, 299–328. Leiden: Brill, 1997.
———. "Covenant in the Qumran Literature." In *The Concept of the Covenant in the Second Temple Period*, edited by Stanley E. Porter and Jacqueline C. R. De Roo, 55–80. Leiden: Brill, 2003.
———. "Daniel in the New Testament: Visions of God's Kingdom." In *The Book of Daniel: Composition and Reception, Volume Two*, edited by John J. Collins and Peter W. Flint, 490–527. Leiden: Brill, 2001.
———. *Fabricating Jesus: How Modern Scholars Distort the Gospels*. Downers Grove, IL: IVP Books, 2006.
———. "From Gospel to Gospel: the Function of Isaiah in the New Testament." In *Writing and Reading the Scroll of Isaiah: Studies of an Interpretive Tradition, Vol 2*, edited by Craig C. Broyles and Craig A. Evans, 651–91. Leiden: Brill, 1997.
———. "Jesus' Action in the Temple: Cleansing or Portent of Destruction." *CBQ* 51 (1989) 237–270.
———. "Jesus and the Continuing Exile of Israel." In *Jesus and the Restoration of Israel: A Critical Assessment of N. T. Wright's Jesus and the Victory of God*, edited by Carey C. Newman, 77–100. Downers Grove, IL: InterVarsity, 1999.
———. *Luke*. Peabody, MA: Hendrickson.
———. *Mark 8:27–16:20*, WBC 34b. Nashville: Thomas Nelson, 2001.
———. "On the Vineyard Parables of Isaiah 5 and Mark 12." *Biblische Zeitschrift* 28, no. 1 (1984) 82–86.
———. "The Temple of Jesus: His Sacrificial Program within a Cultural History of Sacrifice." *Trinity Journal* 14 (1993) 219–21.
Finamore, Stephen. *God, Order, and Chaos: René Girard and the Apocalypse*. Eugene, OR: Wipf & Stock, 2009.
Finlan, Stephen. *Options on Atonement in Christian Thought*. Collegeville, MN: Liturgical, 2007.
———. *Problems with Atonement: The Origins of, and Controversy about, the Atonement Doctrine*. Collegeville, MN: Liturgical, 2005.
Fitzmyer, Joseph A. *The Gospel According to Luke: Introduction, Translation, and Notes*. 2 vols. Garden City, N.Y.: Doubleday & Company, Inc., 1985.
———. *Luke the Theologian: Aspects of His Teaching*. New York: Paulist, 1989.
———. *The One Who is to Come*. Grand Rapids: Eerdmans, 2007.
———. *Tobit*. Berlin: Walter de Gruyter, 2003.
Flanagan, Neal M. *Salvation History: An Introduction to Biblical Theology*. New York: Sheed and Ward, 1964.
Fleming, Chris. *René Girard: Violence and Mimesis*. Malden, MA: Polity, 2004.

Flesher, Paul V. M. "Is Targum Onqelos a Palestinian Targum? The Evidence of Genesis 28–50." *Journal for the Study of the Pseudepigrapha* 19 (1999) 35–79.

Flesher, Paul V. M. and Bruce Chilton. *The Targums: A Critical Introduction*. Waco, TX: Baylor University Press, 2011.

Fodor, Jim. "Christian Discipleship as Participative Imitation: Theological Reflections on Girardian Themes." In *Violence Renounced*, edited by Willard M. Swartley, 246–76. Telford, PA: Cascadia, 2000.

Fornari, Giuseppe. *Fra Dioniso e Cristo: La Sapienza sacrificale greca e la civilta occidentale*. Bologna: Pitagora, 2001.

———. "Labyrinthe Strategies of Sacrifice: *The Cretans* by Euripides." *Contagion* 4 (1997) 163–88.

France, R. T. *The Gospel of Mark: A Commentary on the Greek Text*. Grand Rapids: Eerdmans, 2002.

Fredriksen, Paula. *From Jesus to Christ: The Origins of the New Testament Images of Jesus*. New Haven: Yale University Press, 1988.

Freedman, David N. and David Miano. "People of the New Covenant." In *The Concept of the Covenant in the Second Temple Period*, edited by Stanley E. Porter and Jacqueline C. R. De Roo, 7–26. Leiden: Brill, 2003.

Frei, Hans W. *The Eclipse of Biblical Narrative: A Study in Eighteenth and Nineteenth Century Hermeneutics*. New Haven: Yale University Press, 1974.

———. *The Identity of Jesus Christ: The Hermeneutical Bases of Dogmatic Theology*. Philadelphia: Fortress, 1975.

Fuller, Reginald H. "Double Origin of the Eucharist." *Biblical Research* 8 (1963) 60–72.

Galvin, John P. "The Marvelous Exchange: Raymund Schwager's Interpretation of the History of Soteriology." *The Thomist* 53 (1989) 675–91.

Gamel, Brian K. "Salvation in a Sentence: Mark 15:39 as Markan Soteriology." *Journal of Theological Interpretation* 6 (2012) 65–77.

Gardner, Stephen L. "René Girard's Apocalyptic Critique of Historical Reason: Limiting Politics to Make Way for Faith." *Contagion* 18 (2011) 1–22, 181.

Garrels, Scott R. "Imitation, Mirror Neurons, and Mimetic Desire: Convergence between the Mimetic Theory of René Girard and Empirical Research on Imitation." *Contagion* 12–13 (2006) 47–86.

Gathercole, Simon J. "The Cross and Substitutionary Atonement." *Scottish Bulletin of Evangelical Theology* 21 (2003) 64–73.

George, Augustin. "Le sens de la mort de Jésus pour Luc." *Revue Biblique* 80 (1973) 186–217.

Geyser, A.S. "Jesus, the Twelve and the Twelve Tribes in Matthew." In *Essays on Jewish and Christian Apocalyptic*, edited by A. S. Geyser, 1–19. South Africa: Ntssa, 1981.

Gibbs, Jeffrey A. "The Son of God and the Father's Wrath: Atonement and Salvation in Matthew's Gospel." *CTQ* 72 (2008) 211–25.

Gilbert, Maurice. "Wisdom Literature." In *Jewish Writings of the Second Temple Period*, edited by Michael E. Stone, 283–324. Assen: Van Gorcum, 1984.

Gilmore, Alec. "Date and Significance of the Last Supper." *SJT* 14 (1961) 256–69

Girard, René. "Are the Gospels Mythical?" *First Things* 62 (1996) 27–31.

———. *Battling to the End: Conversations with Benoît Chantre*. Translated by Mary Baker. East Lansing: Michigan State University Press, 2010.

———. *Celui par qui le scandale arrive*. Paris: Brouwer, 2001.

———. *Deceit, Desire, and the Novel: Self and Other in Literary Structure*. Translated by Yvonne Freccero. Baltimore: Johns Hopkins University Press, 1965.
———. *Des choses chachées depuis la fondation du monde*. Paris: Grasset, 1978.
———. *Evolution and Conversion: Dialogues on the Origins of Culture*. London: T & T Clark, 2008.
———. *I See Satan Fall Like Lightning*. Translated by James G. Williams. Maryknoll, N.Y.: Orbis, 2001.
———. *Job: The Victim of His People*. Translated by Yvonne Freccero. Stanford: Stanford University Press, 1987.
———. *La violence et le Sacré*. Paris: Grasset, 1972.
———. *Mensonge romantique et vérité romanesque*. Paris: Grasset, 1961.
———. "Mimetische Theorie und Theologie." In *Vom Fluch und Segen der Sündenböcke*, edited by Józef Niewiadomski and Wolfgang Palaver, 15–29. Thaur: Kulturverlag, 1995.
———. *Resurrection from the Underground: Feodor Dostoevsky*. Edited and Translated by James G. Williams. New York: Crossroad Publishing, 1997.
———. *Sacrifice*. Translated by Matthew Pattillo and David Dawson. East Lansing: Michigan State University Press, 2011.
———. *A Theater of Envy: William Shakespeare*. Oxford: Oxford University Press, 1991.
———. "The Bloody Skin of the Victim." In *The New Visibility of Religion: Studies in Religion and Cultural Hermeneutics*, edited by Graham Ward and Michael Hoelzl, 59–67. London: Continuum, 2008.
———. "The Evangelical Subversion of Myth." In *Politics & Apocalypse*, edited by Robert G. Hamerton-Kelly, 29–49. East Lansing: Michigan State University Press, 2007.
———. *The Girard Reader*. Edited by James G. Williams. New York: Crossroad Publishing, 1996.
———. *The Scapegoat*. Translated by Yvonne Freccero. Baltimore:Johns Hopkins University Press, 1986.
———. *Things Hidden Since the Foundation of the World*. Translated by Stephen Bann and Michael Metteer. Standford: Stanford University Press, 1987.
———. *Violence and the Sacred*. Translated by Patrick Gregory. Baltimore: Johns Hopkins University Press, 1977.
———. "Violence Renounced: Response by René Girard." In *Violence Renounced*, ed. Willard M. Swartley, 308–20. Telford, PA: Cascadia, 2000.
———. "What is a Myth?" In *Myth and Ritual Theory*, edited by Robert A. Segal, 285–303. Oxford: Blackwell, 1998.
Goldberg, Michael. "God, Action, and Narrative: Which Narrative? Which Action? Which God?" In *Why Narrative? Readings in Narrative Theology*, edited by Stanley Hauerwas and L. Gregory Jones, 348–65. Grand Rapids: Eerdmans, 1989.
Goldstein, Jonathan A. "How the Authors of 1 and 2 Maccabees Treated the 'Messianic' Promises." In *Judaisms and Their Messiahs at the Turn of the Christian Era*, edited by Jacob Neusner et al, 69–96. Cambridge: Cambridge University Press, 1987.
Golsan, Richard J. *René Girard and Myth: An Introduction*. New York: Routledge, 2002.
Goodhart, Sandor. *The Prophetic Law: Essays in Judaism, Girardianism, Literary Studies, and the Ethical*. East Lansing: Michigan State University, 2014.

Gorman, Michael J. "Effecting the New Covenant: a (not so) New, New Testament Model for the Atonement." *ExAud* 26 (2010) 26–59.

———. *The Death of the Messiah and the Birth of the New Covenant: A (Not So) New Model of the Atonement.* Eugene, OR: Cascade, 2014.

Gorringe, Timothy. *God's Just Vengeance: Crime, Violence, and the Rhetoric of Salvation.* Cambridge: Cambridge University Press, 1996.

Goulder, Michael D. *Luke: A New Paradigm.* Sheffield: Sheffield Academic, 1989; reprint, 1994.

Goswell, Greg. "The Absence of a Davidic Hope in Ezra-Nehemiah." *Trinity Journal* 33 (2012) 19–31.

Gowan, Donald E. *Theology of the Prophetic Books: The Death and Resurrection of Israel.* Louisville: Westminster John Knox, 1998.

Grabbe, Lester L. "Did all Jews Think Alike? 'Covenant' in Philo and Josephus in the Context of Second Temple Judaic Religion." In *The Concept of the Covenant in the Second Temple Period*, edited by Stanley E. Porter and Jacqueline C.R. de Roo, 251–66. Leiden: Brill, 2003.

Green, Joel B. "The Death of Jesus, God's Servant." In *Reimaging the Death of the Lukan Jesus*, edited by Dennis D. Sylva, 1–28. Frankfurt am Main: Anton Hain, 1990.

———. *The Death of Jesus: Tradition and Interpretation in the Passion Narrative.* Tübingen: J.C.B. Mohr, 1988.

———. "Kaleidoscopic View." In *The Nature of the Atonement: Four Views*, edited by James Beilby and Paul R. Eddy, 157–85. Downers Grove, IL: IVP Academic, 2006.

———. "'The Message of Salvation' in Luke-Acts." *ExAud* 5 (1989) 21–34.

———. "'Was it Not Necessary for the Messiah to Suffer These Things and Enter into His Glory?': The Significance of Jesus' Death for Luke's Soteriology." In *The Spirit and Christ in New Testament and Christian Theology: Essays in Honor of Max Turner*, edited by I. Howard Marshall et al, 71–85. Grand Rapids: Eerdmans, 2012.

Green, Joel B. and Mark D. Baker. *Recovering the Scandal of the Cross: Atonement in New Testament and Contemporary Contexts.* Downers Grove, IL: InterVarsity, 2000.

Gregory of Nyssa. "The Great Catechism." In *Gregory of Nyssa: Dogmatic Treatises, etc.*, vol. 5 *Nicene and Post-Nicene Fathers of the Christian Church*, edited by Philip Schaff and Henry Wace, 5:471–509. Grand Rapids: Eerdmans, 1988.

Grimsrud, Ted. "Scapegoating No More: Christian Pacifism and New Testament Views of Jesus' Death," in *Violence Renounced: René Girard, Biblical Studies and Peacemaking*, edited by Willard M. Swartley, 49-69. Telford, PA: Pandora, 2000.

Guelich, Robert A. *Mark 1–8:26.* Dallas: Word, 1989.

Gundry, Robert H. "Salvation in Matthew." SBLSP 39 (2000) 402–14.

Haenchen, Ernst. *The Acts of the Apostles: A Commentary.* Translated by Bernard Nobel and Gerald Shinn. Translation Revised by R. McL. Wilson. Philadelphia: Westminster, 1971.

Hafemann, Scott. "The 'Temple of the Spirit' as the Inaugural Fulfillment of the New Covenant within the Corinthian Correspondence." *ExAud* 12 (1996) 29–42.

Hahn, Scott. "A Broken Covenant and the Curse of Death: A Study of Hebrews 9:15-22." *CBQ* 66 (2004) 416–36.

———. *Kinship by Covenant: A Canonical Approach to the Fulfillment of God's Saving Promises.* New Haven: Yale University Press, 2009.

Halvorson-Taylor, Martien A. *Enduring Exile: The Metaphorization of Exile in the Hebrew Bible.* Leiden: Brill, 2011.

Ham, Clay. "The Last Supper in Matthew." *BBR* 10 (2000) 59–66.
Hamerton-Kelly, Robert G. "Allegory, Typology and Sacred Violence: Sacrificial Representation and the Unity of the Bible in Paul and Philo." *Studia Philonica Annual* 3 (1991) 53–70.

———. "A Girardian Interpretation of Paul: Rivalry, Mimesis and Victimage in the Corinthian Correspondence." *Semeia* 33 (1985) 65–81.

———. *The Gospel and the Sacred: Poetics of Violence in Mark*. Minneapolis: Fortress, 1994.

———. "Paul's Hermeneutic of the Cross." *Dialog* 32 (1993) 247–54.

———, ed. *Politics & Apocalypse*. East Lansing: Michigan State University Press, 2007.

———. "Sacred Violence and Sinful Desire: Paul's Interpretation of Adam's Sin in the Letter to the Romans." In *Conversation Continues: Studies in Paul & John in Honour of J. Louis Martyn*, edited by Robert T. Fortna and Beverly R. Gaventa, 35–54. Nashville: Abingdon, 1990.

———. "Sacred Violence and the Messiah: The Markan Passion Narrative as a Redefinition of Messianology." In *The Messiah: Developments in Earliest Judaism and Christianity*, edited by James H. Charlesworth, 461–93. Minneapolis: Fortress, 1998.

———. *Sacred Violence: Paul's Hermeneutic of the Cross*. Minneapolis: Fortress,1992.

Hamilton, Victor P. *The Book of Genesis: Chapters 1–17*. Grand Rapids: Eerdmans, 1990.

Hardin, Michael. "Practical Reflections on Nonviolent Atonement." In *René Girard and Sacrifice in Life, Love, and Literature*, edited by Scott Cowdell et al, 247–58. New York: Bloomsbury, 2014.

Harrington, Daniel J. *The Gospel of Matthew*. Collegeville, MN: Liturgical, 1991.

Hasel, Gerhard F. "Polemic Nature of the Genesis Cosmology." *Evangelical Quarterly* 46 (1974) 81–102.

———. "The Significance of the Cosmology in Genesis 1 in Relation to Ancient Near Eastern Parallels." *Andrews University Seminary Studies* 10 (1972) 1–20.

Hatina, Thomas R. "Embedded Scripture Texts and the Plurality of Meaning: The Announcement of the 'Voice from Heaven' in Mark 1.11 as a Case Study." In *The Gospel of Mark*, vol. 1 of *Biblical Interpretation in Early Christian Gospels*, edited by Thomas R. Hatina, 81–99. London: T & T Clark, 2006.

———. "Exile." In *Dictionary of New Testament Background*, edited by Craig A. Evans and Stanley E. Porter, 348–51. Downers Grove, IL: InterVarsity, 2000.

Hedley, Douglas. *Sacrifice Imagined: Violence, Atonement, and the Sacred*. London: Continuum, 2011.

Heider, George C. "Atonement and the Gospels." *Journal of Theological Interpretation* 2 (2008) 259–73.

Heim, S. Mark. *Saved from Sacrifice: A Theology of the Cross*. Grand Rapids: Eerdmans, 2006.

Hefling, Charles. "A View from the Stern: James Alison's Theology (So Far)." *ATR* 81 (1999) 689–710.

Hendel, Ronald S. "Sacrifice as a Cultural System: The Ritual Symbolism of Exodus 24, 3–8." *ZAW* 101 (1989) 366–90.

Hengel, Martin. *The Atonement: The Origins of the Doctrine in the New Testament*. Translated by John Bowden. Philadelphia: Fortress, 1981.

Henriksen, Jan-Olav. *Desire, Gift, and Recognition: Christology and Postmodernity*. Grand Rapids: Eerdmans, 2009.

Hilber, John W. "Theology of Worship in Exodus 24." *JETS* 39 (1996) 177–89.

Hobbes, Thomas. *Leviathan, or the Matter, Forme, & Power of a Common-Wealth Ecclesiasticall and Civill*. London: Green Dragon, 1651. Reprint, *Hobbes's Leviathan*. Oxford: Clarendon, 1929.

Hobson, Theo. "Faith and Rhetorical Violence: A Response to Girard." *Modern Believing* 40 (1999) 34–41.

Hooker, Morna D. "Did the Use of Isaiah 3 to Interpret His Mission Begin with Jesus?" In *Jesus and the Suffering Servant*, edited by William H. Bellinger Jr. and William R. Farmer, 88–103. Harrisburg, PA: Trinity, 1998.

———. "Isaiah in Mark's Gospel." In *Isaiah in the New Testament*, edited by Steve Moyise and Maarten J. J. Menken, 35–49. London: T & T Clark, 2005.

———. *Jesus and the Servant: The Influence of the Servant Concept of Deutero-Isaiah in the New Testament*. London: SPCK, 1959.

Hunsinger, George. "The Politics of the Nonviolent God: Reflections on René Girard and Karl Barth." *SJT* 51 (1998) 61–85.

Iwuamadi, Lawrence. *"He Called unto him the Twelve and began to Send Them Forth": The Continuation of Jesus' Mission According to the Gospel of Mark*. Roma: Editrice Pontificia Università Gregoriana, 2008.

Jaubert, Annie. *Date of the Last Supper*. Translated by I. Rafferty. Staten Island, NY: Alba House, 1965.

Jean, Charles F, ed. and trans. *Archives Royales de Mari*. Vol. 2, *Lettres Diverses*. Paris: Imprimerie Nationalee, 1950.

Jenson, Robert W. "On the Doctrine of Atonement." *Princeton Seminary Bulletin* 27 (2006) 100–108.

Jeremias, Joachim. "Last Supper." *JTS* 50 (1949) 1–10.

———. *The Eucharistic Words of Jesus*. Translated by Norman Perrin. London: SCM, 1966.

Johnson, Luke Timothy. *Hebrews: A Commentary*. Louisville: Westminster John Knox, 2006.

Jones, Ivor H. "Disputed Questions in Biblical Studies: Exile and Eschatology." *ExpTim* 112 (2001) 400–405.

Josephus. *The Works of Josephus: Complete and Unabridged*. Translated by William Whiston. Rev. ed. Peabody, MA: Hendrickson, 1987.

Karris, Robert J. "Luke 23:47 and the Lucan View of Jesus' Death." *JBL* 105 (1986) 65–74.

———. *Luke: Artist and Theologian, Luke's Passion Account as Literature*. New York: Paulist, 1985.

Käsemann, Ernst. *Essays on New Testament Themes*. Translated by W. J. Montague. Naperville, IL: Alec R. Allenson, 1964.

Keim, Paul. "Reading Ancient Near Eastern Literature from the Perspective of Girard's Scapegoat Theory." In *Violence Renounced*, edited by Willard M. Swartley, 157–77. Telford, PA: Cascadia, 2000.

Kelly, Anthony J. "Beyond Locked Doors: The Breath of the Risen One." In *Girard's Mimetic Theory across the Disciplines*, edited by Scott Cowdell et al, 69–85. New York: Continuum, 2012.

Keown, Gerald L., et al. *Jeremiah 26–52*. Dallas: Word, 1995.

Kerr, Fergus. "Rescuing Girard's Argument?" *MT* 8 (1992) 385–99.

Kilmartin, Edward J. *The Eucharist in the Primitive Church*. Englewood Cliffs, NJ: Prentice-Hall, 1965.

Kimball, Charles A., III. "Jesus' Exposition of Scripture in Luke 20:9–19: An Inquiry in Light of Jewish Hermeneutics." *BBR* 3 (1993) 77–92.

Kingsbury, Jack D. "The Parable of the Wicked Husbandmen and the Secret of Jesus' Divine Sonship in Matthew: Some Literary-Critical Observations." *JBL* 105 (1986) 643–55.

Kirwan, Michael. "Being Saved from Salvation: René Girard & the Victims of Religion." *Communio Viatorum* 52 (2010) 27–47.

———. *Discovering Girard*. London: Darton, Longman and Todd, 2004.

———. *Girard and Theology*. London: T & T Clark, 2009.

———. *Philosophy and Theology: Girard and Theology*. London: Continuum, 2009.

Klein, George L. "Reading Genesis 1." *Southwestern Journal of Theology* 44 (2001) 22–38.

Klug, Eugene F. A. "End of the Historical-Critical Method." *Sprinfielder* 38 (1975) 289–302.

Kodell, Jerome. *The Eucharist in the New Testament*. Collegeville, MN: Liturgical, 1988.

Koenig, John. *The Feast of the World's Redemption: Eucharistic Origins and Christian Mission*. Harrisburg, PA: Trinity, 2000.

Koester, Craig R. *Hebrews: A New Translation with Introduction and Commentary*. New York: Doubleday, 2001.

Koet, Bart J. "Isaiah in Luke-Acts." In *Isaiah in the New Testament*, edited by Steve Moyise and Maarten J. J. Menken, 79–100. London: T & T Clark, 2005.

Kümmel, Werner Georg. "Current Theological Accusations against Luke." *Andover Newton Quarterly* 16 (1975) 131–45.

Kutsko, John F. *Between Heaven and Earth: Divine Presence and Absence in the Book of Ezekiel*. Winona Lake, IN: Eisenbrauns, 2000.

Larkin, William J. "Luke's Use of the Old Testament as a Key to His Soteriology." *JETS* 20 (1977) 325–35.

LaVerdiere, Eugene. *Dining in the Kingdom of God: The Origins of the Eucharist in the Gospel of Luke*. Chicago: Liturgy Training, 1994.

Lefebure, Leo D. *Revelation, the Religions, and Violence*. Maryknoll, NY: Orbis, 2000.

Legault, André. "Le baptê de Jésus et la doctrine du Serviteur souffrant." *Sciences ecclésiastiques* 13 (1961) 147–66.

Léon-Dufour, Xavier. *Sharing the Eucharistic Bread: The Witness of the New Testament*. Translated by Matthew J. O'Connell. New York: Paulist, 1987.

Levenson, Jon D. *Resurrection and the Restoration of Israel: The Ultimate Victory of the God of Life*. New Haven: Yale University Press, 2006.

———. *Sinai and Zion: An Entry into the Jewish Bible*. Minneapolis: Winston, 1985.

Levine, Baruch. "René Girard on Job: The Question of the Scapegoat." *Semeia* 33 (1985) 125–33.

Lindars, Barnabas. *New Testament Apologetic: The Doctrinal Significance of the Old Testament Quotations*. Philadelphia: Westminster, 1961.

Lindbeck, George. "Scripture, Consensus, and Community." In *Biblical Interpretation in Crisis: The Ratzinger Conference on Bible and Church*, edited by Richard John Neuhaus, 74–101. Grand Rapids: Eerdmans, 1989.

Liver, J. "The Doctrine of the Two Messiahs in Sectarian Literature in the Time of the Second Commonwealth." *HTR* 52 (1959) 149–86.

Long, Thomas E. *The Viability of a Sacrificial Theology of Atonement: A Critique and Analysis of Traditional and Transformational Views.* Minneapolis: Lutheran University Press, 2006.

Love, Gregory Anderson. *Love, Violence, and the Cross: How the Nonviolent God Saves Us Through the Cross of Christ.* Eugene, OR: Cascade, 2010.

Lucas, Sarah Drews. "War on Terror: The Escalation to Extremes." In *René Girard and Sacrifice in Life, Love, and Literature*, edited by Scott Cowdell et al, 57–66. New York: Bloomsbury, 2014.

Lüdemann, Gerd. *The Acts of the Apostles: What Really Happened in the Earliest Days of the Church.* Amherst, NY: Prometheus, 2005.

Luther, Martin. *Works.* Edited by Jaroslav Pelikan. Saint Louis: Concordia, 1955–1986.

Luomanen, Petri. *Entering the Kingdom of Heaven: A Study on the Structure of Matthew's View of Salvation.* Tübingen: Mohr Siebeck, 1998.

———. "Sacrifices Abolished: The Last Supper in Luke (Codex Bezae) and in the Gospel of the Ebionites." In *Lux Humana, Lux Aeterna: Essays on Biblical and Related Themes in Honour of Lars Aejmelaeus*, edited by Natti Mustakallio et al, 186–208. Helsinki: Finish Exegetical Society, 2005.

Luz, Ulrich. *Matthew 1–7: A Commentary.* Translated by Wilhelm C. Linss. Minneapolis: Augsburg, 1989.

Maag, Victor. "Altestamentliche Anthropogonie in ihrem Verhältnis zur altorientalischen Mythologie." *Asiatische Studien* 9 (1955) 15–44.

Mack, Burton L. "The Innocent Transgressor: Jesus in Early Christian Myth and History." *Semeia* 33 (1985) 135–65.

———. *A Myth of Innocence: Mark and Christian Origins.* Philadelphia: Fortress, 1988.

Madden, Frederic W. *History of Jewish Coinage and of Money in the Old and New Testament.* New York: Ktav, 1967.

Manent, Pierre. "René Girard, la violence et le sacré." *Contrepoint* 14 (1974) 157–70.

Marcus, Joel. *Mark 8–16: A New Translation with Introduction and Commentary.* New Haven: Yale University Press, 2009.

Marshall, I. Howard. "The Hope of a New Age: The Kingdom of God in the New Testament." *Themelios* 11 (1985) 5–15.

———. *Last Supper and Lord's Supper.* Grand Rapids: Eerdmans, 1980.

———. *Luke: Historian & Theologian.* 3d ed. Downers Grove, IL: InterVarsity, 1988.

———. "Review of *Jesus in the Drama of Salvation*." *JTS* 52 (2000) 589–93.

———. "A Son of God or Servant of Yahweh?—A Reconsideration of Mark I.11." *NTS* 15 (1969) 326–36.

———. "Son of Man." In *Dictionary of Jesus and the Gospels*, ed. Joel B. Green et al, 775–81. Downers Grove, IL: InterVarsity, 1992.

McCarthy, Dennis J. *Old Testament Covenant: A Survey of Current Opinions.* Richmond, VA: John Knox, 1972.

———. *Treaty and Covenant: A Study in Form in the Ancient Oriental Documents and in the Old Testament.* Rome: Pontifical Bible Institute, 1963.

McComiskey, Douglas S. "Exile and Restoration from Exile in the Scriptural Quotations and Allusions of Jesus." *JETS* 53 (2010) 673–96.

McGowan, Andrew. "Eating People: Accusations of Cannibalism against Christians in the Second Century." *Journal of Early Christian Studies* 2 (1994) 413–42.

McGuire, Cheryl. "Judaism, Christianity and Girard: The Violent Messiahs." In *Religion, Psychology, and Violence*, vol. 2 of *The Destructive Power of Religion: Violence in*

Judaism, Christianity, and Islam, edited by J. Harold Ellens, 50–85. Westport, Conn.: Praeger, 2004.

McKelvey, R.J. *The New Temple: The Church in the New Testament*. Oxford: Oxford University Press, 1969.

McKenna, Andrew J. *Violence and Difference: Girard, Derrida, and Deconstruction*. Chicago: University of Illinois Press, 1992.

McKnight, Scot. "Jesus and the Twelve." *BBR* 11 (2001) 203–31.

Meier, John P. "The Circle of the Twelve: Did it Exist during Jesus' Public Ministry?" *JBL* 116 (1997) 635–72.

———. "The Eucharist at the Last Supper: Did it Happen?" *Theology Digest* 42 (1995) 335–51.

———. *A Marginal Jew: Rethinking the Historical Jesus*. 4 vols. New York: Doubleday, 1991–2009.

Meilaender, Gilbert. *The Freedom of a Christian: Grace, Vocation, and the Meaning of our Humanity*. Grand Rapids: Brazos, 2006.

Menken, Martinus J. J. "Striking the Shepherd: Early Christian Versions and Interpretations of Zechariah 13,7." *Biblica* 92 (2011) 39–59.

Metzger, Bruce M. *A Textual Commentary on the Greek New Testament*. 2d ed. New York: American Bible Society, 1994.

Meyer, Ben F. *The Aims of Jesus*. San Jose, CA: Pickwick, 2002.

———. "The Expiation Motif in the Eucharistic Words: A Key to the History of Jesus?" In *One Loaf, One Cup: Ecumenical Studies of 1 Cor 11 and Other Eucharistic Texts: The Cambridge Conference on the Eucharist August 1988*, edited by Ben F. Meyer, 11–33. Macon, GA: Mercer University Press, 1993.

Meyers, Carol L., and Eric M. Meyers. *Zechariah 9-14: A New Translation with Introduction and Commentary*. New York: Doubleday, 1993.

Milavec, Aaron A. "Mark's Parable of the Wicked Husbandmen as Reaffirming God's Predilection for Israel." *Journal of Ecumenical Studies* 26 (1989) 289–312.

Milbank, John. *Theology and Social Theory: Beyond Secular Reason*. 2d ed. Oxford: Blackwell Publishing, 2006.

Miller, Marlin E. "Girardian Perspectives and Christian Atonement." In *Violence Renounced*, edited by Willard M. Swartley, 31–48. Telford, PA: Cascadia, 2000.

Miller, Patrick D. "The Book of Jeremiah: Introduction, Commentary, and Reflections." In *The New Interpreter's Bible*, edited by Leander Keck, 6:553-926. Nashville: Abingdon, 2001.

Miller, Stephen R. *Daniel*. Nashville: Broadman & Holman, 1994.

Minear, Paul S. "Note on Luke 22:36." *NovT* 7 (1964) 128–34.

Mitchell, Hinckley G., et al. *A Critical and Exegetical Commentary on Haggai, Zechariah, Malachi and Jonah*. Edinburgh: T & T Clark, 1912, 1980.

Moessner, David P. "'The Christ Must Suffer,' The Church Must Suffer: Rethinking the Theology of the Cross in Luke-Acts." *SBLSP* 29 (1990) 165–95.

Moffitt, David M. *Atonement and the Logic of Resurrection in the Epistle to the Hebrews*. Leiden: Brill, 2011.

Moloney, Francis J. *A Body Broken for a Broken People: Eucharist in the New Testament*. Rev. ed. Peabody, MA: Hendrickson, 1997.

———. *The Gospel of Mark: A Commentary*. Peabody, MA: Hendrickson, 2002.

Moore, Carey A. "Toward the Dating of the Book of Baruch." *CBQ* 36 (1974) 312–20.

Morris, Leon. *The Gospel According to St. Luke: An Introduction and Commentary.* Grand Rapids: Eerdmans, 1974, 1984.
Moss, Charlene M. *The Zechariah Tradition and the Gospel of Matthew.* Berlin: Walter de Gruyter, 2008.
Moyise, Steve. "The Wilderness Quotation in Mark 1.2–3." In *Wilderness: Essays in Honour of Frances Young,* edited by R. S. Sugirtharajah, 78–87. London: T & T Clark, 2005.
Navone, John. *Themes of St. Luke.* Rome: Gregorian University Press, 1970.
Nel, Marius J. "The Forgiveness of Debt in Matthew 6:12, 14–15." *Neot* 47 (2013) 87–106.
Nelson-Pallmeyer, Jack. *Jesus Against Christianity: Reclaiming the Missing Jesus.* Harrisburg, PA: Trinity, 2001.
Neusner, Jacob. *Self-Fulfilling Prophecy: Exile and Return in the History of Judaism.* Boston: Beacon, 1987.
———. *The Mishnah: A New Translation.* New Haven, Conn.: Yale University Press, 1988.
Newell, William Lloyd. *Desire in René Girard and Jesus.* Lanham: Lexington, 2012.
Nickelsburg, George W. E. "The Bible Rewritten and Expanded." In *Jewish Writings of the Second Temple Period: Apocrypha, Pseudepigrapha, Qumran Sectarian Writings, Philo, Josephus,* edited by Michael E. Stone, 89-156. Assen: Van Gorcum, 1984.
———. *Jewish Literature between the Bible and the Mishnah: A Historical and Literary Introduction.* Philadelphia: Fortress, 1981.
———. "Stories of Biblical and Early Post-biblical Times." In *Jewish Writings of the Second Temple Period: Apocrypha, Pseudepigrapha, Qumran Sectarian Writings, Philo, Josephus,* edited by Michael E. Stone, 33–87. Assen: Van Gorcum, 1984.
Nicholson, E. W. "The Covenant Ritual in Exodus XXIV 3-8." *VT* 32 (1982) 74–86.
Nolland, John. *Luke 1–9:20.* Nashville: Thomas Nelson, 1989.
———. *Luke 18:35–24:53.* Dallas: Word, 1993.
———. *The Gospel of Matthew: A Commentary on the Greek Text.* Grand Rapids: Eerdmans, 2005.
North, Robert. "Violence and the Bible: The Girard Connection." *CBQ* 47 (1985) 1–27.
Northey, Wayne. "The Cross: God's Peace Work—Towards a Restorative Peacemaking Understanding of the Atonement." In *Stricken by God? Nonviolent Identification and the Victory of Christ,* edited by Brad Jersak and Michael Hardin, 356–77. Grand Rapids: Eerdmans, 2007.
Nuechterlein, Paul J. "The Work of René Girard as a New Key to Biblical Hermeneutics." *Currents in Theology and Mission* 26 (1999) 196–209.
Oldenhage, Tania. "How to Read a Tainted Text: The Wicked Husbandmen in a Post-Holocaust Context." In *Postmodern Interpretations of the Bible: A Reader,* edited by A. K. M. Adam, 165–76. St. Louis, MO: Chalice, 2001.
Olmstead, Wesley G. *Matthew's Trilogy of Parables: The Nation, the Nations and the Reader in Matthew 21.28–22.14.* Cambridge: Cambridge University Press, 2003.
Ormerod, Neil. "Is all Desire Mimetic? Lonergan and Girard on the Nature of Desire and Authenticity." In *Girard's Mimetic Theory across the Disciplines,* edited by Scott Cowdell et al, 251–62. New York: Continuum, 2012.
O'Toole, Robert F. *The Unity of Luke's Theology: An Analysis of Luke-Acts.* Wilmington, DE: Michael Glazier, 1984.

Palaver, Wolfgang. *René Girard's Mimetic Theory*. Translated by Gabriel Borrud. East Lansing: Michigan State University Press, 2013.
Pao, David W., and Eckhard J. Schnabel. "Luke." In *Commentary on the New Testament Use of the Old Testament*, edited by G. K. Beale and D. A. Carson, 251-414. Grand Rapids: Baker Academic, 2007.
Park, Andrew Sung. *Triune Atonement: Christ's Healing for Sinners, Victims, and the Whole Creation*. Louisville: Westminster John Knox, 2009.
Parker, David C. *Codex Bezae: An Early Christian Manuscript and its Text*. Cambridge: Cambridge University Press, 1992.
———. "Codex Bezae: The Manuscript as Past, Present and Future." In *Bible as Book*, edited by Scot McKendrick and Orlaith O'Sullivan, 43–50. London: Oak Noll, 2003.
———. *The Living Text of the Gospels*. Cambridge: Cambridge University Press, 1997.
Pauli, C.W.H., trans. *The Chaldee Paraphrase on the Prophet Isaiah*. London: London Society's House, 1871.
Perrin, Norman. *Jesus and the Language of the Kingdom: Symbol and Metaphor in New Testament Interpretation*. Philadelphia: Fortress, 1976.
Perry, John M. *Exploring the Evolution of the Lord's Supper in the New Testament*. Kansas City, MO: Sheed & Ward, 1994.
Pesch, Rudolf. *Das Abendmahl und Jesu Todesverständnis*. Freiburg: Herder, 1978.
Peters, Ted. "Atonement and the Final Scapegoat." *Perspectives in Religious Studies* 19 (1992) 151–81.
Philo, *The Works of Philo: Complete and Unabridged*. Translated by C. D. Yonge. Rev. ed. Peabody, MA: Hendrickson, 1993, 2006.
Pilgrim, Walter Edward. "The Death of Christ in Lukan Soteriology." PhD diss., Princeton Theological Seminary, 1971.
Pitre, Brant J. *Jesus, the Tribulation, and the End of the Exile: Restoration Eschatology and the Origin of the Atonement*. Tübingen: Mohr Siebeck, 2005.
———. *Jesus and the Last Supper*. Grand Rapids: Eerdmans, 2015.
Placher, William C. "How Does Jesus Save? An Alternative View of Atonement." *Christian Century* 126, no. 11 (2009) 23–27.
Plummer, Alfred. *A Critical and Exegetical Commentary on the Gospel according to S. Luke*. 5th ed. Edinburgh: T & T Clark, 1981.
Polak, Frank H. "The Covenant at Mount Sinai in the light of Texts from Mari." In *Sefer Moshe: The Moshe Weinfeld Jubilee Volume*, ed. Chaim Cohen et al, 119–34. Winona Lake, IN: Eisenbrauns, 2004.
Poon, Wilson C. K. "Superabundant Table Fellowship in the Kingdom: The Feeding of the Five Thousand and the Meal Motif in Luke." *ExpTim* 114 (2003) 224–30.
Porter, Stanley E. *The Criteria for Authenticity in Historical-Jesus Research: Previous Discussion and New Proposals*. Sheffield, England: Sheffield Academic, 2000.
Propp, William H. C. *Exodus 19–40: A New Translation with Introduction and Commentary*. New York: Doubleday, 2006.
Pryor, John W. "Jesus and Israel in the Fourth Gospel—John 1:11." *NovT* 33 (1990) 201–18.
Putt, B. Keith. "Violent Imitation or Compassionate Repetition? Girard and Caputo on Exemplary Atonement." In *Religion and Violence in a Secular World: Toward a New Political Theology*, edited by Clayton Crockett, 21–45. Charlottesville: University of Virginia Press, 2006.

Ray, Darby K. *Deceiving the Devil: Atonement, Abuse, and Ransom.* Cleveland: Pilgrim, 1998.

Reardon, Timothy W. "Recent Trajectories and Themes in Lukan Soteriology." *Currents in Biblical Research* 12 (2013) 77–95.

Rogers, T. J. "Shaking the Dust Off the Markan Mission Discourse." *JSNT* 27 (2004) 169–92.

Rogness, Michael. "A Canon within the Canon? Yes: Proclaim Christ." *Word & World* 26 (2006) 436, 438.

Root, Michael. "The Narrative Structure of Soteriology." *MT* 2 (1986) 145–58.

Rose, Gillian. *The Broken Middle: Out of Our Ancient Society.* Oxford: Blackwell, 1992.

Rose, Phil. "A Conversation with Rene Girard: (August 2006/May 2007)." *Contagion* 18 (2011) 23–38.

Sanders, E.P. *Jesus and Judaism.* Philadelphia: Fortress, 1985.

———. "Jesus and the Kingdom: The Restoration of Israel and the New People of God." In *Jesus, the Gospels, and the Church: Essays in Honor of William R. Farmer,* edited by E. P. Sanders, 225–39. Macon, GA: Mercer University Press, 1987.

———. *Judaism: Practice and Belief, 63 BCE–66CE.* London: SCM, 1992.

Sarna, Nahum M. *Exodus.* JPS Torah Commentary. Philadelphia: Jewish Publication Society, 1991.

Scaer, Peter J. "The Atonement in Mark's Sacramental Theology." *CTQ* 72 (2008) 227–42.

Scheffler, Eben. "The Meaning of Jesus' Death: The Letter to the Hebrews and Luke's Gospel Compared." *Acta patristica et byzantina* 18 (2007) 145–65.

Schnackenburg, Rudolf. *The Gospel of Matthew.* Translated by Robert R. Barr. Grand Rapids: Eerdmans, 2002.

Schnelle, Udo. *Theology of the New Testament.* Translated by M. Eugene Boring. Grand Rapids: Baker Academic, 2007.

Schroder, Edward H. "Luke's Gospel through a Systematician's Lens." *Currents in Theology and Mission* 3 (1976) 337–46.

Schroeder, Christoph. "'Standing in the Breach': Turning away the Wrath of God." *Int* 52 (1998) 16–23.

Shults, F. LeRon. *Christology and Science.* Grand Rapids: Eerdmans, 2008.

Schwager, Raymund. *Banished from Eden: Original Sin and Evolutionary Theory in the Drama of Salvation.* Translated by James G. Williams. Herefordshire: Gracewing, 2006.

———. *Brauchen wir einen Sündenbock? Gewalt und Erlösung in den biblischen Schriften.* Munich: Kösel, 1978.

———. "Christ's Death and the Prophetic Critique of Sacrifice." *Semiea* 33 (1985) 109–23.

———. *Jesus in the Drama of Salvation: Toward a Biblical Doctrine of Redemption.* Translated by James G. Williams and Paul Haddon. New York: Crossroad Publishing Company, 1999.

———. *Jesus in Heilsdrama: Entwurf einer biblischen Erlösungslehre.* Innsbruck, Austria: Tyrolia, 1990.

———. *Must there be Scapegoats? Violence and Redemption in the Bible.* Leominster, Herefordshire: Gracewing, 2000.

Schwartz, Daniel R. *2 Maccabees.* Berlin: Walter de Gruyter, 2008.

Schweitzer, Albert. *The Mystery of the Kingdom of God: The Secret of Jesus' Messiahship and Passion*. Translated by Walter Lowrie. New York: Macmillan, 1960.

Scott, James M., ed. *Exile: Old Testament, Jewish, and Christian Conceptions*. Leiden: Brill, 1997.

———. *Restoration: Old Testament, Jewish, and Christian Perspectives*. Leiden: Brill, 2001.

———. "Restoration of Israel." In *Dictionary of Paul and His Letters*, edited by Gerald F. Hawthorne et al, 796–805. Downers Grove, IL: InterVarsity, 1993.

Scott, Waldron B. *What About the Cross? Exploring Models of the Atonement*. New York: iUniverse, 2007.

Scubla, Lucien. "The Christianity of René Girard and the Nature of Religion." Translated by Mark R. Anspach. In *Violence and Truth*, edited by Paul Dumouchel, 160–178. Stanford: Stanford University Press, 1988.

Seitz, Christopher R. "The Book of Isaiah 40-66: Introduction, Commentary, and Reflections." In *The New Interpreter's Bible*, ed. Leander E. Keck, 6:309-552. Nashville: Abingdon, 2001.

Senior, Donald P. *The Passion of Jesus in the Gospel of Matthew*. Wilmington, DE: Michael Glazier, 1985.

———. *The Passion Narrative According to Matthew: A Redactional Study*. Leuven: Leuven University Press, 1982.

Shelton, R. Larry. "A Covenant Concept of Atonement." *Wesleyan Theological Journal* 19 (1984) 91–108.

———. *Cross and Covenant: Interpreting the Atonement for 21st Century Mission*. Tyrone, GA: Paternoster, 2006.

Sire, James W. *The Universe Next Door: A Basic Worldview Catalog*. 5th ed. Downers Grove, IL: IVP Academic, 2009.

Smit, Peter-Ben. *Fellowship and Food in the Kingdom: Eschatological Meals and Scenes of Utopian Abundance in the New Testament*. Tübingen: Mohr Siebeck, 2008.

Smith-Christopher, Daniel L. *A Biblical Theology of Exile*. Minneapolis: Fortress, 2002.

Snodgrass, Klyne R. "Reading & Overreading the Parables in Jesus and the Victory of God." In *Jesus & the Restoration of Israel: A Critical Assessment of N. T. Wright's Jesus and the Victory of God*, edited by Carey Newman, 61–76. Downers Grove, IL: InterVarsity, 1999.

———. "Recent Research on the Parable of the Wicked Tenants: An Assessment." *BBR* 8 (1998) 187–216.

Stein, Robert H. *Jesus the Messiah: A Survey of the Life of Christ*. Downers Grove, IL: IVP Academic, 1996.

Stern, Menahem, ed. *Greek and Latin Authors on Jews and Judaism*. Vol. 1, *From Herodotus to Plutarch*. Jerusalem: Israel Academy of Sciences and Humanities, 1976.

Steyn, Gert J. "Soteriological Perspectives in Luke's Gospel." In *Salvation in the New Testament: Perspectives on Soteriology*, edited by Jan G. van der Watt, 67–99. Leiden: Brill, 2005.

Stone, Michael E. "Apocalyptic Literature." In *Jewish Writings of the Second Temple Period*, edited by Michael E. Stone, 383–441. Assen: Van Gorcum, 1984.

Stromberg, Jake. "The 'Root of Jesse' in Isaiah 11:10: Postexilic Judah or Postexilic Davidic King?" *JBL* 127 (2008) 655–69.

Swartley, Willard M., ed. *Violence Renounced: René Girard, Biblical Studies, and Peacemaking*. Telford, PA: Cascadia, 2000.

Talbert, Charles H. *Reading Luke: A Literary and Theological Commentary on the Third Gospel*. New York: Crossroad, 1982.

Talmon, Shemaryahu. "The Community of the Renewed Covenant: Between Judaism and Christianity." In *The Community of the Renewed Covenant: The Notre Dame Symposium on the Dead Sea Scrolls*, edited by Eugene C. Ulrich and James C. VanderKam, 3–24. Notre Dame, IN: University of Notre Dame Press, 1994.

Tan, Kim Huat. *The Zion Traditions and the Aims of Jesus*. Cambridge: Cambridge University Press, 1997.

Tannehill, Robert C. *The Narrative Unity of Luke-Acts: A Literary Interpretation*. Vol. 1, *The Gospel According to Luke*. 2 vols. Philadelphia: Fortress, 1986.

———. "The Story of Israel within the Lukan Narrative." In *Jesus and the Heritage of Israel: Luke's Narrative Claim upon Israel's Legacy*, edited by David P. Moessner, 325–39. Harrisburg, PA: Trinity, 1999.

———. "Study in the Theology of Luke-Acts." *AThR* 43 (1961) 195–203.

The Targum of the Minor Prophets. Translated by Kevin J. Cathcart and Robert P. Gordon. Wilmington, DE: Michael Glazier, 1989.

The Targum Onqelos to Exodus. Translated by Bernard Grossfeld. Wilmington, DE: Michael Glazier, 1988.

Targum Pseudo-Jonathan: Exodus. Translated by Michael Maher. Collegeville, MN: Liturgical, 1994.

Taylor, Vincent. *The Passion Narrative of St Luke: A Critical and Historical Investigation*. Edited by Owen E. Evans. Cambridge: Cambridge University Press, 1972.

Theissen, Gerd and Annette Merz. *The Historical Jesus: A Comprehensive Guide*. Minneapolis: Fortress, 1998.

Torrance, Thomas F. *Atonement: The Person and Work of Christ*. Edited by Robert T. Walker. Downers Grove, IL: IVP Academic, 2009.

Tuckett, Christopher. "Isaiah in Q." In *Isaiah in the New Testament*, edited by Steve Moyise and Maarten J. J. Menken, 51–61. London: T & T Clark, 2005.

Tyson, Joseph B. *The Death of Jesus in Luke-Acts*. Columbia: University of South Carolina Press, 1986.

Urs von Balthasar, Hans. *The Glory of the Lord: A Theological Aesthetics*. Vol. 7, *Theology: The New Covenant*. Edited by John Riches. Translated by Brian McNeil. 3d ed. San Francisco: Ignatius, 1990.

———. *The Glory of the Lord: A Theological Aesthetics*. Vol. 6, *Theology: The Old Covenant*. Edited by John Riches. Translated by Brian McNeil and Erasmo Leiva-Merikakis. San Francisco: Ignatius, 1991.

Valadier, Paul. "Bouc émissaire et revelation chrétienne selon René Girard." *Etudes* 357 (1982) 251–60.

———. "René Girard revisité." *Etudes* 396 (2002) 773–77.

van Aarde, Andries G. "ΙΗΣΟΥΣ, the Davidic Messiah, as Political Saviour in Matthew's History." In *Salvation in the New Testament: Perspectives on Soteriology*, edited by Jan G. van der Watt, 7–31. Leiden: Brill, 2005.

van den Brink, Gijsbert. "Narrative, Atonement, and the Christian Conception of the Good Life." In *Religion and the Good Life*, edited by Marcel Sarot and Wessel Stoker, 113–29. Assen: Royal van Gorcum, 2004.

VanderKam, James C. "Exile in Jewish Apocalyptic Literature." In *Exile*, edited by James M. Scott, 89–109. Leiden: Brill, 1997.
VanderKam, James C. and Peter Flint. *The Meaning of the Dead Sea Scrolls: Their Significance for Understanding the Bible, Judaism, Jesus, and Christianity*. New York: HarperSanFrancisco, 2002.
Van der Watt, Jan G., ed. *Salvation in the New Testament: Perspectives on Soteriology*. Leiden: Brill, 2005.
van Henten, J. W. *The Maccabean Martyrs as Saviours of the Jewish People: A Study of 2 and 4 Maccabees*. Leiden: Brill, 1997.
Vanhoozer, Kevin J. "The Atonement in Postmodernity: Guilt, Goats and Gifts." In *The Glory of the Atonement: Biblical, Historical & Practical Perspectives*, edited by Charles E. Hill and Frank A. James III, 367–407. Downers Grove, IL: InterVarsity, 2004.
———. *The Drama of Doctrine: A Canonical-Linguistic Approach to Christian Theology*. Louisville: Westminster John Knox, 2005.
van Zyl, Hermie C. "The Soteriological Meaning of Jesus' Death in Luke Acts: A Survey of Possibilities." *Verbum et ecclesia* 23 (2002) 533–57.
Vattimo, Gianni. *After Christianity*. New York: Columbia University Press, 2002.
Vattimo, Gianni and René Girard. *Christianity, Truth, and Weakening Faith: A Dialogue*. Edited by Pierpaolo Antonello. Translated by William McCuaig. New York: Columbia University Press, 2010.
Vermes, Geza. *Jesus the Jew: A Historian's Reading of the Gospels*. New York: Macmillan Publishing, 1973.
———. *The Complete Dead Sea Scrolls in English*. Rev. ed. London: Penguin, 2004.
Vidu, Adonis. *Atonement, Law, and Justice: The Cross in Historical and Cultural Contexts*. Grand Rapids: Baker Academic, 2014.
Volf, Miroslav. *Exclusion and Embrace: A Theological Exploration of Identity, Otherness, and Reconciliation*. Nashville: Abingdon, 1996.
Vööbus, Arthur. "A New Approach to the Problem of the Shorter and Longer Text in Luke." *NTS* 15 (1969) 457–63.
Wacks, Mel. *The Handbook of Biblical Numismatics from Abraham to the Crusaders*. Houston: Israel Numismatic Service, 1976.
Waetjen, Herman C. "Genealogy as the Key to the Gospel according to Matthew." *JBL* 95 (1967) 205–30.
Wagner, J. Ross. "Psalm 118 in Luke-Acts: Tracing a Narrative Thread." In *Early Christian Interpretations of the Scriptures of Israel*, edited by Craig A. Evans and James A. Sanders, 154–78. Sheffield: Sheffield Academic, 1997.
Wallace, Daniel B. *Greek Grammar Beyond the Basics: An Exegetical Syntax of the New Testament*. Grand Rapids: Zondervan, 1996.
Wallace, Mark I. "Postmodern Biblicism: The Challenge of René Girard for Contemporary Theology." *MT* 5 (1989) 309–25.
Watts, Rikki E. *Isaiah's New Exodus in Mark*. Grand Rapids: Baker, 2000.
———. "Jesus' Death, Isaiah 53, and Mark 10:45: A Crux Revisited." In *Jesus and the Suffering Servant*, edited by William H. Bellinger Jr. and William R. Farmer, 125–51. Harrisburg, PA: Trinity, 1998.
Weatherly, Jon A. "Eating and Drinking in the Kingdom of God: The Emmaus Episode and the Meal Motif in Luke-Acts." In *Christ's Victorious Church*, edited by Jon A. Weatherly, 18–33. Eugene, OR: Wipf and Stock, 2001.

Weaver, J. Denny. *The Nonviolent Atonement*. Grand Rapids: Eerdmans, 2001.
Weinberger, Theodore. "Soteriology and the Promise of Narrative Theology." *Andover Newton Review* 2 (1991) 44–57.
Weinfeld, Moshe. "בְּרִית, bᵉrîth." In *Theological Dictionary of the Old Testament*, edited by G. Johannes Botterweck et al, 2:275-78. 15 vols. Grand Rapids: Eerdmans, 1975-2015.
Weiss, Johannes. *Jesus' Proclamation of the Kingdom of God*. Edited and translated by Richard H. Hiers and David L. Holland. Philadelphia: Fortress, 1971.
Weitzman, Steven. "Allusion, Artifice, and Exile in the Hymn of Tobit." *JBL* 115 (1996) 49–61.
Westermann, Claus. *Isaiah 40–66*. Philadelphia: Westminster, 1969.
Williams, Delores S. *Sisters in the Wilderness: The Challenge of Womanist God-Talk*. Maryknoll, NY: 1993.
Williams, James G. *The Bible, Violence, and the Sacred: Liberation from the Myth of Sanctioned Violence*. New York: HarperSanFrancisco, 1991.
Williams, Rowan. "Between Politics and Metaphysics: Reflections in the Wake of Gillian Rose." *MT* 11 (1995) 3–22.
Wink, Walter. *Engaging the Powers: Discernment and Resistance in a World of Domination*. Minneapolis: Fortress, 1992.
Wise, Michael O. "The Origins and History of the Teacher's Movement." In *The Oxford Handbook of Dead Sea Scrolls*, edited by John J. Collins and Timothy H. Lim. Oxford: Oxford University Press, 2010. http://www.oxfordhandbooks.com/view/10.1093/oxfordhb/9780199207237.001.0001/oxfordhb-9780199207237.
Witherington, Ben, III. *The Christology of Jesus*. Minneapolis: Fortress, 1990.
———. *The Gospel of Mark: A Socio-Rhetorical Commentary*. Grand Rapids: Eerdmans, 2001.
Wolff, Hans W. "Das Kerygma des Jahwisten." *Evangelische Theologie* 24 (1964) 73–98.
———. "The Kerygma of the Yahwist." Translated by Wilbur A. Benwar. *Int* 20 (1966) 131–58.
Wolters, Al. "The Messiah in the Qumran Documents." In *The Messiah in the Old and New Testaments*, ed. Stanley E. Porter, 75–89. Grand Rapids: Eerdmans, 2007.
Wright, N. T. *Evil and the Justice of God*. Downers Grove, IL: IVP, 2006.
———. *Jesus and the Victory of God*. Minneapolis: Fortress, 1996.
———. *The New Testament and the People of God*. Minneapolis: Fortress, 1992.
———. "The Reasons for Jesus' Crucifixion." In *Stricken by God? Nonviolent Identification and the Victory of Christ*, edited by Brad Jersak and Michael Hardin, 78–149. Grand Rapids: Eerdmans, 2007.
———. *The Resurrection of the Son of God*. Minneapolis: Fortress, 2003.
Zehnle, Richard. "Salvific Character of Jesus' Death in Lucan Soteriology." *TS* 30 (1969) 420–44.
Zimmerli, Walther. *Ezekiel 1: A Commentary on the Book of the Prophet Ezekiel, Chapters 1–24*. Edited by Frank Moore Cross et al. Translated by Ronald E. Clements. Philadelphia: Fortress, 1979.

Subject Index

Abelard, Peter, xiii–xiv, 53
Abraham, 10, 59, 70, 76, 92, 94–96, 128n134
Abrahamic covenant, 69, 94, 96, 128n134
Adam, 9, 74, 213n70
Adam and Eve, 9, 213n70
Alison, James, xviii, 12n54, 40–44, 47, 52n2, 140, 152, 207, 209, 212n65
Anselm, xiii–xv, 51n1, 52–53, 162n10
atonement, xix–xx, 25, 37, 40, 44–50, 51n1, 53, 106–7n60, 127n124, 139–45, 153–57, 161–62, 166–67, 170, 174, 176, 178–xiii–xiv, 80, 184, 187, 190, 203–5, 211, 223, 227–34
atonement theories, xiii–xiv, 51n1, 153, 227–34

baptism of Jesus, 102–5, 107n60, 130, 151
Bartlett, Anthony, xviii, 46–49, 176, 204n42

covenant, xix–xx, 30–31, 35–36, 39, 42–45, 49–50, 56–64, 66–73, 75–82, 85, 90–91, 94–96, 99n28, 101, 103–4, 113n77, 120, 123, 129, 130, 138–48, 150, 153, 155–57, 161–63, 165–66, 169–70, 172–76, 178, 180–82, 184, 187–92, 200, 202–4, 208, 210–11, 219–20, 222–23, 229–34
covenant sacrifice, xix, 30, 43, 49, 138–48, 153, 156, 161–62, 174–75, 178, 202–4, 208, 222

cross, xiii–xx, 6n28, 7–8, 17, 21–22, 28–33, 43–48, 50, 53–54, 125, 133, 134, 142n32, 143–44, 153–55, 162, 164, 166, 170, 174, 179, 183–86, 190n60, 191, 193, 195, 205–34
crucifixion, xix, 7, 21, 44, 120, 127n126, 134, 147n52, 150–51, 154–57, 165, 177, 180n35, 182, 184, 206–8, 228–29
Cyrus of Persia, 17, 65n35, 82–84, 87–88, 129, 233

David, 61, 68, 76–81, 92–96, 103–4, 129, 149, 186n52, 191
Davidic covenant, 61, 68, 76–79, 96, 103, 130

Eucharist, xiii, xivn5, 37, 39, 45–48, 143n33, 151, 154, 160, 168–71, 183–84, 187, 207–8
exile, xix, 17, 58–59, 61–69, 74–77, 80–93, 96, 100–102, 109, 112–14, 123, 129–30, 148–51, 156, 163–64, 173, 189, 191, 194, 196–97, 201, 219, 223, 232, 233
Exodus (under Moses), 11–13, 35, 37, 38, 42–43, 59, 61, 64, 94, 139, 168, 173

Garden of Eden, 9, 59, 213n70
Garden of Gethsemane, 151, 154, 157, 165, 206
Girard, René, xiv–xx, 1–57, 65n36, 66n41, 90, 120, 124, 125n114, 132–33, 142n32, 192–234

257

SUBJECT INDEX

Gospels (in the New Testament), ix, xiiin4, xiv–xx, 5–8, 10n49, 15–26–28, 30, 36, 38–39, 41–42, 44–45, 48–50, 52n2, 53–58, 64, 82, 90–135, 147n54, 152n64, 154, 158, 161, 163, 168, 174–75, 190–208, 211, 219–20, 222–27, 230, 232–33
Gospel (Good News), 42, 47, 98–102, 124, 198

Hamerton-Kelly, Robert, 37–39, 49n107, 153n71, 196n8, 204
Hasmoneans, 85–86
Hebrews, Book of, xvn11, xix, 142–45, 180, 201–3
Heim, S. Mark, xviii, 44–46, 49n106–107, 204n41, 205n43, 208–9, 216
hermeneutics, 31n18, 55–56, 193–201

idols, 62, 72–73
idolatry, 61, 67, 73–75, 112, 195
Isaac, 10

Jacob, 65, 70, 109
Job, Book of, 14–15, 55, 223–25
John the Baptist, 24, 94–95, 99–102, 113, 124n113, 162, 185n49, 196
Joseph, son of Jacob, 5–6, 10–11, 34–37, 55, 225
Joseph, husband of Mary, 93–95, 163
Josephus, 34n35, 79–80, 86–87, 89, 97n20, 110n71, 131, 152n65

kingdom of God, 17–18, 20, 29–32, 58, 98–99, 107–20, 128–30, 134, 137, 146, 148, 151, 153, 156–57, 159, 166–69, 176–77, 181–82, 188, 199–200, 204n39, 208, 213, 215, 217

Last Supper, xiv, xvi–xvii, xix–xx, 27, 29–30, 34, 37, 39, 42–46, 48–49, 90, 106, 133–40, 145–48, 151, 153, 156–59, 161–66, 168–70, 172–93, 201–5, 208, 210–11, 219–20, 226, 233

Mary, mother of Jesus, 94–95, 163
Messiah, 76n72, 77n74, 78–81, 86, 92–95, 106n60, 111, 123, 126n122, 134, 137n10, 148–51, 155, 163–64, 177, 183–92, 204, 207, The Death of the Messiah, 106, 134, 148, 177, 183–90, 204, 207
mimesis (mimetic theory), xviii, 1–5, 7–12, 14, 19–23, 25, 34–38, 40n57, 46–49, 52–53, 124, 195–99, 201, 203, 205, 212, 217, 228–29
Moses, xix, 11, 60, 67, 69, 71–72, 80, 87, 93–96, 139, 141, 143, 161–62, 165

new covenant, xx, 31, 42, 45, 66–72, 95–96, 99n28, 140, 144, 146, 162, 169–70, 172–74, 176, 178, 180–84, 187–92, 208, 222, 229, 232
new exodus, 38, 64–66, 70, 81, 85, 87, 89, 94, 96, 98, 101, 129–30, 196, 201
nonviolence, 18, 20n99, 25, 30, 35

Parable of the Wicked Tenants, 19, 28, 117, 124–29, 159, 197–99
Passover, 42, 135–39, 148, 156, 158–59, 165, 168–69, 173
penal substitution. *See* substitutionary sacrifice

ransom, saying, xix, 36–39, 48–49, 106, 151–53, 164, 174–76, 182–85, 203–4, 226
ransom, theology and language of, 52, 140n23, 187
redemption, xvn11, 33–34, 41, 48–49, 51, 64, 75, 94–97, 109, 111–14, 124, 129, 138n13, 144, 152–53, 171, 173, 182–87, 190, 204, 208, 218–19
restoration of Israel, xix, 17, 38–39, 56, 58, 63–98, 100, 102, 104, 109, 111–14, 119–20, 123–24, 129–30, 132–34, 139, 145, 147–48, 151, 155–56, 159, 163, 166–68, 172–74, 177, 191–92,

194, 196–97, 199–201, 203–5, 219, 223, 232–33
resurrection, 7–8, 20, 22–25, 30–31, 40–41, 44–45, 48, 52–53, 74, 102, 125, 133, 144, 149, 151, 164–66, 180, 182–92, 209–13, 226n15

sacrifice, xv, xix, 3–4, 10, 15–18, 20, 25, 30, 37–39, 43–45, 48–50, 76, 120–23, 128n128, 135, 136n9, 138n13, 139–47, 152–53, 156, 158, 161–62, 168, 172, 175–76, 178, 189, 191, 201–5, 208–9, 215–17, 219–20, 222–23, 225
scapegoat Mechanism, xviii, 2–8, 11, 15n69, 16–21, 24, 35, 38–40, 52, 54–55, 132, 153n71, 193, 195, 197–98, 200, 206–7, 212–16, 218n85, 219–21, 223, 225
Schwager, Raymund, xviii, 27–34, 37, 40–41, 47, 49n106–107, 66n41, 124, 148n57, 198–99, 204n39, 207, 209, 215, 225–26
satisfaction (for sin), xiii–xvi, 30, 228, 232
Satan, 14, 18–19, 46, 199–200, 214, 216

servant of YHWH, 16, 30, 43, 69, 103–7, 130, 146–47, 152–53, 161, 177, 197, 207n49, 223n5
spirit, the divine, 69, 72–74, 79, 82, 102–5, 115, 129–30, 151, 191–92
substitutionary sacrifice, xv–xvi, 28, 38, 140, 147n55, 153n71, 171n11, 179n34, 180n34, 208, 222, 227–29, 232

Targums, 105n54, 114n79, 126n122, 127, 141–43, 145, 202
temple, of Jerusalem, 38–39, 74–77, 81n92, 82–83, 85–86, 88, 95, 96n13, 99n28, 111, 117, 120–24, 126–30, 138, 152n65, 155–57, 165, 185, 199, 204
temple cleansing, 38–39, 61, 63, 120–24, 126–27, 130, 138, 156

violence, xiii, 3–13, 16, 18, 21–23, 28, 30–38, 41, 44–49, 52, 56, 126n114, 199–200, 203, 205–8, 210–11, 213–20, 222, 225–26, 230, 233

Williams, James, 34–37, 49, 176n18, 204n42, 205n43, 220n87
Wright, N.T., 82, 88–90, 94, 112, 228

Ancient Document Index

Old Testament

Genesis

1:2	74
2:7	74
3–11	59
3	9
3:14–22	59
4	9–10
9:16	69n49
12:2–3	59
17:7	69n49
17:13	69n49
17:19	69n49
22	10
22:2	103n44
22:12	103n44
22:16	103n44

Exodus

1:15–22	93
6:6	186n52
6:7	67, 101n35
12:28	165
13:13	186n52
13:15	186n52
15:13	186n52
19:5–6	59
20:3	60
20:13–17	60
20:17	12
23	99n28
23:20	99
24	142–43
24:5–8	142n32
24:8	xix, 43, 139–41, 145–46, 161–63, 174, 202–3
30:11–16	121
34:20	186n52

Leviticus

4:7	147
4:18	147
4:25	147
4:30	147
4:35	147
17:4	146
17:14	172
19:20	186n52
25:25	186n52
25:29	185n51
25:30	186n52
25:33	186n52
25:48–49	186n52
25:48	185n51
25:54	186n52
26:12	67, 101n35
26:33	150
26:38	150
27:13	186n52
27:15	186n52
27:19–20	186n52
27:27–29	186n52
27:31	186n52
27:33	186n52

Numbers

18:15	186n52
18:17	186n52
23:21	108
35:33	146

Deuteronomy

4:27	150
7:8	186n52
9:26	186n52
13:5	186n52
14:24–26	121
15:15	186n52
16:3	138
18:15	93
19:10	146
21:7	146
21:8	186n52
23:1–8	75
24:18	186n52
30:15	191
30:16–18	60–61
34:10	93

Ruth

1:16	67n43, 101n35

1 Samuel

8:7	109
12:12	109n68
13:14	61

2 Samuel

4:9	186n52
7:12–16	61, 77
7:14	103
7:23	186n52
23:5	69n49
24:14	149

1 Kings

1:19	186n52
13:1–4	62
13:33–34	62
16:32	62
18:1—19:37	62
23:5	69

2 Kings

10:29	62n30
13:2	62n30
13:11	62n30
14:24	62n30
15:9	62n30
15:18	62n30
15:24	62n30
15:28	62n30
17:7–8	62
17:15	62
22:8	67
24:3–4	63

1 Chronicles

16:17	69n49
16:31	108n67
16:35	151
17:21	186n52
21:13	149
28:5	108n67

2 Chronicles

13:8	108n67
36:5–16	63

Ezra

1:1–5	82n96
9:9	82

Nehemiah

1:10	186n52
9:36	82

ANCIENT DOCUMENT INDEX   263

Esther

4:17	186n52

Job

1:1—2:10	14
16:12–21	224
16:19–21	14
19:2–7	224
19:25–27	14, 224
30:9–15	14, 224
38:1–42:6	15

Psalms

2:7	103
7:2	186n52
10:16	108n67
17:9b–12	13
22:28	108n67
24:8–10	108n67
25:22	186n52
26:11	186n52
31:5	186n52
32:7	186n52
34:22	186n52
44:26	186n52
47:2	108n67
47:8	109
49:7	186n52
49:8	185n51
49:15	186n52
55:18	186n52
59:1	186n52
69:18	186n52
71:23	186n52
72:14	186n52
74:2	186n52
77:15	186n52
78:42	186n52
93:1	108n67
95:3	108n67
96:10	108n67
97:1	108n67
99:1–4	108n67
103:4	186n52
103:19	108n67
105:10	69n49
106:10	186n52
106:41	150
107:2	186n52
111:9	185n51
118:22–23	124–26
118:22	19, 28
118:23	19n93
119:134	186n52
119:154	186n52
130:7–8	185n51
130:8	186n52
136:24	186n52
137:8–9	14
144:10	186n52
145:11–13	108n67

Proverbs

23:11	186n52

Isaiah

1—39	100
5:1–7	125
5:2	127
6:5	108n67
8:14–15	126
9:1–2	114
9:2	95n11
11:1	77
11:10	77
16:4–5	77
19:4	149
19:12	149
33:22	109n69
35:8–10	101
35:9	186n52
36—39	62
39:5–8	100
40—66	100
40	101, 196–97, 201
40:1–5	100–101
40:3–5	101, 197
40:3–4	17, 65, 196
40:3	99–100

Isaiah (continued)

40:9	98n26
41:14	186n52
42:1–4	105–6
42:1	103–4
42:6–7	95n11
42:6	69, 146
43:1	186n52
43:14	186n52
44:6	109
44:22–24	186n52
44:28	75
49:1–6	105
49:8	69, 146
49:11	65
50:4–9	105
51:11	186n52
51:17	154
51:22	154
52:3	186n52
52:7	98, 98n26, 109n69
52:13—53:12	16, 105–6, 151, 177n22
53	16, 22n107, 30, 107n60
53:4	16, 106, 161,
53:11	152–53
53:12	106, 147, 177
54:10	69
55:3	69
56—66	100n32
56:7	75, 76, 121n96
60:6	98n26
60:7	75
61	188
61:1	98n26
61:8	69
62:12	186n52
63:4	185n51
63:9	186n52

Jeremiah

7:11	121n96
8:19	108n67
9:16	150
10:10	108n67
10:14	73n66
11:4	67n43, 101n35
15:21	186n52
23:5–6	78
23:7–8	64
25:11–12	83n102
25:15–17	154
29:10	83n102
30:22	67n43, 101n35
31	146, 172
31:11	186n52
31:31–34	67, 162–63, 173
31:31	174
31:32	173
31:34	173, 180
32:28	67n43, 101n35
33:15	78
33:17	78n76
33:21	78n76
38:16	149–50
44:18–19	109
44:27–28	109
48:15	108n67
49:12	154
51:7	154
51:57	108n67
50:5	68

Lamentations

1:3	151
2:9	151
3:58	186n52
4:20	151
5:8	186n52

Ezekiel

4:13	151
6:5	74
6:9	151
8:4	123n108
9:3	123n108
10:18–19	123n108
11:17	64
11:22–25	123n108

12:15-16	150-51	4:10-12	117-18
14:4	73	4:22	118
16:59-63	68	4:27	186n52
16:60	68	6:28	186n52
20:23	151	7	118-19
20:32	73	7:13-14	110, 152n68
20:33	109n70	7:13	118
20:34	63-64	7:22	114-15
20:37	69	7:27	110
22:15	151	9:1-2	83
23:31-33	154	9:24	84
28:25	65n34	9:25	84
30:23	150	9:26	110
30:26	150	11:31	117
31:11	150	12:4	115
31:17	150		
34:23-34	78		
34:11-13	65n34	Hosea	
34:25	69		
36:24	65n34	3:5	78
36:25-26	73	6:6	20
36:28	65n34, 67n43, 101n35	7:13	186n52
		8:10	150
37:1-14	165, 192	13:14	186n52
37:3	73		
37:5	73	Joel	
37:7	166		
37:11-14	73	2:28-29	74
37:12	74, 166		
37:14	74		
37:24-25	78	Amos	
37:26	69	9:11	78
37:27	67n43, 101n35		
39:26-28	65n34		
40:1—44:3	74	Micah	
		4:1-2	75-76
Daniel		4:10	186n52
		5:2	78
2:19	116	6:4	186n52
2:27	116		
2:30	116		
2:32-33	110	Habakkuk	
2:35	110		
2:44-45	116	2:16	154
2:44	110		
2:47	116		
3:88	186n52		

Zephaniah

3:15	109n70, 186n52

Zechariah

4:7–9	126
9	163
9:11	145–46, 161, 174

10:8	186n52
12:2	154
13:7	154, 165, 206

Malachi

1:4	108n67
3:1	99n28

Apocrypha

Baruch

2:35	70
3:8	84
5:5–9	65n36
5:5–7	196n7
5:506	65

1 Esdras

8:74–77	83n99

Judith

8:22	84n106

2 Maccabees

1:27	66n38, 83n99
2:1–8	85
2:7	85
2:17–18	85
2:18	65–66
10:1–8	85

Sirach

36:13–16	65
48:10	65n37

Tobit

13:5	83
14:5–7	75
14:5	83

Pseudepigrapha

Assumption of Moses

10:1	112
10:7–9	112

2 Baruch

29:3	78n79
39:7	78n79
40:1–2	78

70:9	78n79
72:1–6	78n79

1 Enoch

46:1–4	111n72
90:28–29	75
91:13	75n70

4 Ezra

12:11	111n72
12:31–32	111n72
12:32	78
13:40–47	87
14:47	87

Jubilees

1:15	76n71
1:17	76n71
22:14–15	70
22:30	70

Psalms of Solomon

11:2–3	66
11:4	65n36, 196n7
17:21–32	123n110
17:21–22	78
17:28	66n39
18:5	78

Sibylline Oracles

3:294	76
3:652–56	78
3:652	81n92
3:767–74	111
5:414–33	123n110

Testament of Dan

5:13	112

Testament of Judah

24:4	78

New Testament

Matthew

1:1–17	163
1:1	92
1:6	92
1:17	92
1:21	163
2:13–23	93
3:1–6	162
3:2	115, 159n3
3:3	100n30
3:11	102
3:17	103n43, 104n48
4:13–16	113
4:17	113, 115
4:23	98
5:1	93n5
6:9–13	165
6:12	164
6:23–35	164
8	106
8:17	106
8:29	159
9:2	180n37
9:5–6	180n37
9:13	20
9:35	98n24
10:1–5	97n16
11:1	97n16
11:5	98n24
11:25	159n2
12:1	159n2
12:9–14	105
12:16	105
12:18–21	105
12:18	103n44, 104n48, 105
12:19	105
12:21	105
12:28	115
12:31	180n37
13:11	116
13:30	159
13:31–32	118
14:1	159n2
16:21–23	164

Matthew (continued)

16:27	119n92
16:3	159
17:22	164
18:6–9	20
18:21	180n37
19:28	97
20:17	97n16
20:18	164
20:20	49
20:28	xivn5, 106n58, 164, 171n9, 174
21:12–17	120
21:31	125n114
21:33–44	28, 124, 197
21:34	159
21:41	125n114, 159,
21:42	19, 28n5, 28n6
21:43	128
21:44	126–27n123
23:27	19
23:35	18n88
24:14	98n24
24:15	117
24:30	119n92
24:45	159n2
26:1	164n12
26:2	168n1
26:4	164n12
26:6	164n12
26:13	98n24
26:14	97n16
26:17	158, 164n12, 168n1
26:18	159, 168n1
26:19	164n12, 165, 168n1
26:20	97n16
26:26–29	xivn5, xvi,
26:26–28	160
26:26	164n12
26:28	31n19, 49, 161, 163, 180n37
26:31–35	165
26:31	206
26:36	164n12
26:39	206
26:47	97n16
26:49–51	164n12
26:63	164n12
26:64	119n92
26:71	164n12
27:1	164n12
27:11	164n12
27:11	164n12
27:20	164n12
27:22	164n12
27:27	164n12
27:37	164n12
27:51–53	165
27:51	166
27:52–53	166
27:55	164n12
27:57	164n12

Mark

1:1	98
1:2–3	99
1:4	162, 180n37
1:8	102
1:10–11	103
1:11	104
1:14–15	98n23
1:15	115
2:5–10	180n37
3:16	97n16
3:23	19
3:28–29	180n37
4:2	155n76
4:10	97n16
4:11	116
6:7	97n16
6:16	24
8:27–33	155
8:29	148
8:30	119n92
8:31	148
8:32	149
8:35	98n23
9:12	149
9:31	149–50, 157
9:35	97n16
10:29	98n23

10:32	97n16
10:33-34	150
10:33	157, 232
10:38-39	107n60
10:38	151, 154
10:44	151
10:45	xivn5, 36, 38, 49, 106n58, 151-53, 171n9, 174,
11:14	122
11:15-19	120
11:17	121
11:20	122
12:1-12	197
12:1-11	28, 124
12:9	125n114
12:10-11	19, 28n6, 125
12:10	28
13:10	98n23
13:14	117
13:26	119n92
14:1	168n1
14:9	98n23
14:12	135, 158, 168n1
14:13	168n1
14:14	168n1
14:17	135, 137
14:18-21	137
14:21	149
14:22-25	xivn5
14:22-24	xvi, 160, 170
14:22	137
14:23	154, 160
14:24	31n19, 49, 99n28, 139, 146-47, 153,
14:25	146-47, 148, 153n72
14:26	136, 153,
14:27	154, 206
14:36	154, 206
14:49	149
14:62	119
14:64	230
15:34	155
15:38	155
15:39	127n126, 155
16:15	98n23

Luke

1:19	98n25
1:32	94
1:55	94
1:68-69	94
1:68	184-85
1:72-73	95
1:76-77	95, 185n49
1:77	180n37, 185
1:78-79	95
2:10	98n25
2:11	95
2:25	95
2:26	95
2:32	177
2:38	185
3:3	180n37, 185n49
3:4-6	100n30
3:16	102
3:22	103n43
4:18	98n25, 188
4:43	98
2:29-32	95
2:38	96
5:20-24	180n37
7:22	98n25
7:34	181
7:37	181
7:41-43	181
7:47-49	180n37
7:48	181
7:49	181
8:1	98n25
8:10	116
9:6	98n25
9:10-17	187n55
9:16	183n42
9:26	119n92
11:20	115
12:35-38	175
12:50	107n60
13:18-19	118
16:16	98n25
19:45-48	120
20:1	98n25
20:9-19	197
20:9-18	28, 124

Luke (continued)

20:17–18	117
20:17	19, 28n5, 28n6
20:18	126
20:19	127
21:27	119n92
22:1	168n1
22:7	168
22:8	168
22:9	168n1
22:11	168n1
22:13	168n1
22:14–20	xivn5
22:14	175n16
22:15–20	xvi
22:15–16	168
22:16	169
22:17–18	168, 169n5
22:19–20	169–71, 179, 189
22:19	171, 183n42
22:20	31n19, 172
22:24–27	48
22:25–26	174
22:27	174–75
22:28–30	176
22:29–30	97
22:29	188
22:35–37	177n22
22:36	177
22:37	106, 177
22:39–46	177n22
22:42	206
22:67–69	119n92
23:12	21
23:32	177
24	190
24:16	182
24:19	182
24:21	182, 186
24:25–26	183
24:26	29, 207
24:34	188
24:35	187
24:39	187n55
24:42–43	187
24:45	187
24:46–47	187–89
24:46	107n60, 186
24:27	183, 189
24:30	183
24:31	183
27:47	180n37

John

1:11	213n70
1:23	100n30
6:51	171n10
8:43–44	18
11:45–53	45
11:50	21
12:34	118, 119n92
15:25	7, 22
20:23	180n37

Acts

1:15–26	97
2:1–21	102
2:38	180
2:42	183n42
3:13	177n22
3:26	177n22
4:11	28n6
4:27	177n22
4:30	177n22
5:31	180n37
5:45	98n25
7:56	119n92
8:4	98n25
8:12	98n25
8:26–40	106n60
8:32–33	177n22
10:36	98n25
10:43	180n37
11:20	98n25
13	190
13:29	107n60
13:32	98n25
13:38–39	189
13:38	180n37
14:7	98n25
14:15	98n25
14:21	98n25

15:7	98n25	**Titus**	
15:35	98n25		
16:10	98n25	2:14	171n10, 186n52
20:24	98n25		
26:18	180n37	**Hebrews**	
		2:6	119n92
1 Corinthians		7:22	31n19
		8:1–13	143
3:11	28n6	8:1–10	31n19
5:7	136	9:12	185n50
11:23	135	9:15–22	144
11:25	31n19	9:15	144
15:3–6	97	9:18–20	142–43
20:28	179	9:22	143, 180n37
		9:26	143
2 Corinthians		10	202
		12:24	31n19
3:6	31n19	13:20	31n19
8:5	171n9		
		James	
Galatians		5:15	180n37
1:4	171n10		
		1 Peter	
Ephesians		1:18–19	186n52
2:20	28n6	2:7	28n6
Colossians		**Revelation**	
1:14	180n37	1:13	119n92
		14:14	119n92
1 Timothy			
2:6	171n9–10		

Dead Sea Scrolls

CD		**1Q28b**	
6:19	71n57	5	79n84
7:19	79n84		
8.20–21	71n57	**1QM**	
12:22	79n80		
19.33	71n57	2:2–3	66n39
20:10–12	71n57		

1QpHab

2:3–6	71n57

1QS

1:16–26	71
5:4–6	71n57
5:8–9	71n57
8:5–11	127
9:11	79

1QSa

2:11–21	79n80

4Q252

5:1–6	79

4Q161

Frs. 8–10	79

4Q174

	128n128
1:11–12	79

4Q251

	79

4Q285

7	79

4Q504

	142n32

4Q521

	79

4Q525

	108n64

11QT

18:14–16	66n39
19:10	76n71

Rabbinic Writings

Mishnah Pesaḥ

10:2–7	139n16, 169n3
10:5	171n8

Targum Isaiah

5:2	127n124
9:102	114n79

Targum Jonathan

126n122

Targum Onqelos

Exodus 24:8	141–42

Targum Pseudo-Jonathan

Exodus 24:8	141–42

www.ingramcontent.com/pod-product-compliance
Lightning Source LLC
Chambersburg PA
CBHW071239230426
43668CB00011B/1503